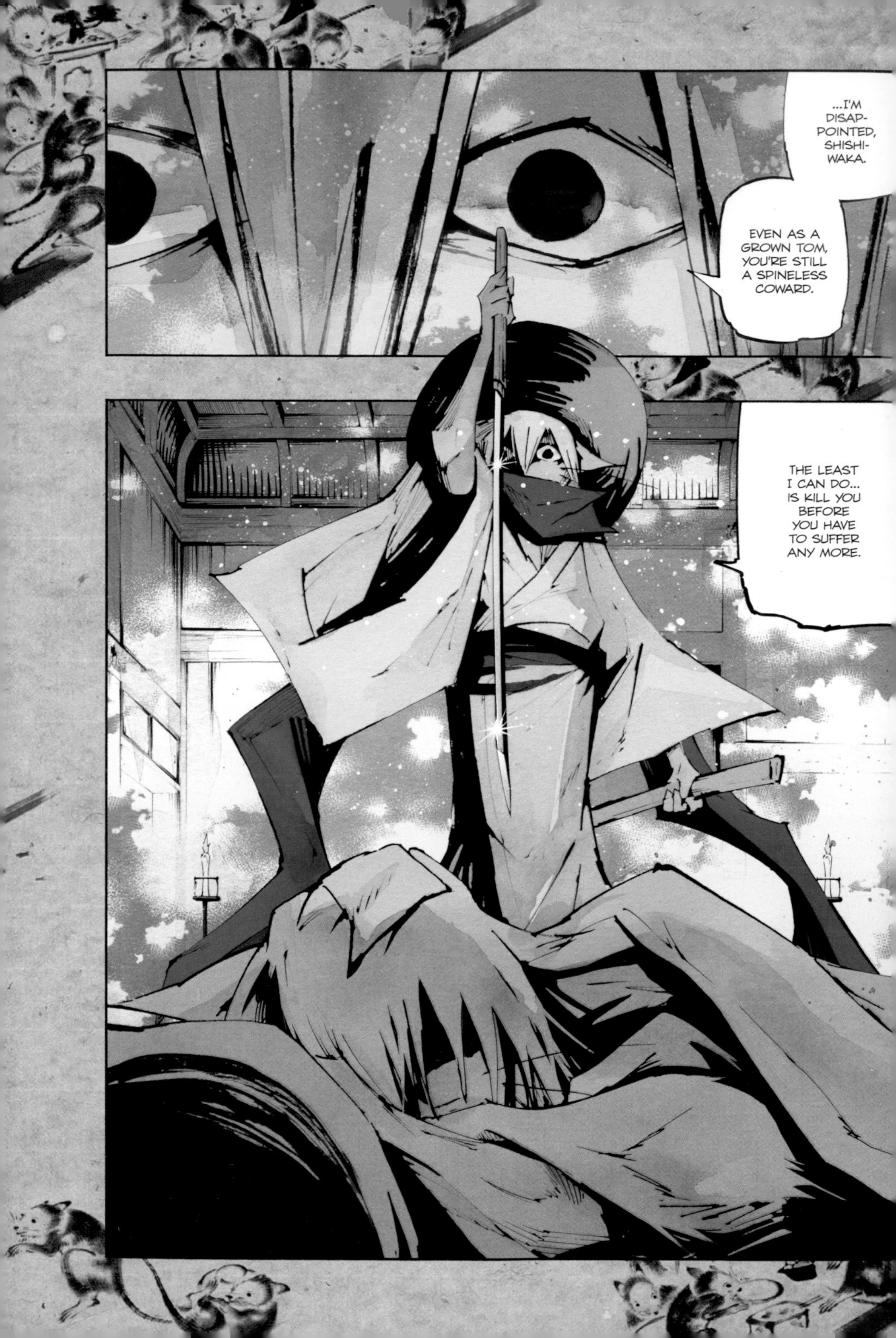
...I'M DISAP-POINTED, SHISHI-WAKA.
EVEN AS A GROWN TOM, YOU'RE STILL A SPINELESS COWARD.
THE LEAST I CAN DO... IS KILL YOU BEFORE YOU HAVE TO SUFFER ANY MORE.

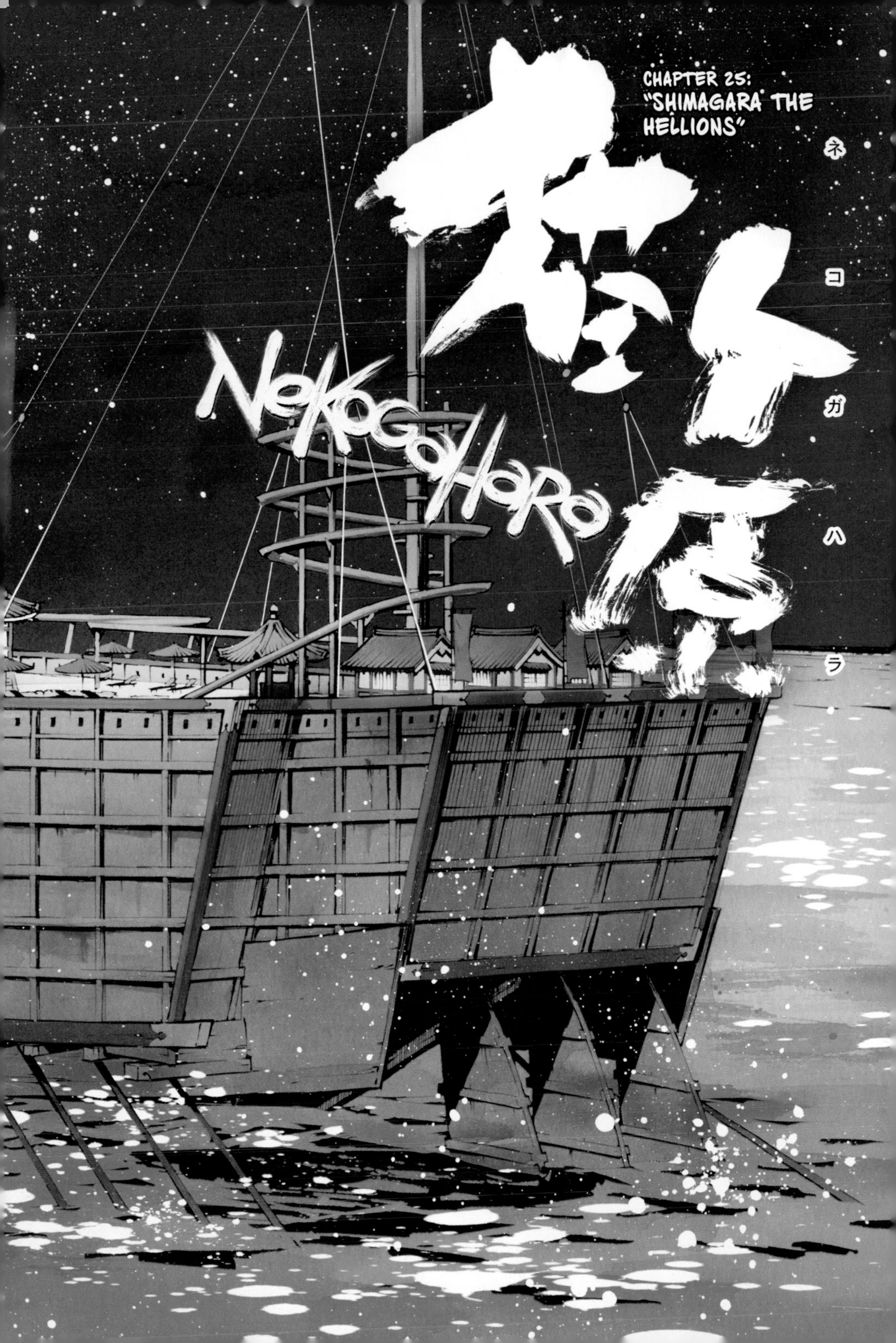
CHAPTER 25:
"SHIMAGARA THE HELLIONS"
NekogaHara
猫ヶ原
ネコガハラ

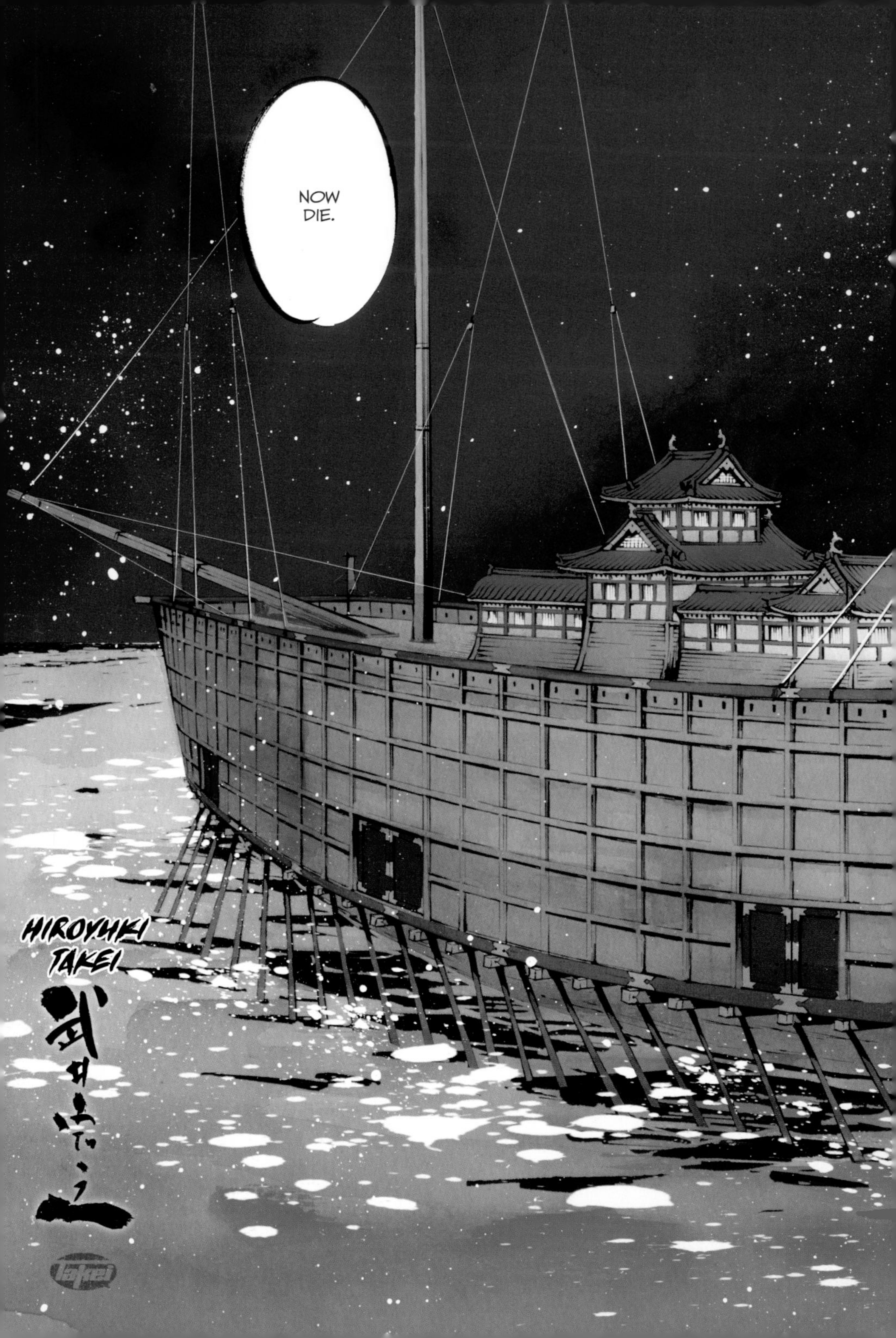
NOW DIE.
HIROYUKI TAKEI

NEKOGAHARA VOLUME FIVE CONTENTS

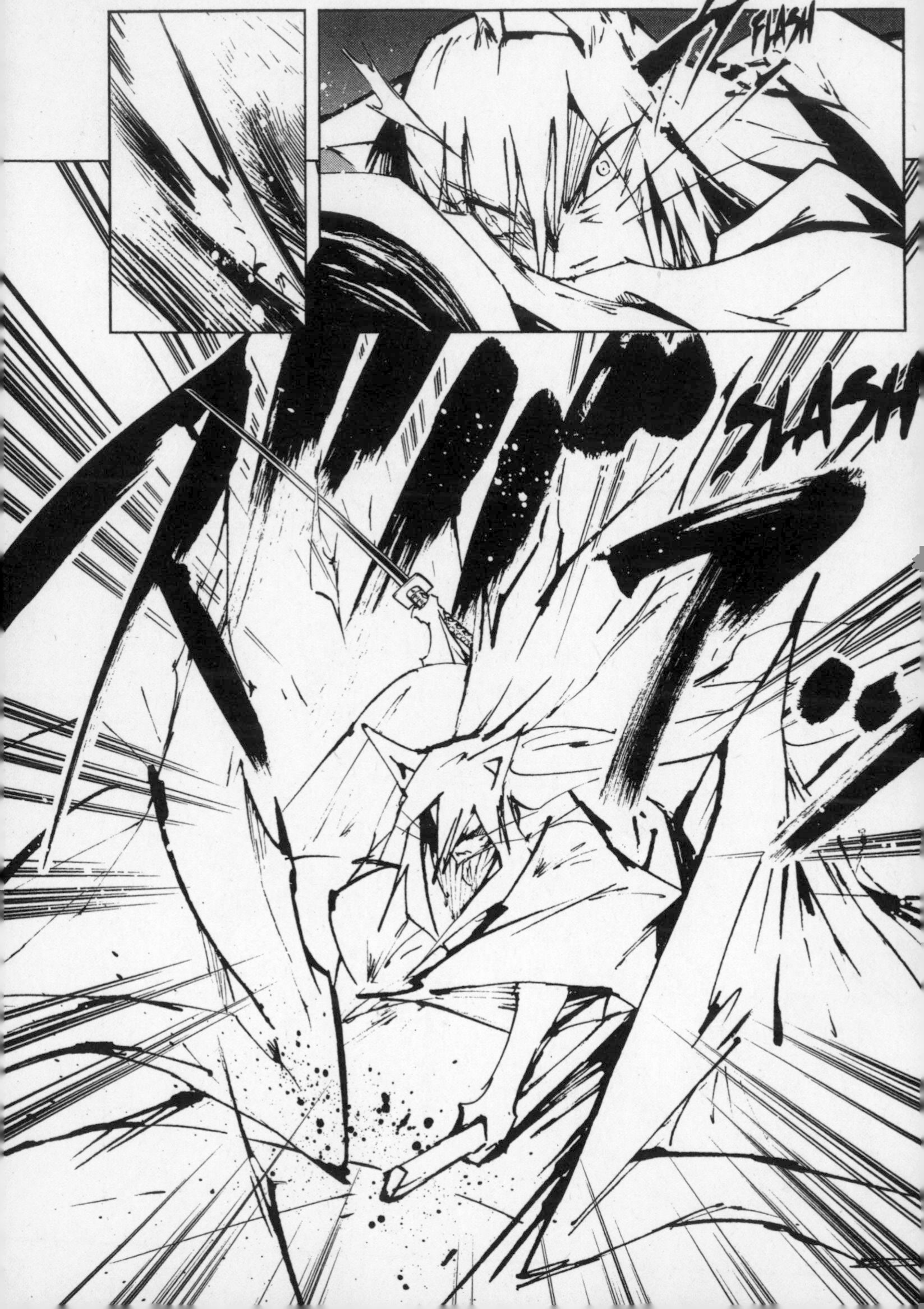
FLASH
SLASH

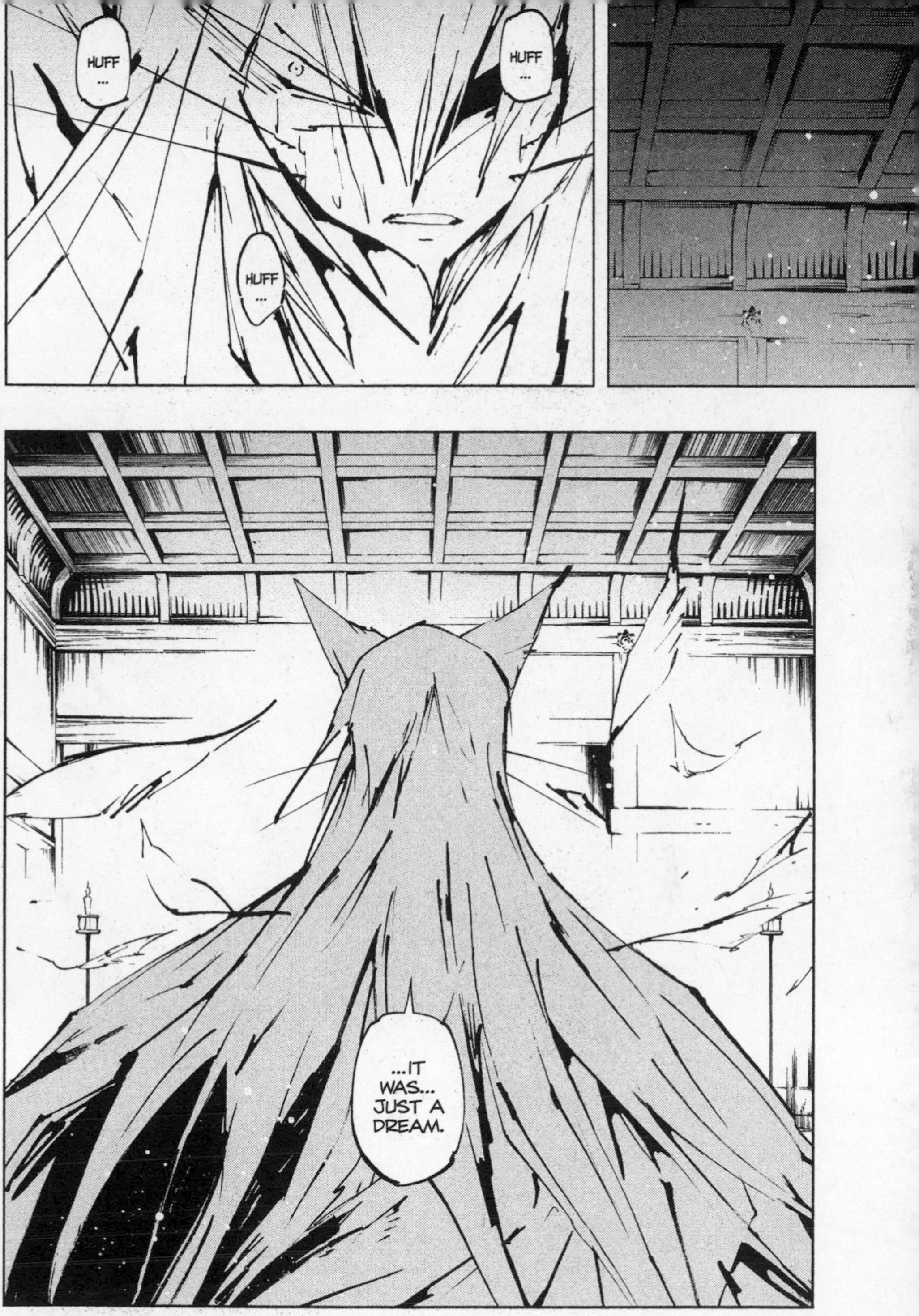
HUFF ...
HUFF ...
HUFF ...
...IT WAS... JUST A DREAM.

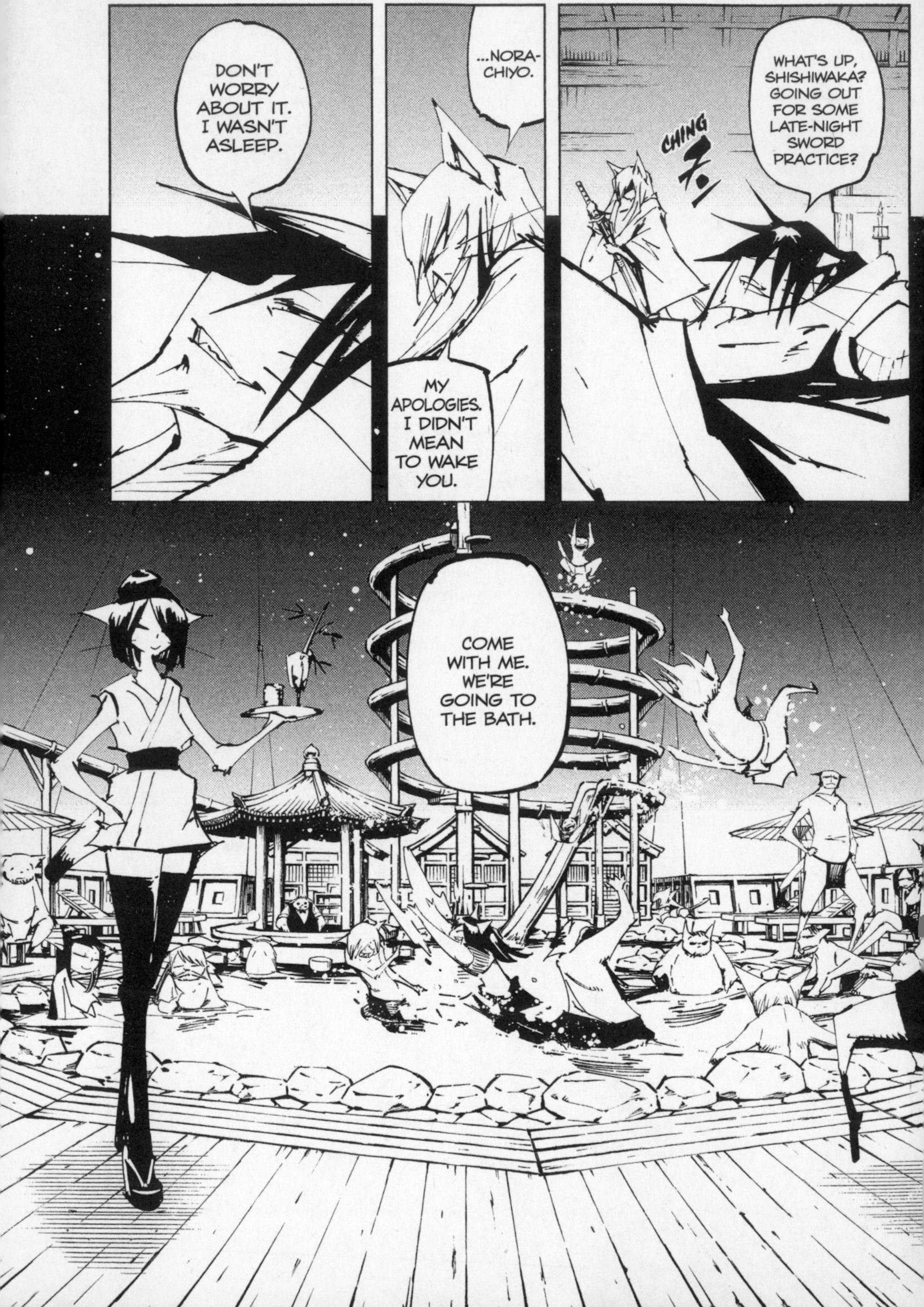
WHAT'S UP, SHISHIWAKA? GOING OUT FOR SOME LATE-NIGHT SWORD PRACTICE?
CHING
...NORACHIYO.
MY APOLOGIES. I DIDN'T MEAN TO WAKE YOU.
DON'T WORRY ABOUT IT. I WASN'T ASLEEP.
COME WITH ME. WE'RE GOING TO THE BATH.

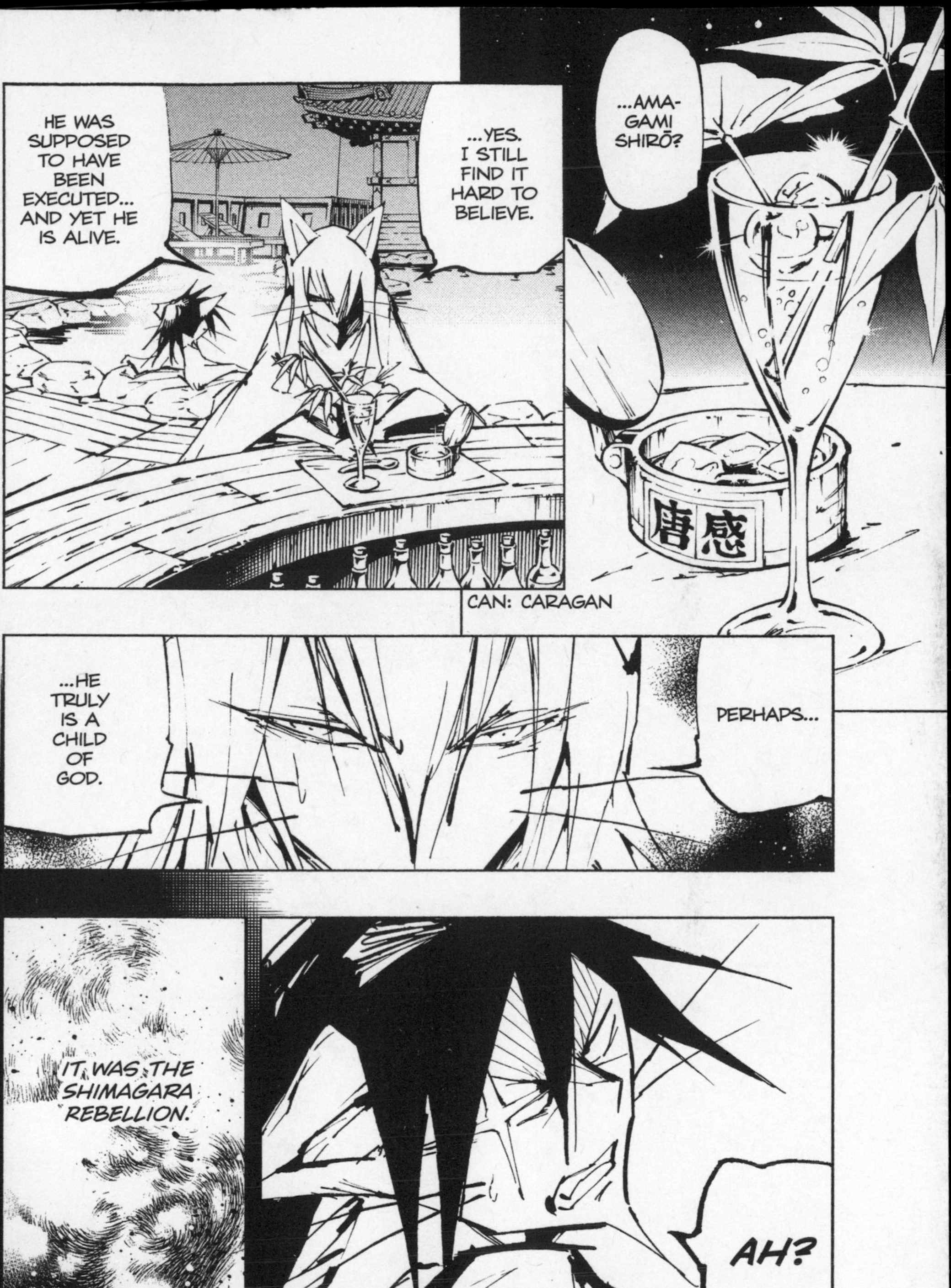
...AMA-GAMI SHIRŌ?
唐感
...YES. I STILL FIND IT HARD TO BELIEVE.
HE WAS SUPPOSED TO HAVE BEEN EXECUTED... AND YET HE IS ALIVE.
CAN: CARAGAN
PERHAPS...
...HE TRULY IS A CHILD OF GOD.
AH?
IT WAS THE SHIMAGARA REBELLION.

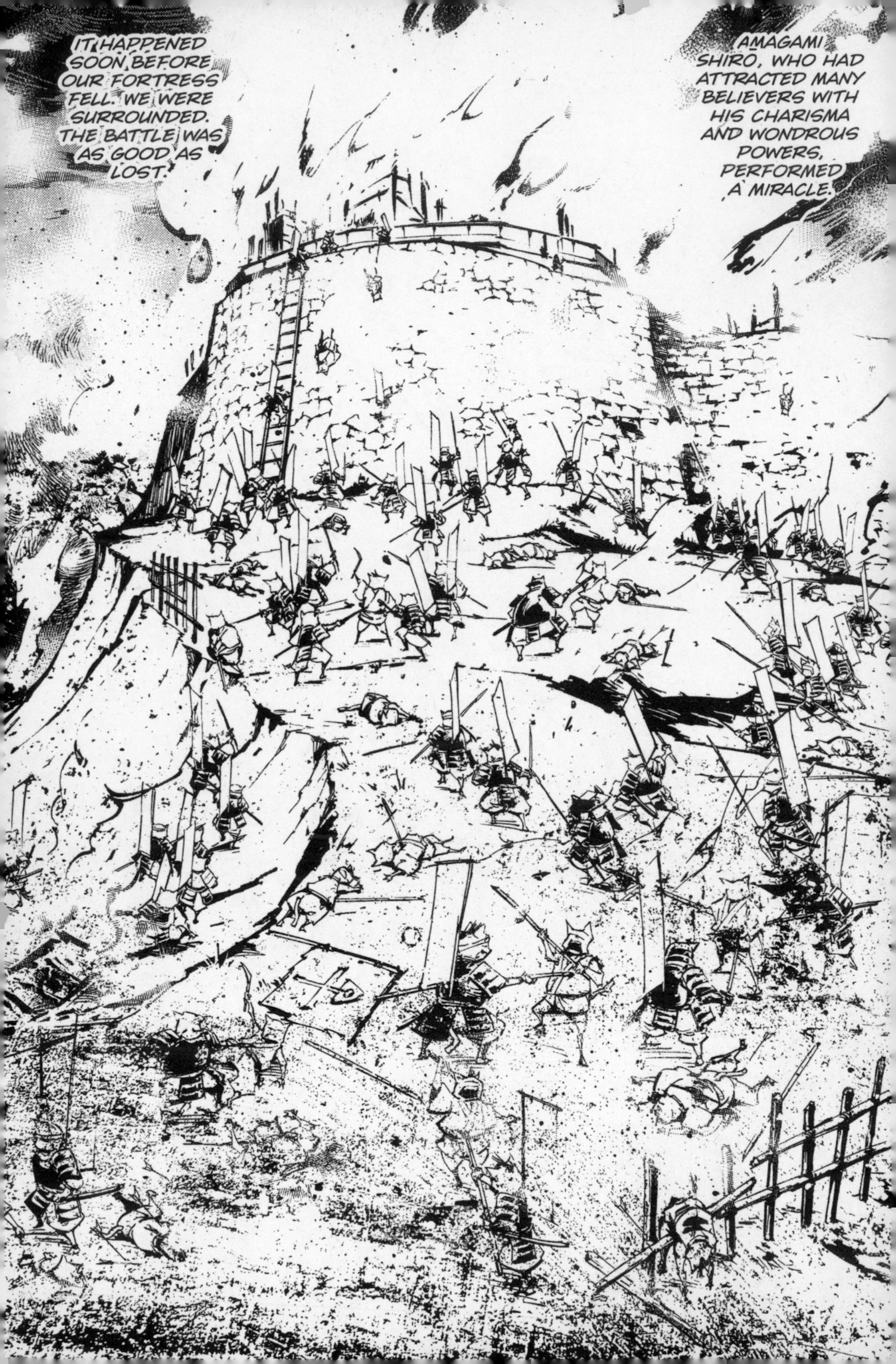
AMAGAMI SHIRO, WHO HAD ATTRACTED MANY BELIEVERS WITH HIS CHARISMA AND WONDROUS POWERS, PERFORMED A MIRACLE.
IT HAPPENED SOON BEFORE OUR FORTRESS FELL. WE WERE SURROUNDED. THE BATTLE WAS AS GOOD AS LOST.

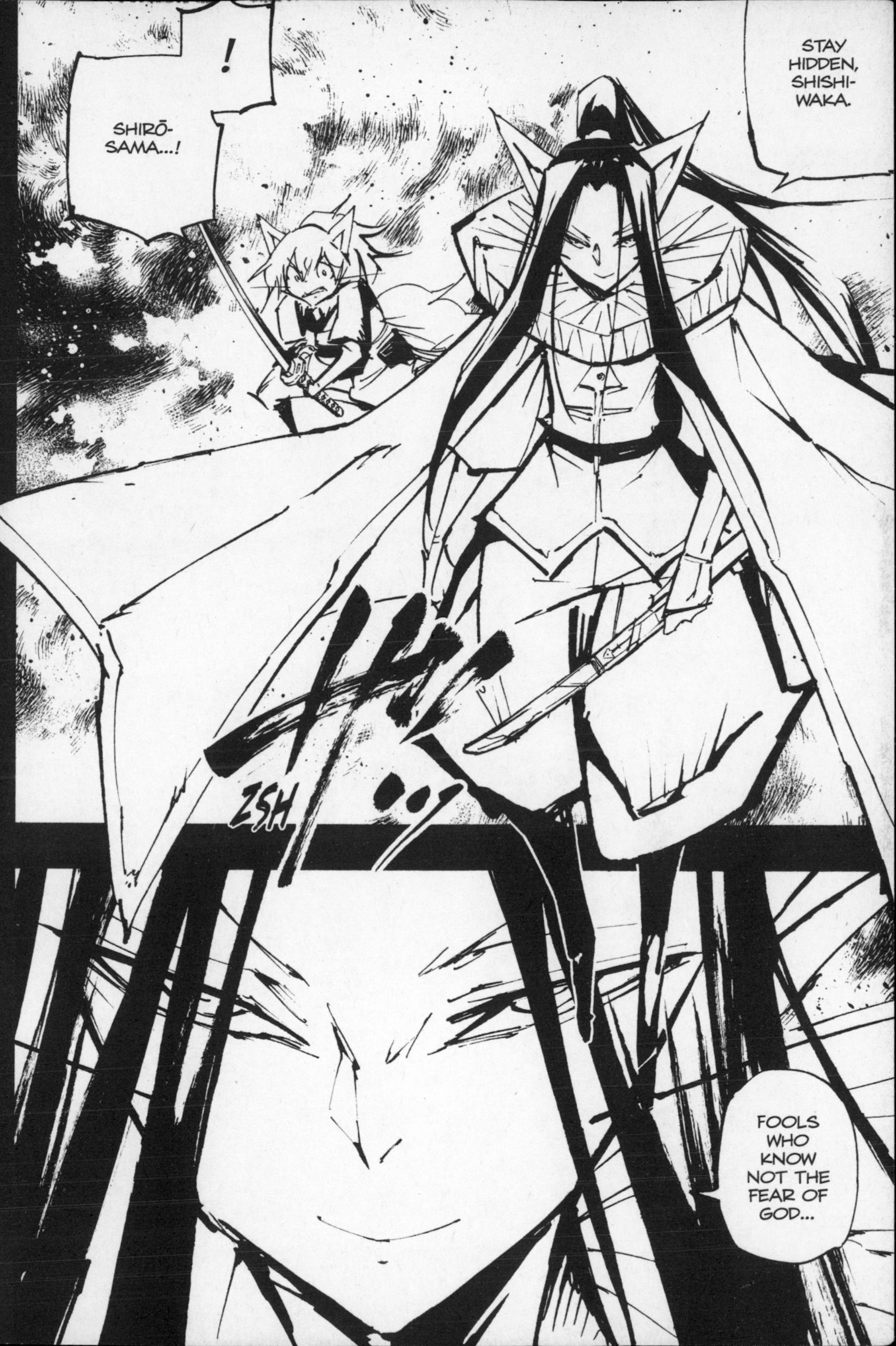
STAY HIDDEN, SHISHI-WAKA.
!
SHIRŌ-SAMA...!
ZSH
FOOLS WHO KNOW NOT THE FEAR OF GOD...

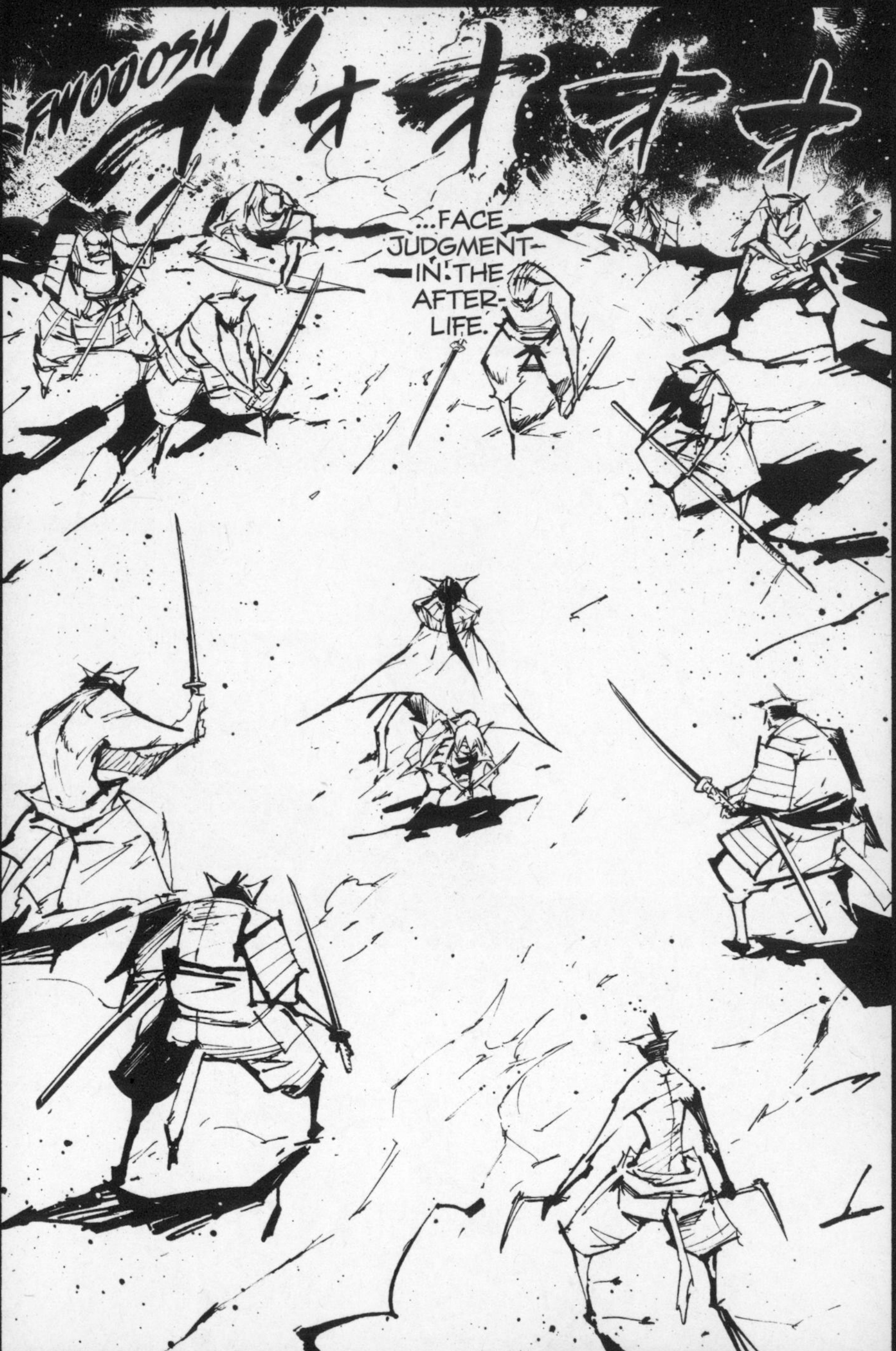
FWOOOSH
ゴハォオオオオ
...FACE JUDGMENT IN THE AFTER-LIFE.

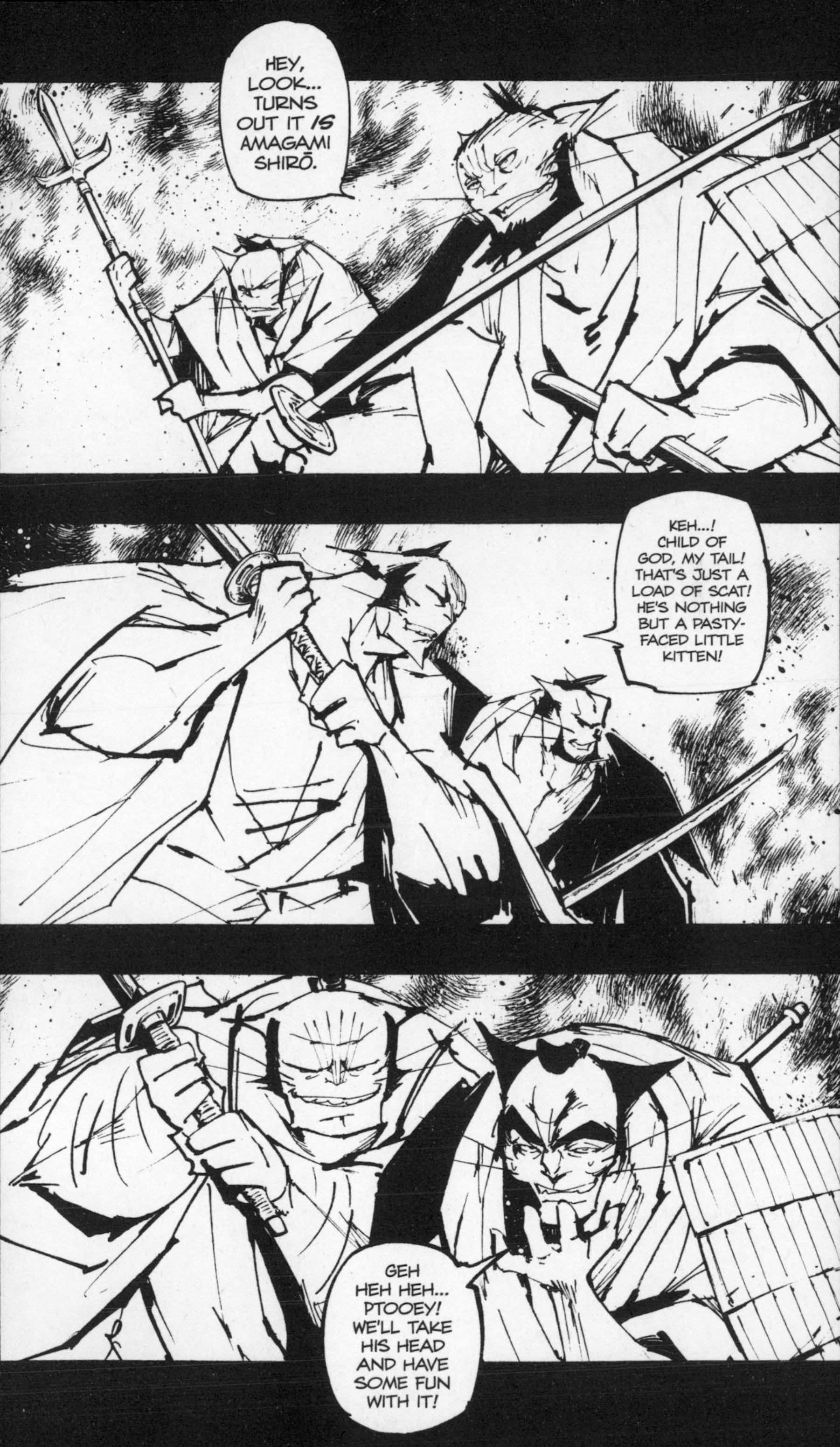
HEY, LOOK... TURNS OUT IT *IS* AMAGAMI SHIRŌ.
KEH...! CHILD OF GOD, MY TAIL! THAT'S JUST A LOAD OF SCAT! HE'S NOTHING BUT A PASTY-FACED LITTLE KITTEN!
GEH HEH HEH... PTOOEY! WE'LL TAKE HIS HEAD AND HAVE SOME FUN WITH IT!

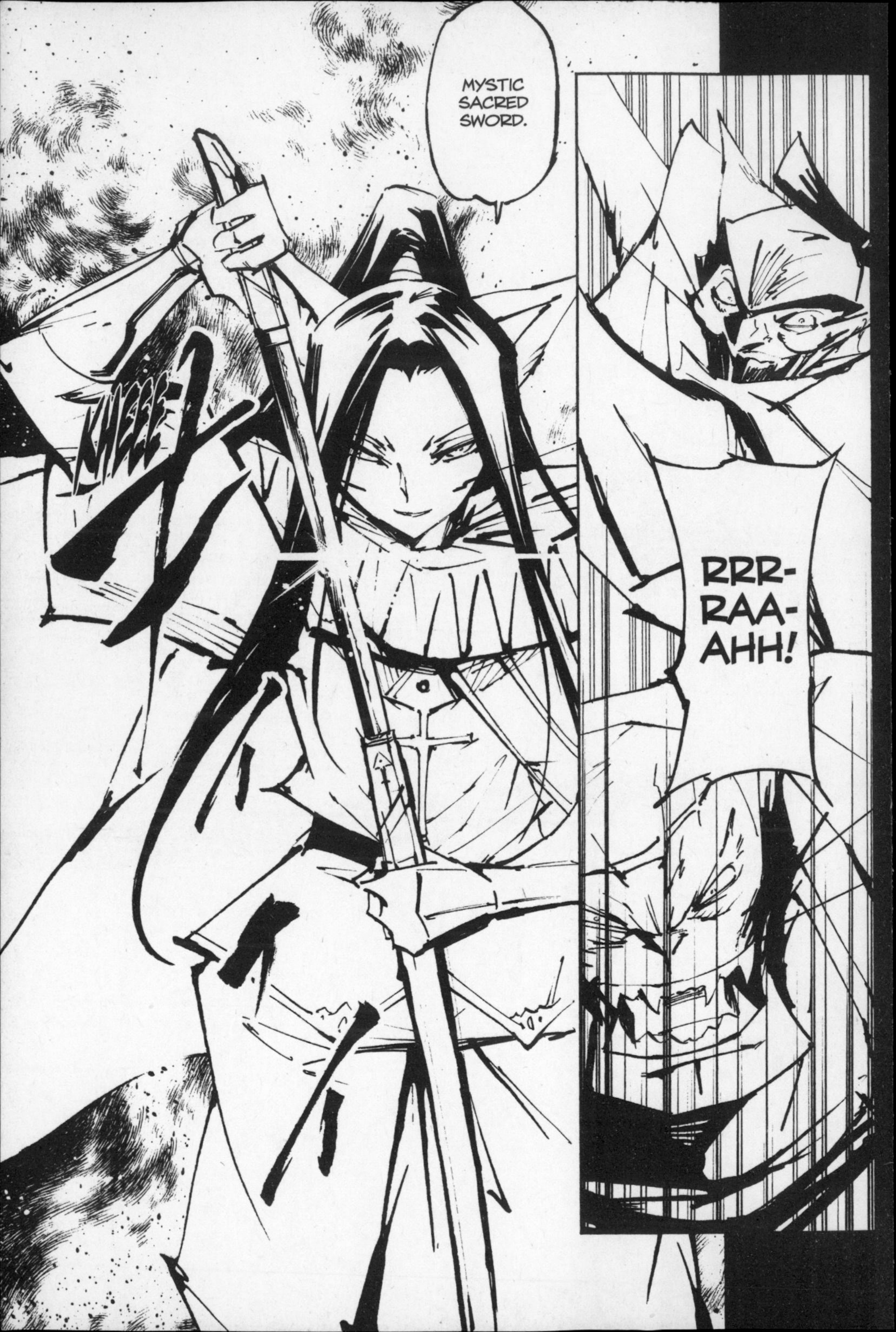
RRR-RAA-AHH!
MYSTIC SACRED SWORD.
KHEEE

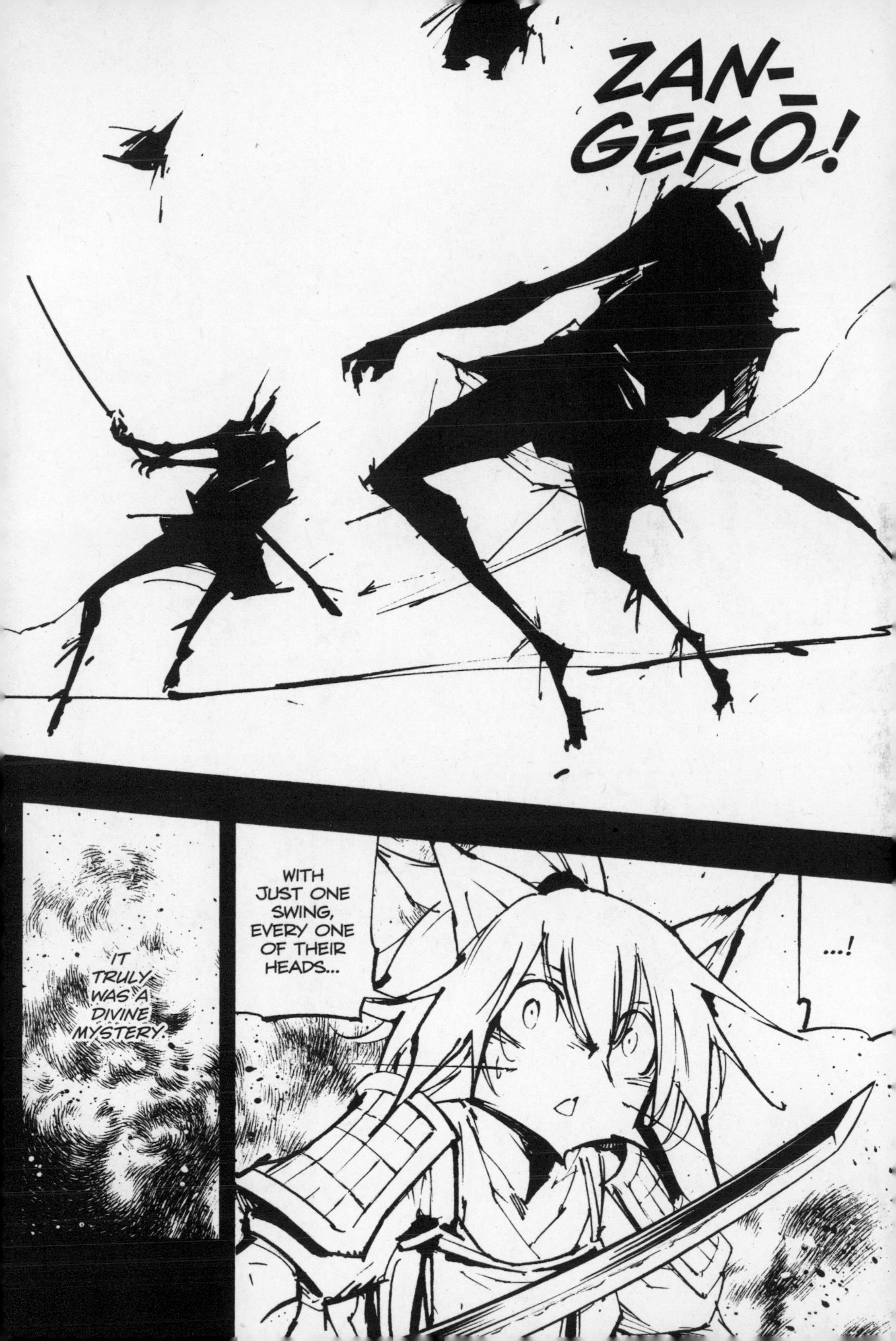

ZAN-GEKŌ!
...!
WITH JUST ONE SWING, EVERY ONE OF THEIR HEADS...
IT TRULY WAS A DIVINE MYSTERY.

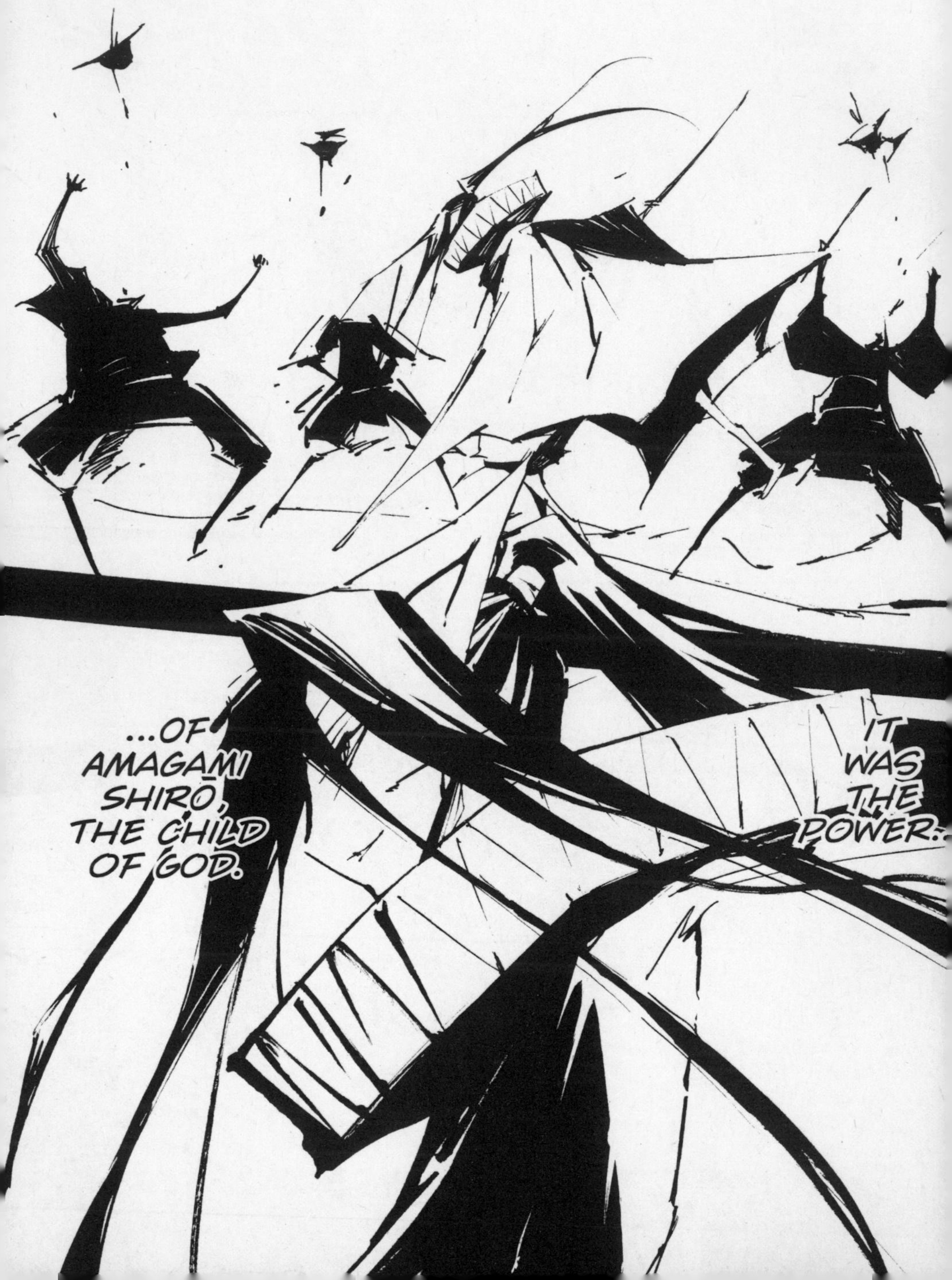
IT WAS THE POWER...
...OF AMAGAMI SHIRŌ, THE CHILD OF GOD.

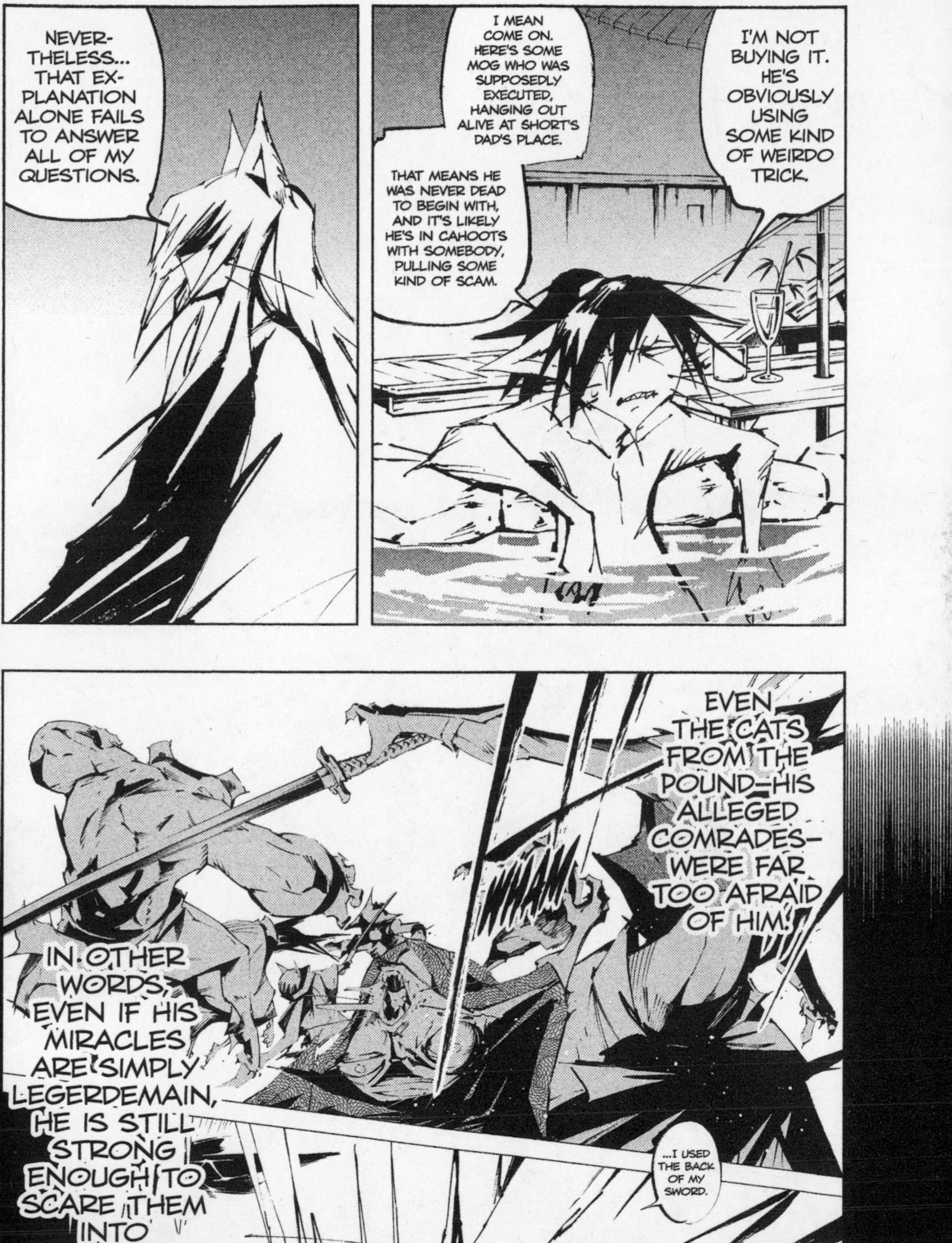
I'M NOT BUYING IT. HE'S OBVIOUSLY USING SOME KIND OF WEIRDO TRICK.
I MEAN COME ON. HERE'S SOME MOG WHO WAS SUPPOSEDLY EXECUTED, HANGING OUT ALIVE AT SHORT'S DAD'S PLACE.
THAT MEANS HE WAS NEVER DEAD TO BEGIN WITH, AND IT'S LIKELY HE'S IN CAHOOTS WITH SOMEBODY, PULLING SOME KIND OF SCAM.
NEVER-THELESS... THAT EX-PLANATION ALONE FAILS TO ANSWER ALL OF MY QUESTIONS.
EVEN THE CATS FROM THE POUND—HIS ALLEGED COMRADES—WERE FAR TOO AFRAID OF HIM!
IN OTHER WORDS, EVEN IF HIS MIRACLES ARE SIMPLY LEGERDEMAIN, HE IS STILL STRONG ENOUGH TO SCARE THEM INTO SUBMISSION.
...I USED THE BACK OF MY SWORD.

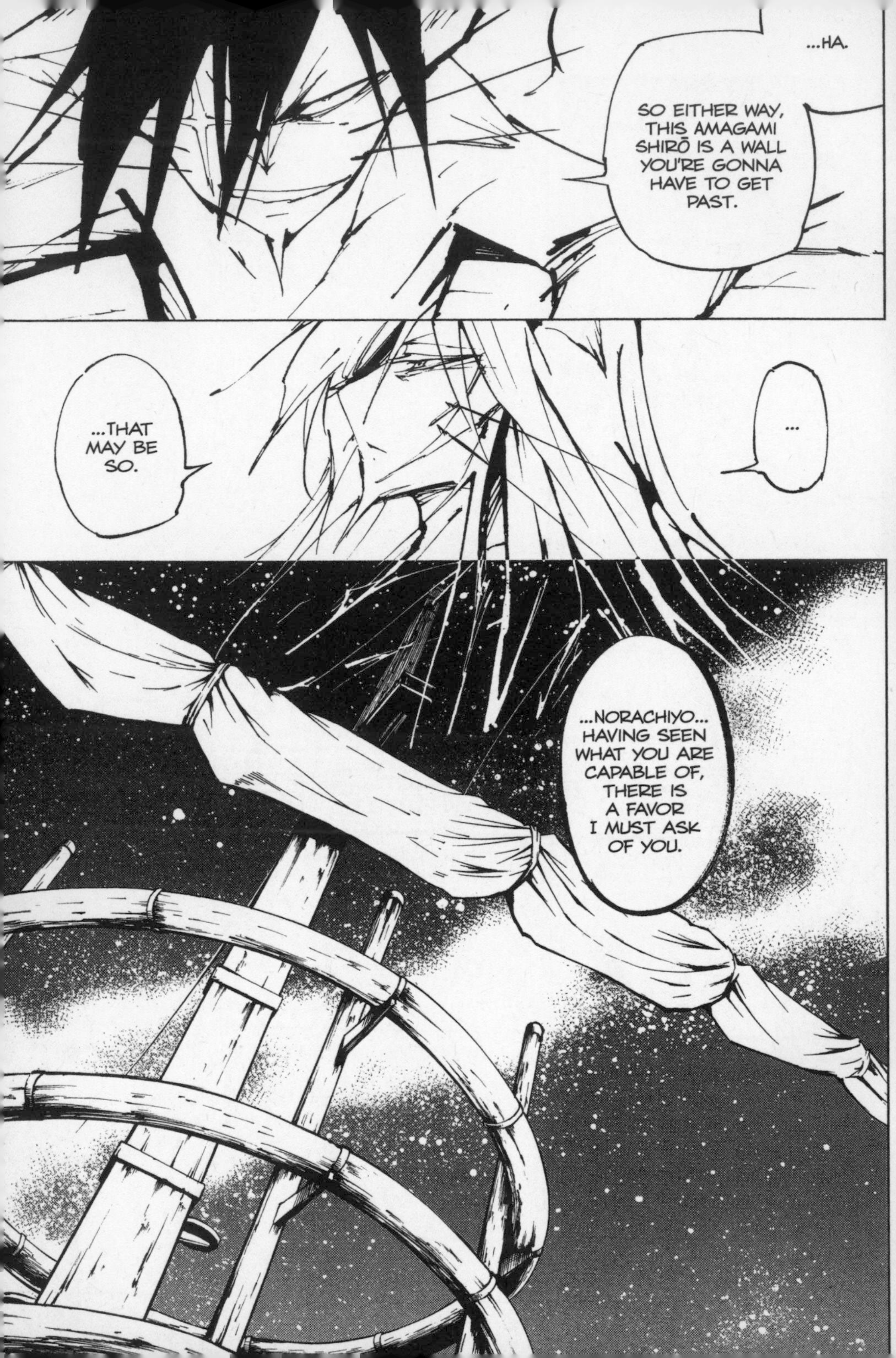
...HA.
SO EITHER WAY, THIS AMAGAMI SHIRŌ IS A WALL YOU'RE GONNA HAVE TO GET PAST.
...
...THAT MAY BE SO.
...NORACHIYO... HAVING SEEN WHAT YOU ARE CAPABLE OF, THERE IS A FAVOR I MUST ASK OF YOU.

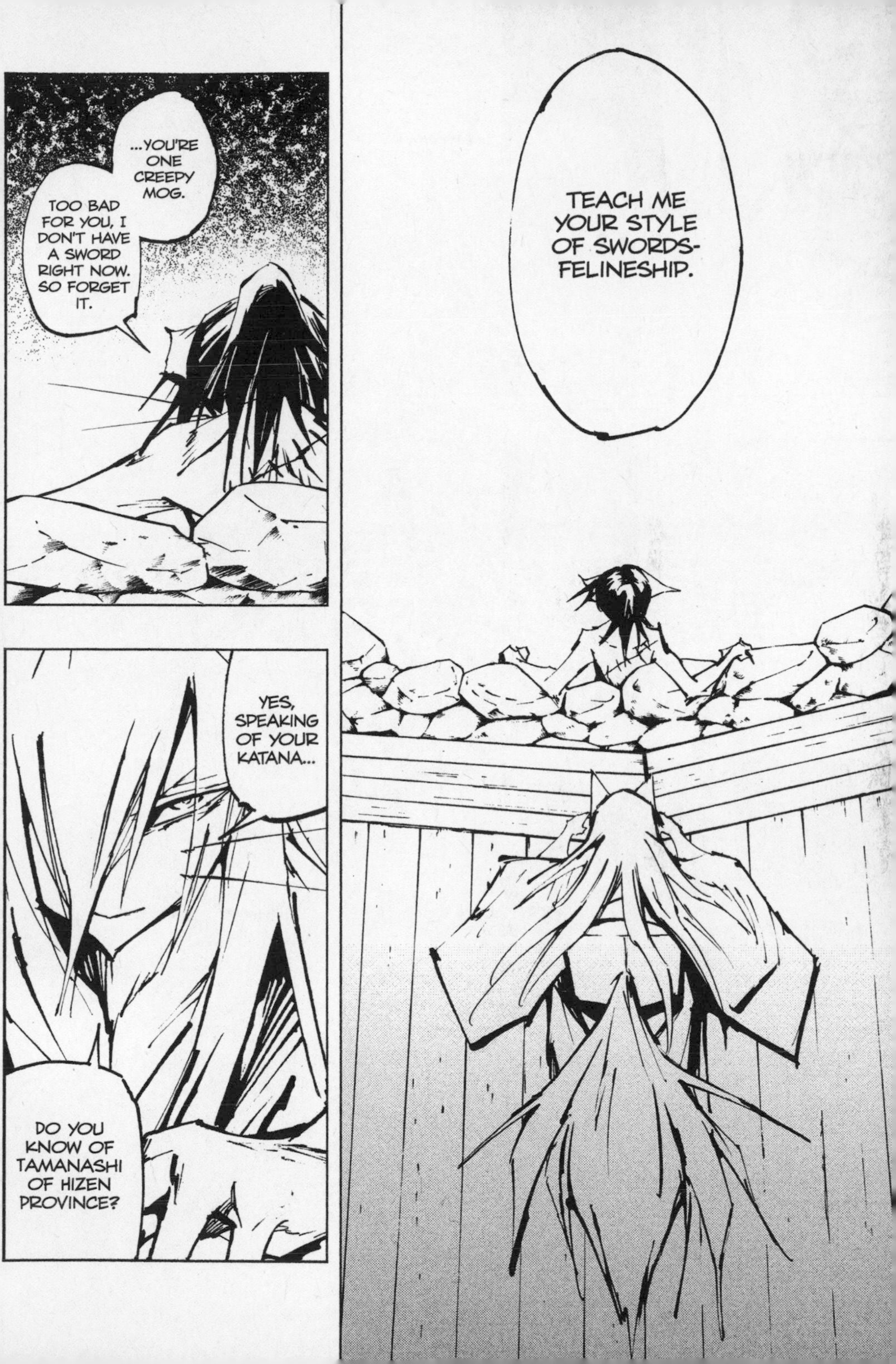
TEACH ME YOUR STYLE OF SWORDS-FELINESHIP.
...YOU'RE ONE CREEPY MOG.
TOO BAD FOR YOU, I DON'T HAVE A SWORD RIGHT NOW. SO FORGET IT.
YES, SPEAKING OF YOUR KATANA...
DO YOU KNOW OF TAMANASHI OF HIZEN PROVINCE?

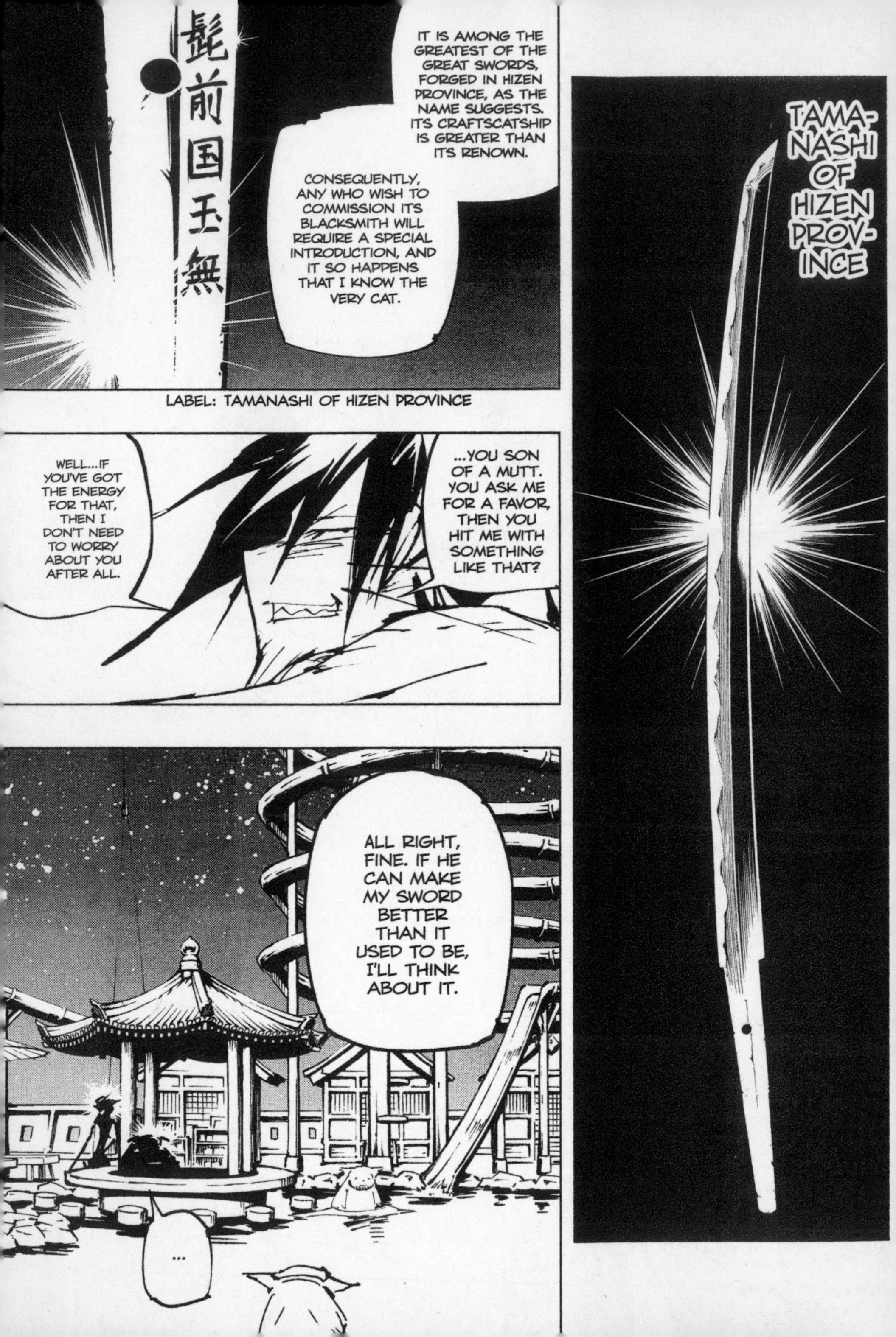
TAMA-NASHI OF HIZEN PROV-INCE
髭前国玉無
IT IS AMONG THE GREATEST OF THE GREAT SWORDS, FORGED IN HIZEN PROVINCE, AS THE NAME SUGGESTS. ITS CRAFTSCATSHIP IS GREATER THAN ITS RENOWN.
CONSEQUENTLY, ANY WHO WISH TO COMMISSION ITS BLACKSMITH WILL REQUIRE A SPECIAL INTRODUCTION, AND IT SO HAPPENS THAT I KNOW THE VERY CAT.
LABEL: TAMANASHI OF HIZEN PROVINCE
...YOU SON OF A MUTT. YOU ASK ME FOR A FAVOR, THEN YOU HIT ME WITH SOMETHING LIKE THAT?
WELL...IF YOU'VE GOT THE ENERGY FOR THAT, THEN I DON'T NEED TO WORRY ABOUT YOU AFTER ALL.
ALL RIGHT, FINE. IF HE CAN MAKE MY SWORD BETTER THAN IT USED TO BE, I'LL THINK ABOUT IT.
...

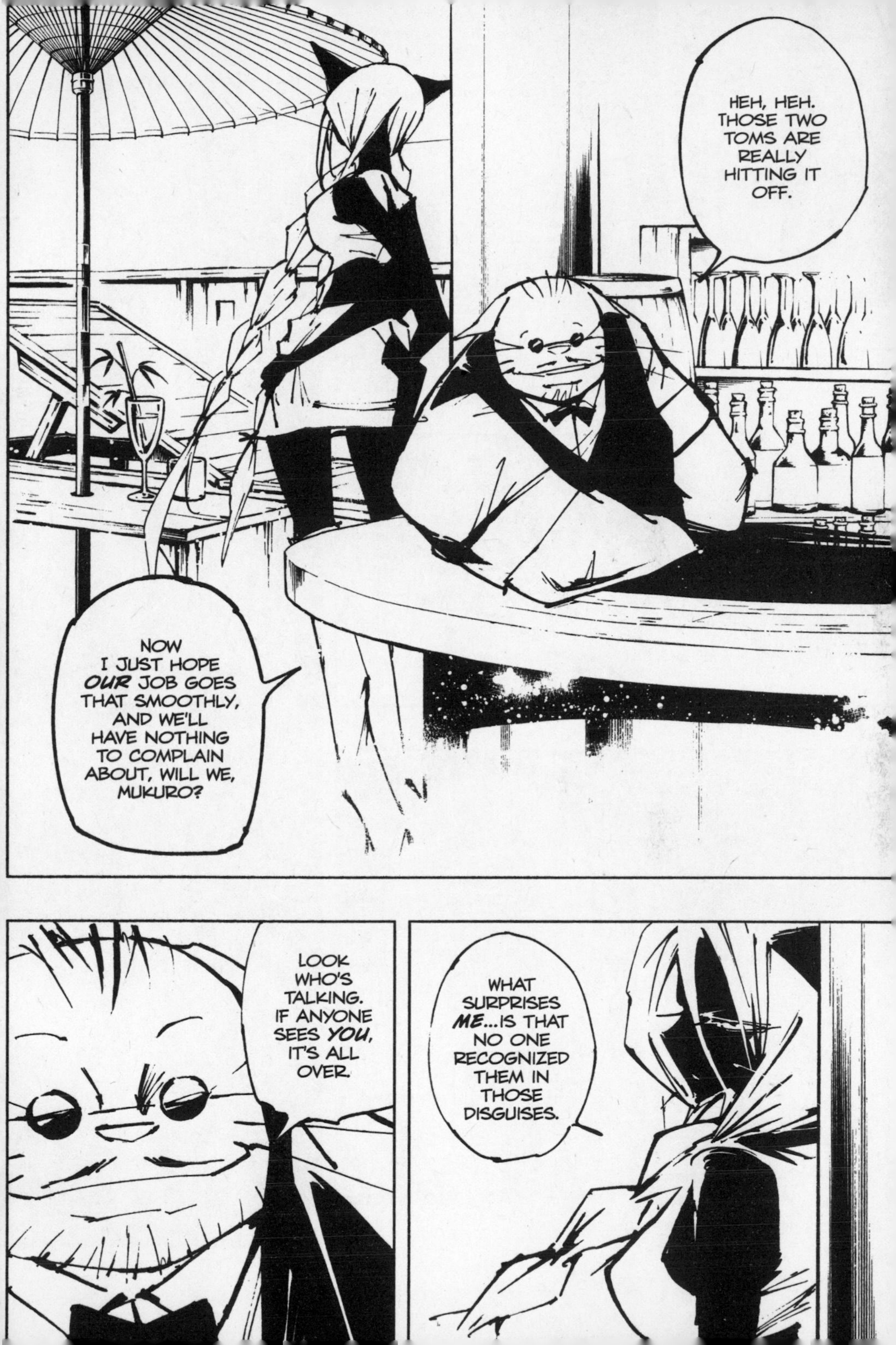
HEH, HEH. THOSE TWO TOMS ARE REALLY HITTING IT OFF.
NOW I JUST HOPE OUR JOB GOES THAT SMOOTHLY, AND WE'LL HAVE NOTHING TO COMPLAIN ABOUT, WILL WE, MUKURO?
WHAT SURPRISES ME...IS THAT NO ONE RECOGNIZED THEM IN THOSE DISGUISES.
LOOK WHO'S TALKING. IF ANYONE SEES YOU, IT'S ALL OVER.

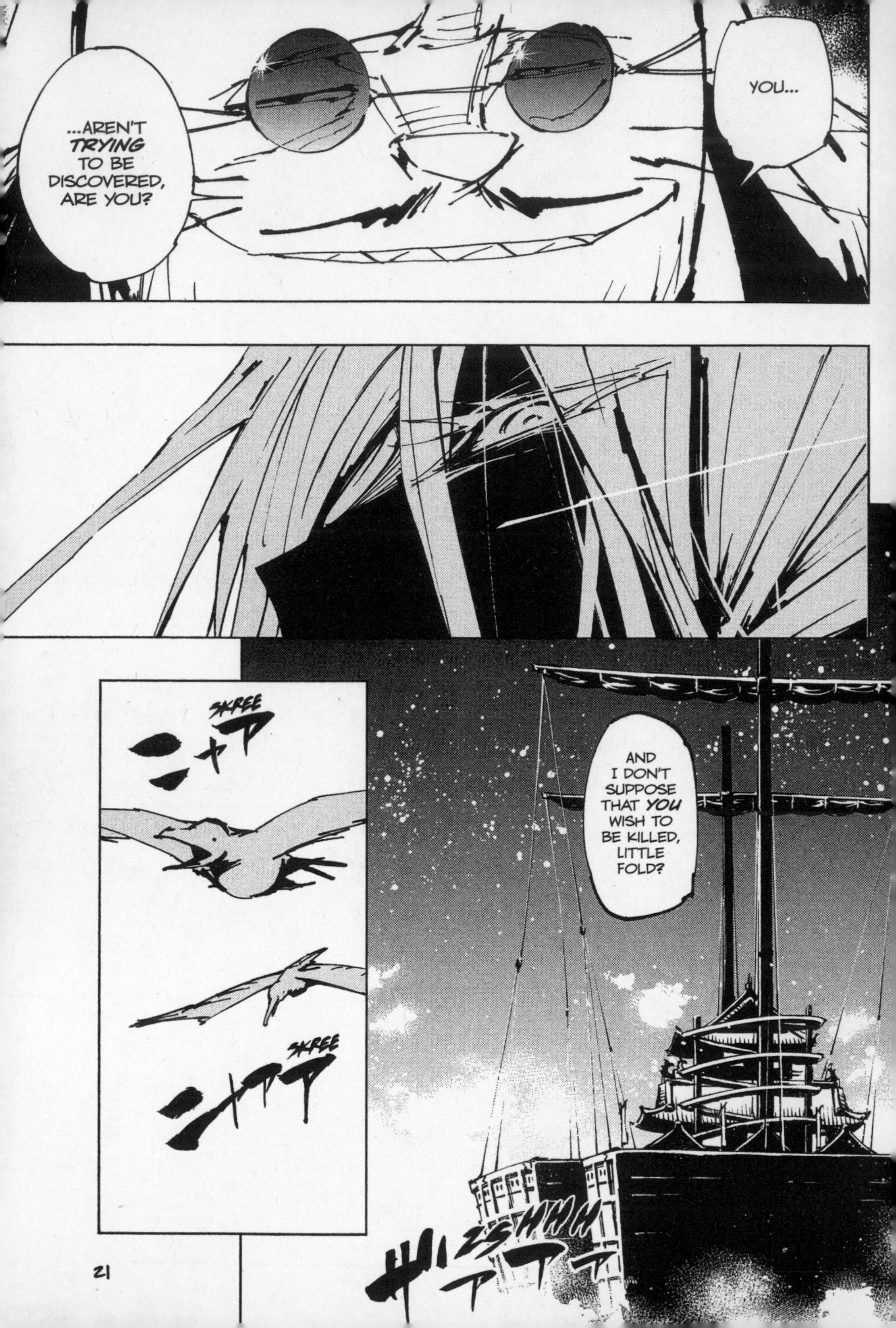
YOU...
...AREN'T *TRYING* TO BE DISCOVERED, ARE YOU?
AND I DON'T SUPPOSE THAT *YOU* WISH TO BE KILLED, LITTLE FOLD?
ZSHHHH
SKREE
SKREE

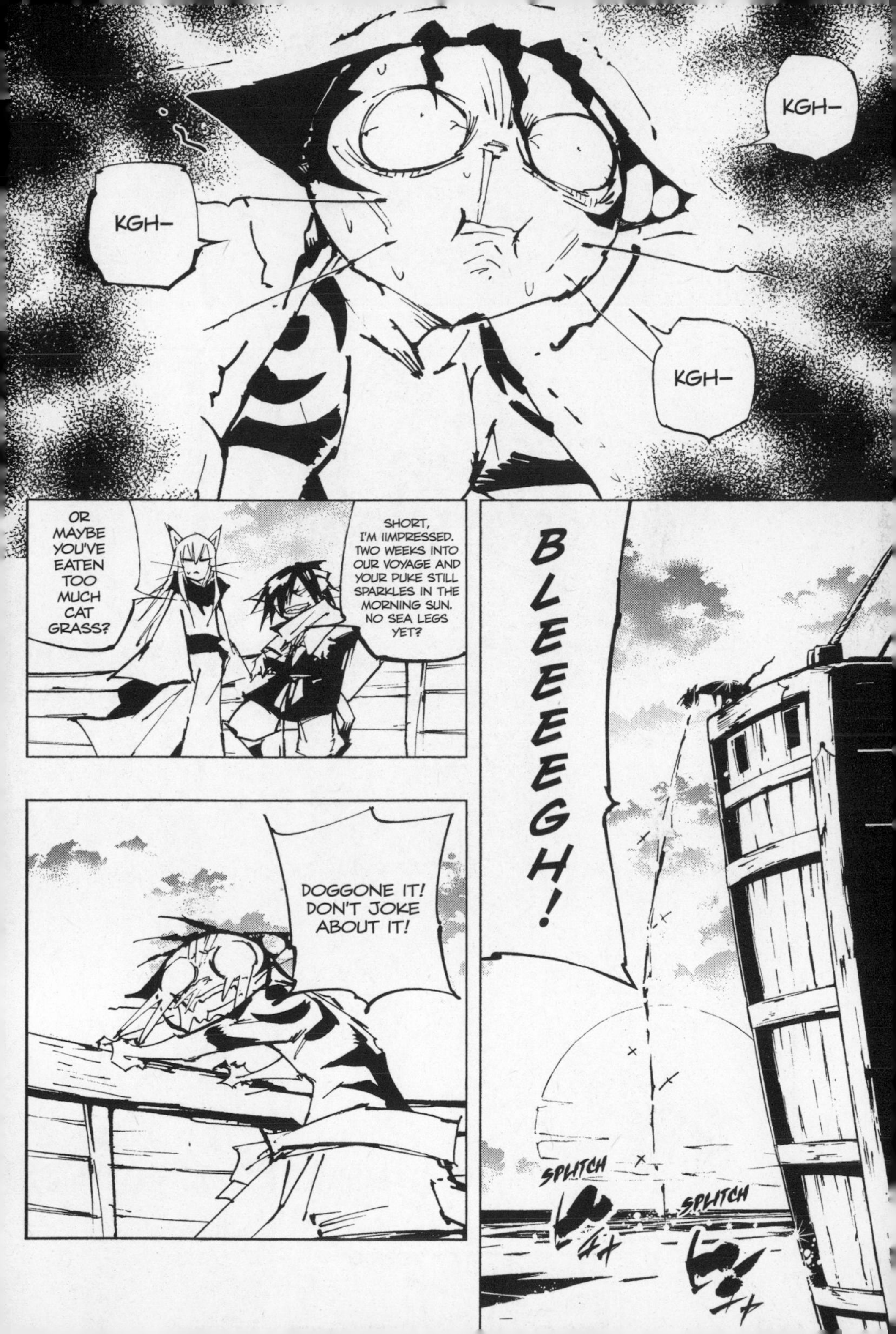
KGH–
KGH–
KGH–
BLEEEEEGH!
SPLITCH
SPLITCH
SHORT, I'M IIMPRESSED. TWO WEEKS INTO OUR VOYAGE AND YOUR PUKE STILL SPARKLES IN THE MORNING SUN. NO SEA LEGS YET?
OR MAYBE YOU'VE EATEN TOO MUCH CAT GRASS?
DOGGONE IT! DON'T JOKE ABOUT IT!

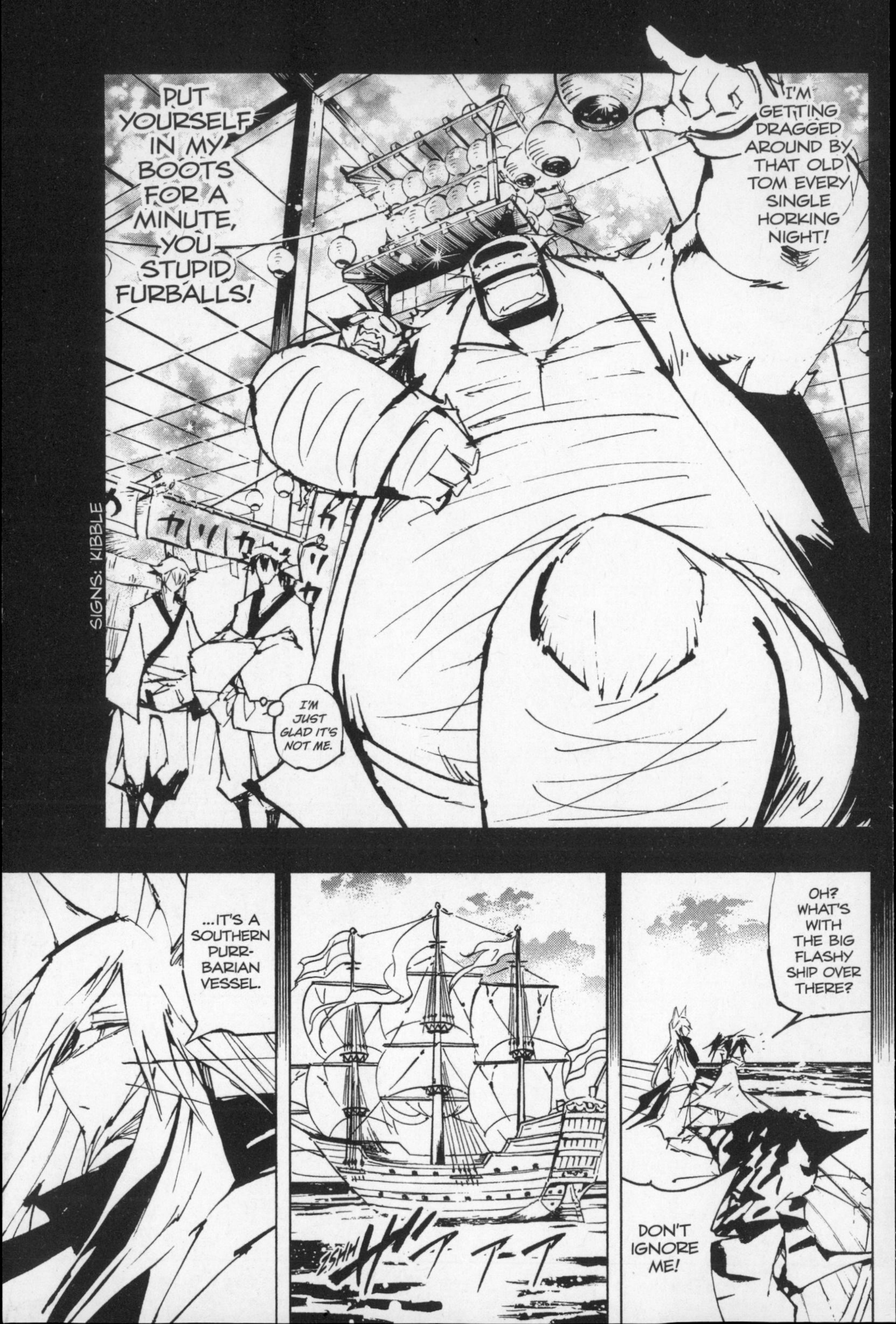
I'M GETTING DRAGGED AROUND BY THAT OLD TOM EVERY SINGLE HORKING NIGHT!
PUT YOURSELF IN MY BOOTS FOR A MINUTE, YOU STUPID FURBALLS!
SIGNS: KIBBLE
I'M JUST GLAD IT'S NOT ME.
OH? WHAT'S WITH THE BIG FLASHY SHIP OVER THERE?
DON'T IGNORE ME!
SHHH
...IT'S A SOUTHERN PURR-BARIAN VESSEL.

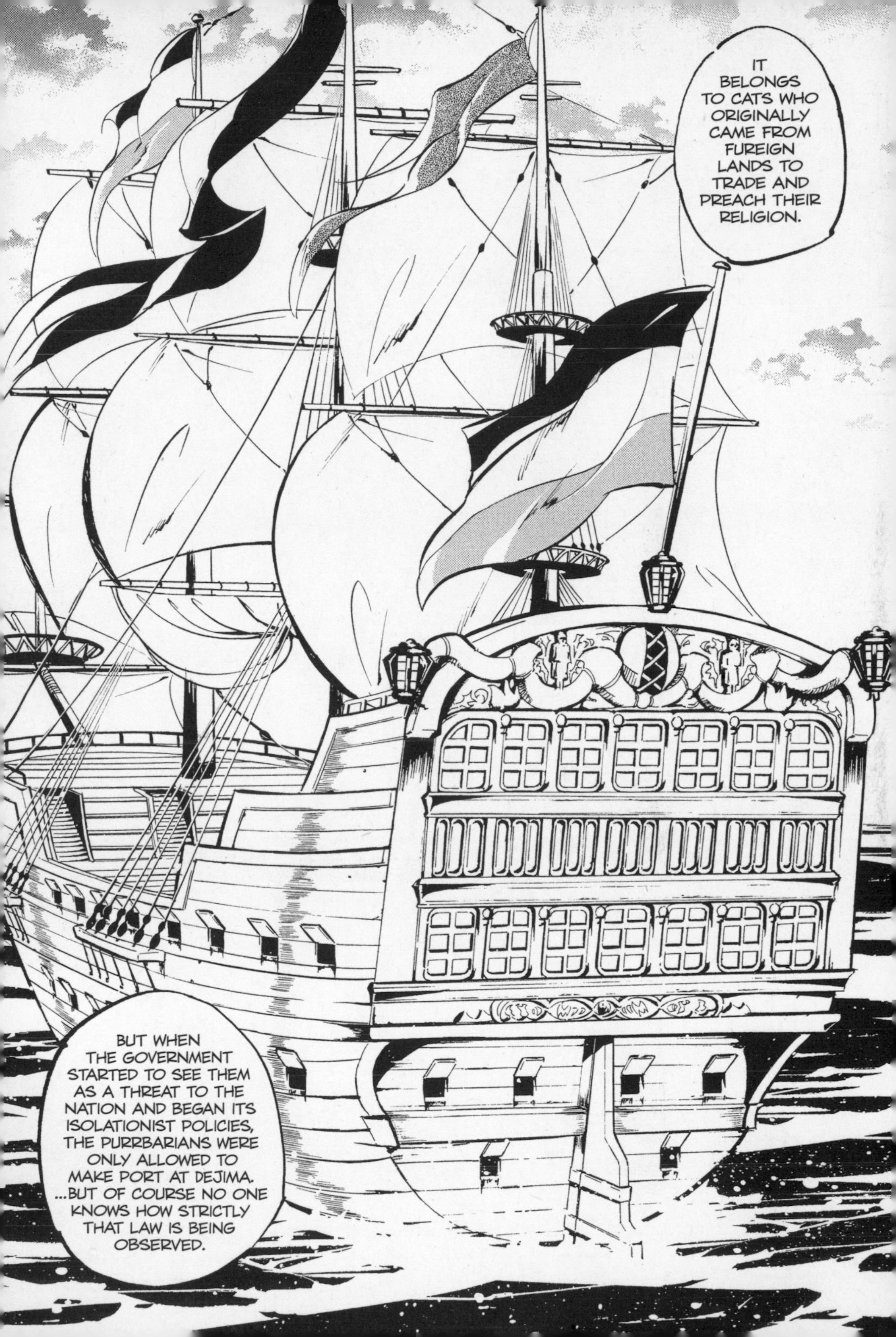
IT BELONGS TO CATS WHO ORIGINALLY CAME FROM FUREIGN LANDS TO TRADE AND PREACH THEIR RELIGION.
BUT WHEN THE GOVERNMENT STARTED TO SEE THEM AS A THREAT TO THE NATION AND BEGAN ITS ISOLATIONIST POLICIES, THE PURRBARIANS WERE ONLY ALLOWED TO MAKE PORT AT DEJIMA. ...BUT OF COURSE NO ONE KNOWS HOW STRICTLY THAT LAW IS BEING OBSERVED.

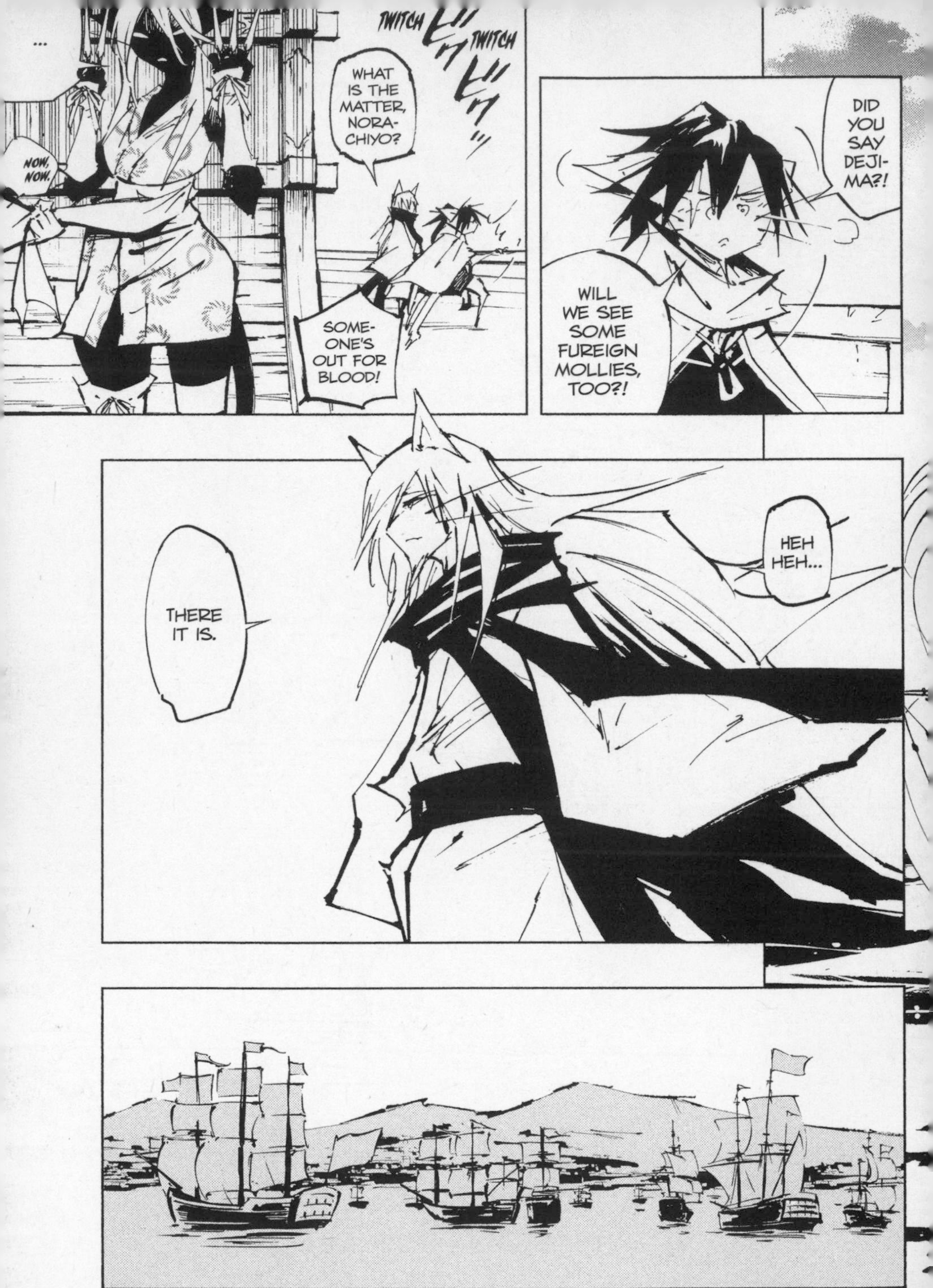
DID YOU SAY DEJIMA?!
WILL WE SEE SOME FUREIGN MOLLIES, TOO?!
TWITCH
TWITCH
WHAT IS THE MATTER, NORA-CHIYO?
SOME-ONE'S OUT FOR BLOOD!
NOW, NOW.
...
HEH HEH...
THERE IT IS.

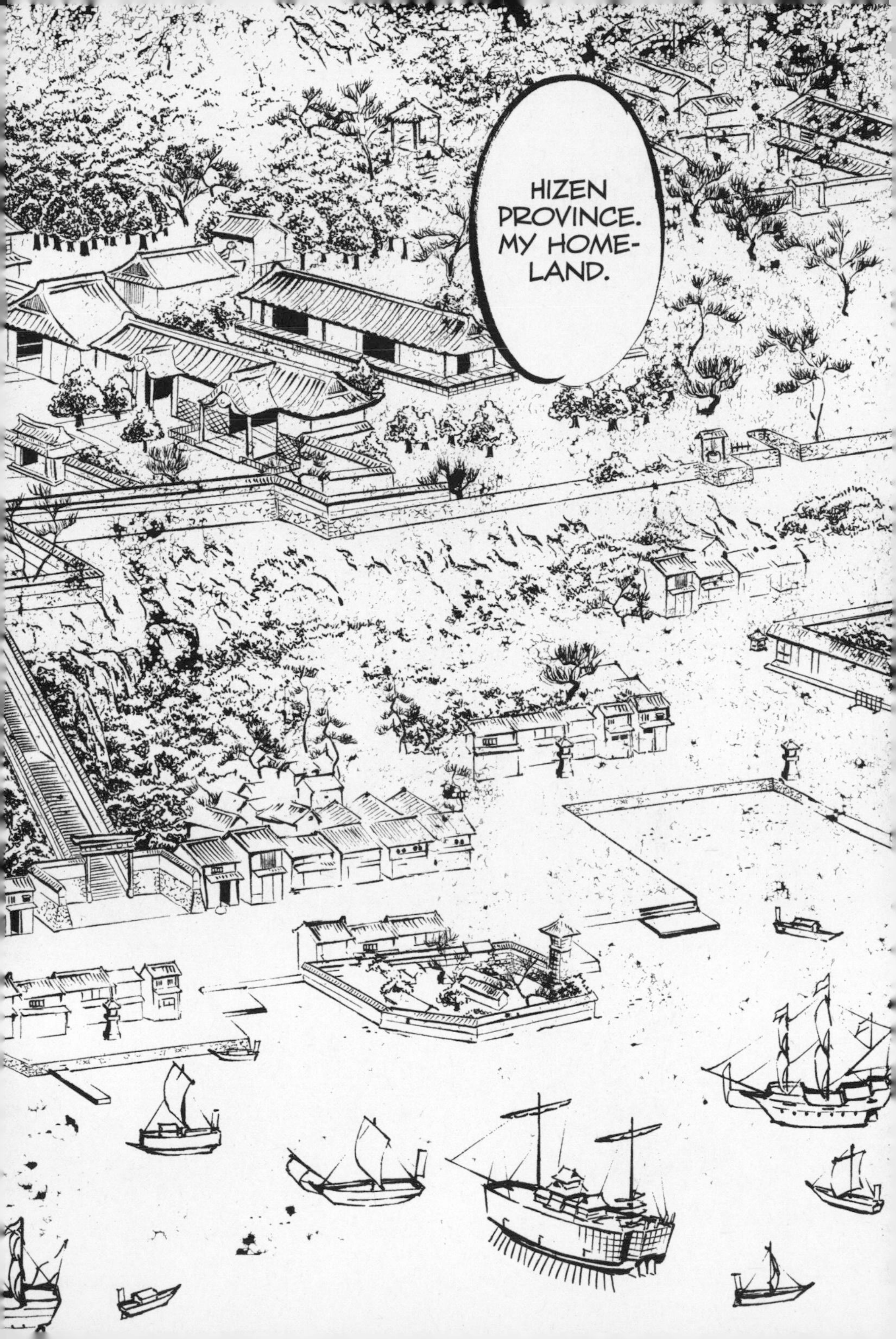
HIZEN PROVINCE. MY HOME-LAND.

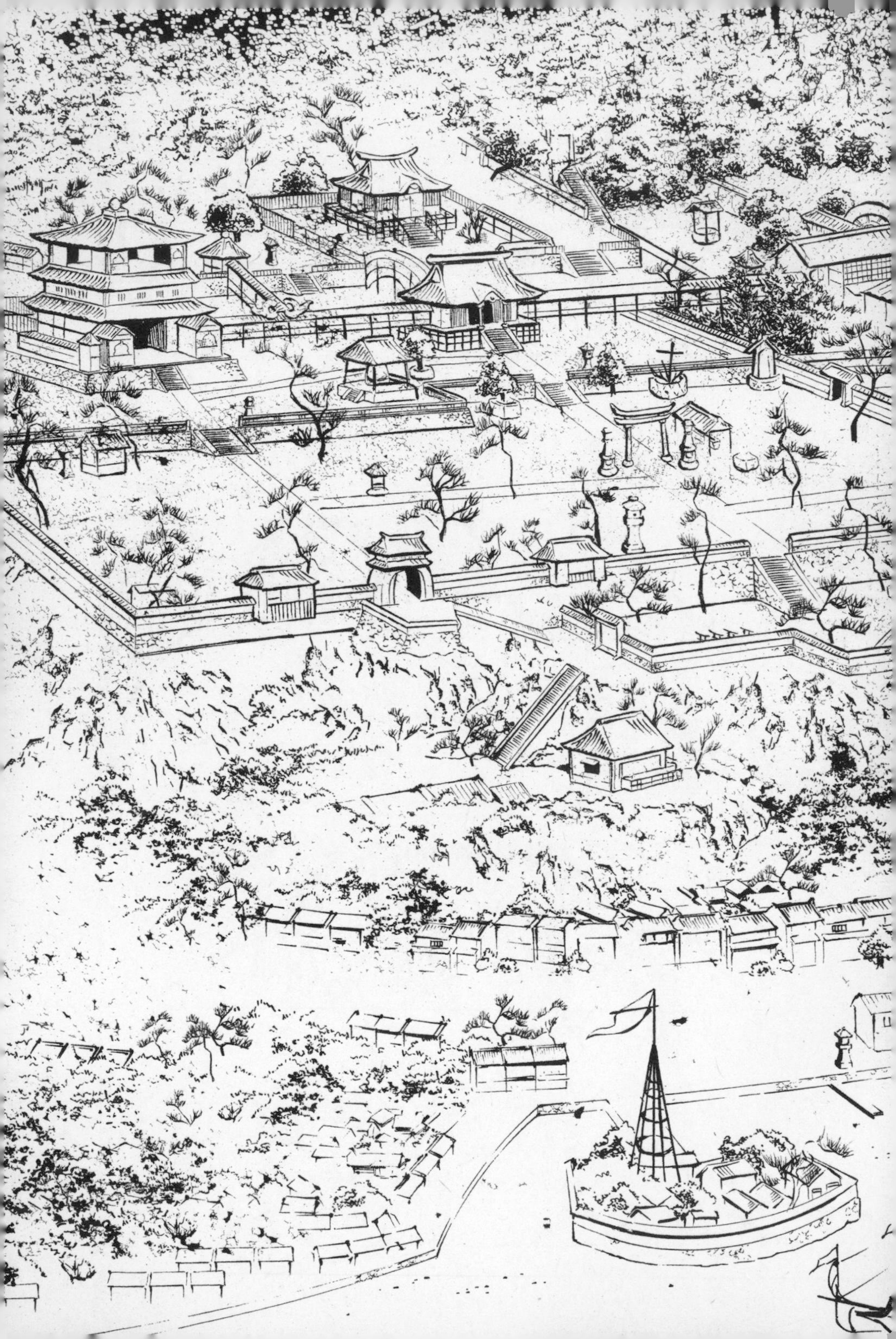

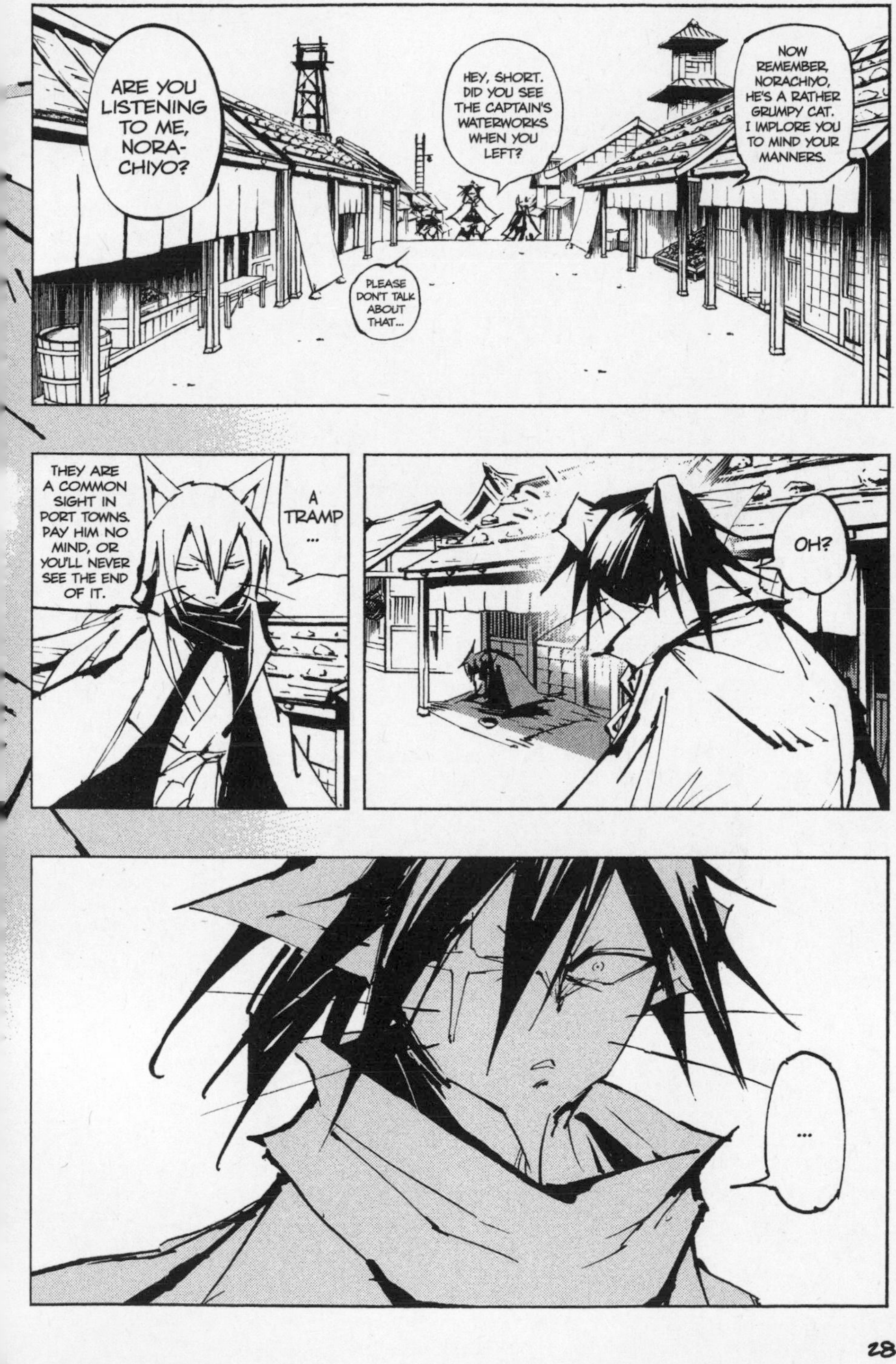
NOW REMEMBER, NORACHIYO, HE'S A RATHER GRUMPY CAT. I IMPLORE YOU TO MIND YOUR MANNERS.
HEY, SHORT. DID YOU SEE THE CAPTAIN'S WATERWORKS WHEN YOU LEFT?
ARE YOU LISTENING TO ME, NORA-CHIYO?
PLEASE DON'T TALK ABOUT THAT...
OH?
A TRAMP ...
THEY ARE A COMMON SIGHT IN PORT TOWNS. PAY HIM NO MIND, OR YOU'LL NEVER SEE THE END OF IT.
...

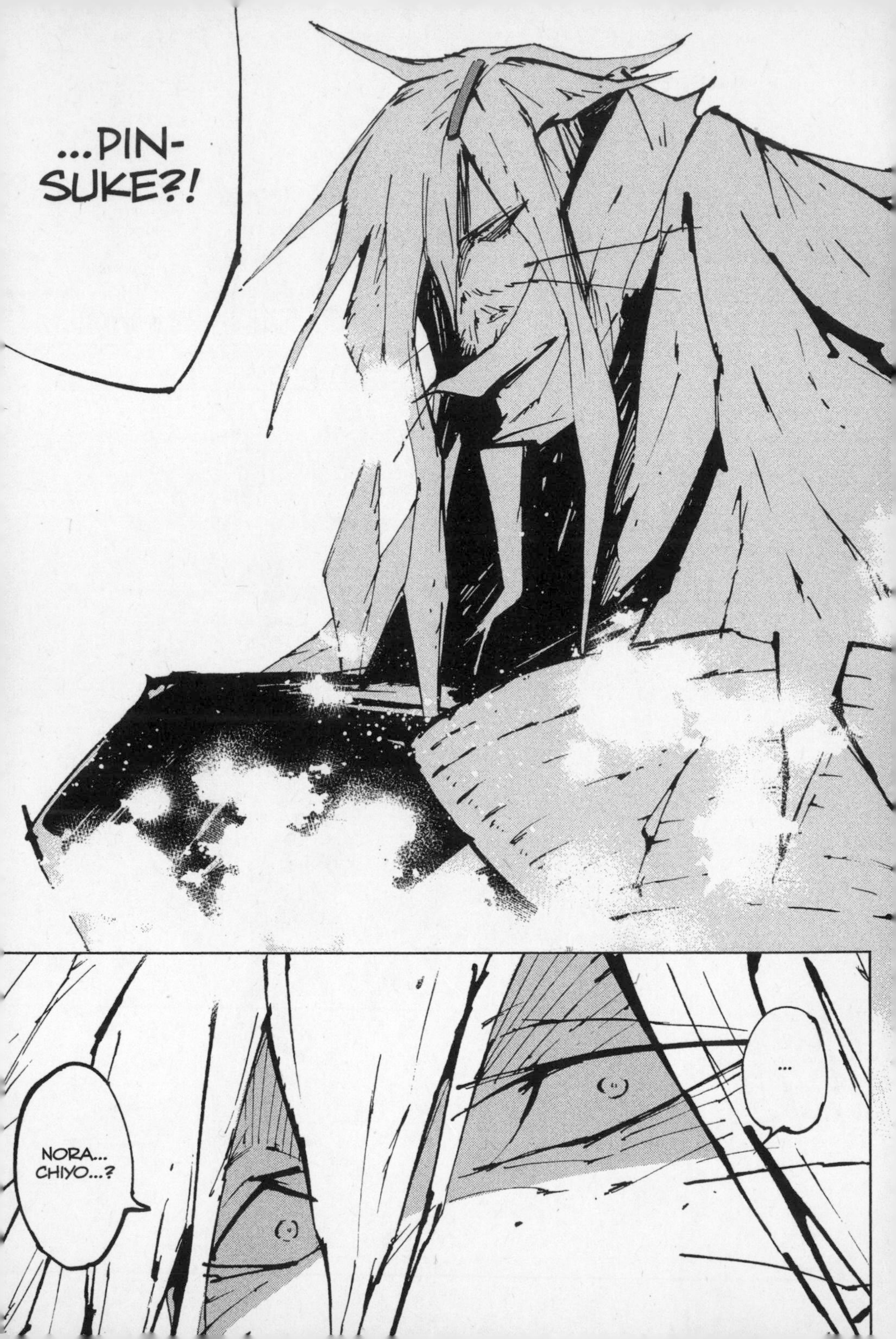
...PIN-SUKE?!
...
NORA... CHIYO...?

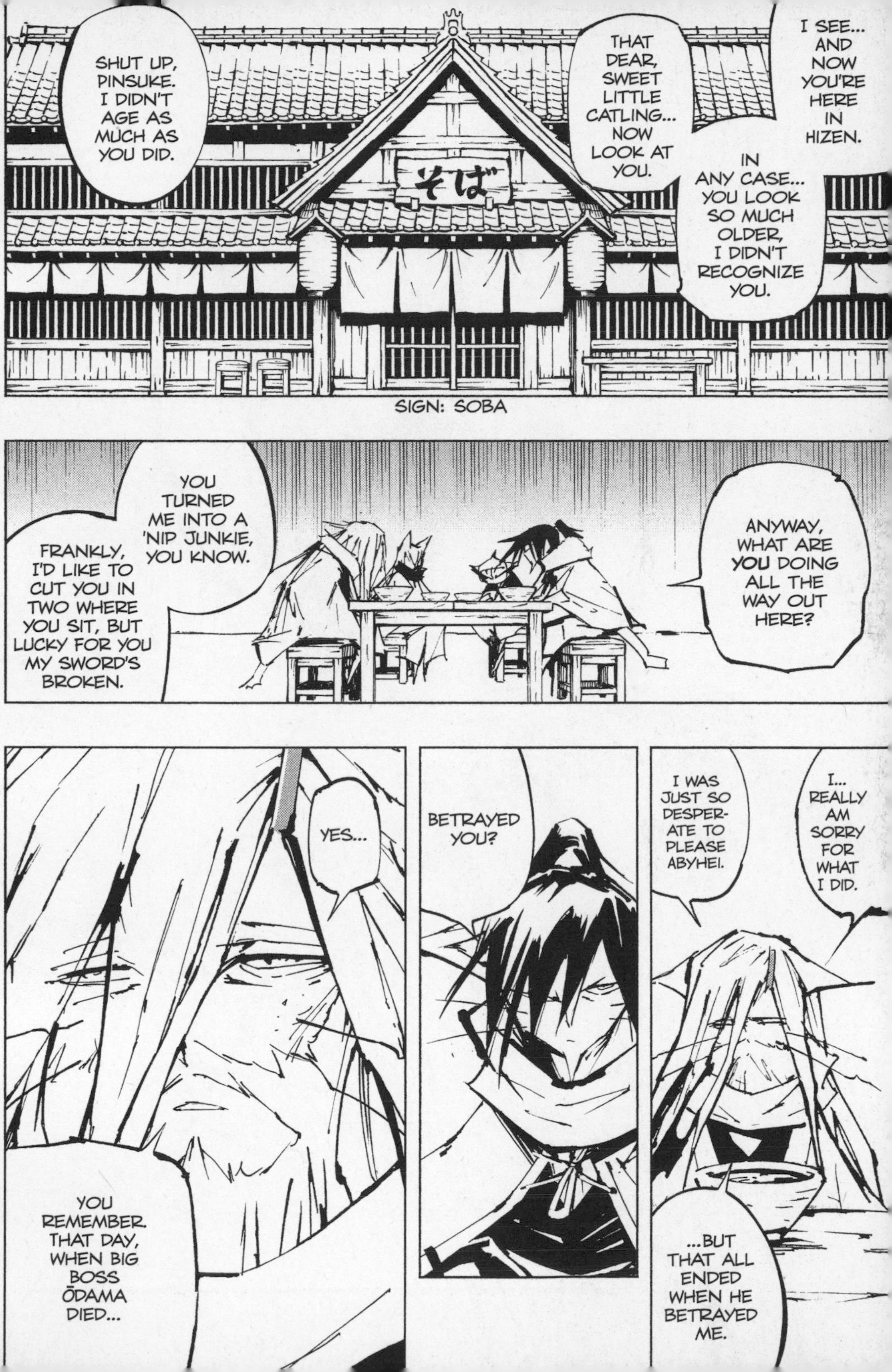
I SEE... AND NOW YOU'RE HERE IN HIZEN.
IN ANY CASE... YOU LOOK SO MUCH OLDER, I DIDN'T RECOGNIZE YOU.
THAT DEAR, SWEET LITTLE CATLING... NOW LOOK AT YOU.
SHUT UP, PINSUKE. I DIDN'T AGE AS MUCH AS YOU DID.
そば
SIGN: SOBA
ANYWAY, WHAT ARE YOU DOING ALL THE WAY OUT HERE?
YOU TURNED ME INTO A 'NIP JUNKIE, YOU KNOW.
FRANKLY, I'D LIKE TO CUT YOU IN TWO WHERE YOU SIT, BUT LUCKY FOR YOU MY SWORD'S BROKEN.
I... REALLY AM SORRY FOR WHAT I DID.
I WAS JUST SO DESPERATE TO PLEASE ABYHEI.
...BUT THAT ALL ENDED WHEN HE BETRAYED ME.
BETRAYED YOU?
YES...
YOU REMEMBER THAT DAY, WHEN BIG BOSS ŌDAMA DIED...

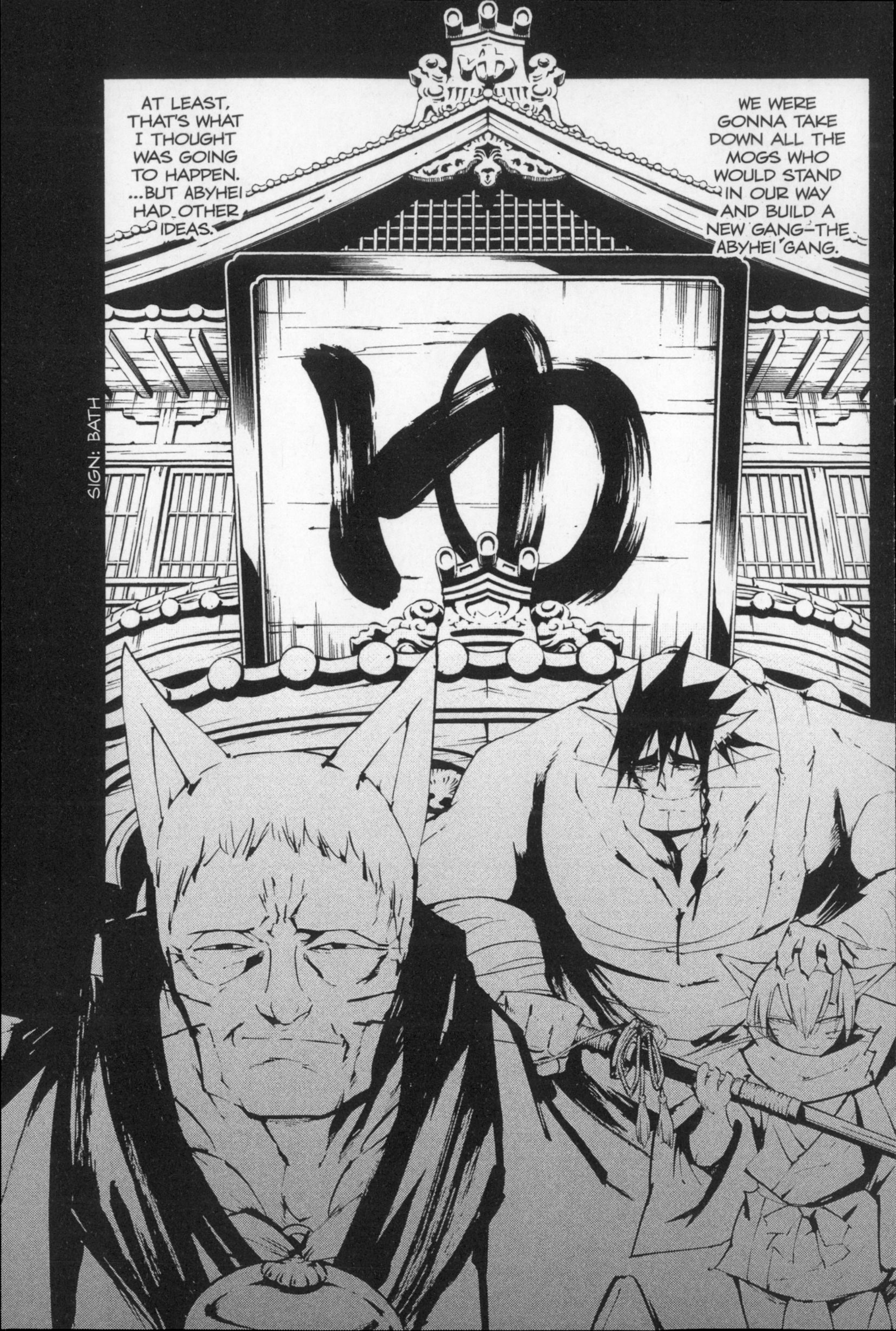
WE WERE GONNA TAKE DOWN ALL THE MOGS WHO WOULD STAND IN OUR WAY AND BUILD A NEW GANG–THE ABYHEI GANG.
AT LEAST, THAT'S WHAT I THOUGHT WAS GOING TO HAPPEN. ...BUT ABYHEI HAD OTHER IDEAS.
SIGN: BATH

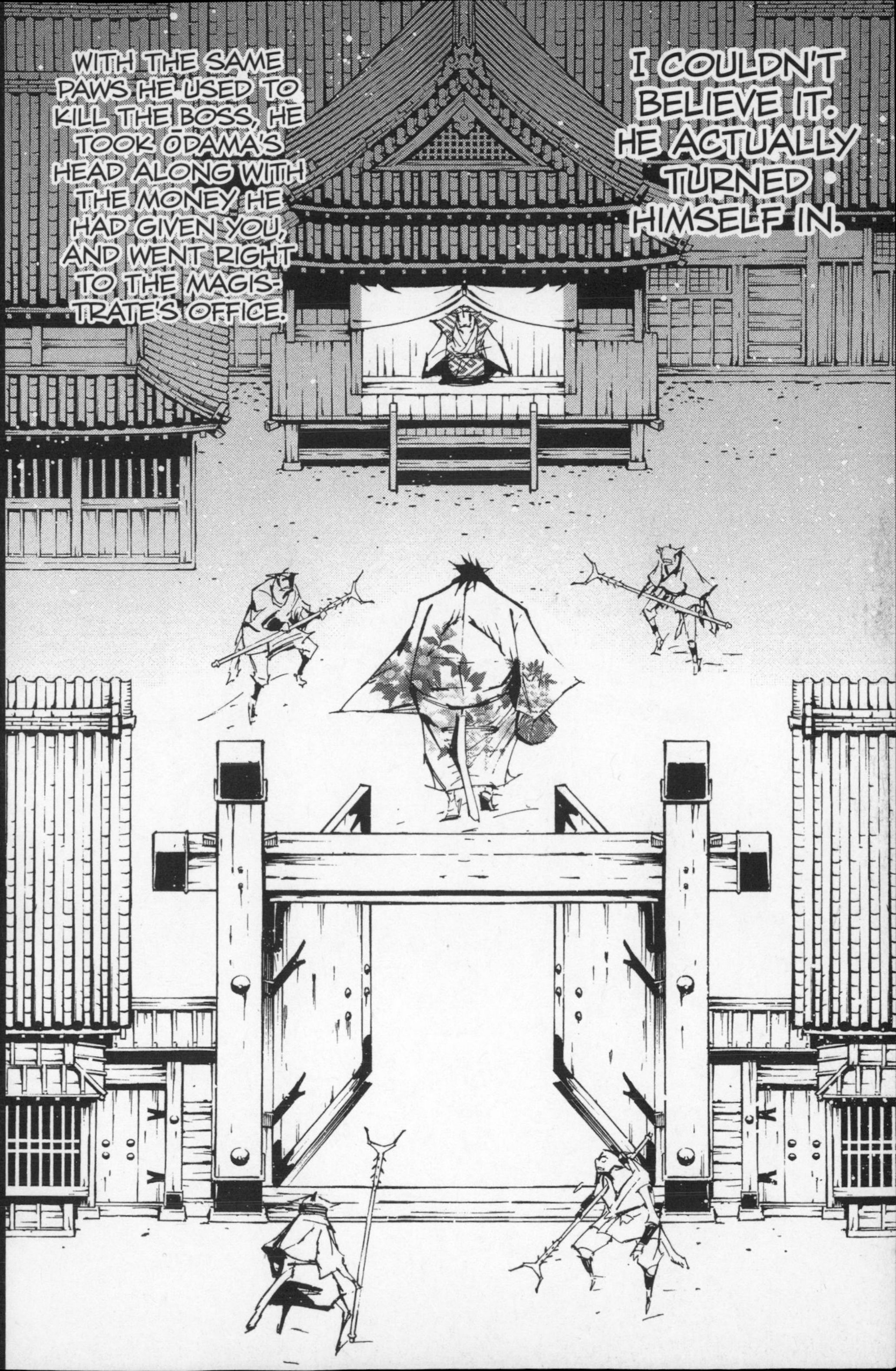
I COULDN'T BELIEVE IT. HE ACTUALLY TURNED HIMSELF IN.
WITH THE SAME PAWS HE USED TO KILL THE BOSS, HE TOOK ŌDAMA'S HEAD ALONG WITH THE MONEY HE HAD GIVEN YOU, AND WENT RIGHT TO THE MAGIS-TRATE'S OFFICE.

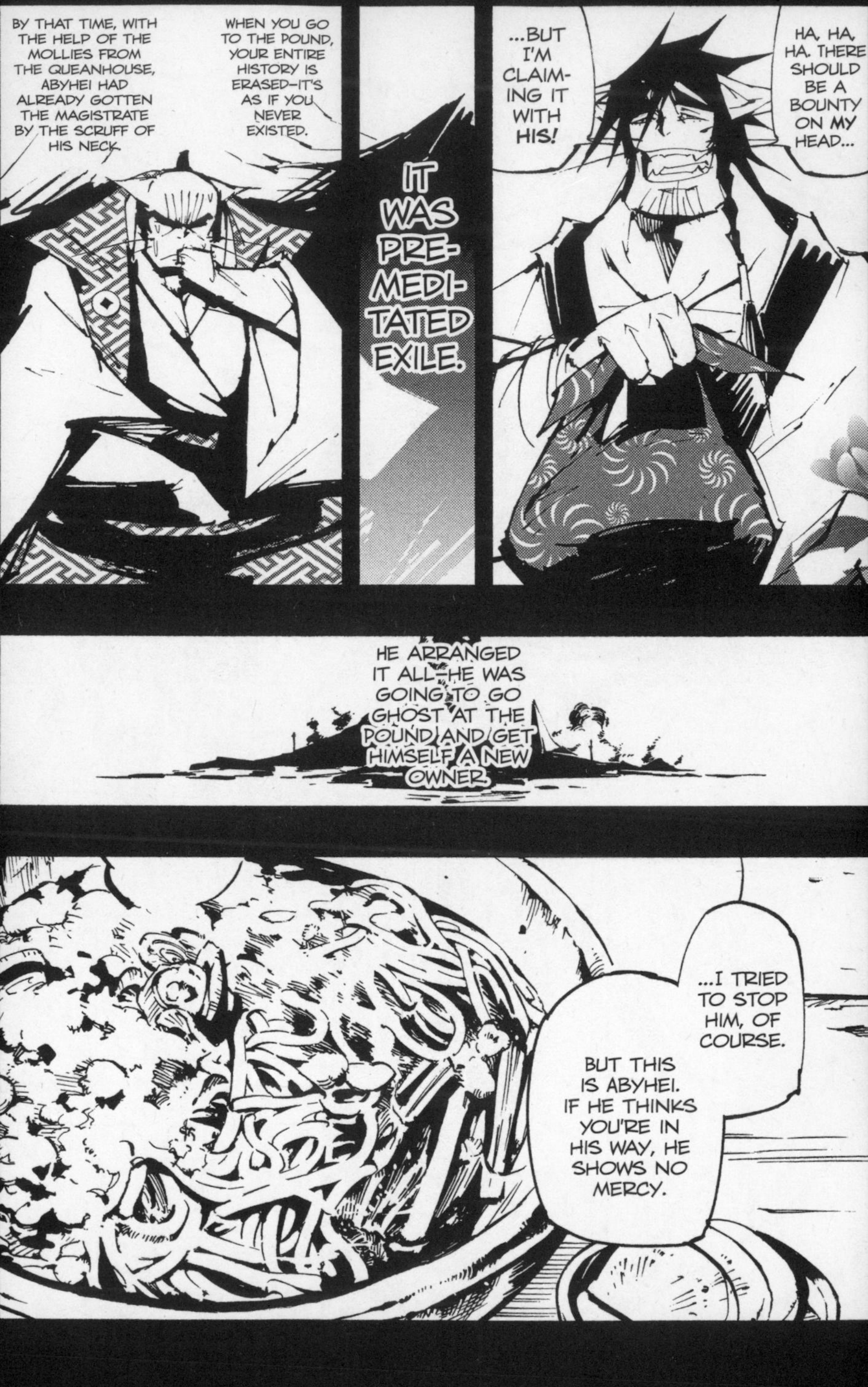
HA, HA, HA. THERE SHOULD BE A BOUNTY ON MY HEAD...
...BUT I'M CLAIMING IT WITH HIS!
IT WAS PRE-MEDITATED EXILE.
WHEN YOU GO TO THE POUND, YOUR ENTIRE HISTORY IS ERASED—IT'S AS IF YOU NEVER EXISTED.
BY THAT TIME, WITH THE HELP OF THE MOLLIES FROM THE QUEANHOUSE, ABYHEI HAD ALREADY GOTTEN THE MAGISTRATE BY THE SCRUFF OF HIS NECK.
HE ARRANGED IT ALL—HE WAS GOING TO GO GHOST AT THE POUND AND GET HIMSELF A NEW OWNER.
...I TRIED TO STOP HIM, OF COURSE.
BUT THIS IS ABYHEI. IF HE THINKS YOU'RE IN HIS WAY, HE SHOWS NO MERCY.

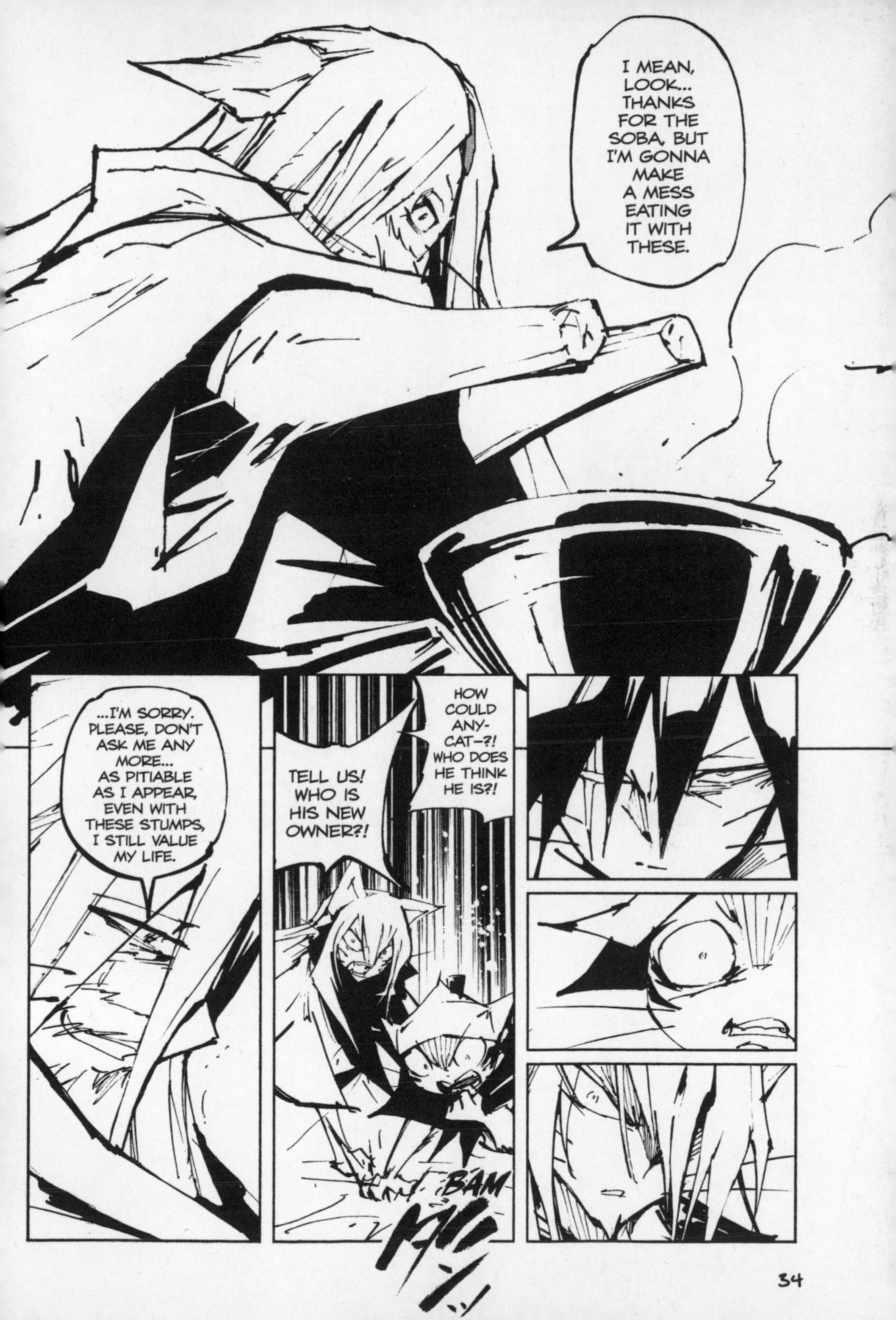
I MEAN, LOOK... THANKS FOR THE SOBA, BUT I'M GONNA MAKE A MESS EATING IT WITH THESE.
HOW COULD ANY-CAT-?! WHO DOES HE THINK HE IS?!
TELL US! WHO IS HIS NEW OWNER?!
BAM
...I'M SORRY. PLEASE, DON'T ASK ME ANY MORE... AS PITIABLE AS I APPEAR, EVEN WITH THESE STUMPS, I STILL VALUE MY LIFE.

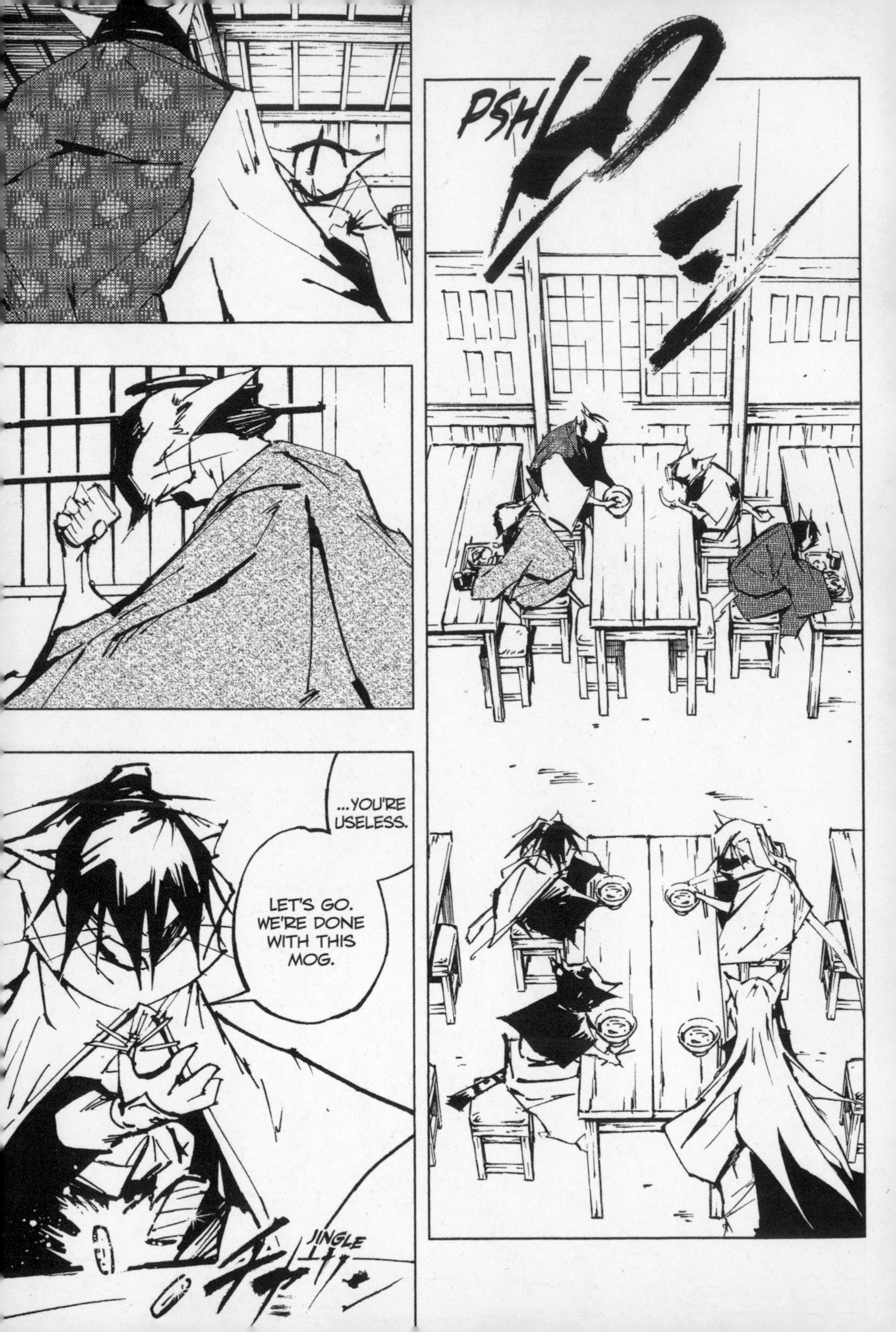
PSH
...YOU'RE USELESS.
LET'S GO. WE'RE DONE WITH THIS MOG.
JINGLE

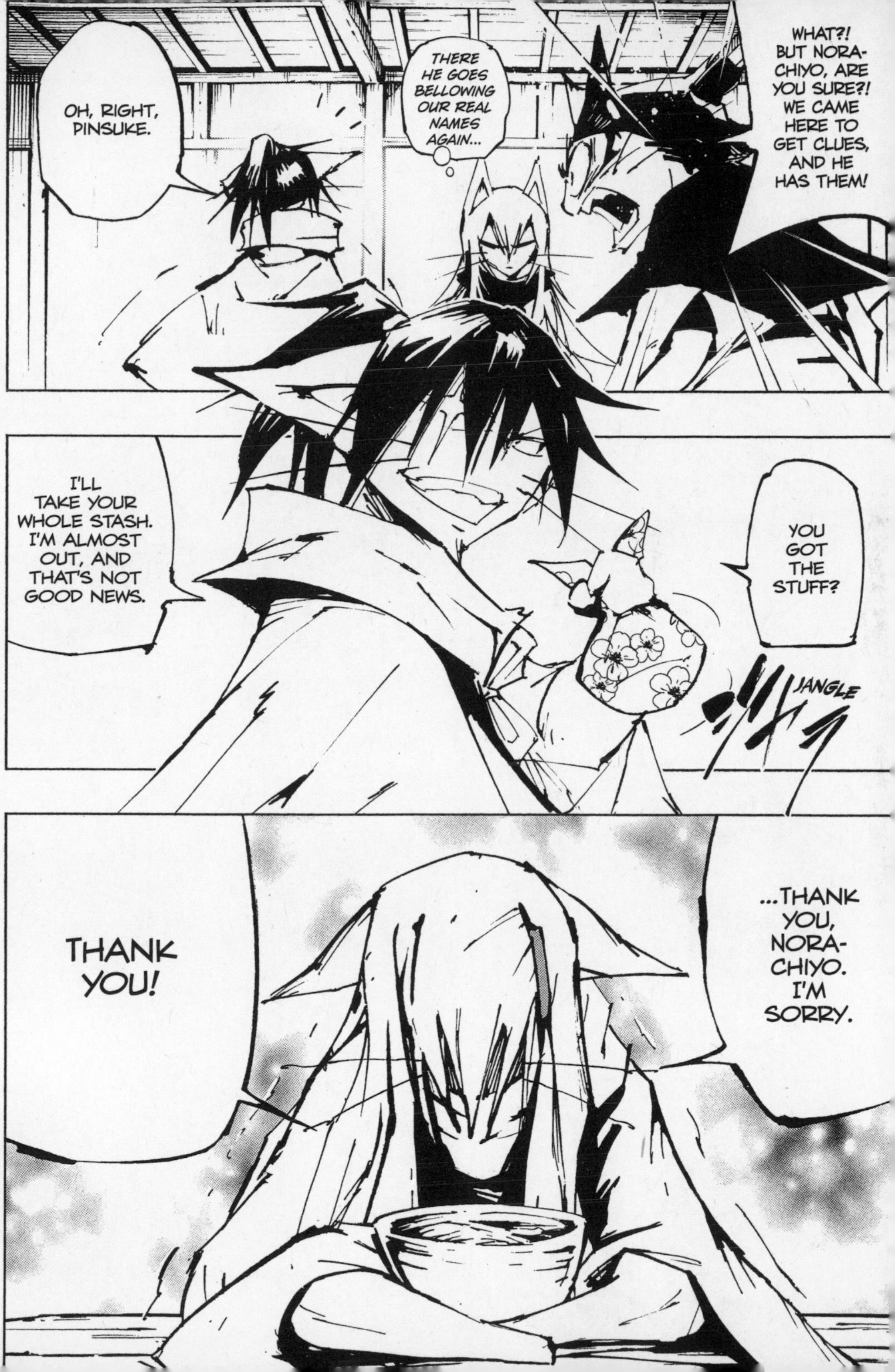
WHAT?! BUT NORA-CHIYO, ARE YOU SURE?! WE CAME HERE TO GET CLUES, AND HE HAS THEM!
THERE HE GOES BELLOWING OUR REAL NAMES AGAIN...
OH, RIGHT, PINSUKE.
YOU GOT THE STUFF?
JANGLE
I'LL TAKE YOUR WHOLE STASH. I'M ALMOST OUT, AND THAT'S NOT GOOD NEWS.
...THANK YOU, NORA-CHIYO. I'M SORRY.
THANK YOU!

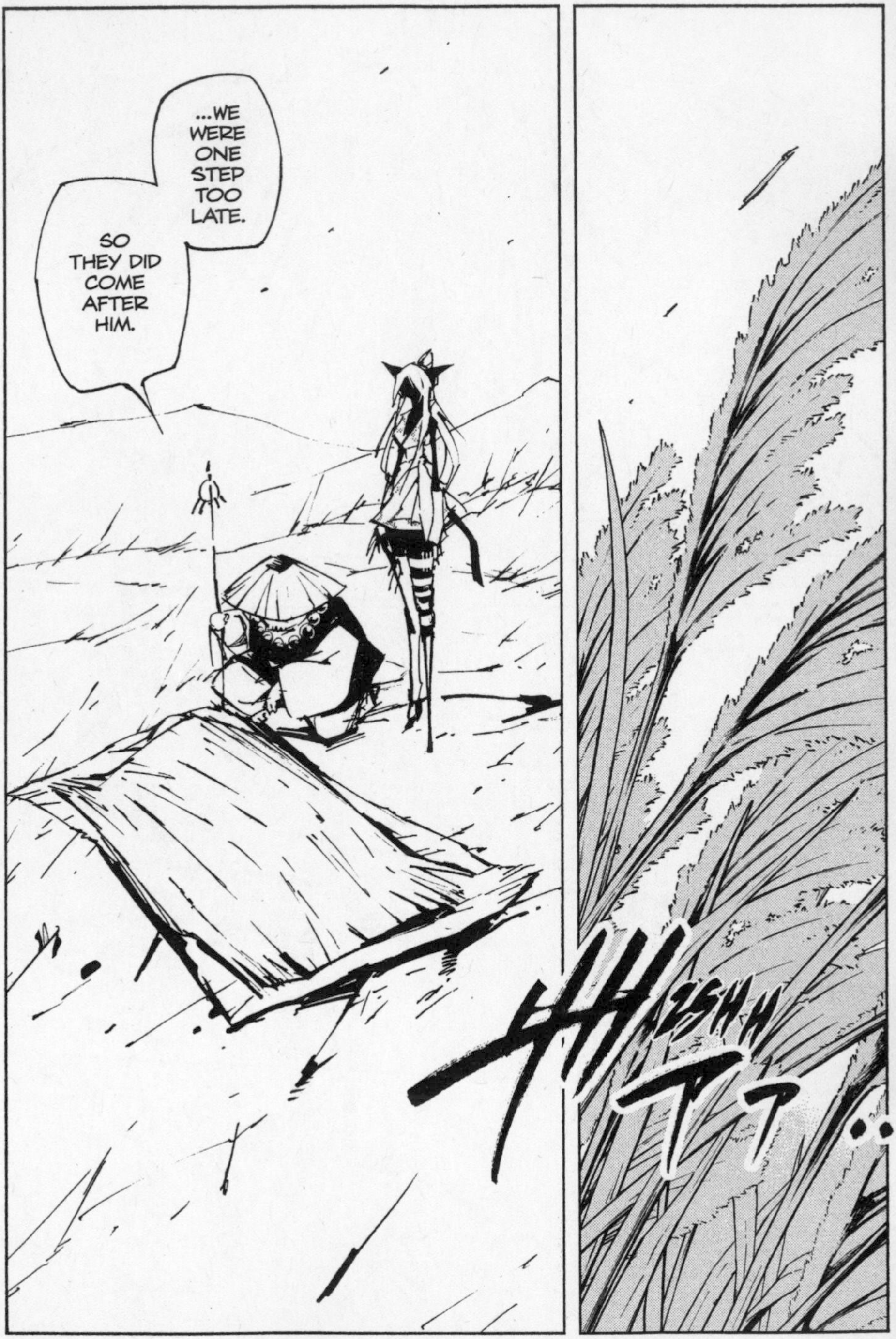
ZSHH
...WE WERE ONE STEP TOO LATE.
SO THEY DID COME AFTER HIM.

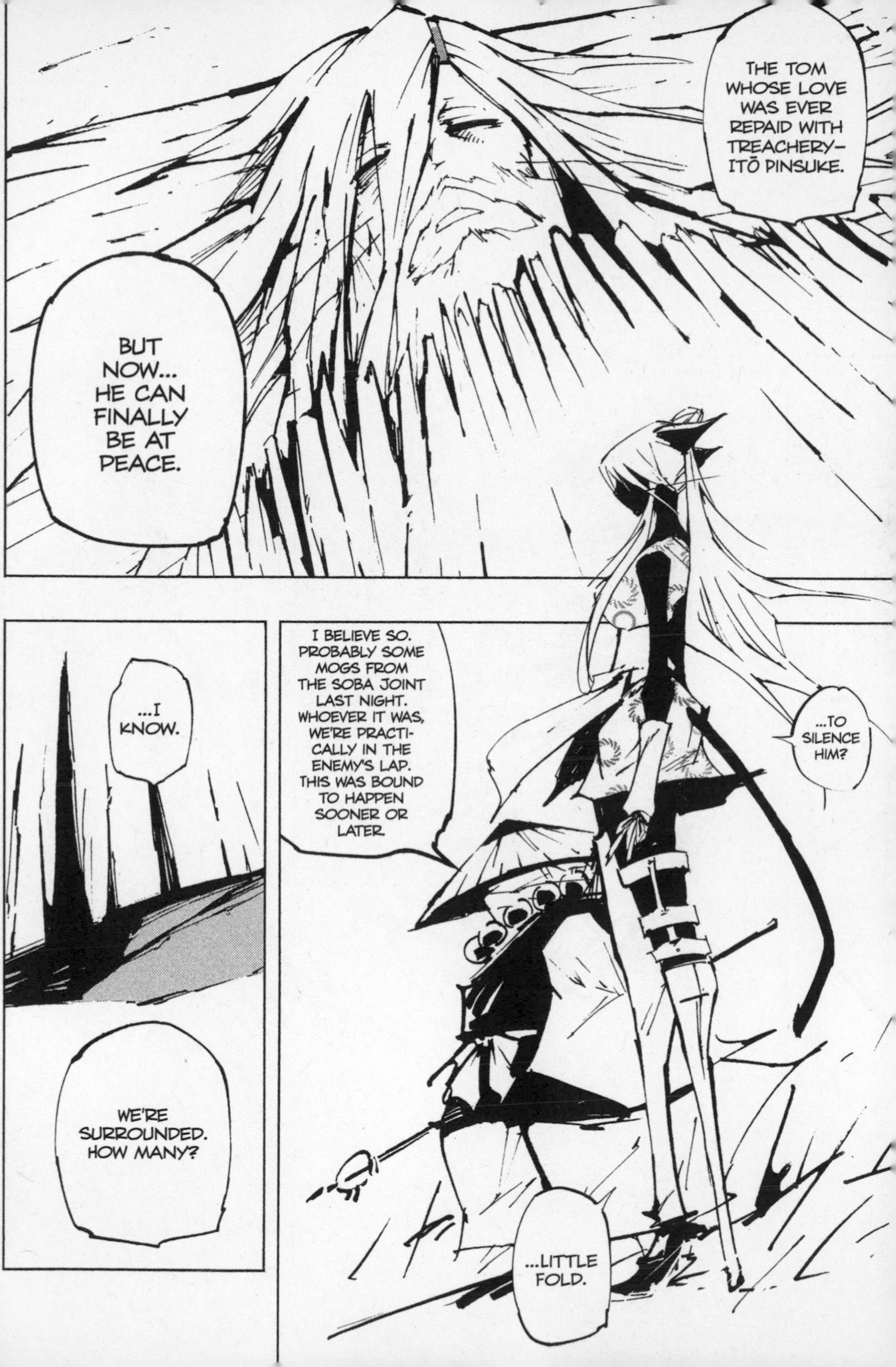
THE TOM WHOSE LOVE WAS EVER REPAID WITH TREACHERY– ITŌ PINSUKE.
BUT NOW... HE CAN FINALLY BE AT PEACE.
...TO SILENCE HIM?
I BELIEVE SO. PROBABLY SOME MOGS FROM THE SOBA JOINT LAST NIGHT. WHOEVER IT WAS, WE'RE PRACTI- CALLY IN THE ENEMY'S LAP. THIS WAS BOUND TO HAPPEN SOONER OR LATER.
...LITTLE FOLD.
...I KNOW.
WE'RE SURROUNDED. HOW MANY?

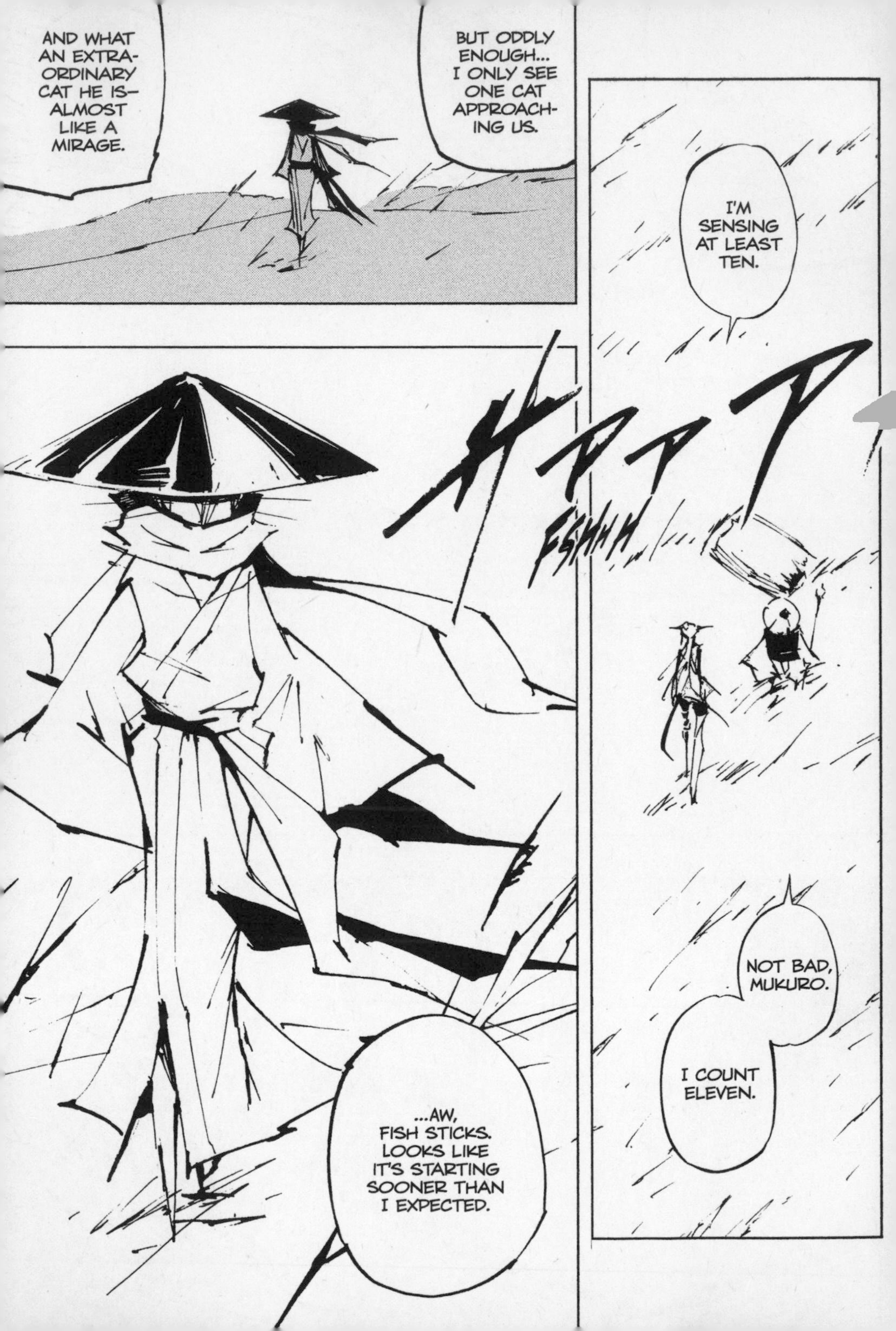
BUT ODDLY ENOUGH... I ONLY SEE ONE CAT APPROACHING US.
AND WHAT AN EXTRA-ORDINARY CAT HE IS—ALMOST LIKE A MIRAGE.
I'M SENSING AT LEAST TEN.
FSHHH
NOT BAD, MUKURO.
I COUNT ELEVEN.
...AW, FISH STICKS. LOOKS LIKE IT'S STARTING SOONER THAN I EXPECTED.

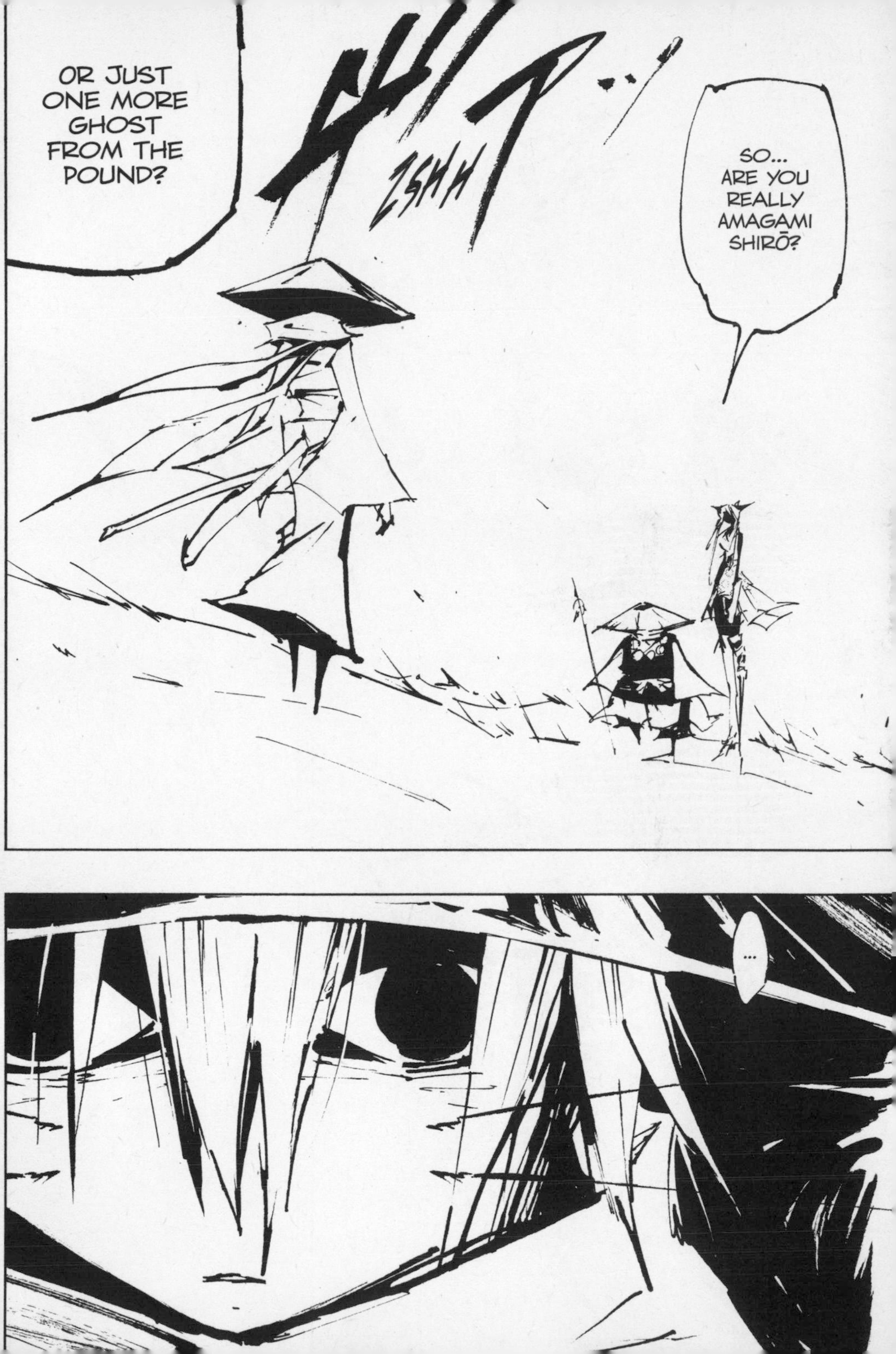
SO... ARE YOU REALLY AMAGAMI SHIRŌ?
OR JUST ONE MORE GHOST FROM THE POUND?
ZSHH
...

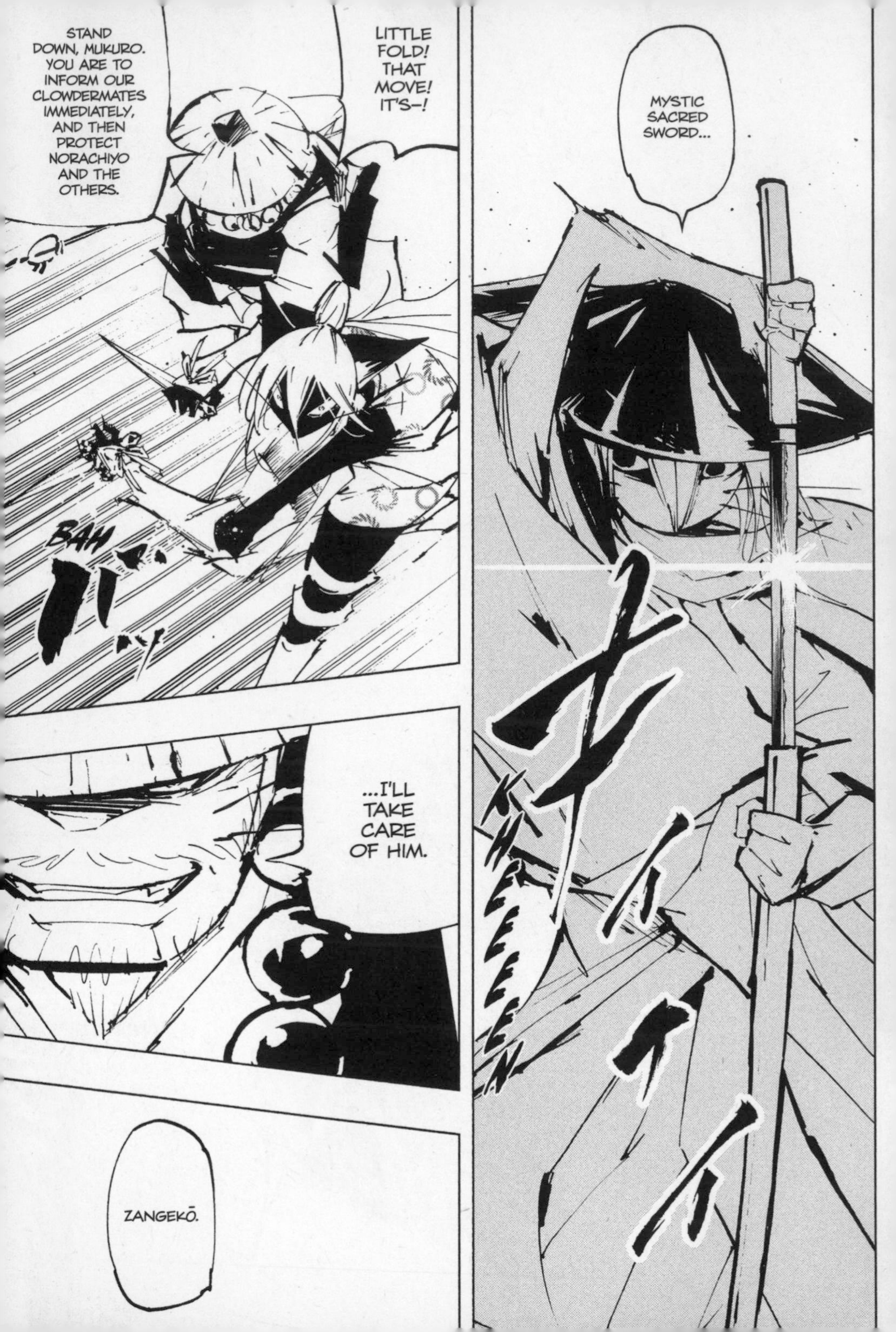
MYSTIC SACRED SWORD...
LITTLE FOLD! THAT MOVE! IT'S–!
STAND DOWN, MUKURO. YOU ARE TO INFORM OUR CLOWDERMATES IMMEDIATELY, AND THEN PROTECT NORACHIYO AND THE OTHERS.
BAH
...I'LL TAKE CARE OF HIM.
ZANGEKŌ.

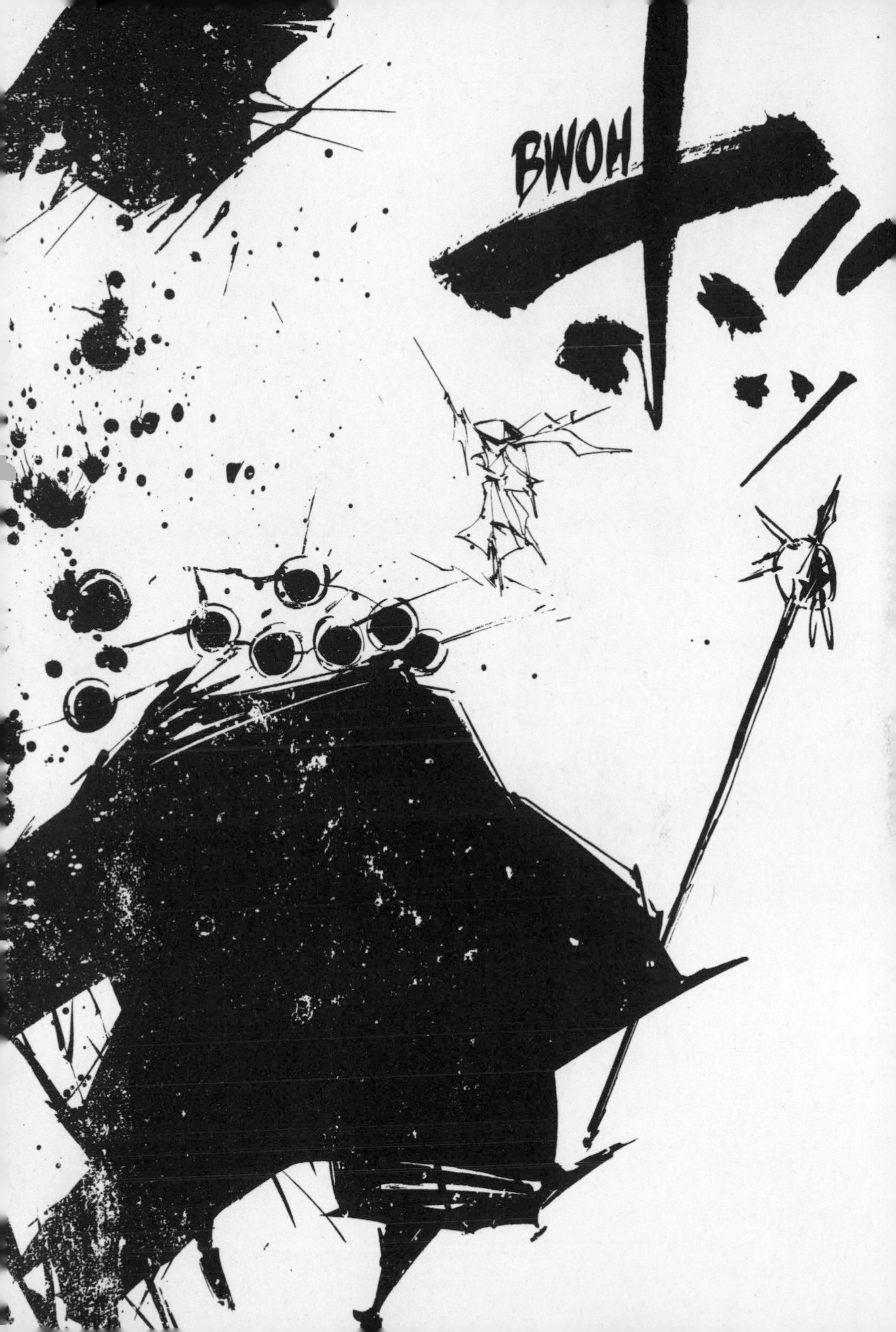
BWOH

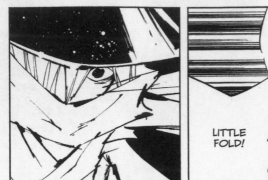

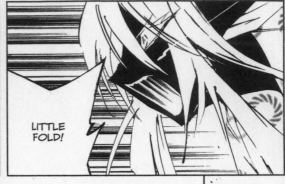

LITTLE FOLD!

STUMPED...

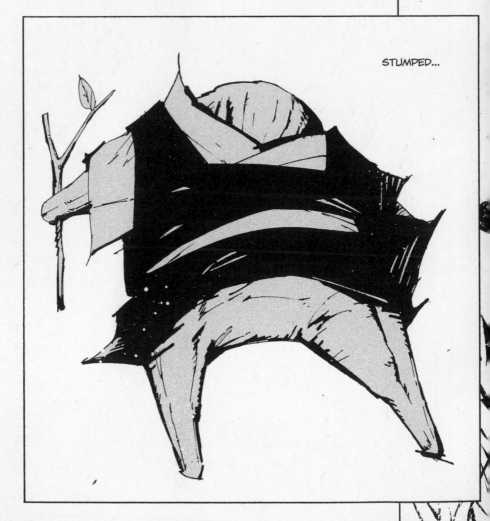

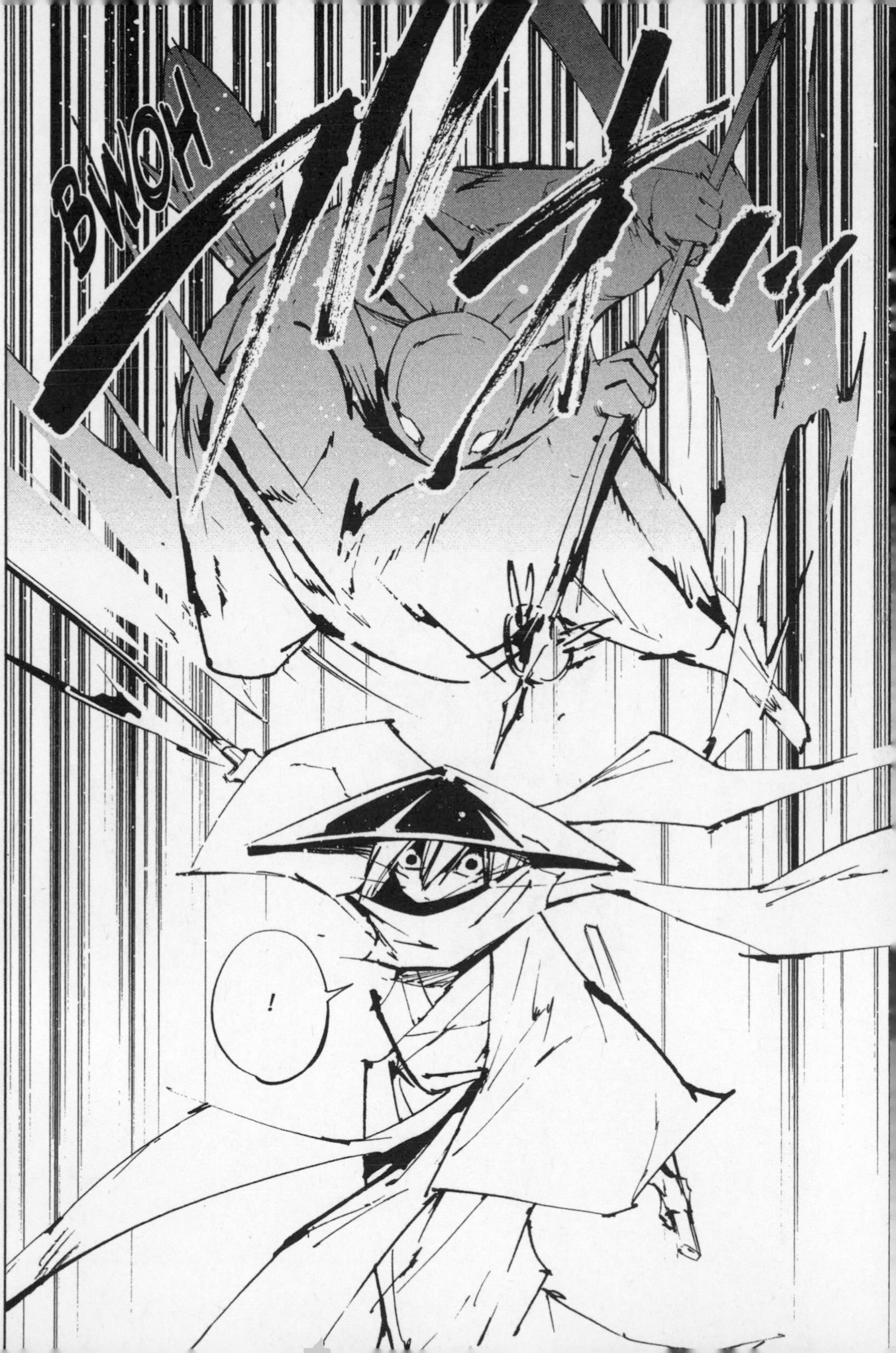
BWOH
!

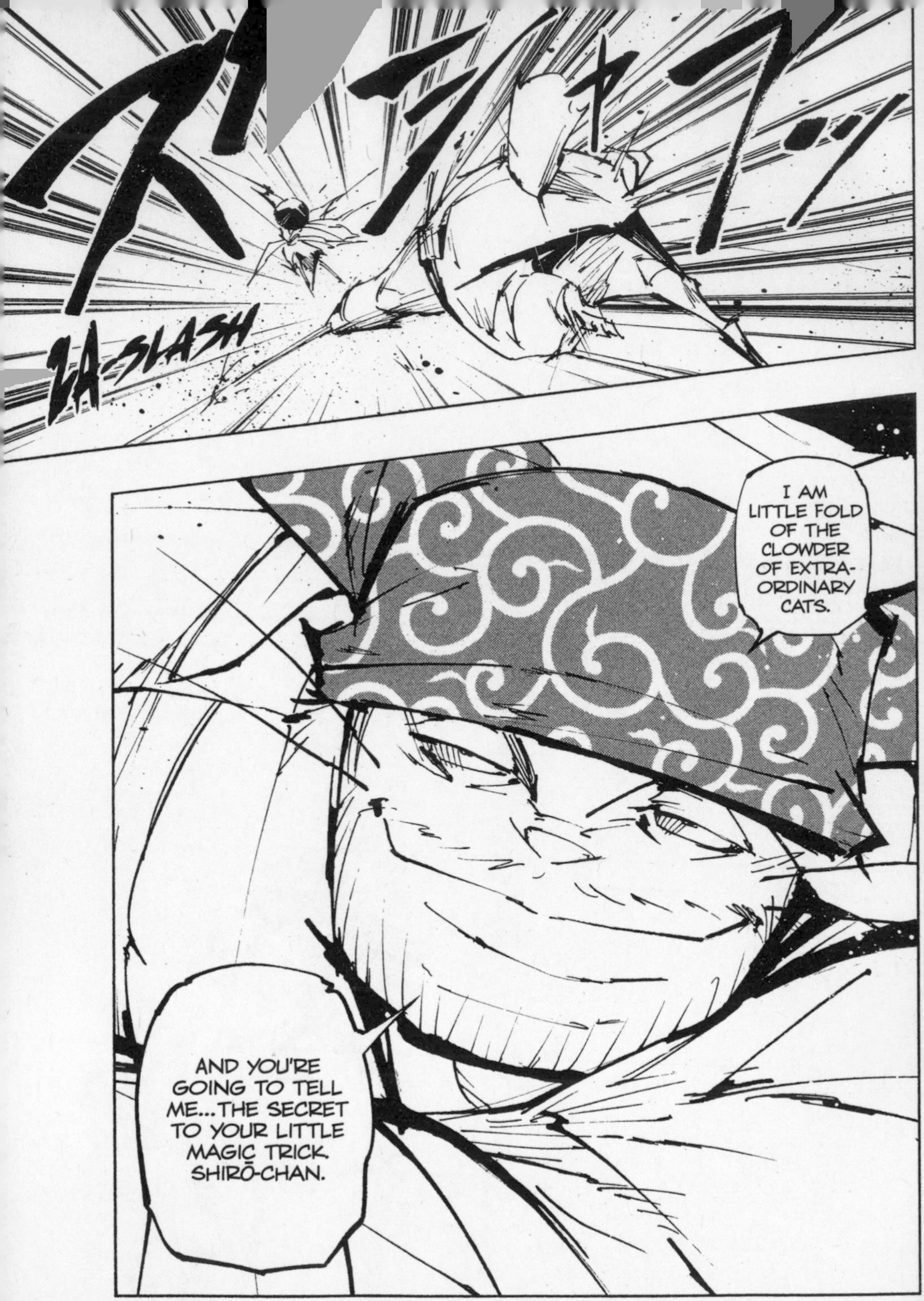
ZA-SLASH
I AM LITTLE FOLD OF THE CLOWDER OF EXTRA-ORDINARY CATS.
AND YOU'RE GOING TO TELL ME...THE SECRET TO YOUR LITTLE MAGIC TRICK SHIRŌ-CHAN.

猫ヶ原

ネコガハラ

NeKoGaHara

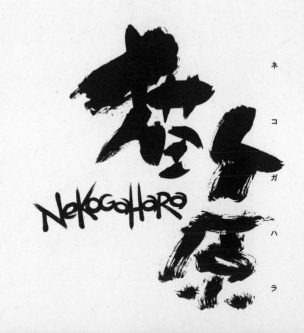

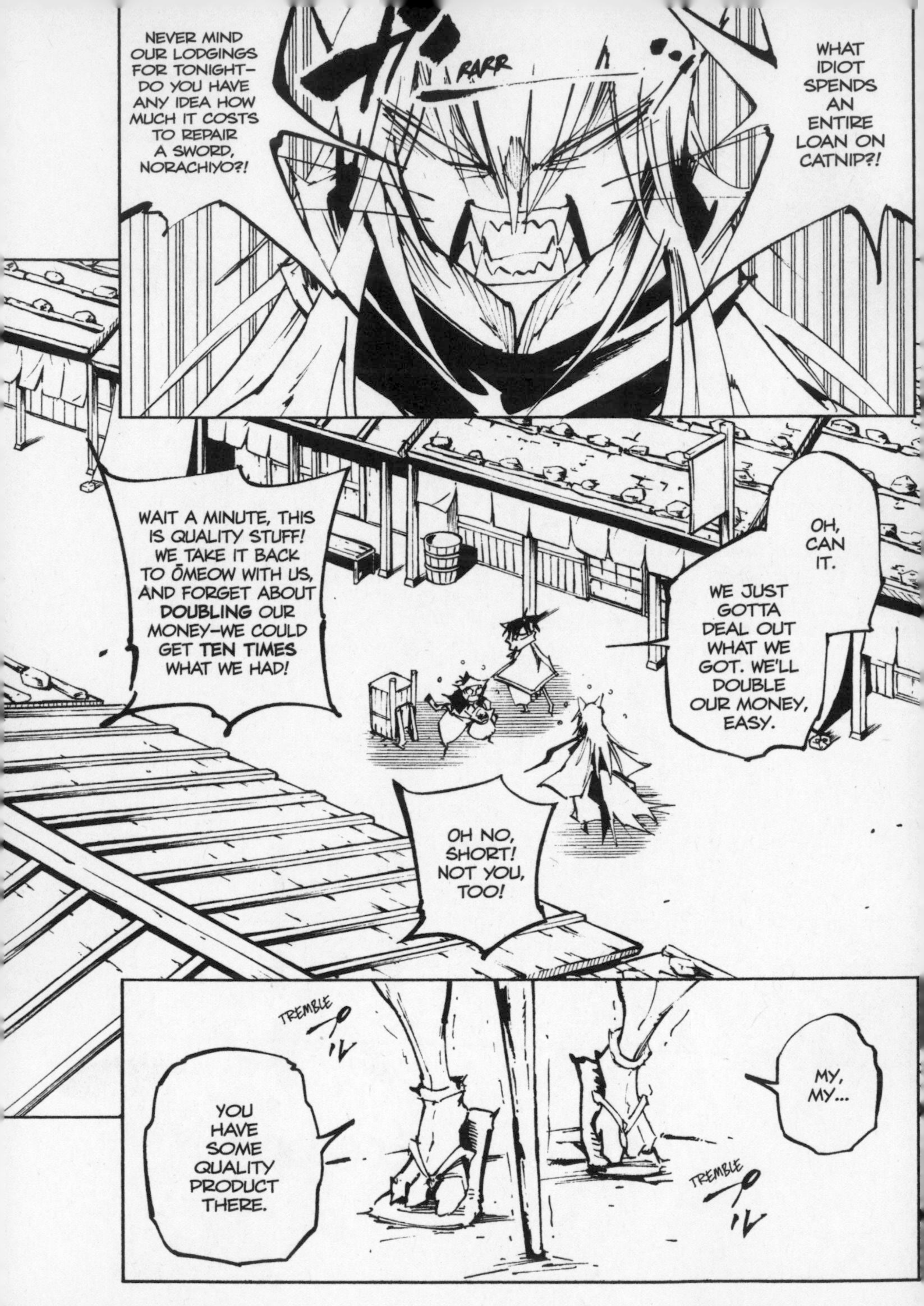
WHAT IDIOT SPENDS AN ENTIRE LOAN ON CATNIP?!
RARR
NEVER MIND OUR LODGINGS FOR TONIGHT—DO YOU HAVE ANY IDEA HOW MUCH IT COSTS TO REPAIR A SWORD, NORACHIYO?!
OH, CAN IT.
WE JUST GOTTA DEAL OUT WHAT WE GOT. WE'LL DOUBLE OUR MONEY, EASY.
WAIT A MINUTE, THIS IS QUALITY STUFF! WE TAKE IT BACK TO ŌMEOW WITH US, AND FORGET ABOUT **DOUBLING** OUR MONEY—WE COULD GET **TEN TIMES** WHAT WE HAD!
OH NO, SHORT! NOT YOU, TOO!
MY, MY...
TREMBLE
YOU HAVE SOME QUALITY PRODUCT THERE.
TREMBLE

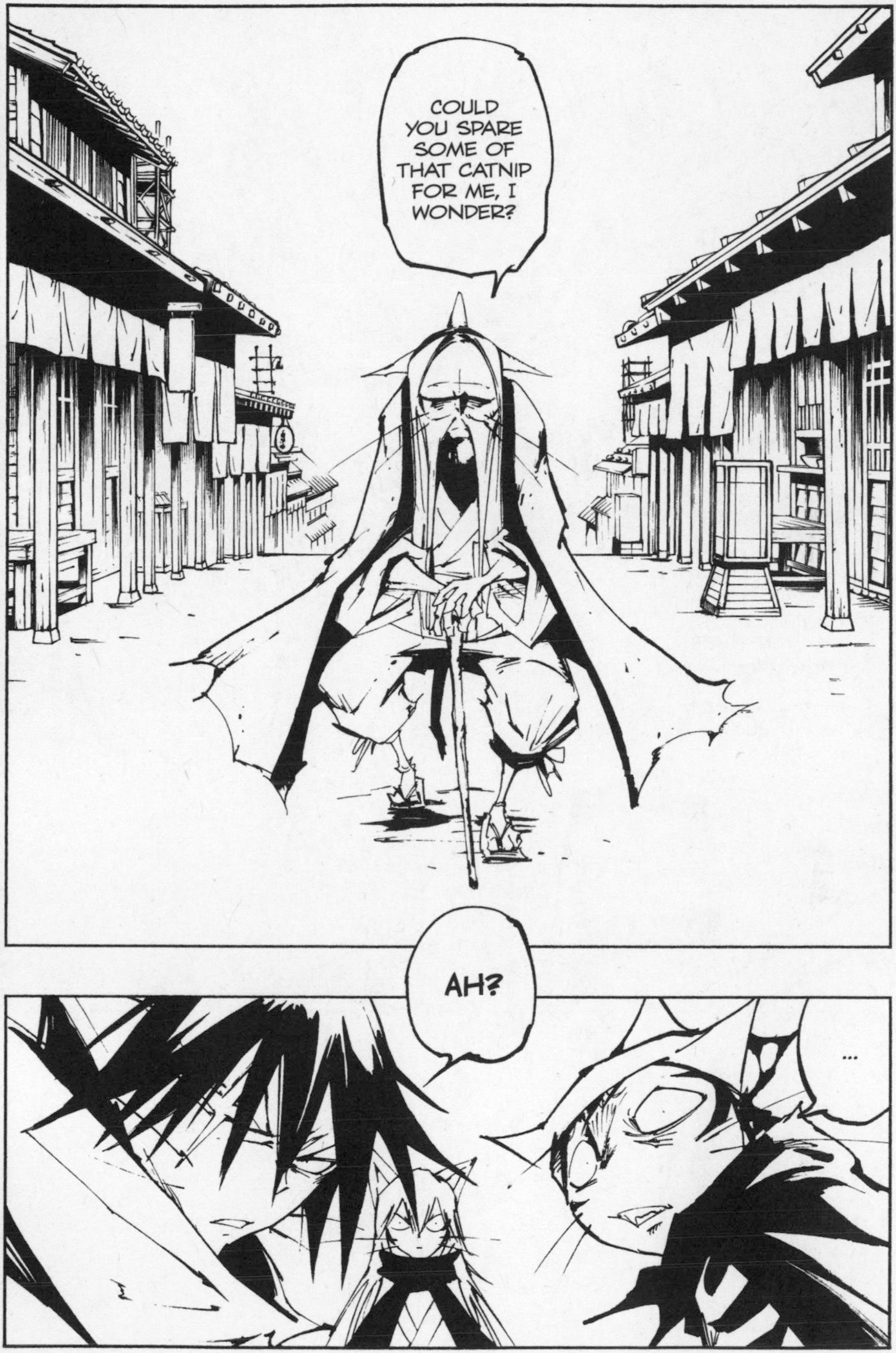
COULD YOU SPARE SOME OF THAT CATNIP FOR ME, I WONDER?
AH?
...

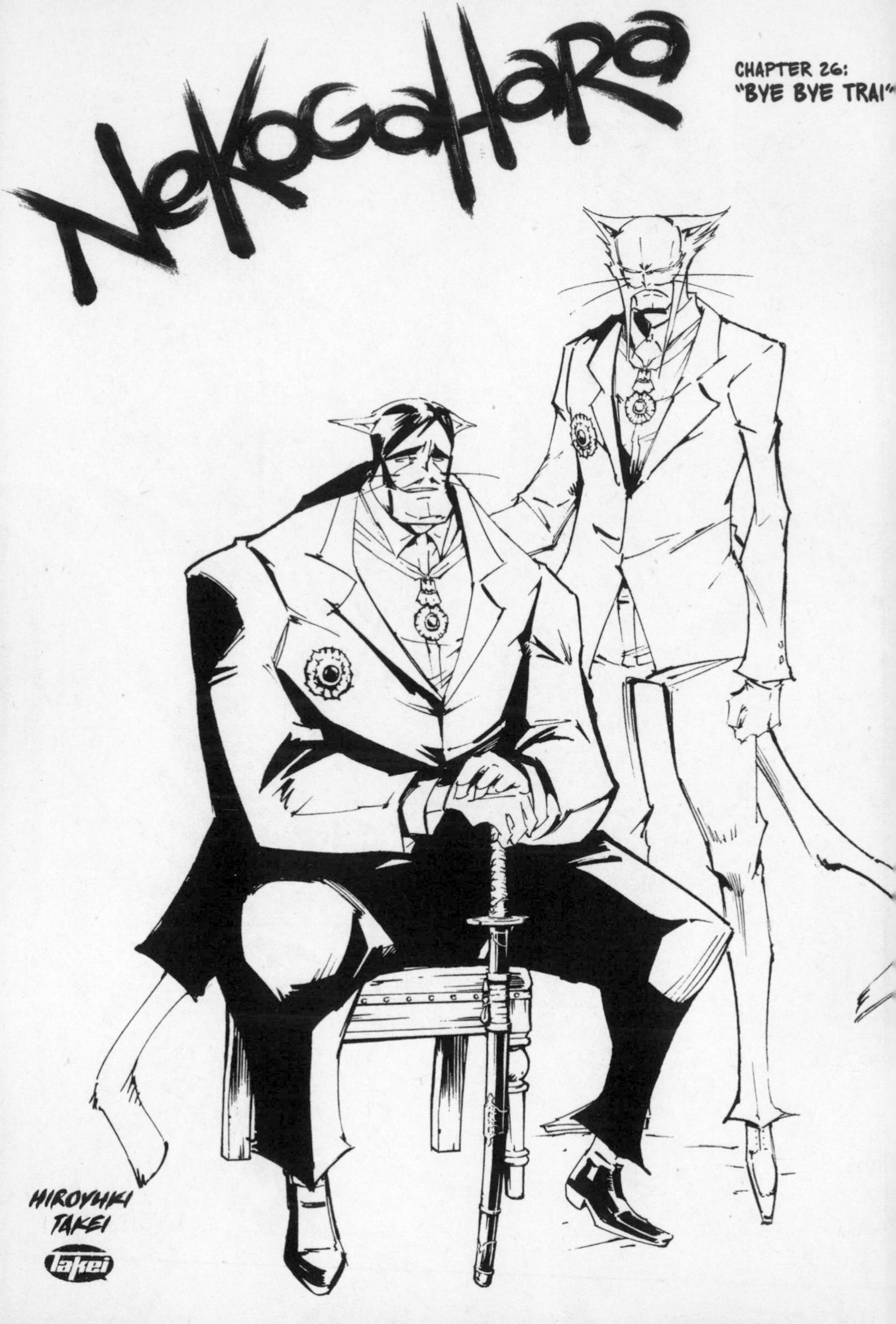
NekogaHara
CHAPTER 26:
"BYE BYE TRAI"
HIROYUKI
TAKEI
Takei

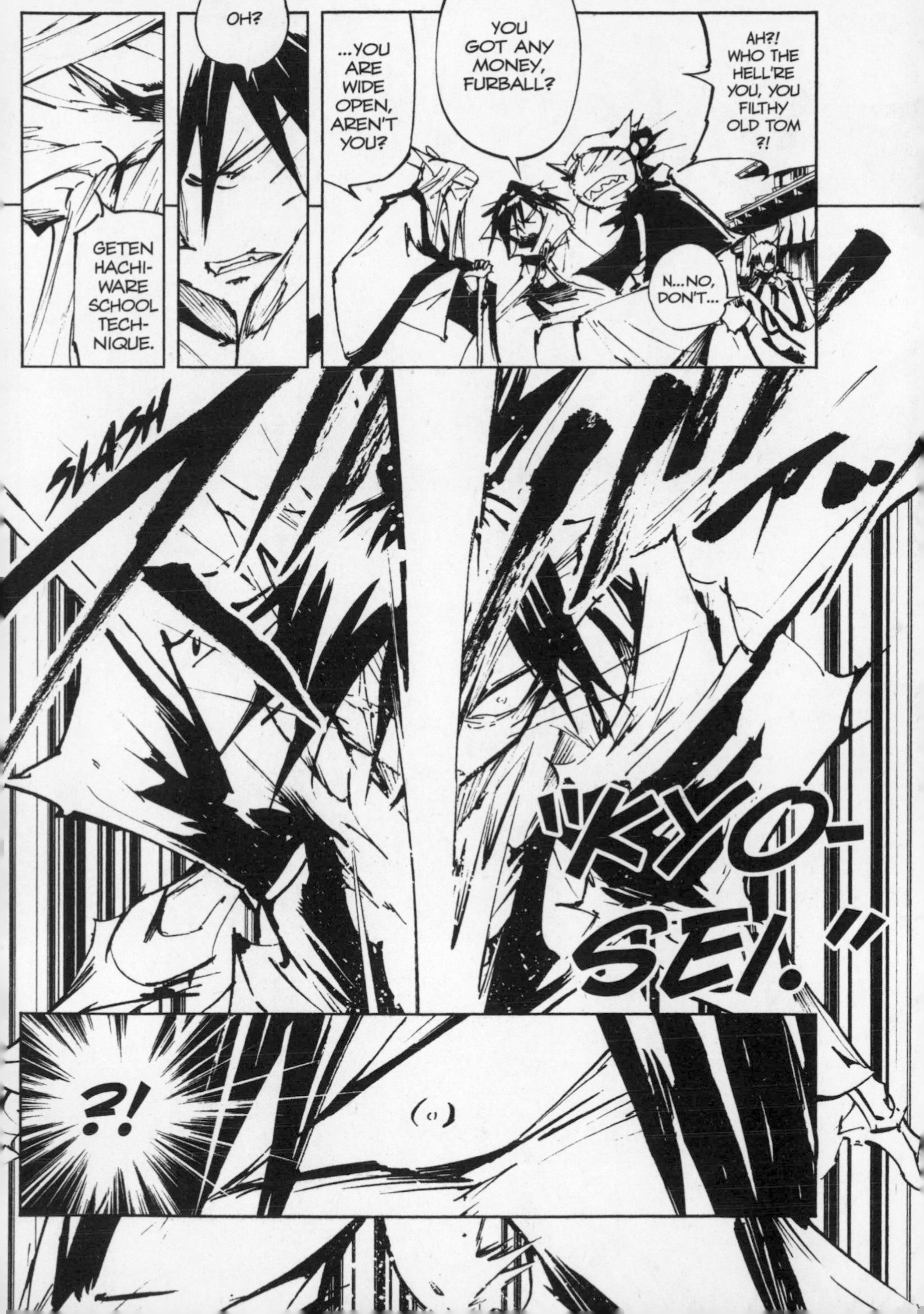
AH?! WHO THE HELL'RE YOU, YOU FILTHY OLD TOM ?!
YOU GOT ANY MONEY, FURBALL?
...YOU ARE WIDE OPEN, AREN'T YOU?
N...NO, DON'T...
OH?
GETEN HACHI-WARE SCHOOL TECH-NIQUE.
"KYO-SEI!"
SLASH
?!

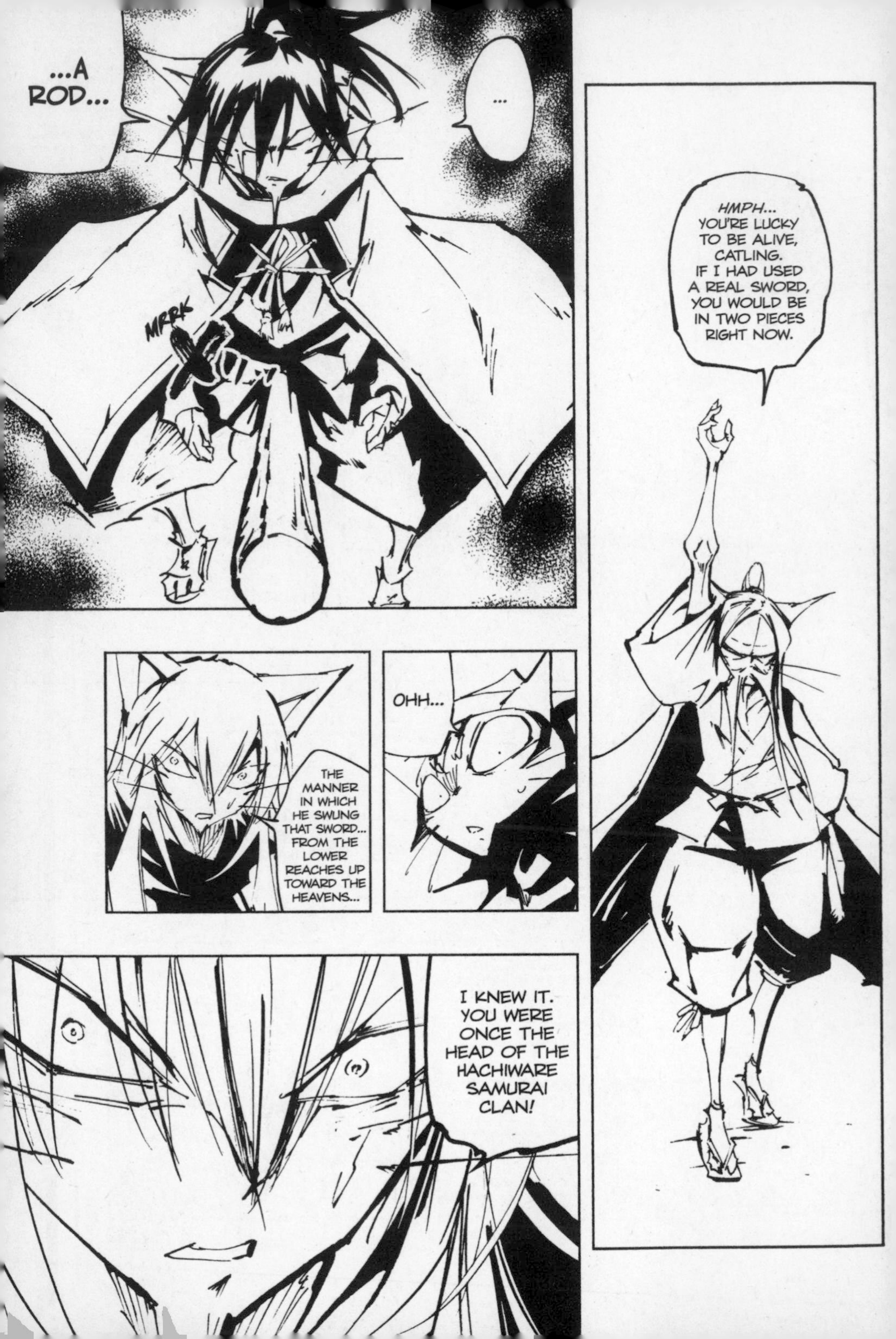
HMPH... YOU'RE LUCKY TO BE ALIVE, CATLING. IF I HAD USED A REAL SWORD, YOU WOULD BE IN TWO PIECES RIGHT NOW.
...
...A ROD...
MRRK
OHH...
THE MANNER IN WHICH HE SWUNG THAT SWORD... FROM THE LOWER REACHES UP TOWARD THE HEAVENS...
I KNEW IT. YOU WERE ONCE THE HEAD OF THE HACHIWARE SAMURAI CLAN!

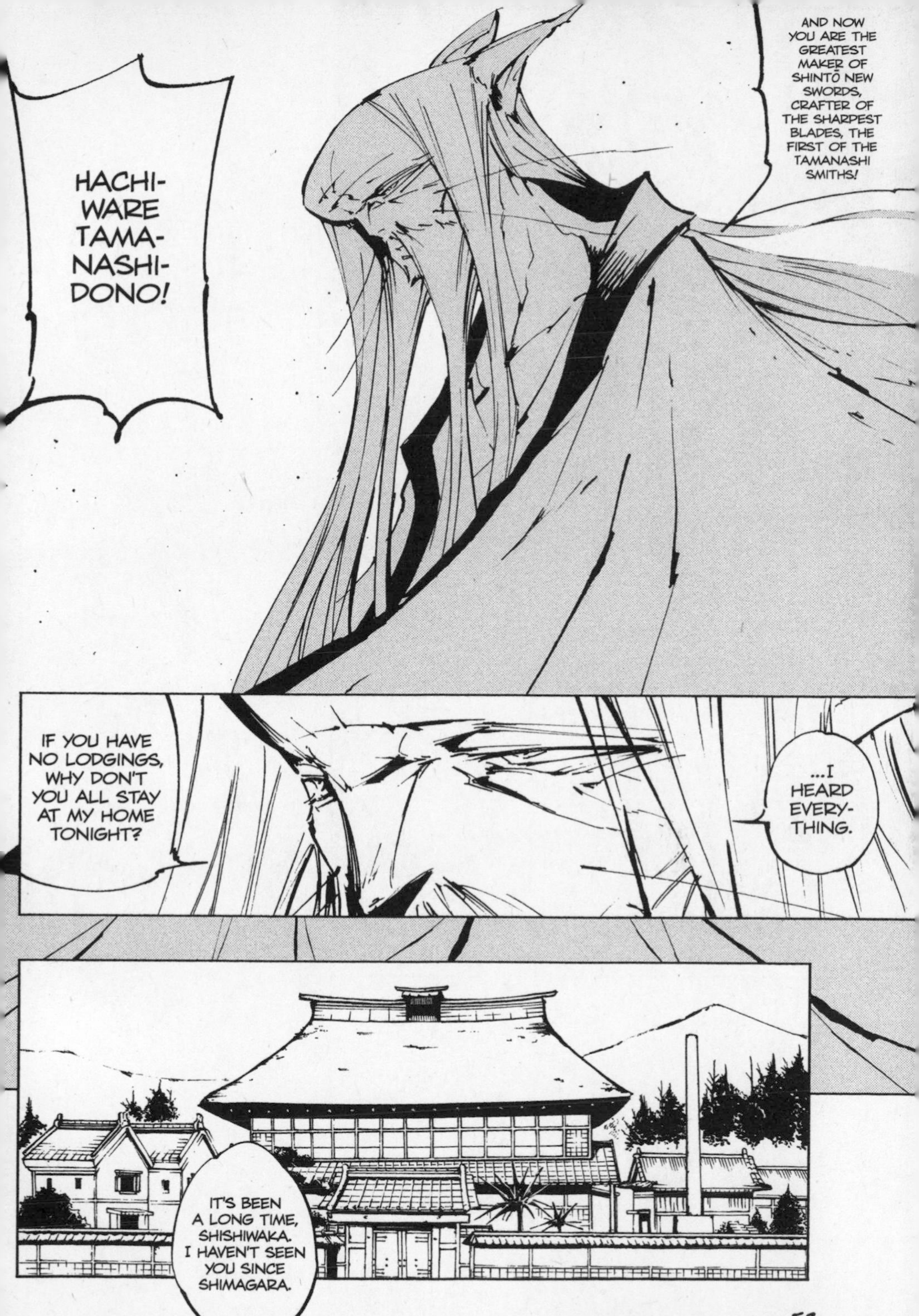
AND NOW YOU ARE THE GREATEST MAKER OF SHINTŌ NEW SWORDS, CRAFTER OF THE SHARPEST BLADES, THE FIRST OF THE TAMANASHI SMITHS!
HACHI-WARE TAMA-NASHI-DONO!
...I HEARD EVERY-THING.
IF YOU HAVE NO LODGINGS, WHY DON'T YOU ALL STAY AT MY HOME TONIGHT?
IT'S BEEN A LONG TIME, SHISHIWAKA. I HAVEN'T SEEN YOU SINCE SHIMAGARA.

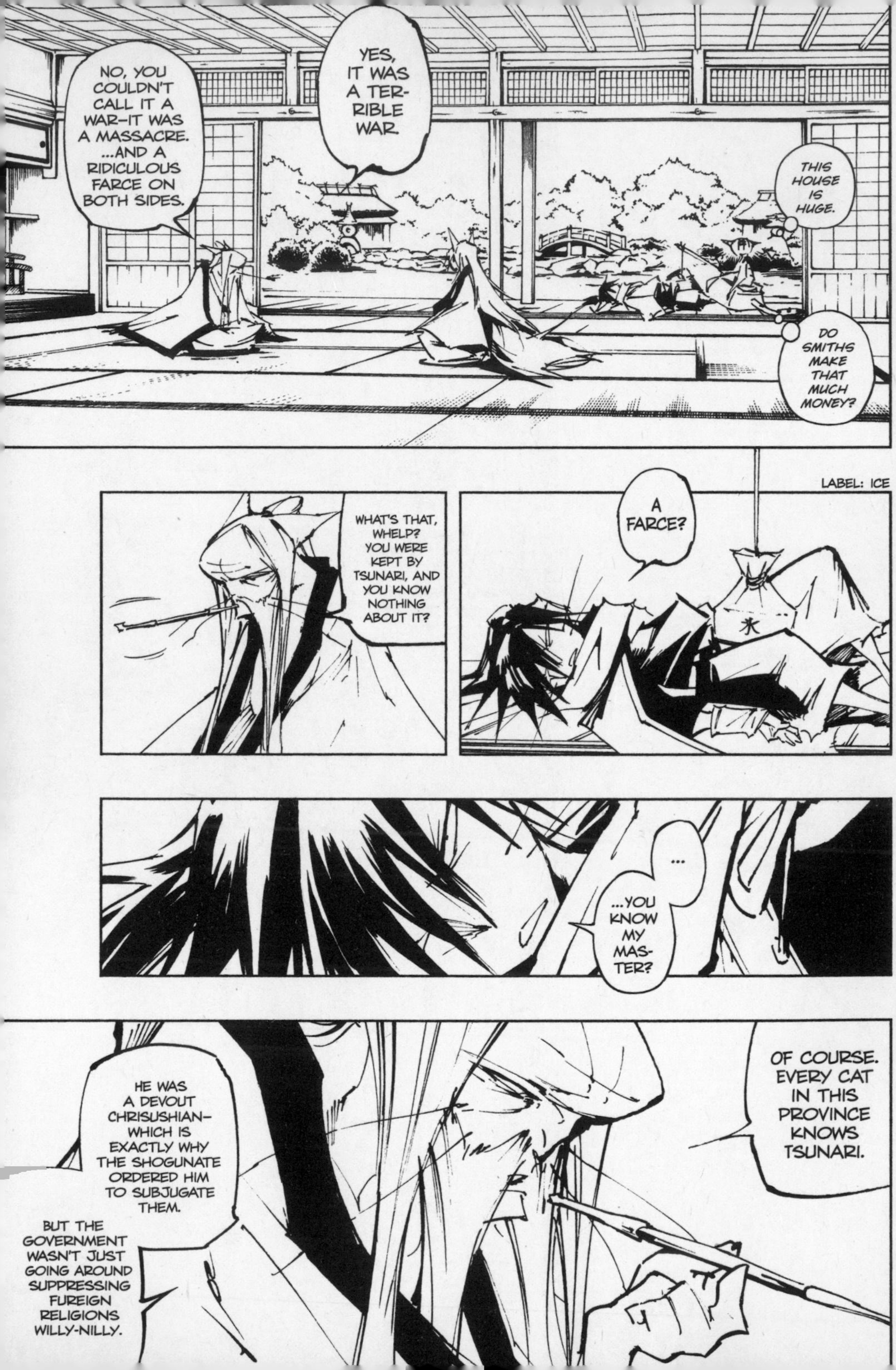
THIS HOUSE IS HUGE.
DO SMITHS MAKE THAT MUCH MONEY?
YES, IT WAS A TER-RIBLE WAR.
NO, YOU COULDN'T CALL IT A WAR—IT WAS A MASSACRE. ...AND A RIDICULOUS FARCE ON BOTH SIDES.
LABEL: ICE
A FARCE?
WHAT'S THAT, WHELP? YOU WERE KEPT BY TSUNARI, AND YOU KNOW NOTHING ABOUT IT?
...
...YOU KNOW MY MAS-TER?
OF COURSE. EVERY CAT IN THIS PROVINCE KNOWS TSUNARI.
HE WAS A DEVOUT CHRISUSHIAN—WHICH IS EXACTLY WHY THE SHOGUNATE ORDERED HIM TO SUBJUGATE THEM.
BUT THE GOVERNMENT WASN'T JUST GOING AROUND SUPPRESSING FUREIGN RELIGIONS WILLY-NILLY.

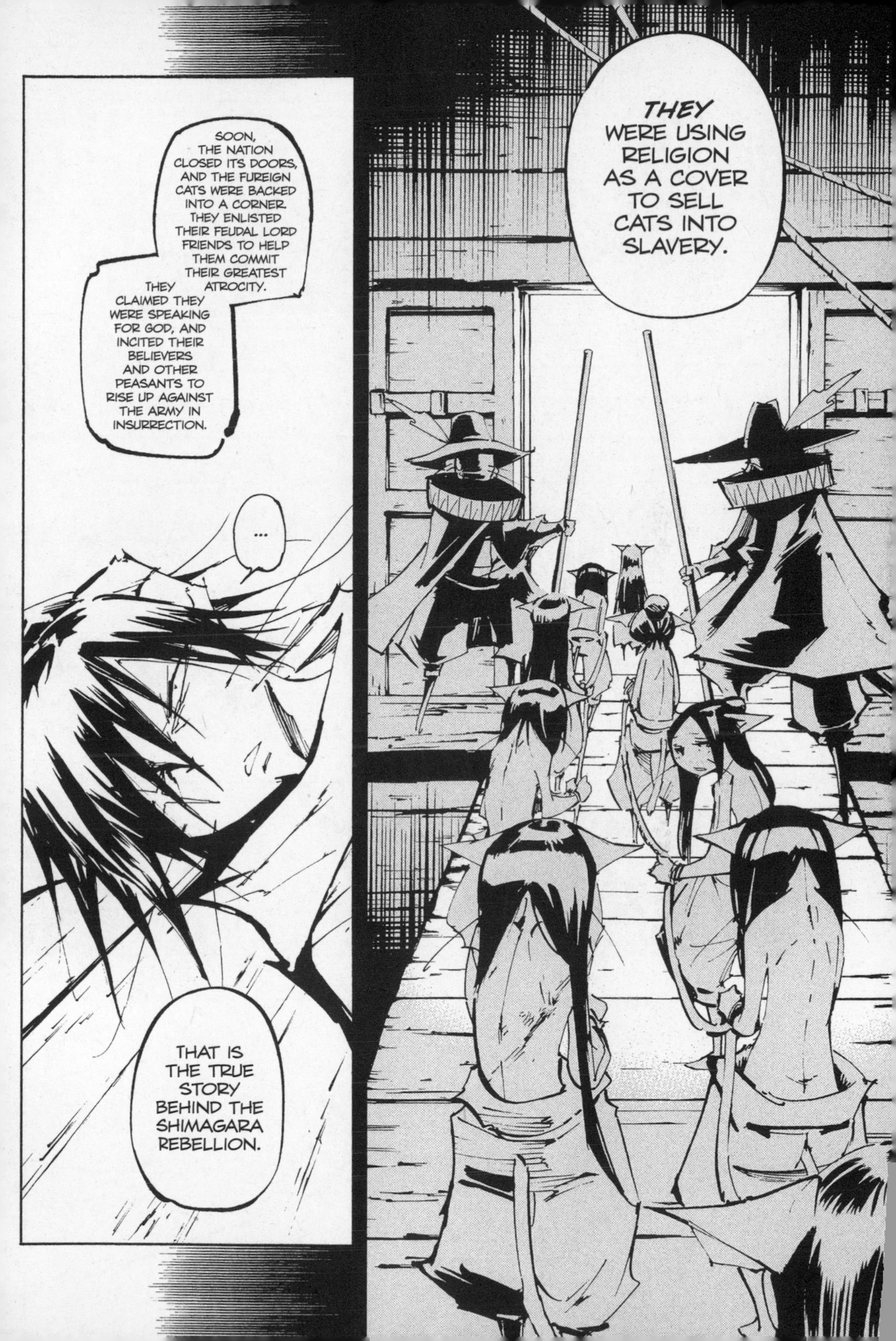
THEY WERE USING RELIGION AS A COVER TO SELL CATS INTO SLAVERY.
SOON, THE NATION CLOSED ITS DOORS, AND THE FUREIGN CATS WERE BACKED INTO A CORNER. THEY ENLISTED THEIR FEUDAL LORD FRIENDS TO HELP THEM COMMIT THEIR GREATEST ATROCITY. THEY CLAIMED THEY WERE SPEAKING FOR GOD, AND INCITED THEIR BELIEVERS AND OTHER PEASANTS TO RISE UP AGAINST THE ARMY IN INSURRECTION.
...
THAT IS THE TRUE STORY BEHIND THE SHIMAGARA REBELLION.

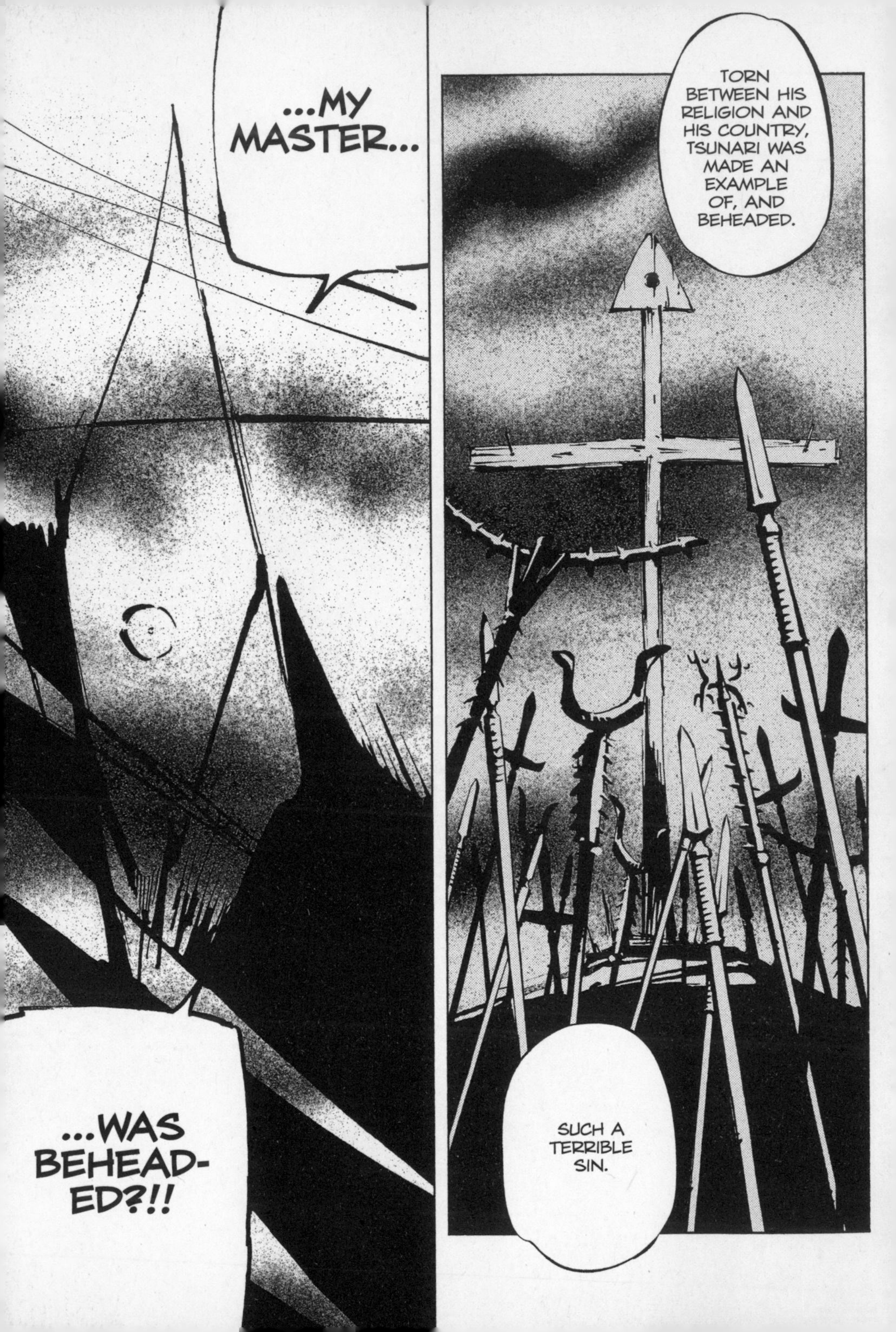
TORN BETWEEN HIS RELIGION AND HIS COUNTRY, TSUNARI WAS MADE AN EXAMPLE OF, AND BEHEADED.
SUCH A TERRIBLE SIN.
...MY MASTER...
...WAS BEHEAD-ED?!!

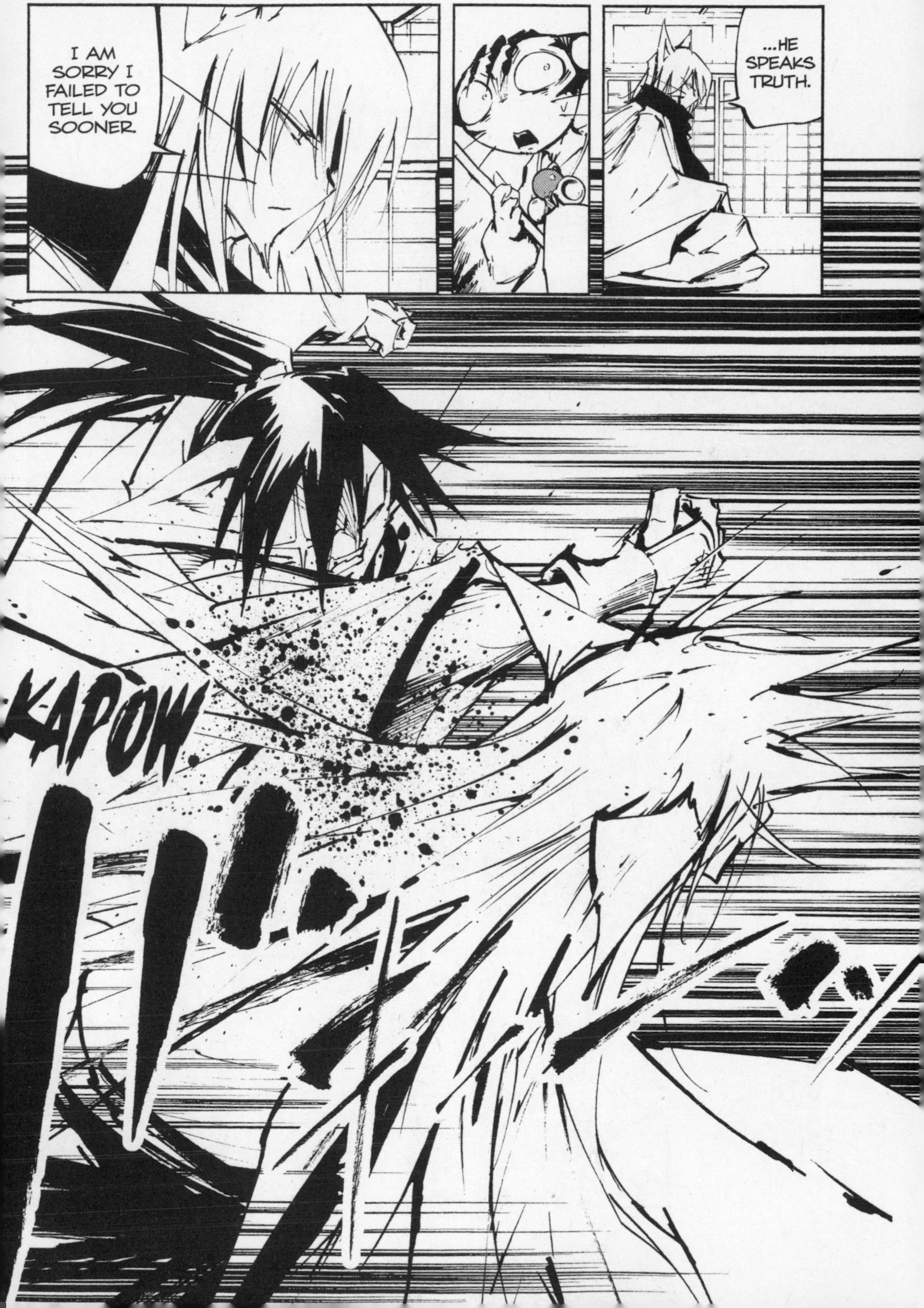
...HE SPEAKS TRUTH.
I AM SORRY I FAILED TO TELL YOU SOONER.
KAPOW

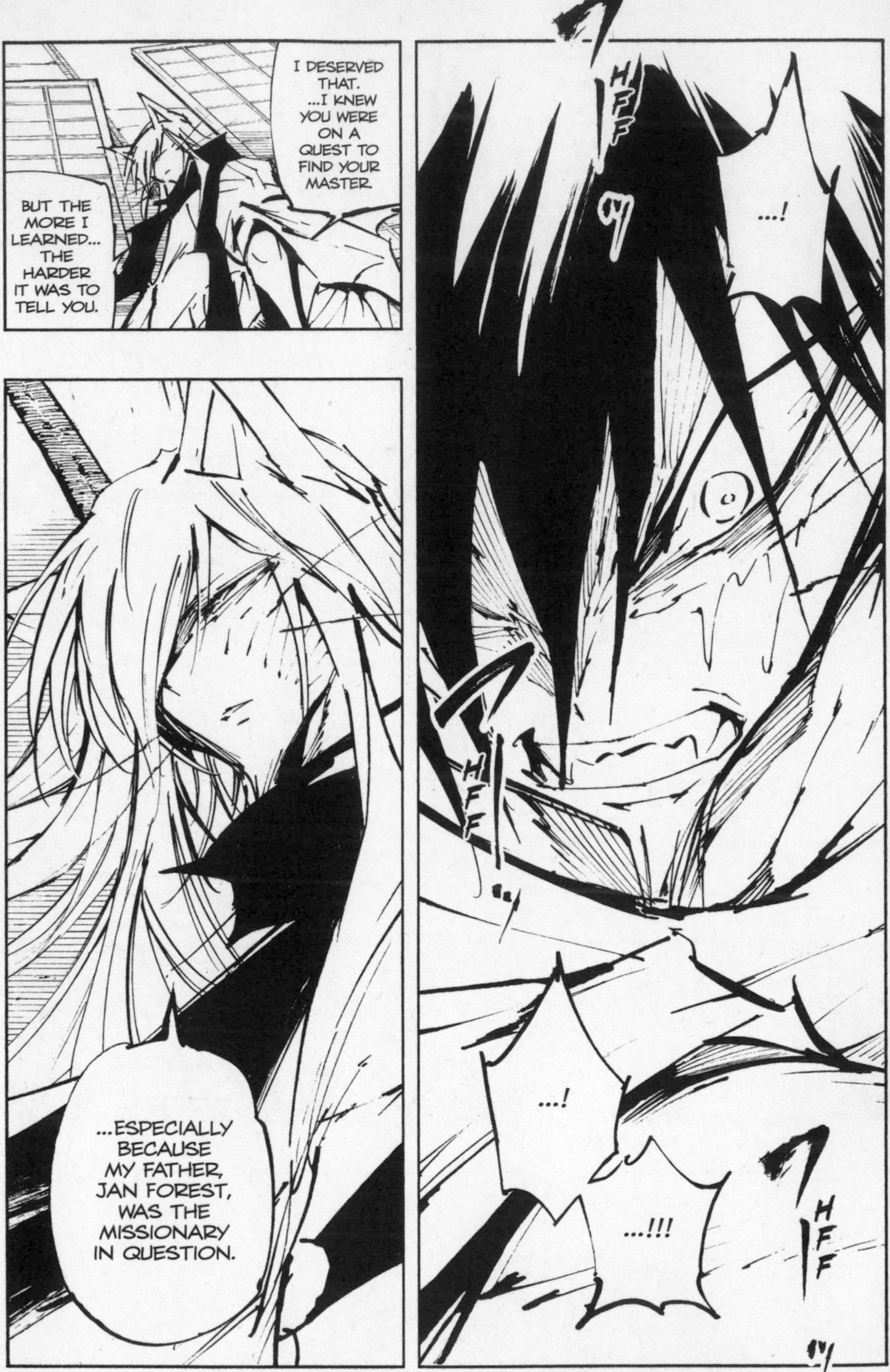
HFF
...!
HFF
...!
...!!!
HFF
I DESERVED THAT. ...I KNEW YOU WERE ON A QUEST TO FIND YOUR MASTER
BUT THE MORE I LEARNED... THE HARDER IT WAS TO TELL YOU.
...ESPECIALLY BECAUSE MY FATHER, JAN FOREST, WAS THE MISSIONARY IN QUESTION.

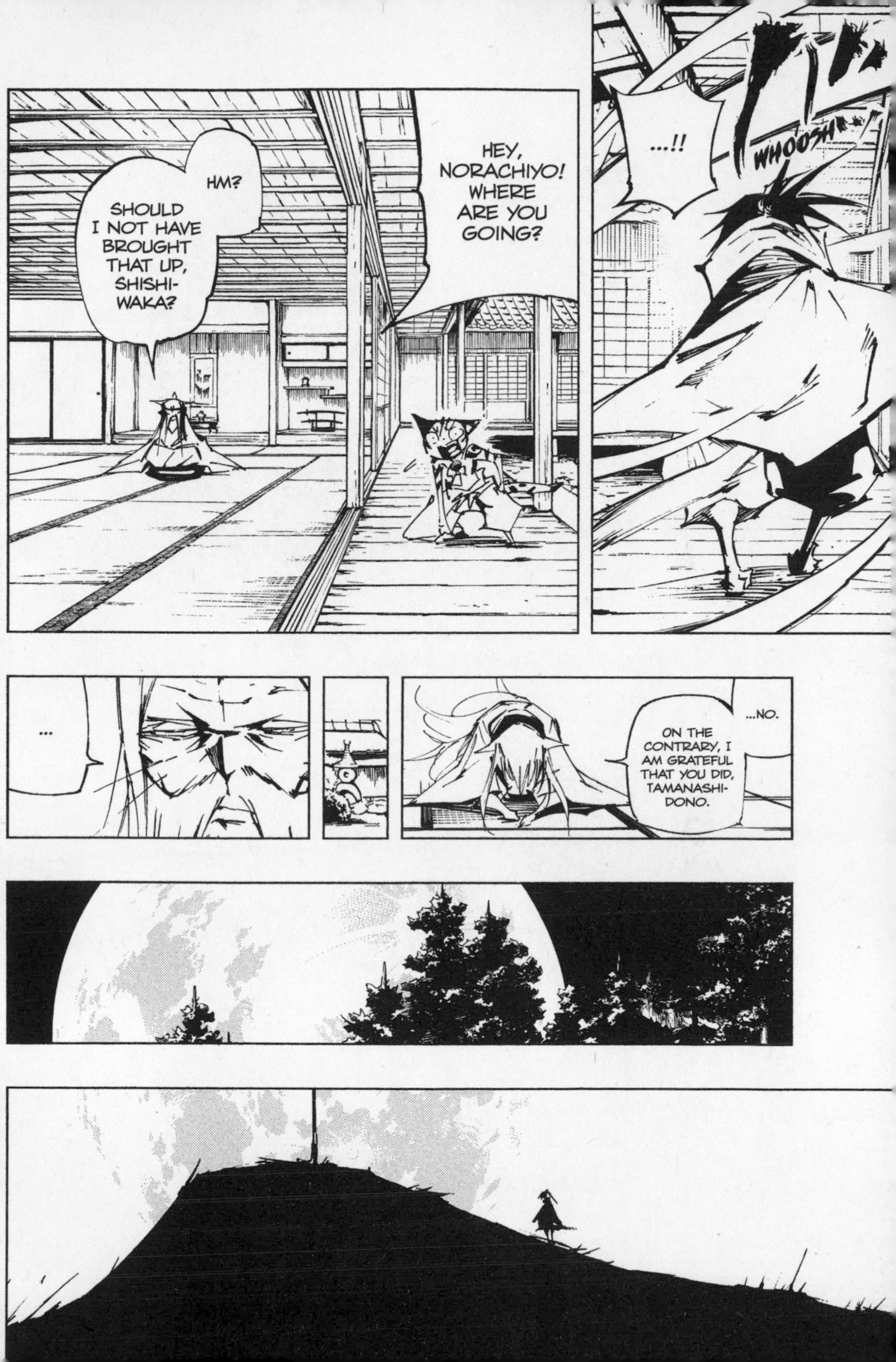
...!!
WHOOSH
HEY, NORACHIYO! WHERE ARE YOU GOING?
HM?
SHOULD I NOT HAVE BROUGHT THAT UP, SHISHI-WAKA?
...NO.
ON THE CONTRARY, I AM GRATEFUL THAT YOU DID, TAMANASHI-DONO.
...

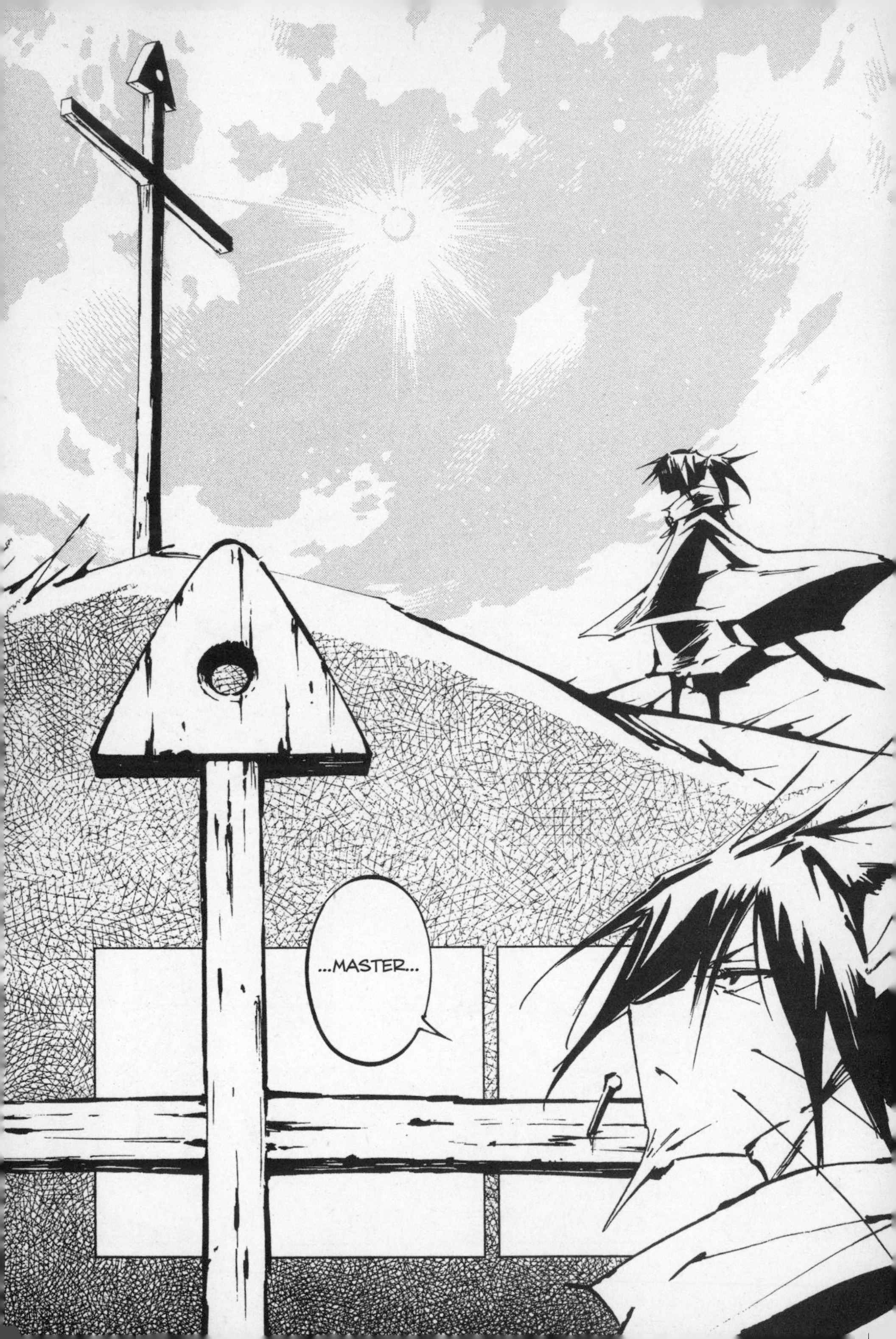
...MASTER...

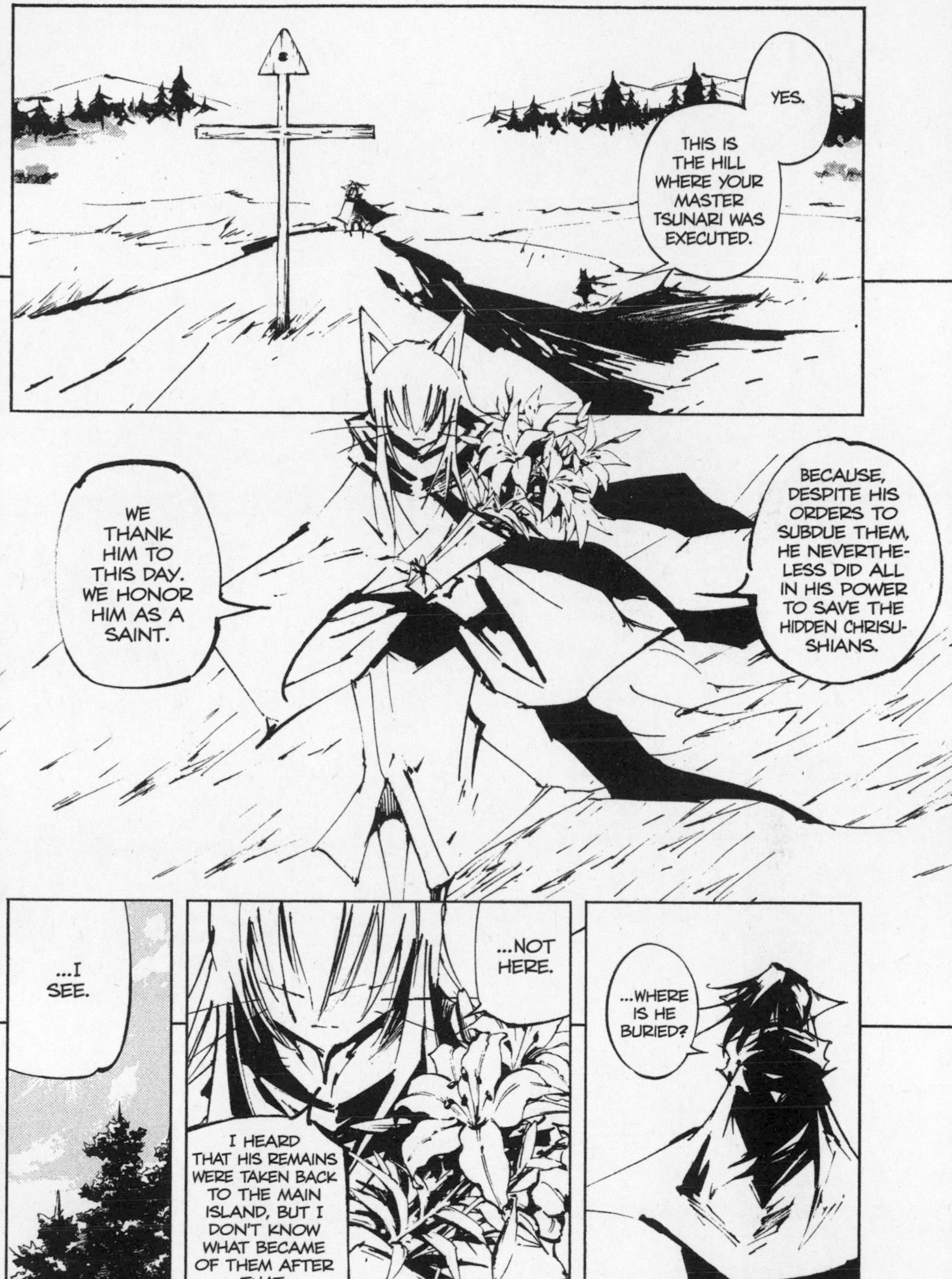
YES.
THIS IS THE HILL WHERE YOUR MASTER TSUNARI WAS EXECUTED.
BECAUSE, DESPITE HIS ORDERS TO SUBDUE THEM, HE NEVERTHELESS DID ALL IN HIS POWER TO SAVE THE HIDDEN CHRISUSHIANS.
WE THANK HIM TO THIS DAY. WE HONOR HIM AS A SAINT.
...WHERE IS HE BURIED?
...NOT HERE.
I HEARD THAT HIS REMAINS WERE TAKEN BACK TO THE MAIN ISLAND, BUT I DON'T KNOW WHAT BECAME OF THEM AFTER THAT.
...I SEE.

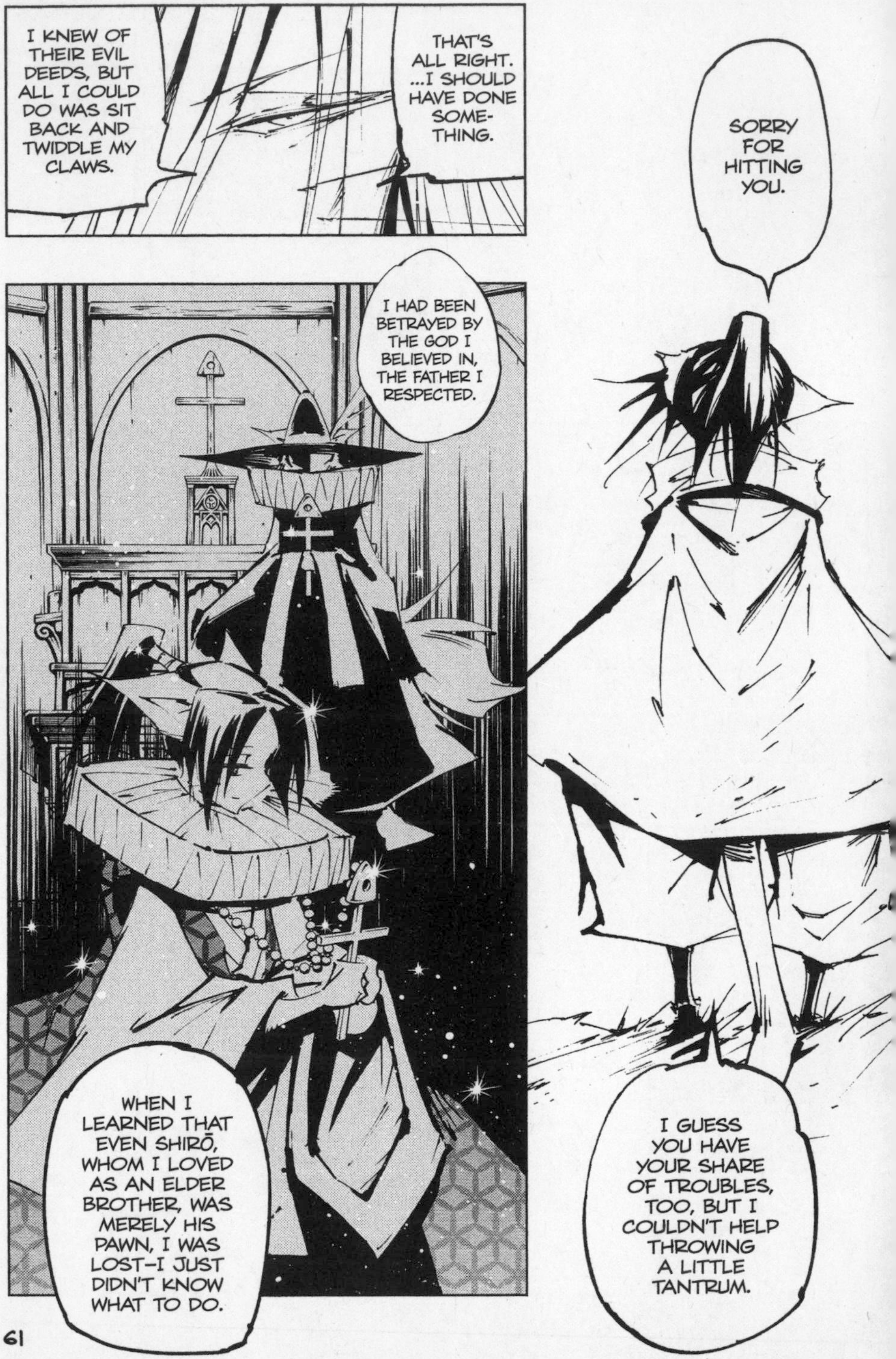
SORRY FOR HITTING YOU.
I GUESS YOU HAVE YOUR SHARE OF TROUBLES, TOO, BUT I COULDN'T HELP THROWING A LITTLE TANTRUM.
THAT'S ALL RIGHT. ...I SHOULD HAVE DONE SOME-THING.
I KNEW OF THEIR EVIL DEEDS, BUT ALL I COULD DO WAS SIT BACK AND TWIDDLE MY CLAWS.
I HAD BEEN BETRAYED BY THE GOD I BELIEVED IN, THE FATHER I RESPECTED.
WHEN I LEARNED THAT EVEN SHIRŌ, WHOM I LOVED AS AN ELDER BROTHER, WAS MERELY HIS PAWN, I WAS LOST–I JUST DIDN'T KNOW WHAT TO DO.

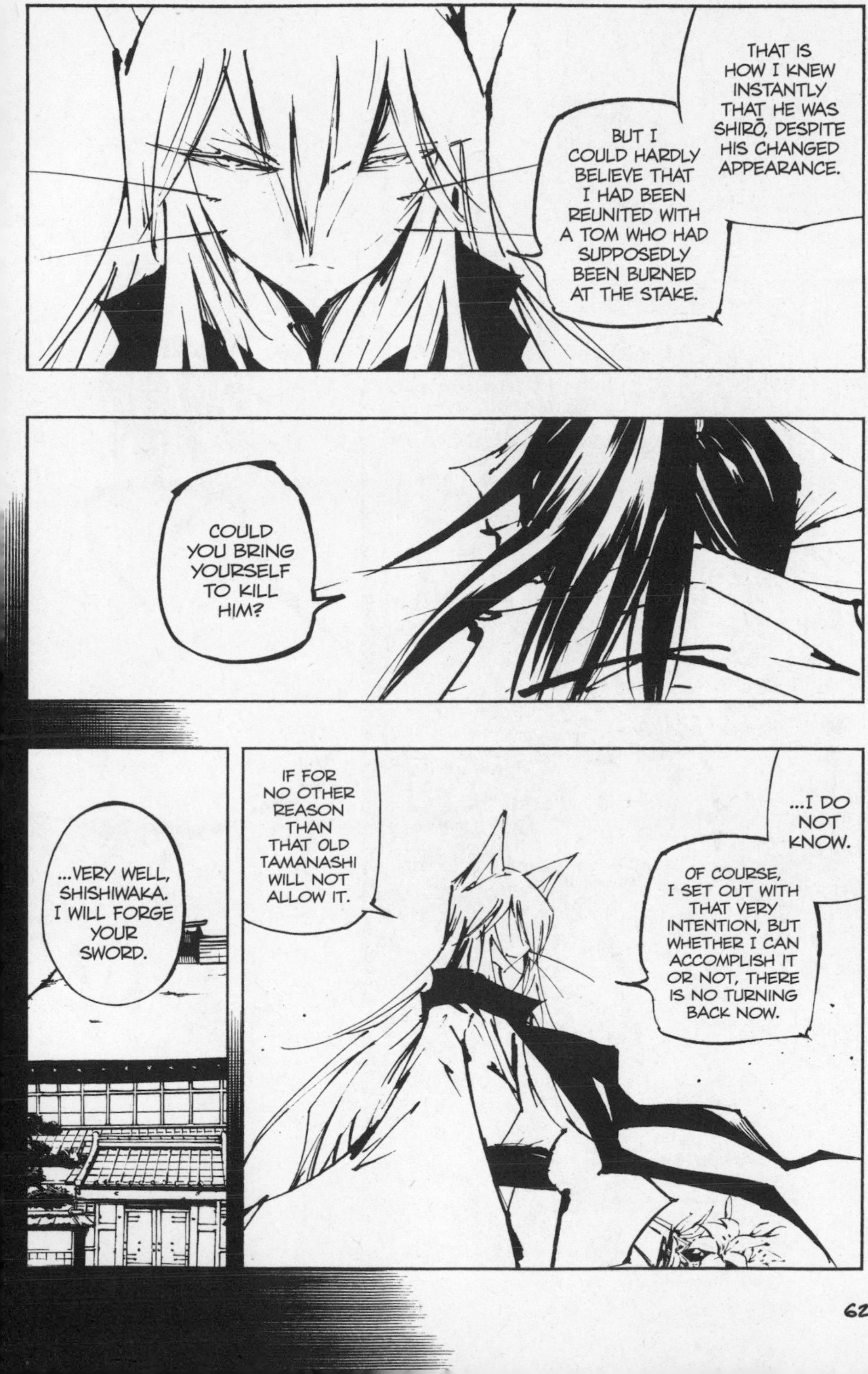
THAT IS HOW I KNEW INSTANTLY THAT HE WAS SHIRŌ, DESPITE HIS CHANGED APPEARANCE.
BUT I COULD HARDLY BELIEVE THAT I HAD BEEN REUNITED WITH A TOM WHO HAD SUPPOSEDLY BEEN BURNED AT THE STAKE.
COULD YOU BRING YOURSELF TO KILL HIM?
...I DO NOT KNOW.
OF COURSE, I SET OUT WITH THAT VERY INTENTION, BUT WHETHER I CAN ACCOMPLISH IT OR NOT, THERE IS NO TURNING BACK NOW.
IF FOR NO OTHER REASON THAN THAT OLD TAMANASHI WILL NOT ALLOW IT.
...VERY WELL, SHISHIWAKA. I WILL FORGE YOUR SWORD.

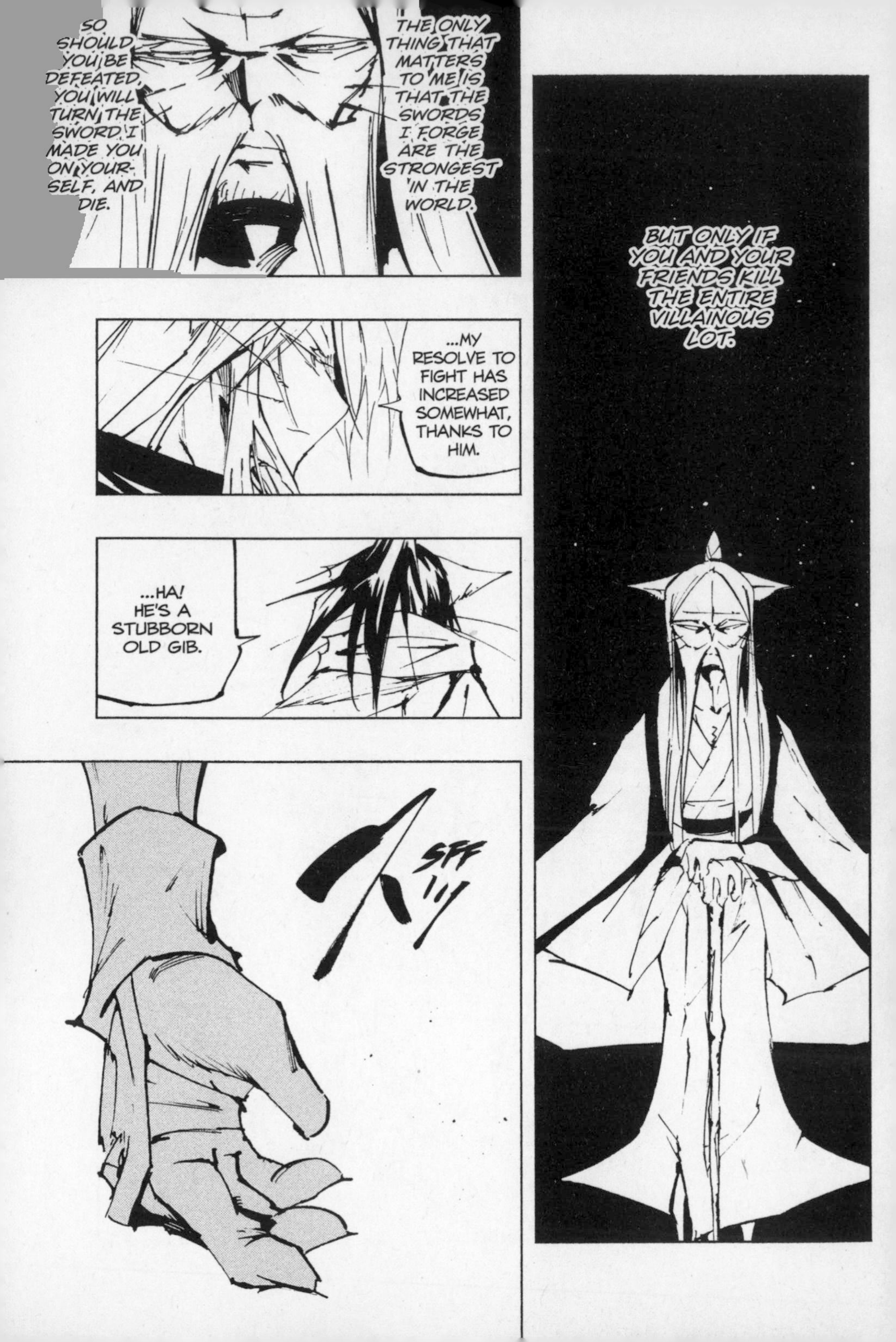
BUT ONLY IF YOU AND YOUR FRIENDS KILL THE ENTIRE VILLAINOUS LOT.
THE ONLY THING THAT MATTERS TO ME IS THAT THE SWORDS I FORGE ARE THE STRONGEST IN THE WORLD.
SO SHOULD YOU BE DEFEATED, YOU WILL TURN THE SWORD I MADE YOU ON YOURSELF, AND DIE.
...MY RESOLVE TO FIGHT HAS INCREASED SOMEWHAT, THANKS TO HIM.
...HA! HE'S A STUBBORN OLD GIB.
SFF

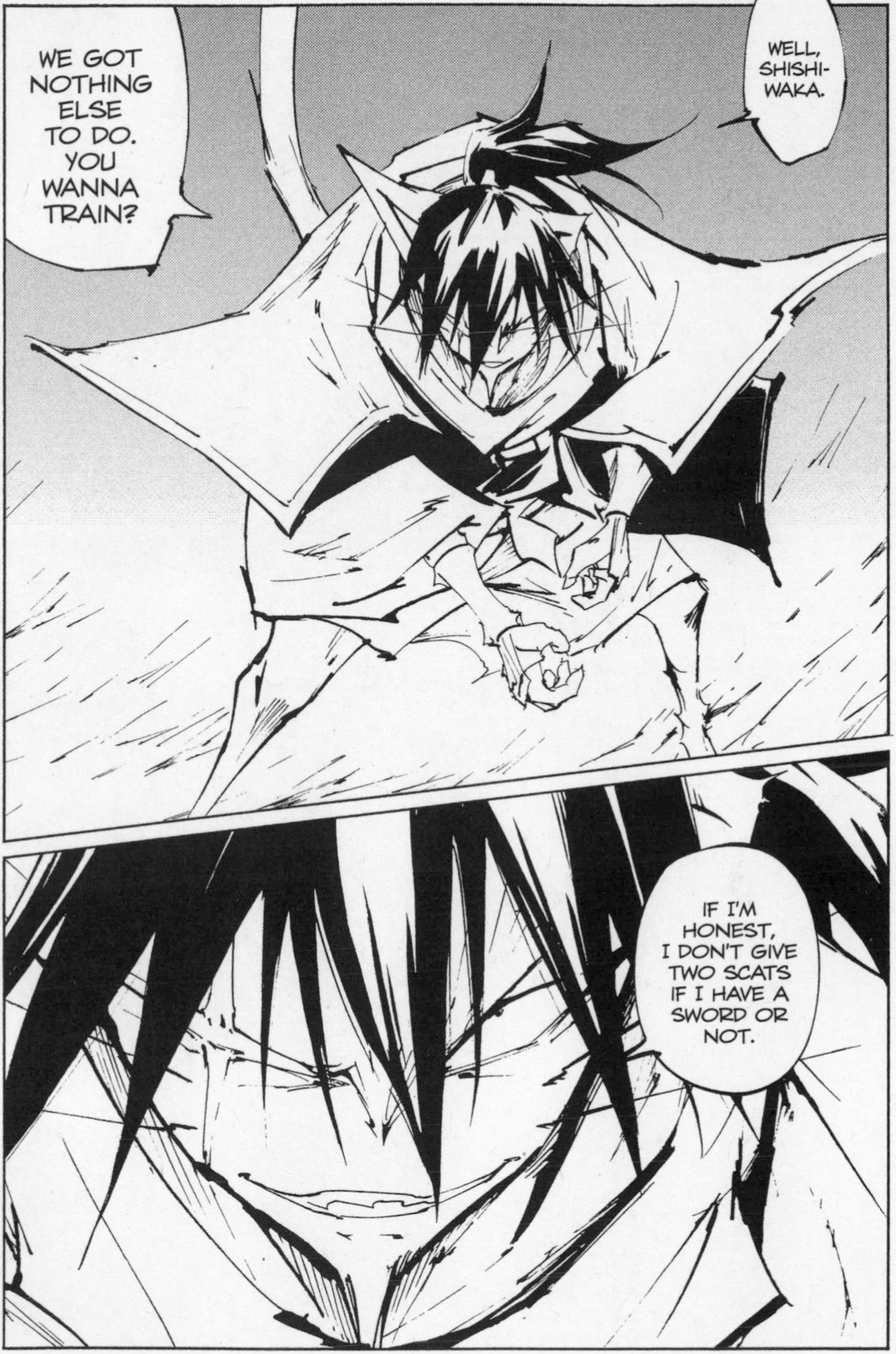
WELL, SHISHI-WAKA.
WE GOT NOTHING ELSE TO DO. YOU WANNA TRAIN?
IF I'M HONEST, I DON'T GIVE TWO SCATS IF I HAVE A SWORD OR NOT.

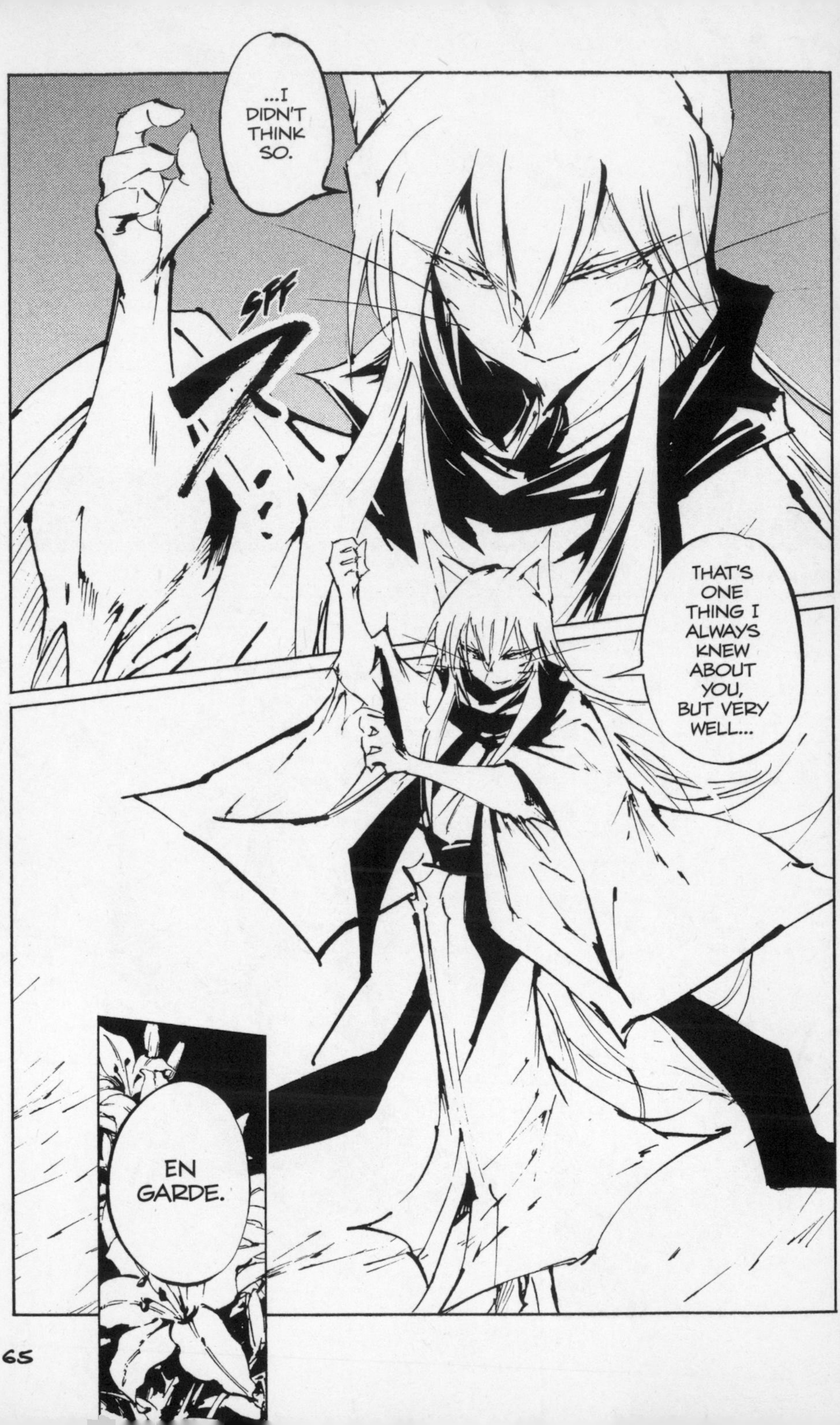
...I DIDN'T THINK SO.
SFF
THAT'S ONE THING I ALWAYS KNEW ABOUT YOU, BUT VERY WELL...
EN GARDE.

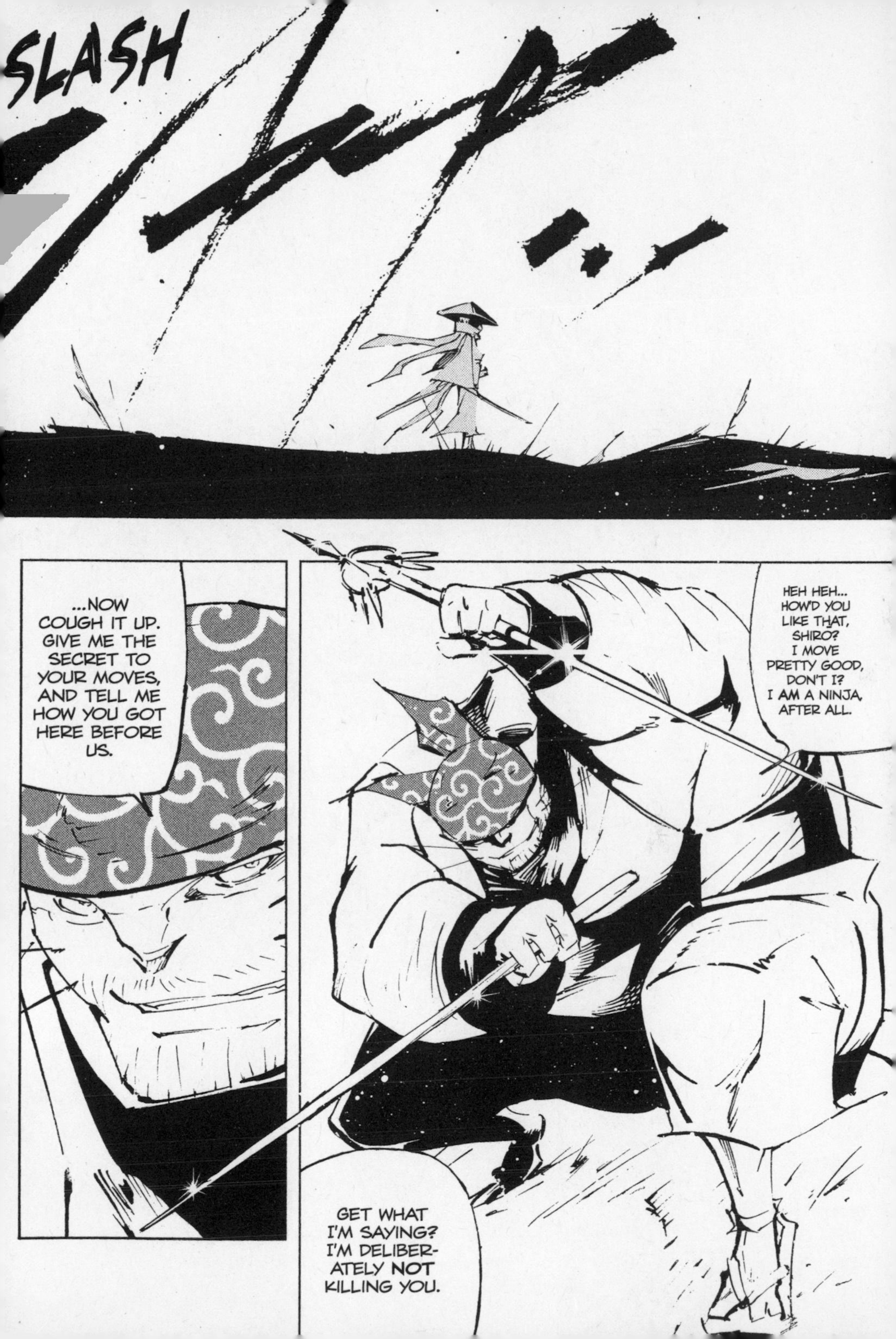
SLASH
HEH HEH... HOW'D YOU LIKE THAT, SHIRO? I MOVE PRETTY GOOD, DON'T I? I AM A NINJA, AFTER ALL.
GET WHAT I'M SAYING? I'M DELIBER-ATELY NOT KILLING YOU.
...NOW COUGH IT UP. GIVE ME THE SECRET TO YOUR MOVES, AND TELL ME HOW YOU GOT HERE BEFORE US.

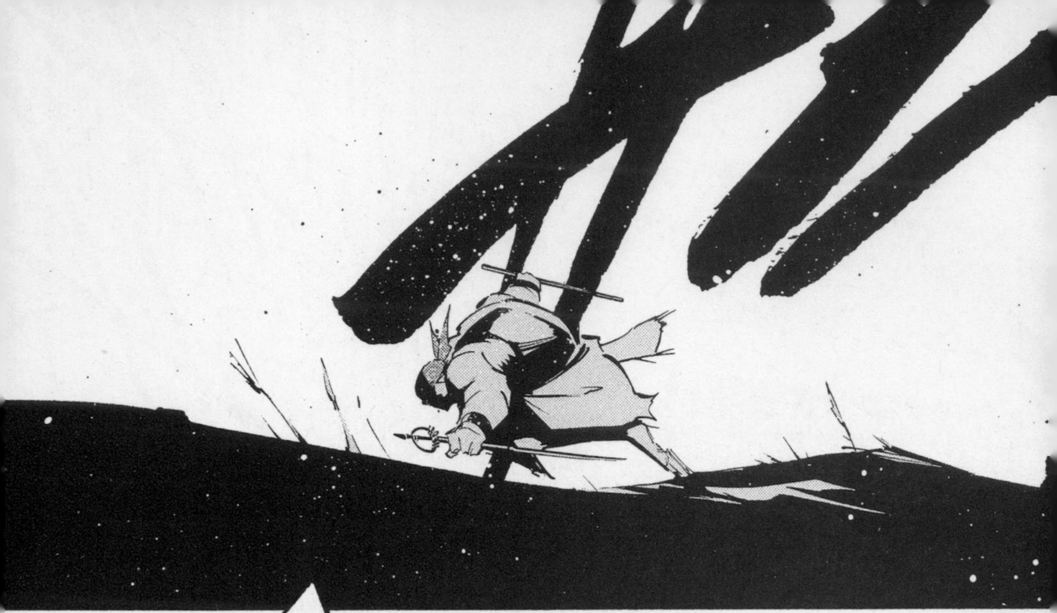

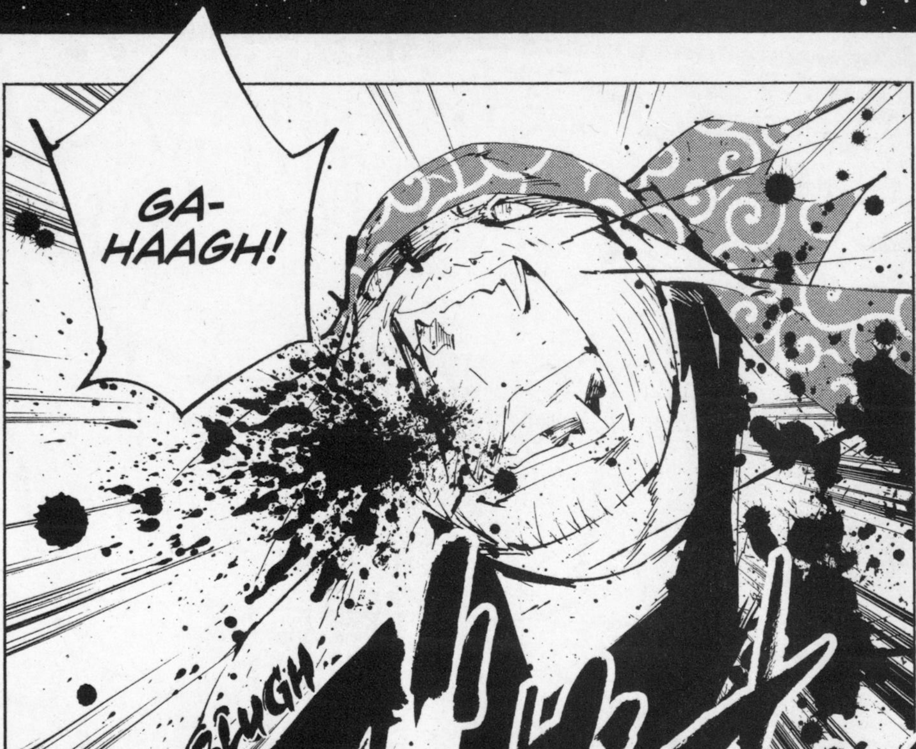
GA-HAAGH!
GA-BLUGH

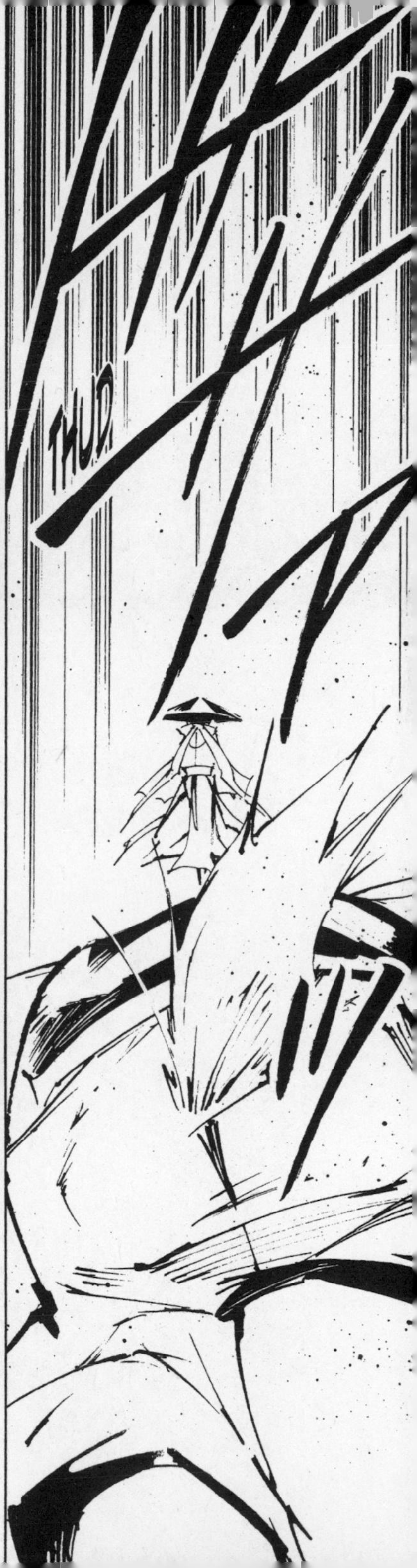
THUD

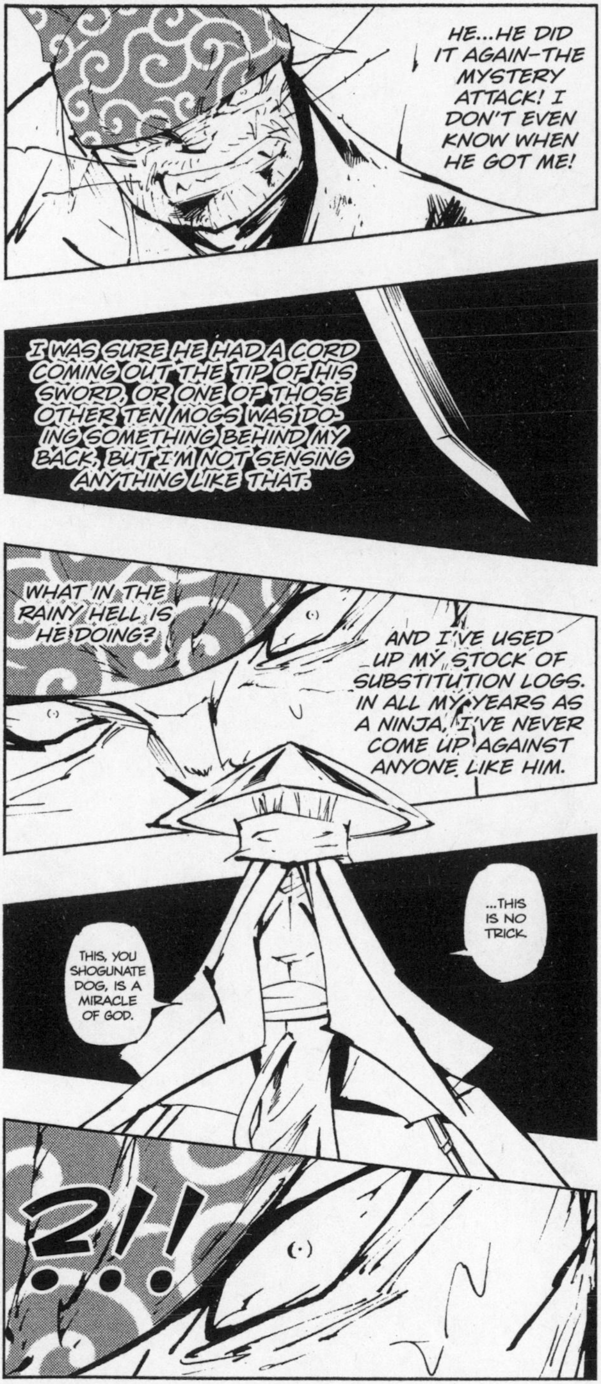
HE...HE DID IT AGAIN–THE MYSTERY ATTACK! I DON'T EVEN KNOW WHEN HE GOT ME!
I WAS SURE HE HAD A CORD COMING OUT THE TIP OF HIS SWORD, OR ONE OF THOSE OTHER TEN MOGS WAS DOING SOMETHING BEHIND MY BACK, BUT I'M NOT SENSING ANYTHING LIKE THAT.
WHAT IN THE RAINY HELL IS HE DOING?
AND I'VE USED UP MY STOCK OF SUBSTITUTION LOGS. IN ALL MY YEARS AS A NINJA, I'VE NEVER COME UP AGAINST ANYONE LIKE HIM.
...THIS IS NO TRICK
THIS, YOU SHOGUNATE DOG, IS A MIRACLE OF GOD.
?!!

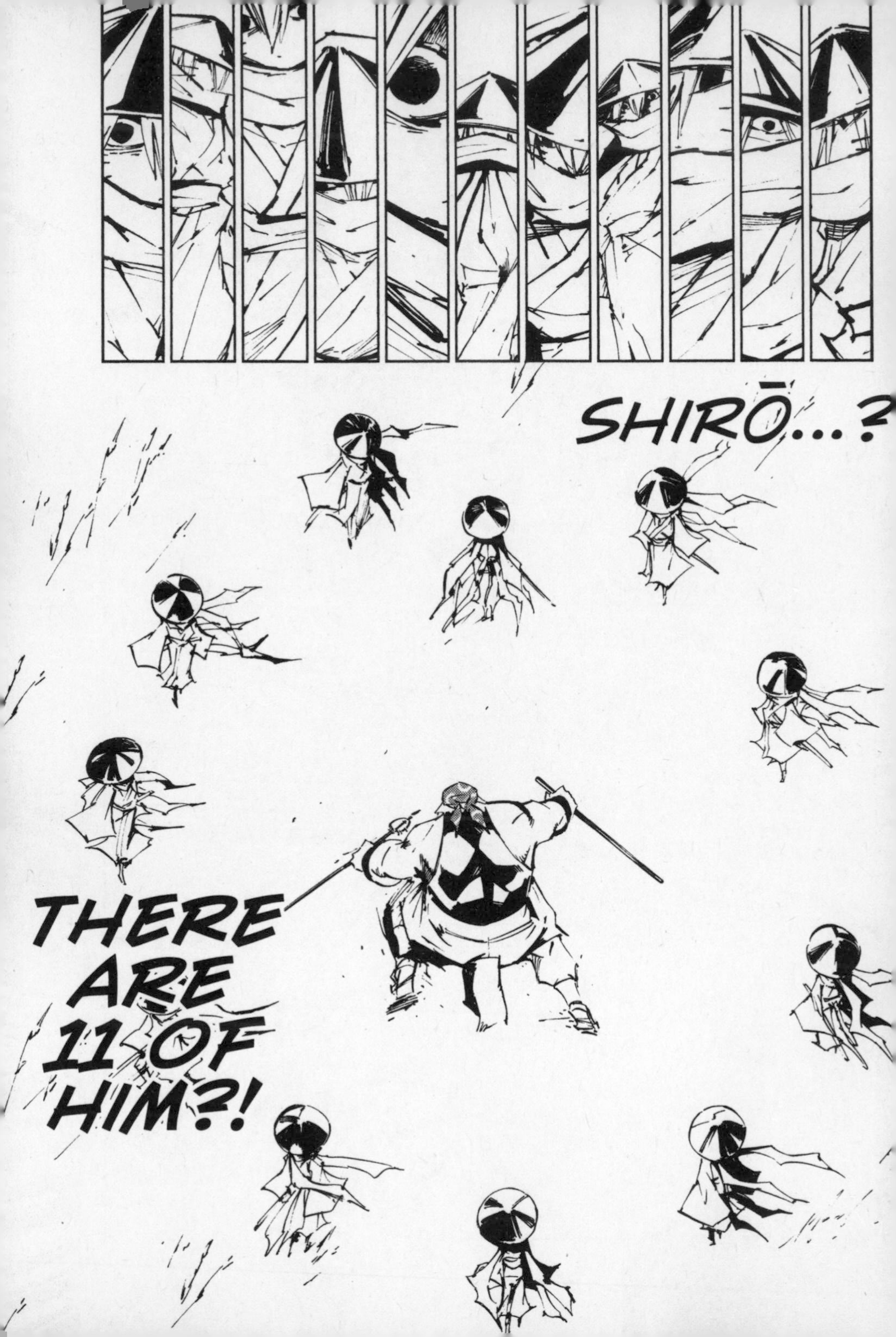
SHIRŌ...?
THERE ARE 11 OF HIM?!

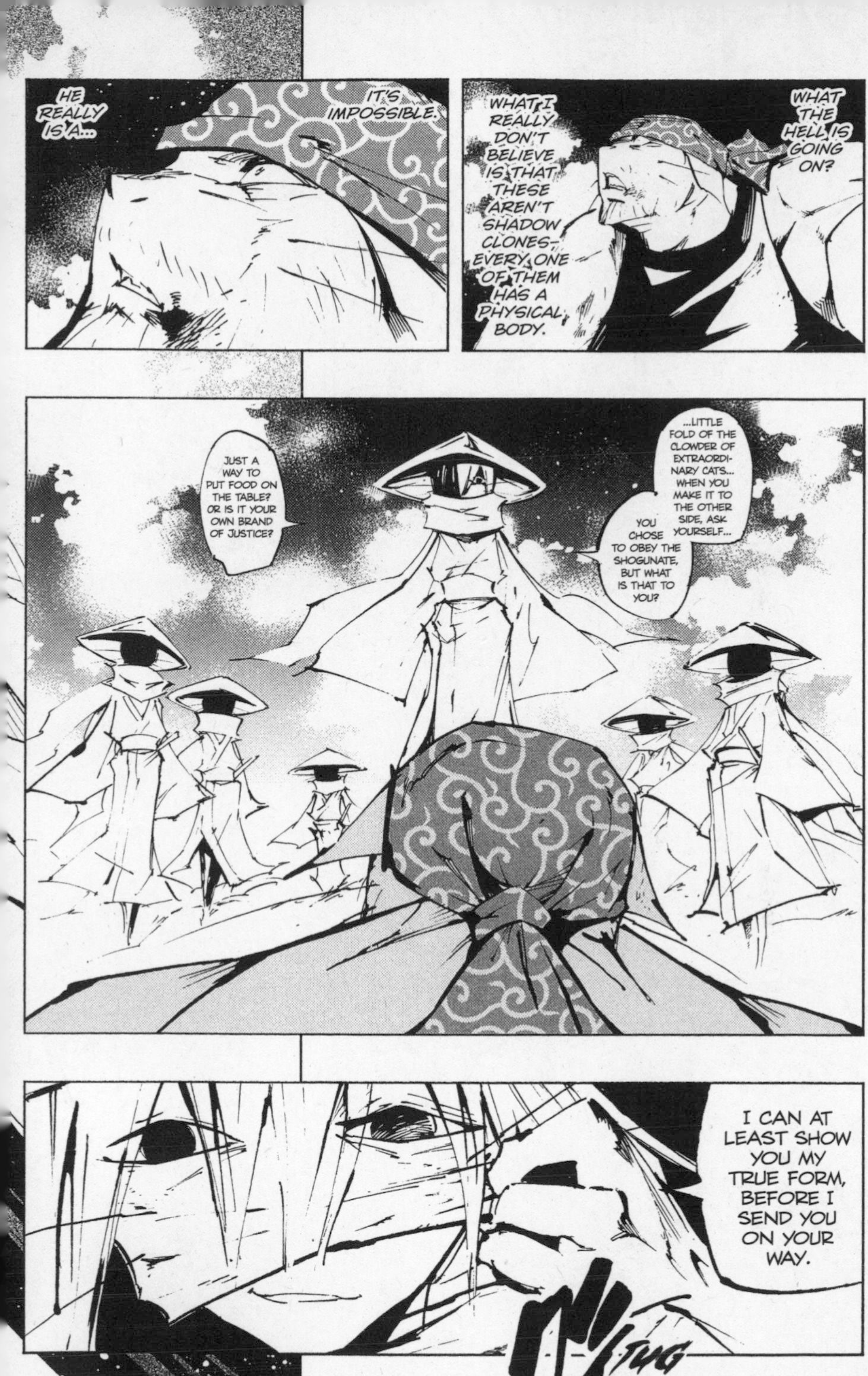

WHAT THE HELL IS GOING ON?
WHAT I REALLY DON'T BELIEVE IS THAT THESE AREN'T SHADOW CLONES—EVERY ONE OF THEM HAS A PHYSICAL BODY.
IT'S IMPOSSIBLE.
HE REALLY IS A...
...LITTLE FOLD OF THE CLOWDER OF EXTRAORDINARY CATS... WHEN YOU MAKE IT TO THE OTHER SIDE, ASK YOURSELF...
YOU CHOSE TO OBEY THE SHOGUNATE, BUT WHAT IS THAT TO YOU?
JUST A WAY TO PUT FOOD ON THE TABLE? OR IS IT YOUR OWN BRAND OF JUSTICE?
I CAN AT LEAST SHOW YOU MY TRUE FORM, BEFORE I SEND YOU ON YOUR WAY.
TUG

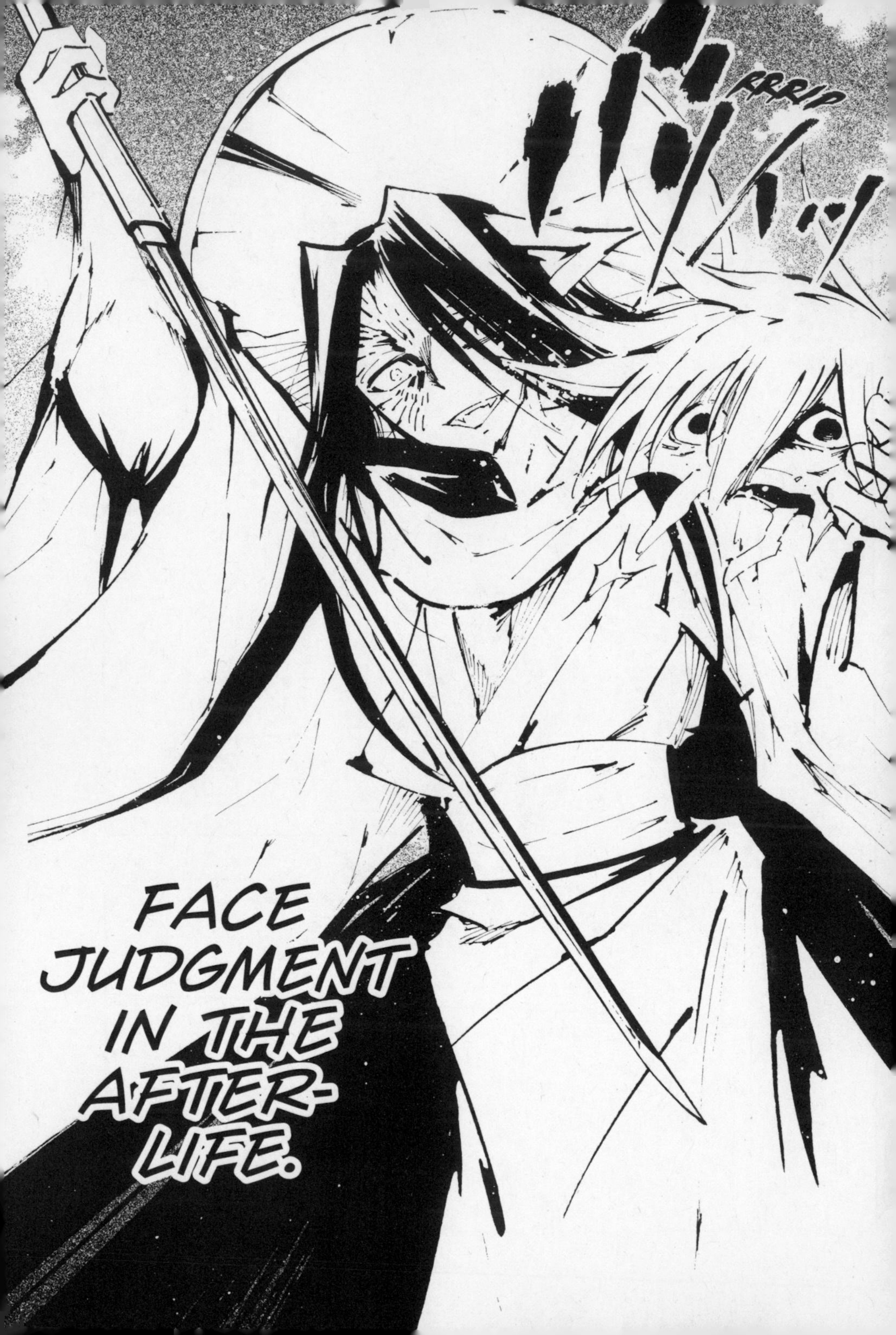
RRRIP
FACE JUDGMENT IN THE AFTER-LIFE.

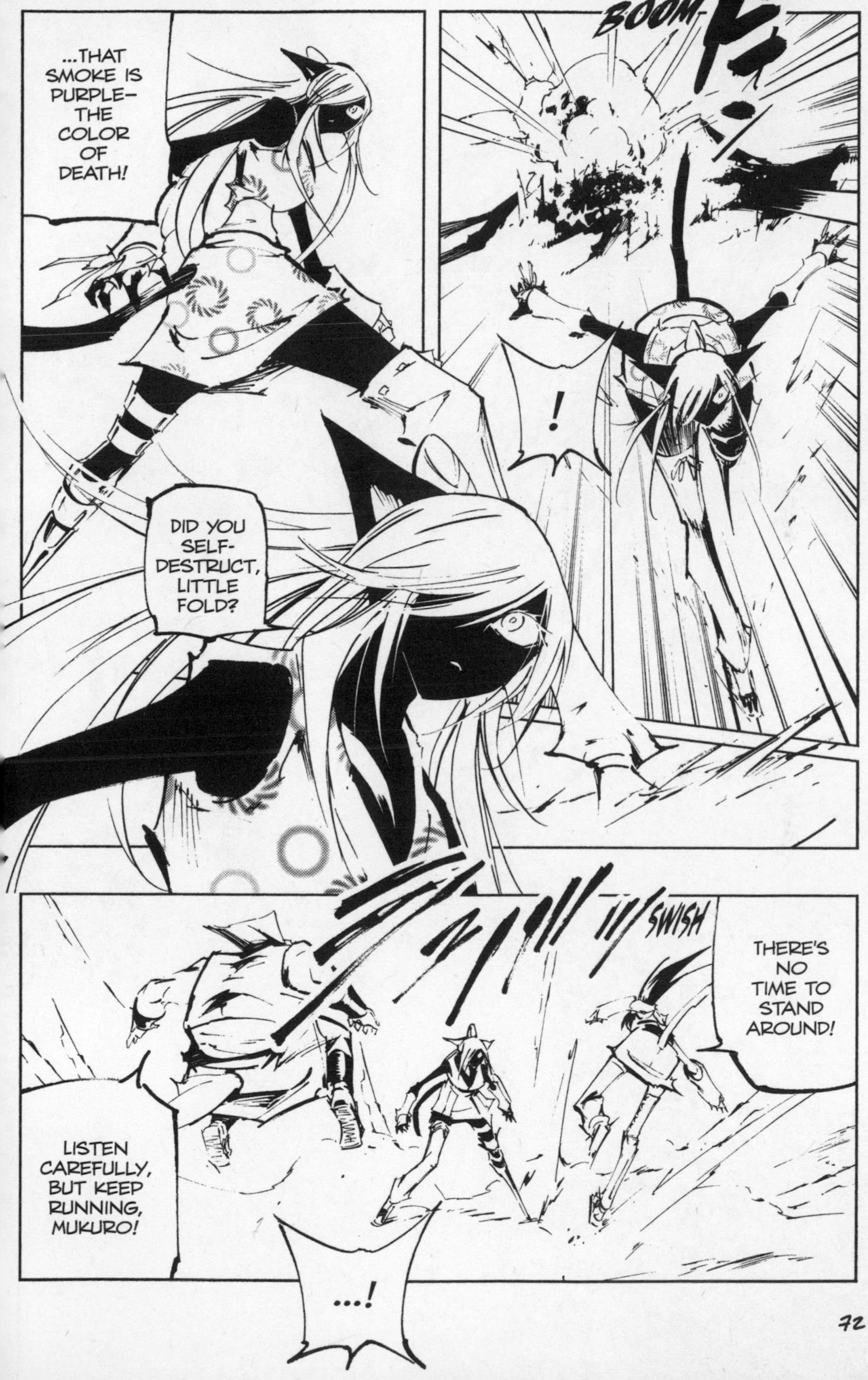
BOOM
!
...THAT SMOKE IS PURPLE— THE COLOR OF DEATH!
DID YOU SELF-DESTRUCT, LITTLE FOLD?
SWISH
THERE'S NO TIME TO STAND AROUND!
LISTEN CAREFULLY, BUT KEEP RUNNING, MUKURO!
...!

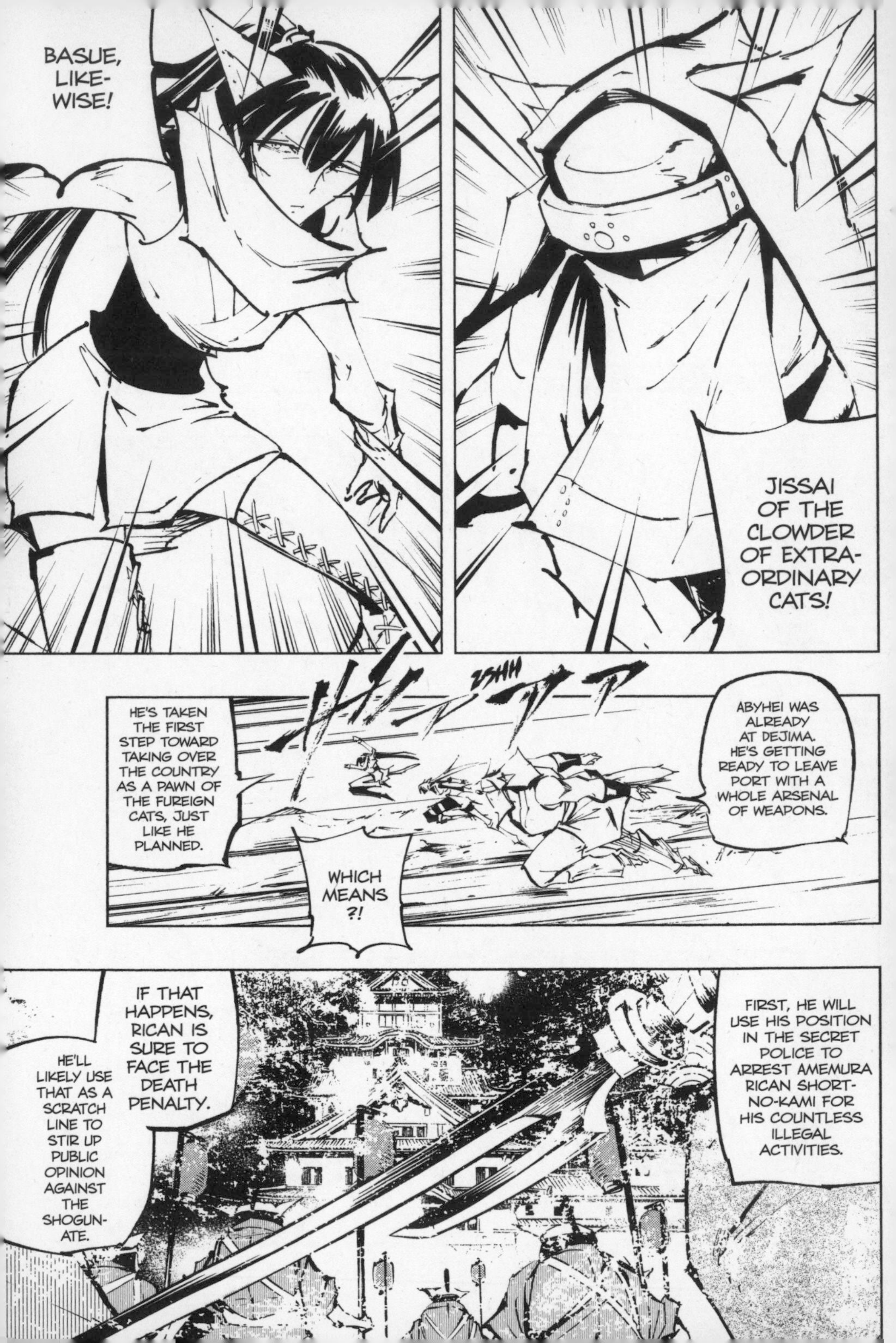
JISSAI OF THE CLOWDER OF EXTRA-ORDINARY CATS!
BASUE, LIKE-WISE!
ZSHH
ABYHEI WAS ALREADY AT DEJIMA. HE'S GETTING READY TO LEAVE PORT WITH A WHOLE ARSENAL OF WEAPONS.
HE'S TAKEN THE FIRST STEP TOWARD TAKING OVER THE COUNTRY AS A PAWN OF THE FUREIGN CATS, JUST LIKE HE PLANNED.
WHICH MEANS?!
FIRST, HE WILL USE HIS POSITION IN THE SECRET POLICE TO ARREST AMEMURA RICAN SHORT-NO-KAMI FOR HIS COUNTLESS ILLEGAL ACTIVITIES.
IF THAT HAPPENS, RICAN IS SURE TO FACE THE DEATH PENALTY.
HE'LL LIKELY USE THAT AS A SCRATCH LINE TO STIR UP PUBLIC OPINION AGAINST THE SHOGUN-ATE.

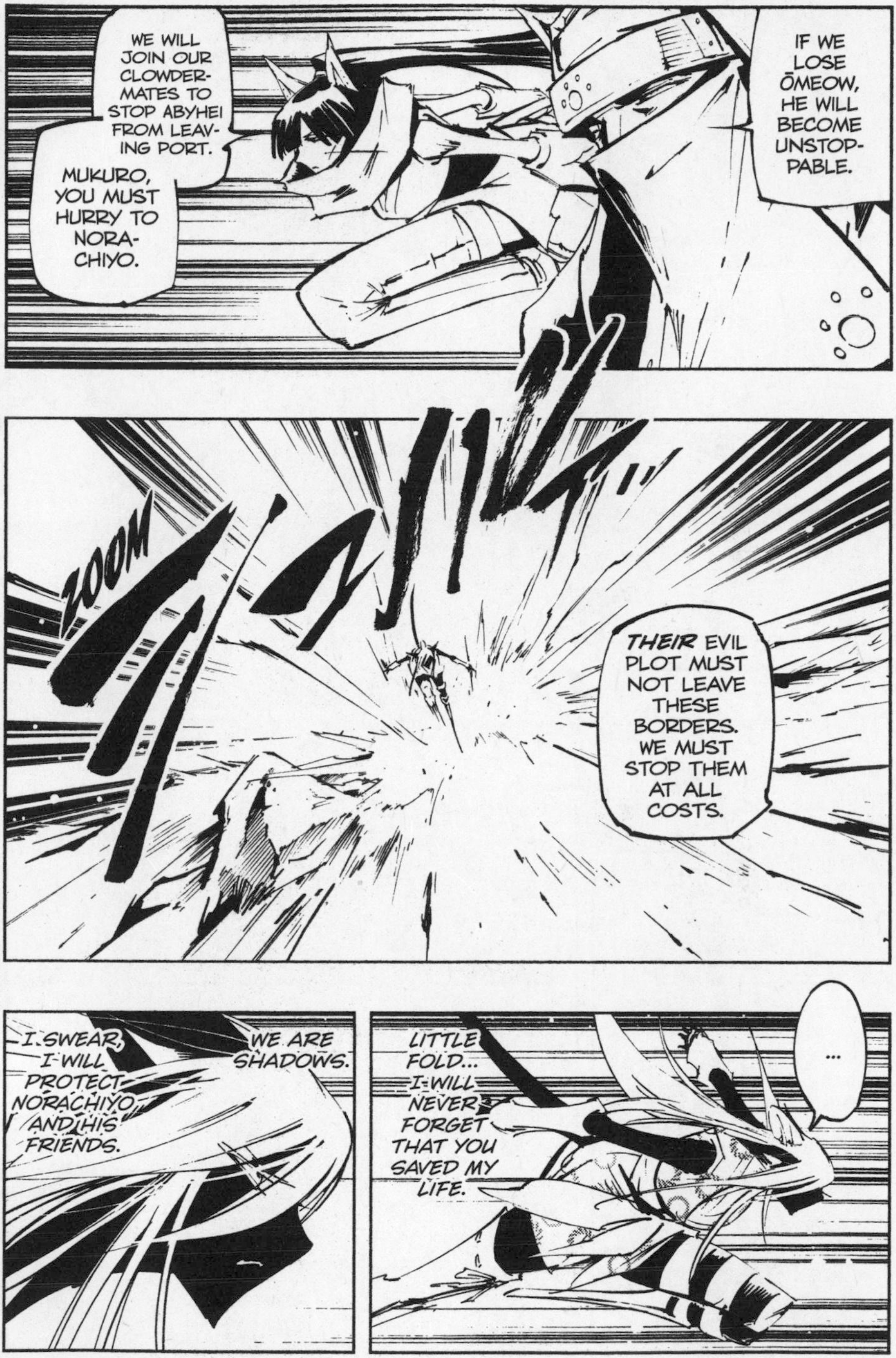
IF WE LOSE ŌMEOW, HE WILL BECOME UNSTOP-PABLE.
WE WILL JOIN OUR CLOWDER-MATES TO STOP ABYHEI FROM LEAV-ING PORT.
MUKURO, YOU MUST HURRY TO NORA-CHIYO.
THEIR EVIL PLOT MUST NOT LEAVE THESE BORDERS. WE MUST STOP THEM AT ALL COSTS.
ZOOM
...
LITTLE FOLD... I WILL NEVER FORGET THAT YOU SAVED MY LIFE.
WE ARE SHADOWS.
I SWEAR, I WILL PROTECT NORACHIYO AND HIS FRIENDS.

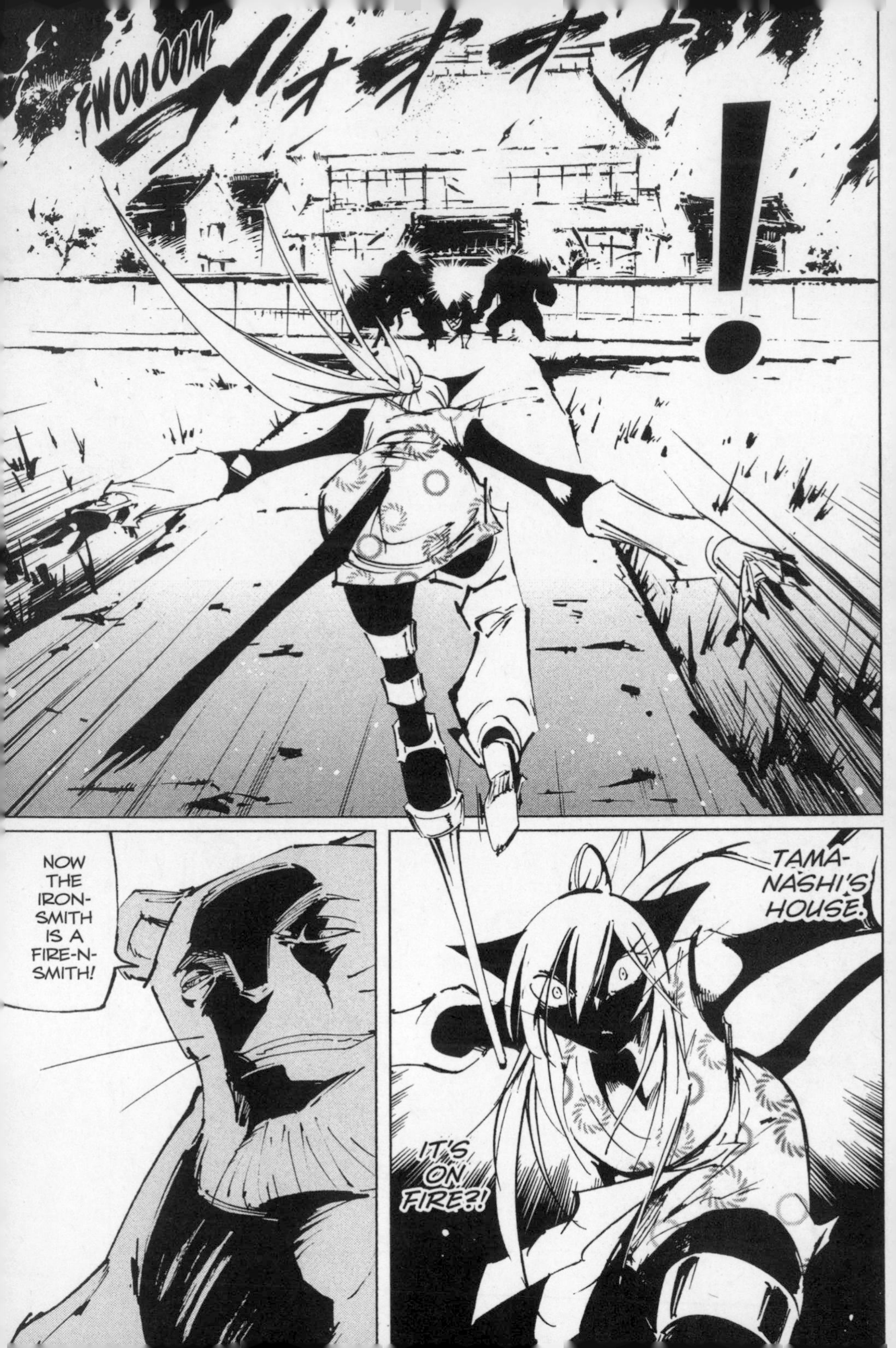
FWOOOM
TAMA-NASHI'S HOUSE.
IT'S ON FIRE?!
NOW THE IRON-SMITH IS A FIRE-N-SMITH!

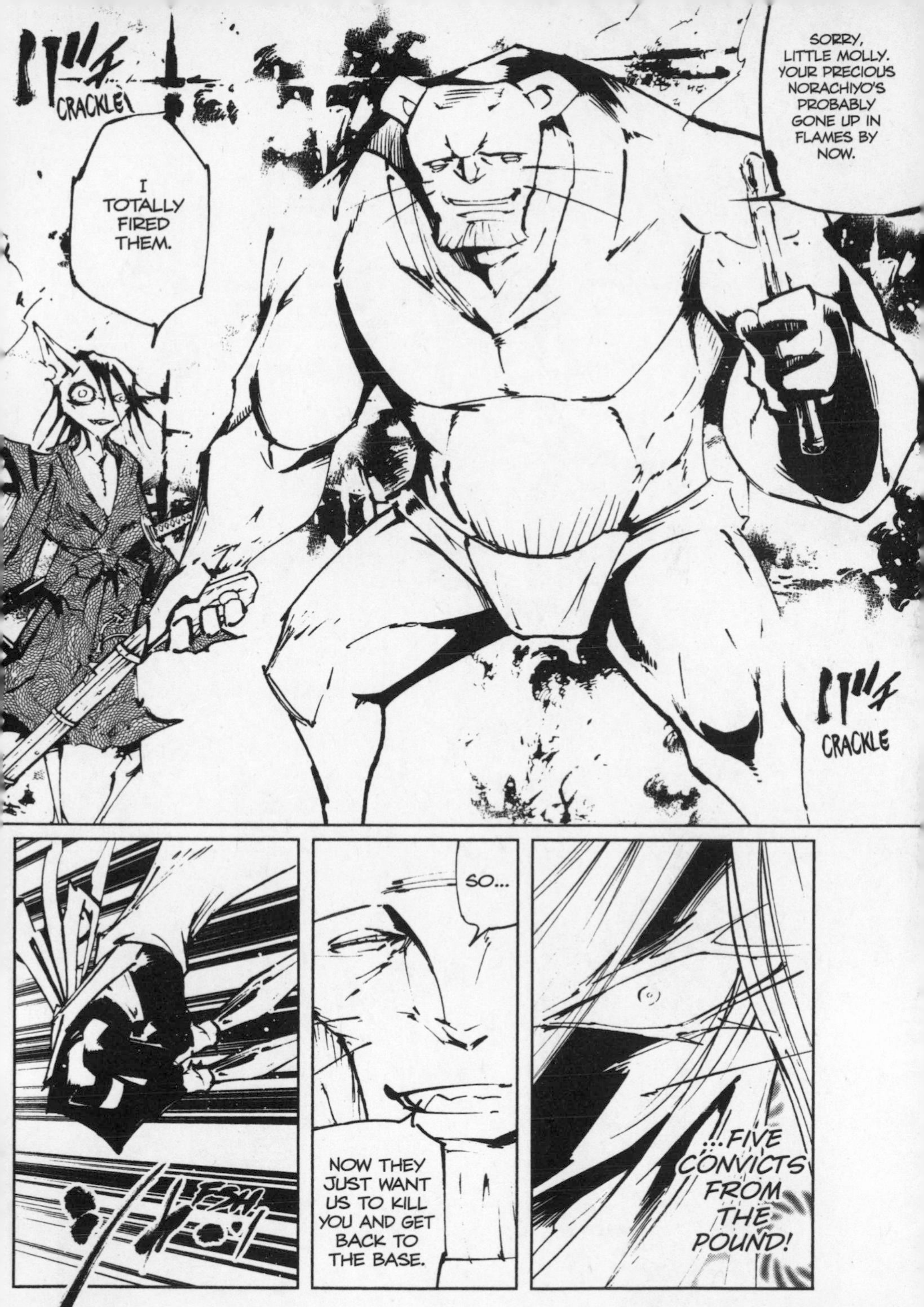
SORRY, LITTLE MOLLY. YOUR PRECIOUS NORACHIYO'S PROBABLY GONE UP IN FLAMES BY NOW.
CRACKLE
I TOTALLY FIRED THEM.
CRACKLE
...FIVE CONVICTS FROM THE POUND!
SO...
NOW THEY JUST WANT US TO KILL YOU AND GET BACK TO THE BASE.
FSH

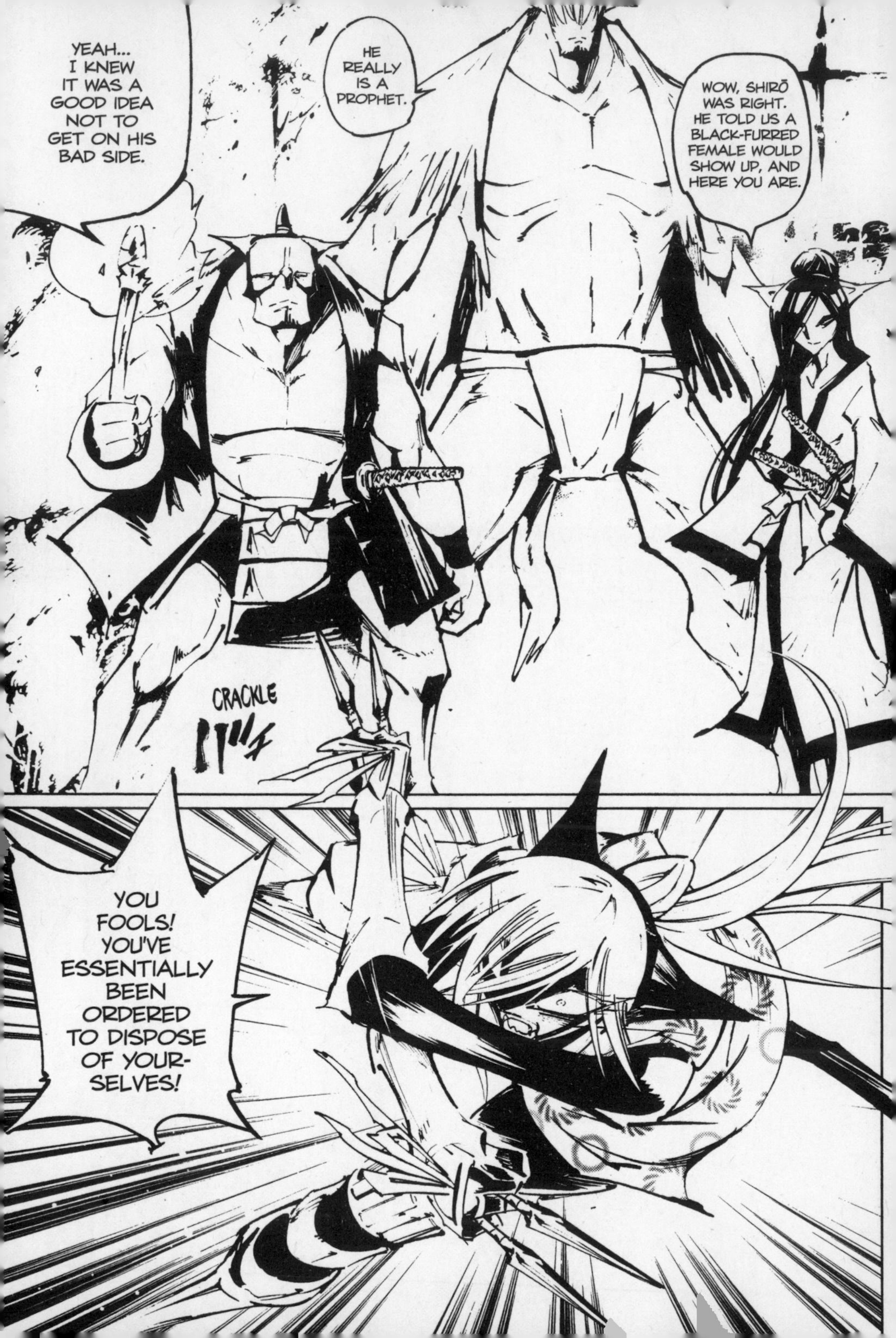
WOW, SHIRŌ WAS RIGHT. HE TOLD US A BLACK-FURRED FEMALE WOULD SHOW UP, AND HERE YOU ARE.
HE REALLY IS A PROPHET.
YEAH... I KNEW IT WAS A GOOD IDEA NOT TO GET ON HIS BAD SIDE.
CRACKLE
YOU FOOLS! YOU'VE ESSENTIALLY BEEN ORDERED TO DISPOSE OF YOUR-SELVES!

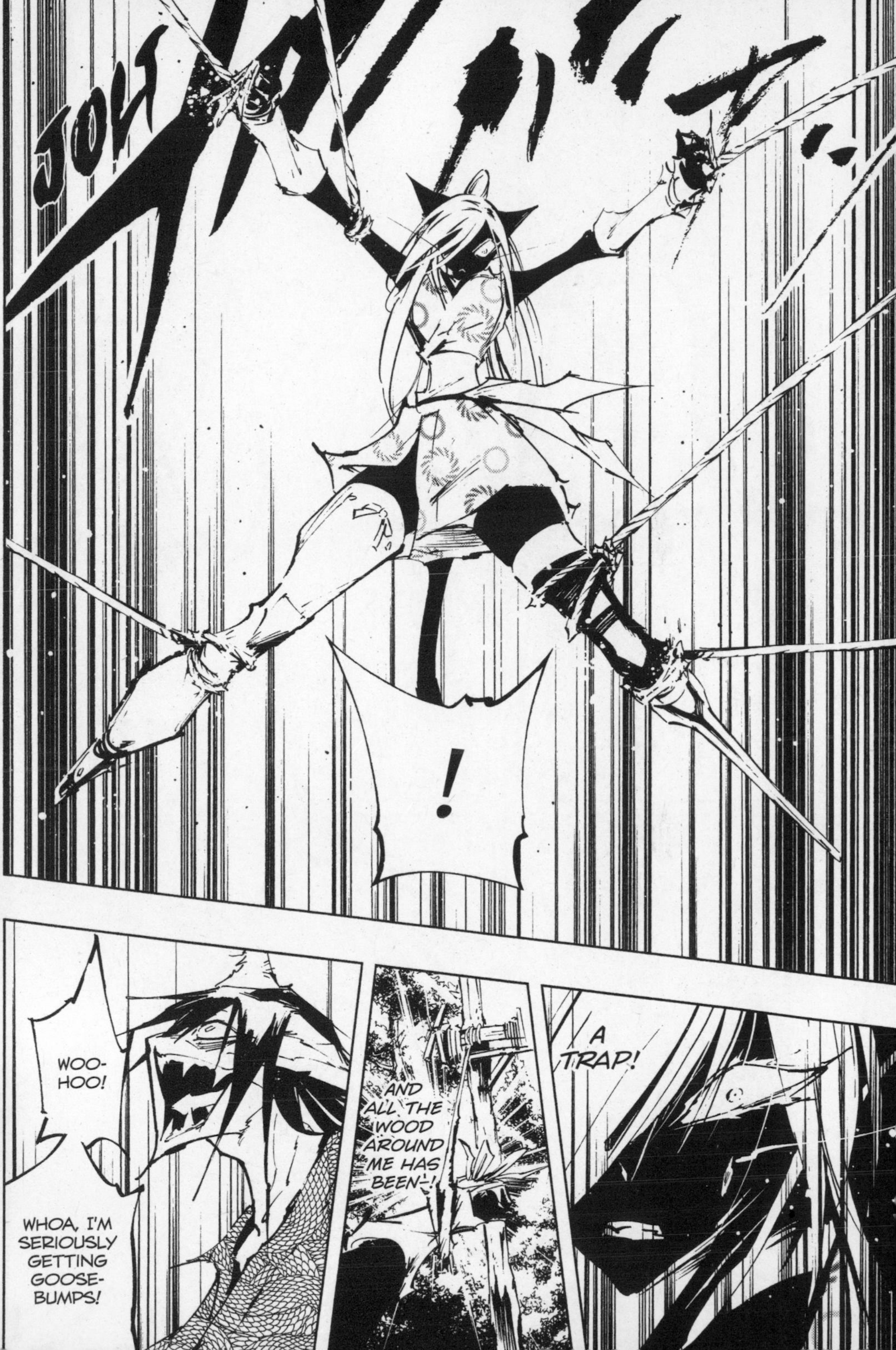
JOLT
!
A TRAP!
AND ALL THE WOOD AROUND ME HAS BEEN--!
WOO-HOO!
WHOA, I'M SERIOUSLY GETTING GOOSE-BUMPS!

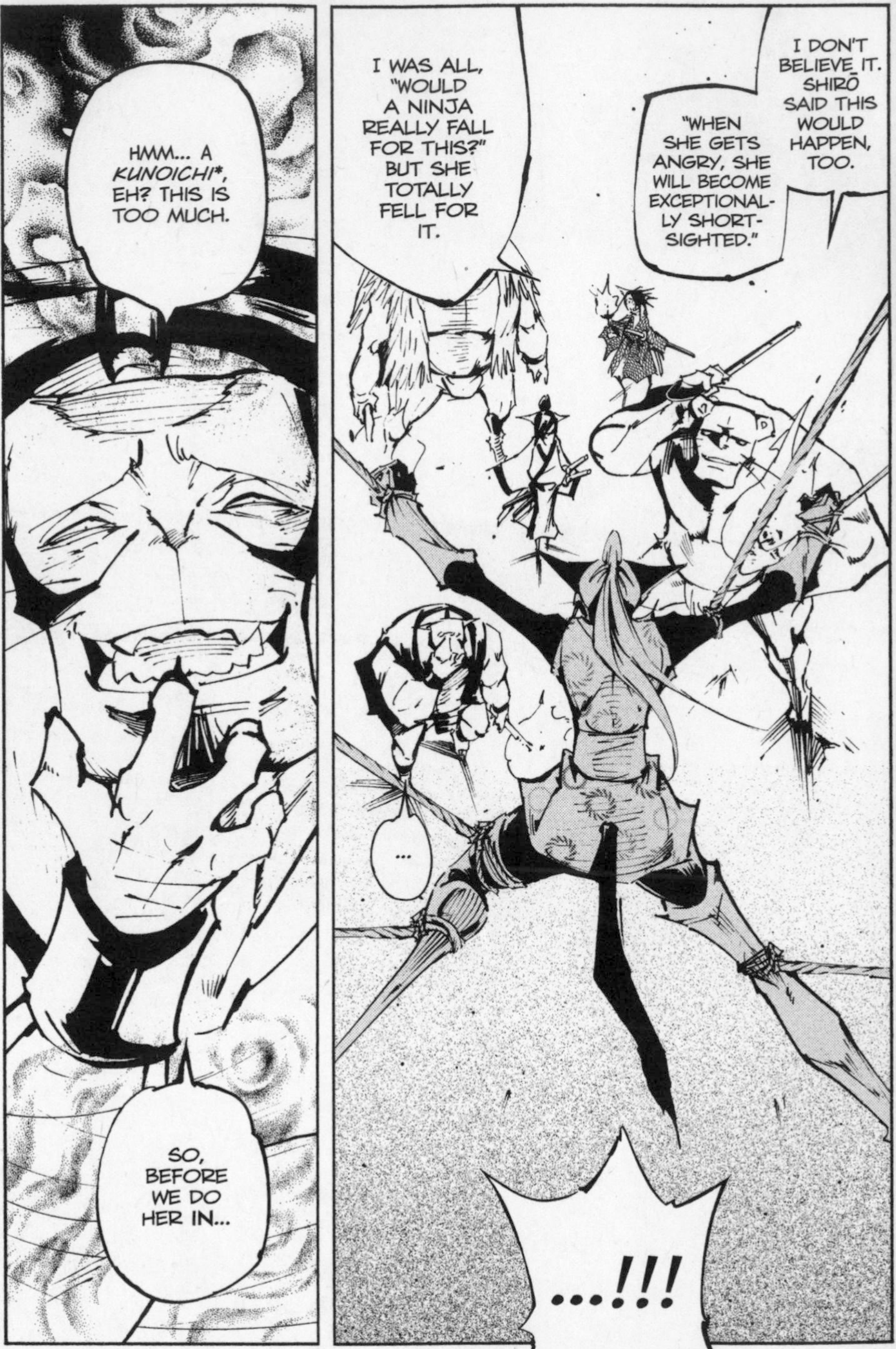
I DON'T BELIEVE IT. SHIRŌ SAID THIS WOULD HAPPEN, TOO.
"WHEN SHE GETS ANGRY, SHE WILL BECOME EXCEPTIONAL-LY SHORT-SIGHTED."
I WAS ALL, "WOULD A NINJA REALLY FALL FOR THIS?" BUT SHE TOTALLY FELL FOR IT.
...
...!!!
HMM... A KUNOICHI*, EH? THIS IS TOO MUCH.
SO, BEFORE WE DO HER IN...

*A FEMALE NINJA

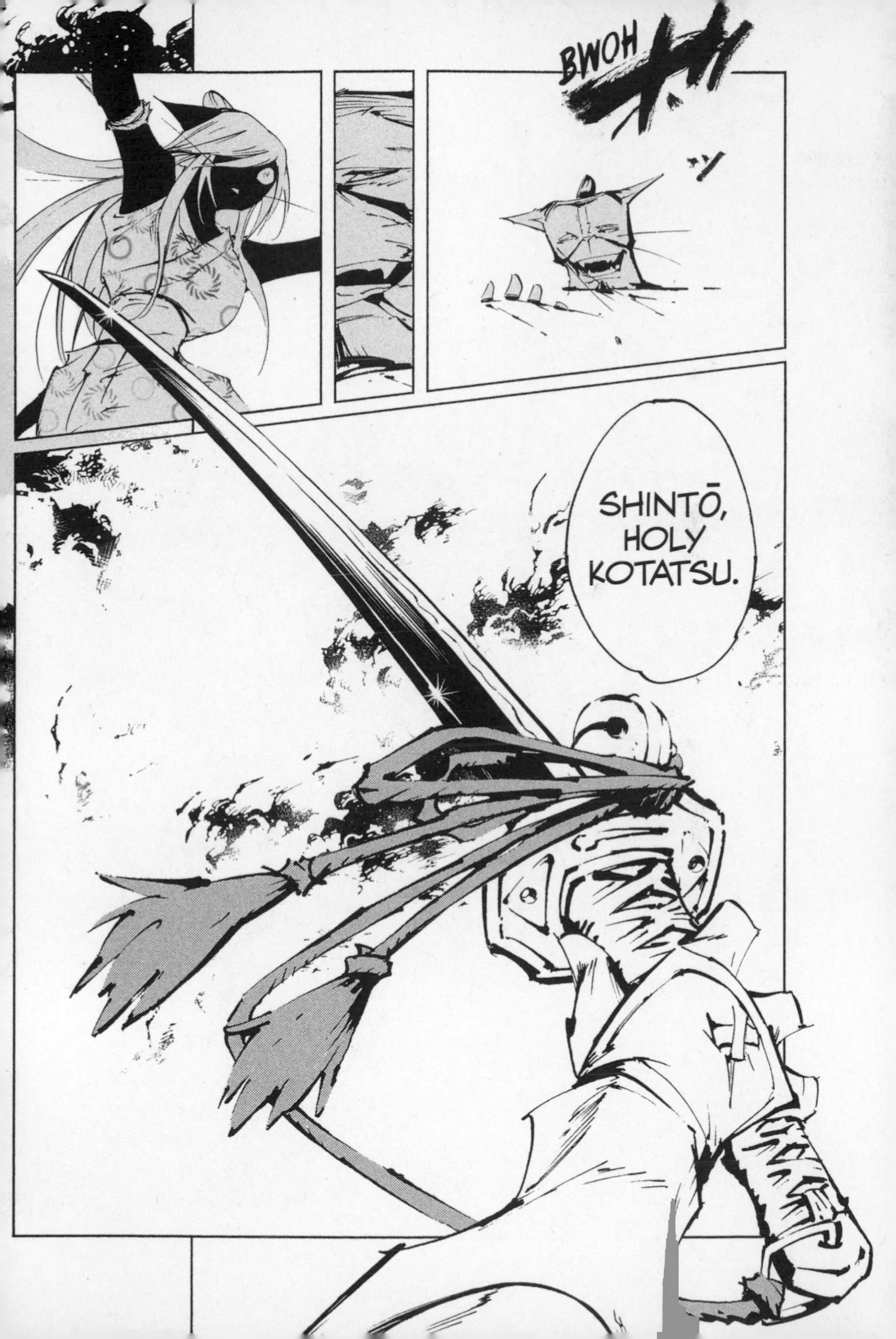
BWOH
SHINTŌ, HOLY KOTATSU.

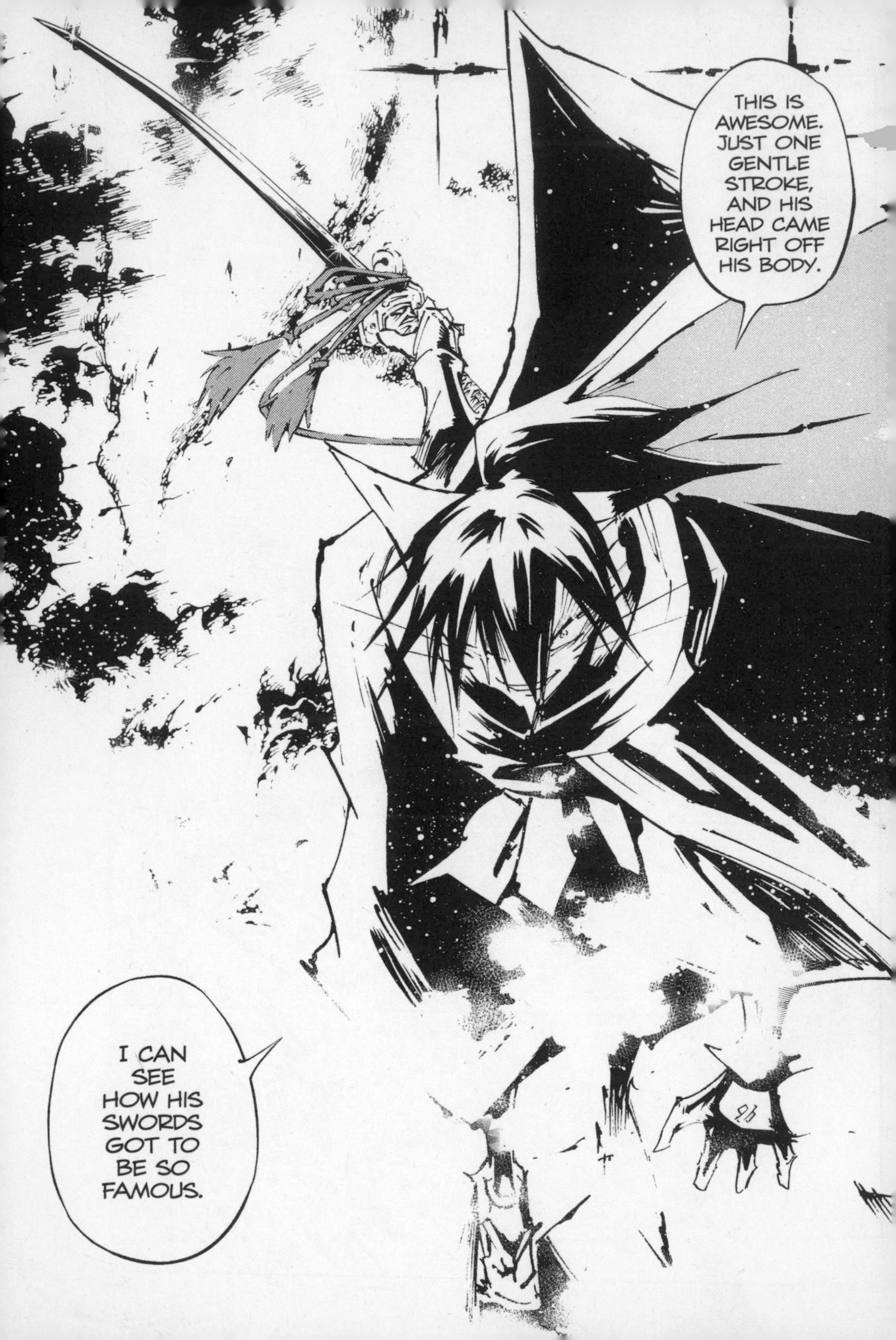
THIS IS AWESOME. JUST ONE GENTLE STROKE, AND HIS HEAD CAME RIGHT OFF HIS BODY.
I CAN SEE HOW HIS SWORDS GOT TO BE SO FAMOUS.

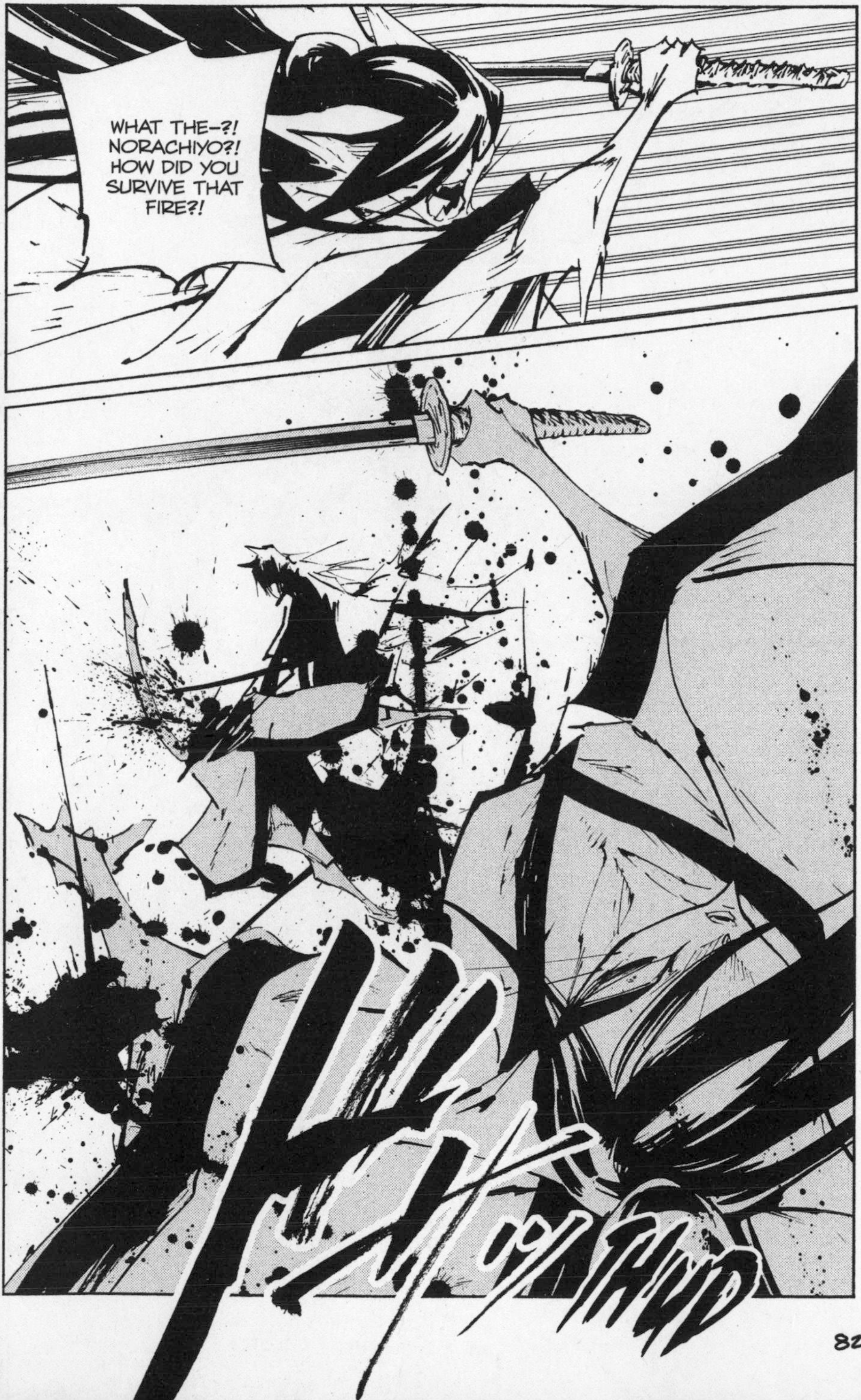
WHAT THE-?! NORACHIYO?! HOW DID YOU SURVIVE THAT FIRE?!
THUD

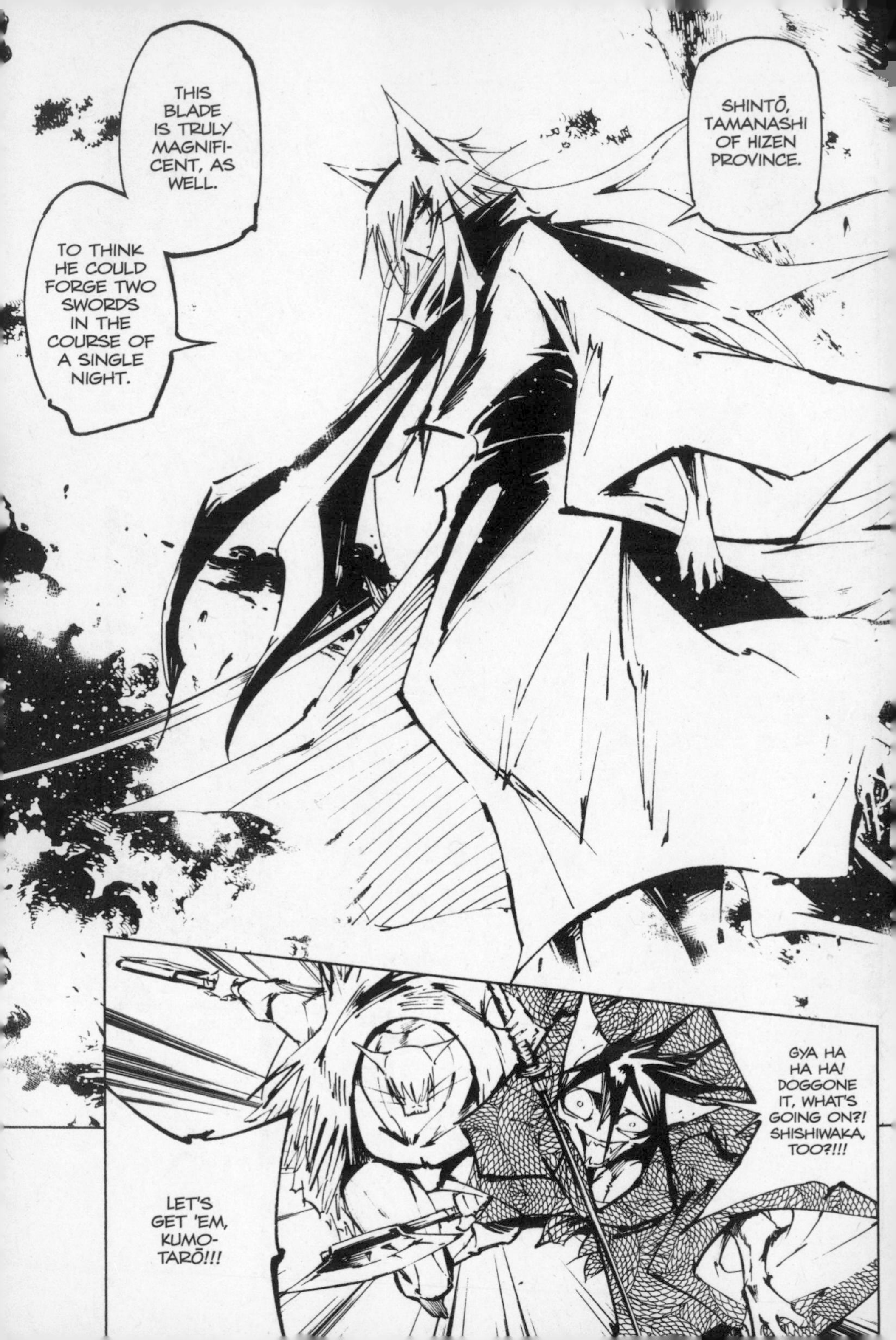
SHINTŌ, TAMANASHI OF HIZEN PROVINCE.
THIS BLADE IS TRULY MAGNIFI-CENT, AS WELL.
TO THINK HE COULD FORGE TWO SWORDS IN THE COURSE OF A SINGLE NIGHT.
GYA HA HA HA! DOGGONE IT, WHAT'S GOING ON?! SHISHIWAKA, TOO?!!!
LET'S GET 'EM, KUMO-TARŌ!!!

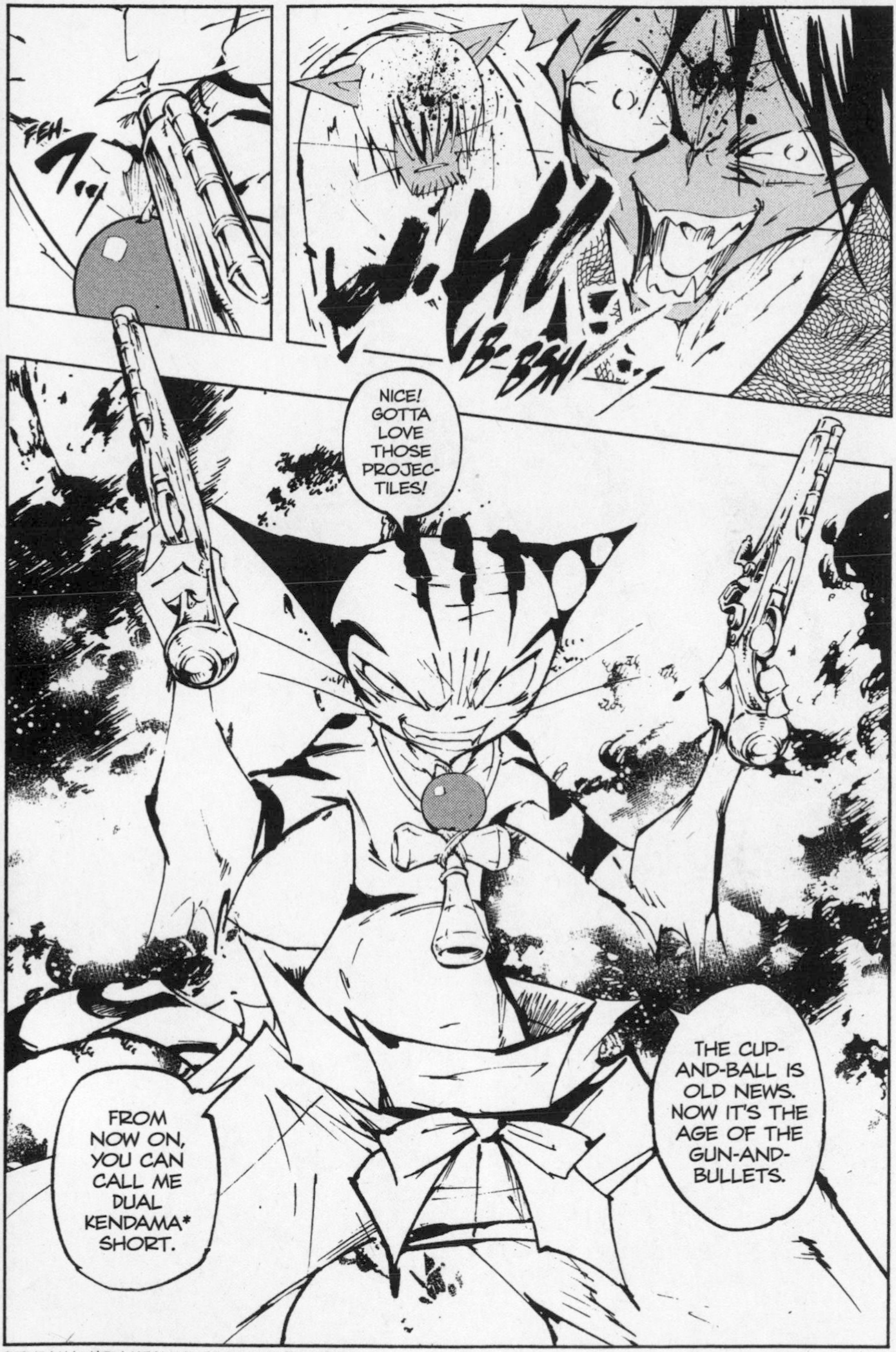
B-BSH
FEH-
NICE! GOTTA LOVE THOSE PROJEC-TILES!
THE CUP-AND-BALL IS OLD NEWS. NOW IT'S THE AGE OF THE GUN-AND-BULLETS.
FROM NOW ON, YOU CAN CALL ME DUAL KENDAMA* SHORT.

*KENDAMA: NOW MEANING "GUN AND BULLETS"

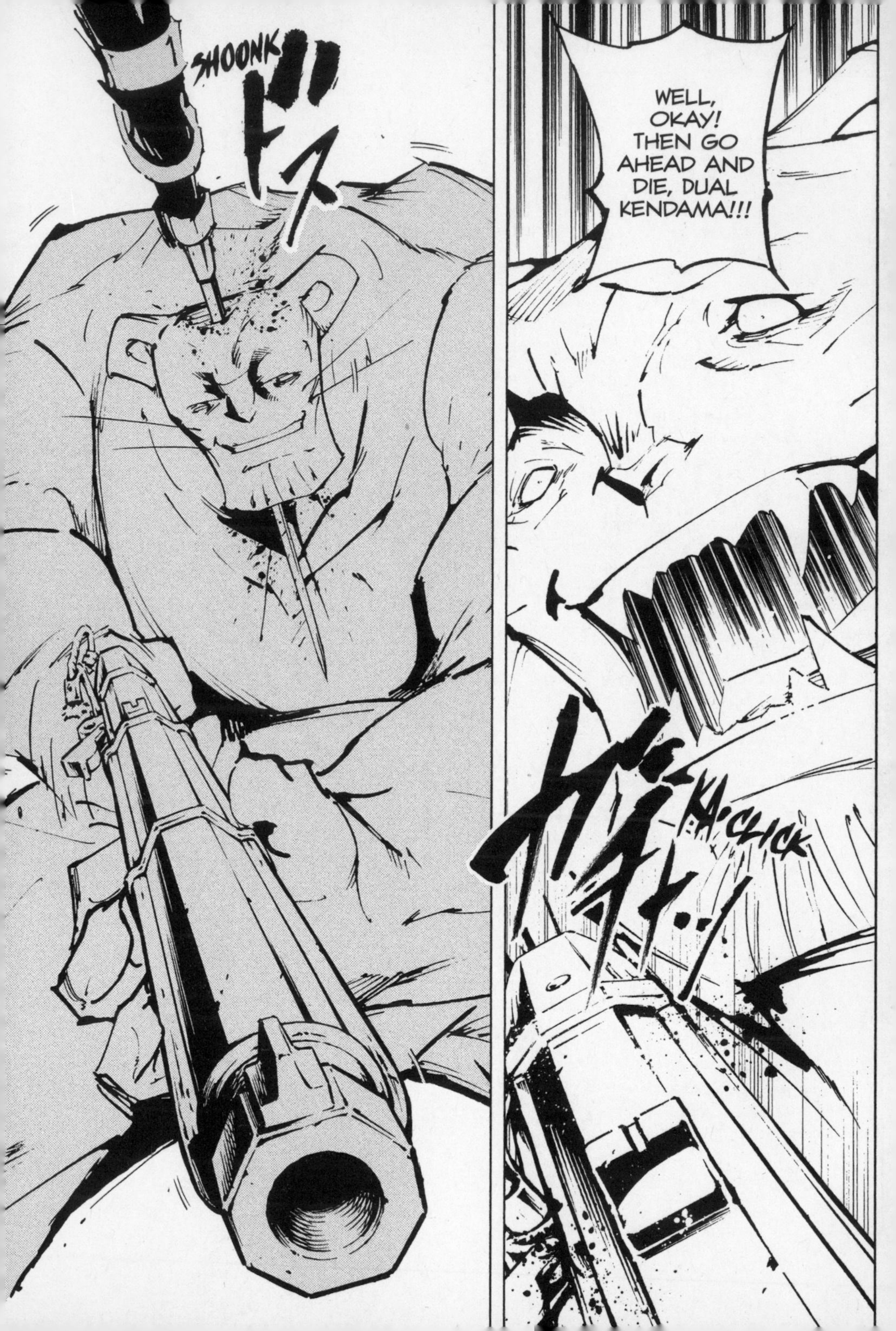
WELL, OKAY! THEN GO AHEAD AND DIE, DUAL KENDAMA!!!
KA-CLICK
SHOONK

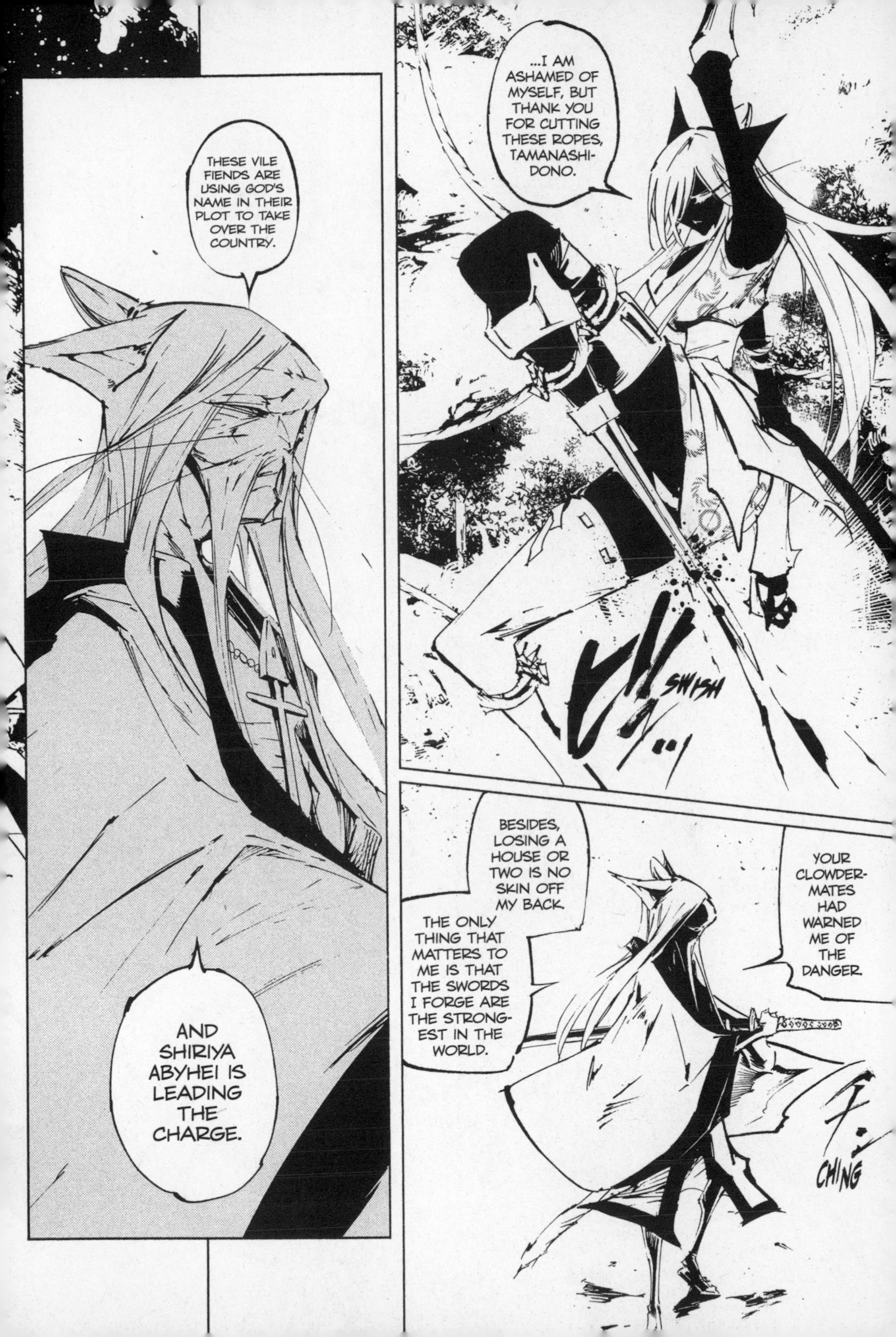
...I AM ASHAMED OF MYSELF, BUT THANK YOU FOR CUTTING THESE ROPES, TAMANASHI-DONO.
SWISH
YOUR CLOWDER-MATES HAD WARNED ME OF THE DANGER.
BESIDES, LOSING A HOUSE OR TWO IS NO SKIN OFF MY BACK.
THE ONLY THING THAT MATTERS TO ME IS THAT THE SWORDS I FORGE ARE THE STRONG-EST IN THE WORLD.
CHING
THESE VILE FIENDS ARE USING GOD'S NAME IN THEIR PLOT TO TAKE OVER THE COUNTRY.
AND SHIRIYA ABYHEI IS LEADING THE CHARGE.

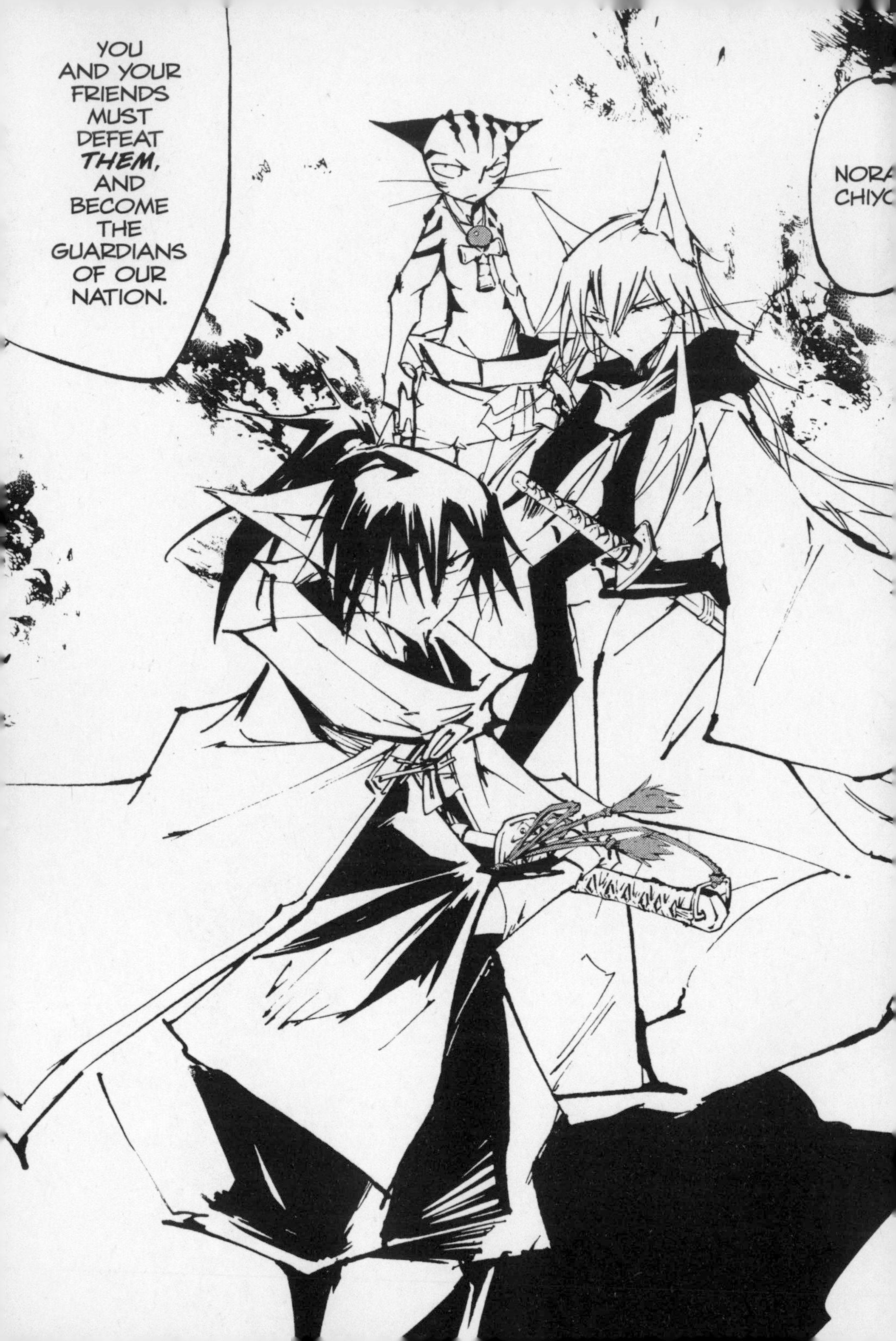
NORA CHIYO
YOU AND YOUR FRIENDS MUST DEFEAT *THEM,* AND BECOME THE GUARDIANS OF OUR NATION.

猫ヶ原

NeKoGaHara

ネコガハラ

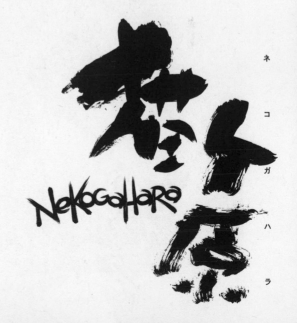

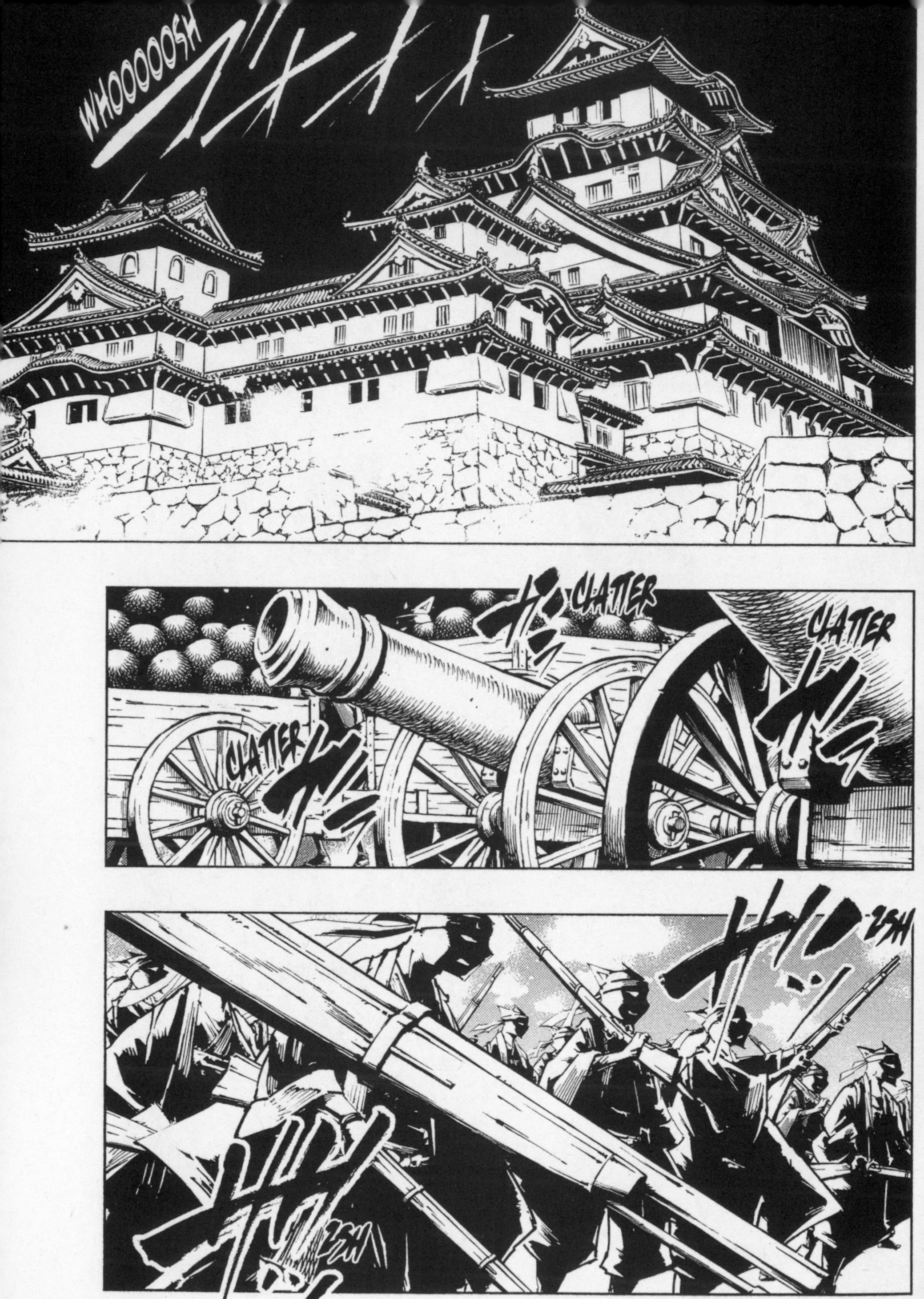
WHOOOOOSH
CLATTER
CLATTER
CLATTER
-ZSH
ZSH

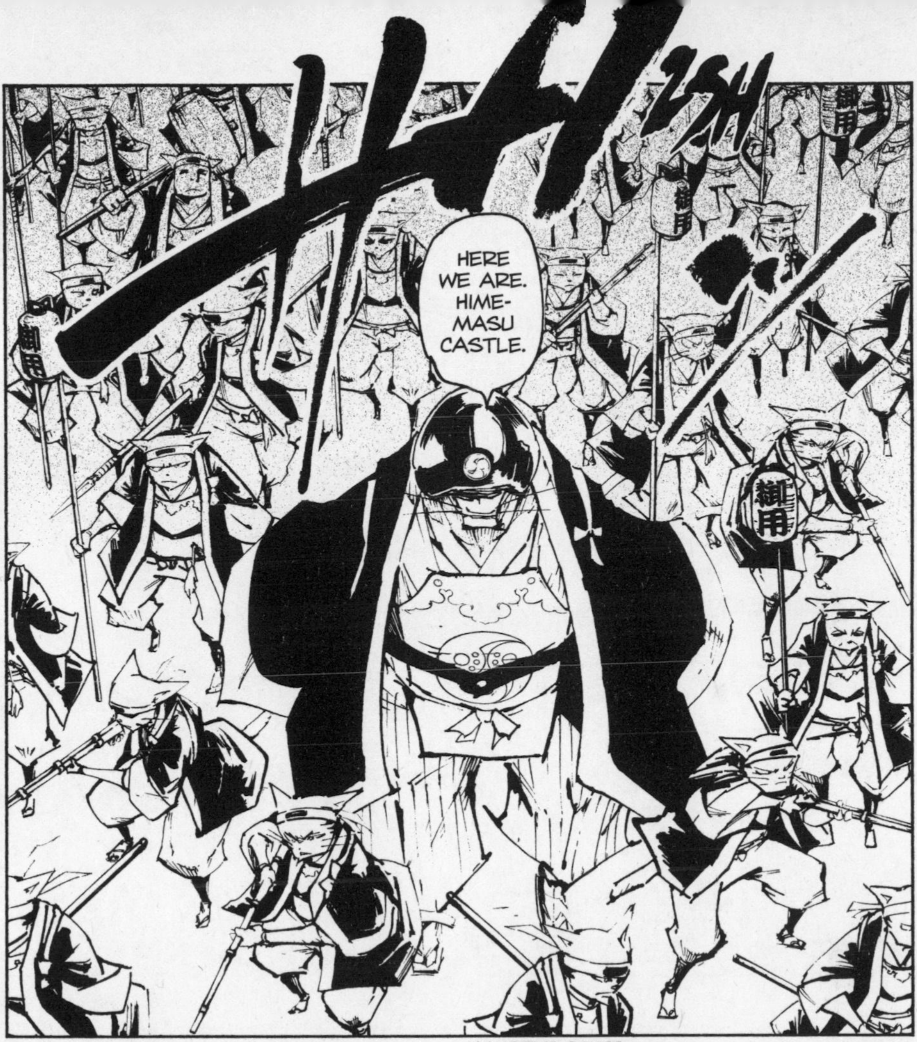
ZSH
御用
HERE WE ARE. HIME-MASU CASTLE.

LANTERNS: POLICE

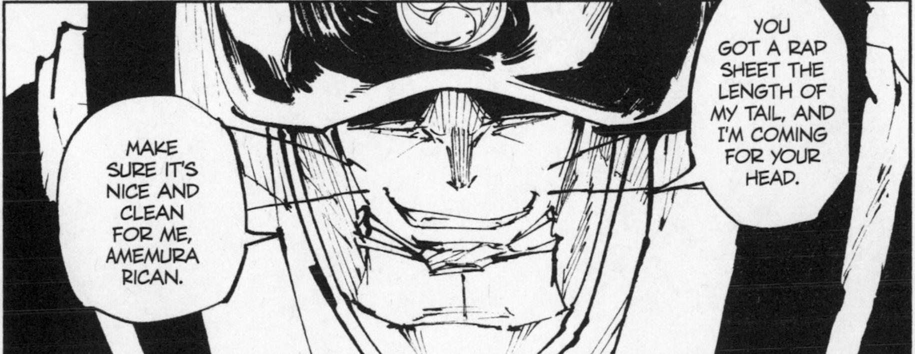
YOU GOT A RAP SHEET THE LENGTH OF MY TAIL, AND I'M COMING FOR YOUR HEAD.
MAKE SURE IT'S NICE AND CLEAN FOR ME, AMEMURA RICAN.

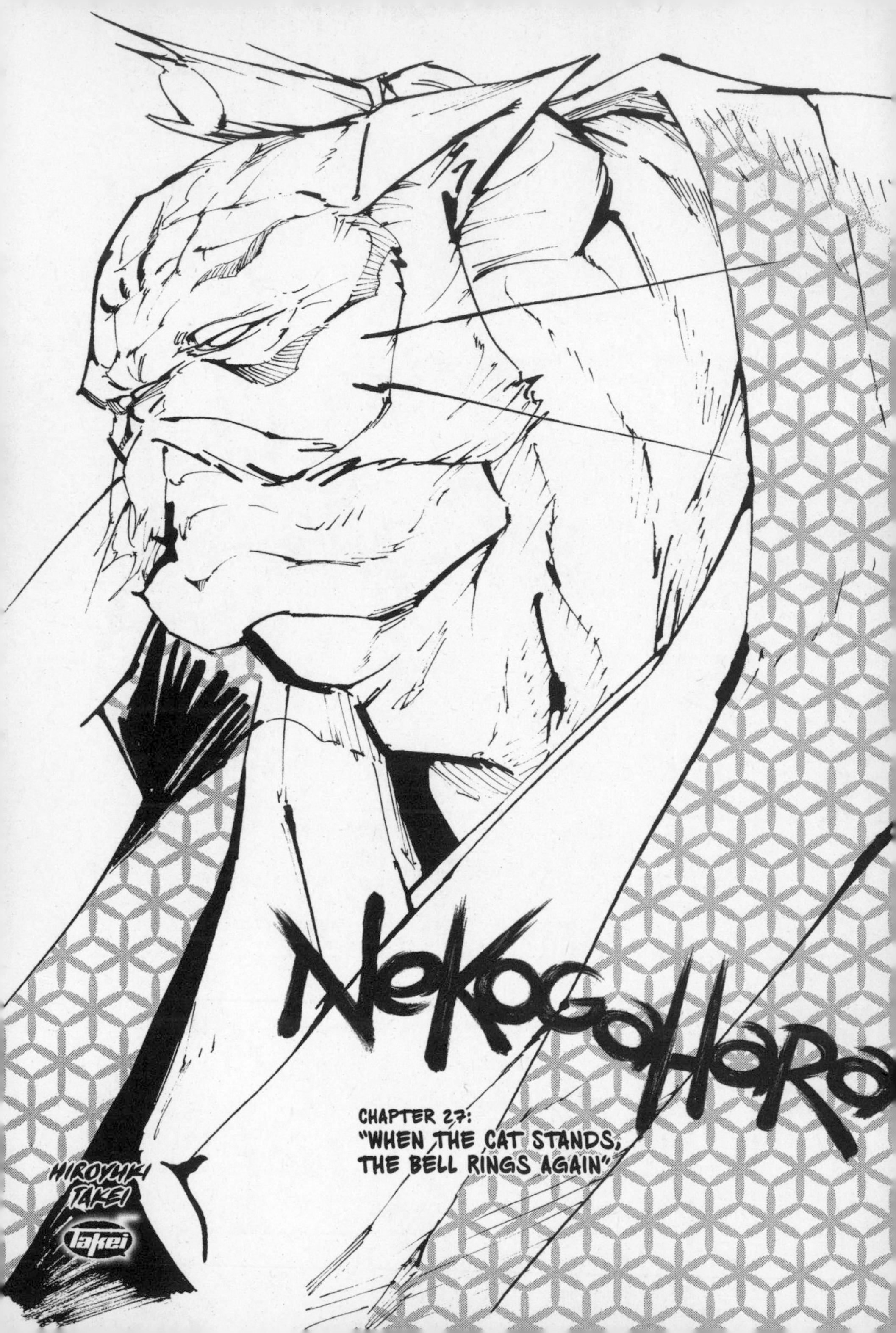
NekoGaHara
CHAPTER 27:
"WHEN THE CAT STANDS, THE BELL RINGS AGAIN"
HIROYUKI TAKEI
Takei

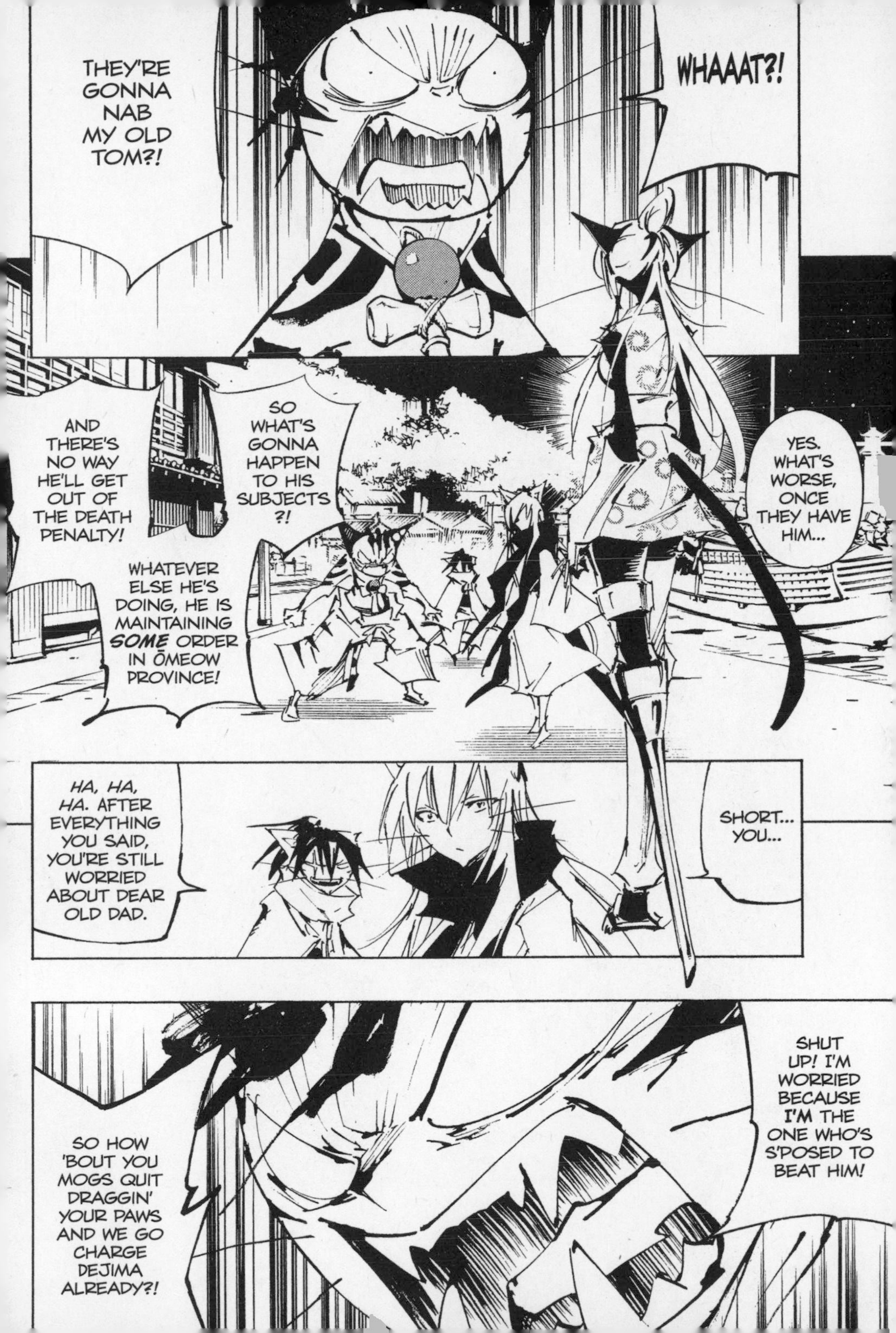
WHAAAT?!
THEY'RE GONNA NAB MY OLD TOM?!
YES. WHAT'S WORSE, ONCE THEY HAVE HIM...
SO WHAT'S GONNA HAPPEN TO HIS SUBJECTS ?!
AND THERE'S NO WAY HE'LL GET OUT OF THE DEATH PENALTY!
WHATEVER ELSE HE'S DOING, HE IS MAINTAINING *SOME* ORDER IN ŌMEOW PROVINCE!
SHORT... YOU...
HA, HA, HA. AFTER EVERYTHING YOU SAID, YOU'RE STILL WORRIED ABOUT DEAR OLD DAD.
SHUT UP! I'M WORRIED BECAUSE **I'M** THE ONE WHO'S S'POSED TO BEAT HIM!
SO HOW 'BOUT YOU MOGS QUIT DRAGGIN' YOUR PAWS AND WE GO CHARGE DEJIMA ALREADY?!

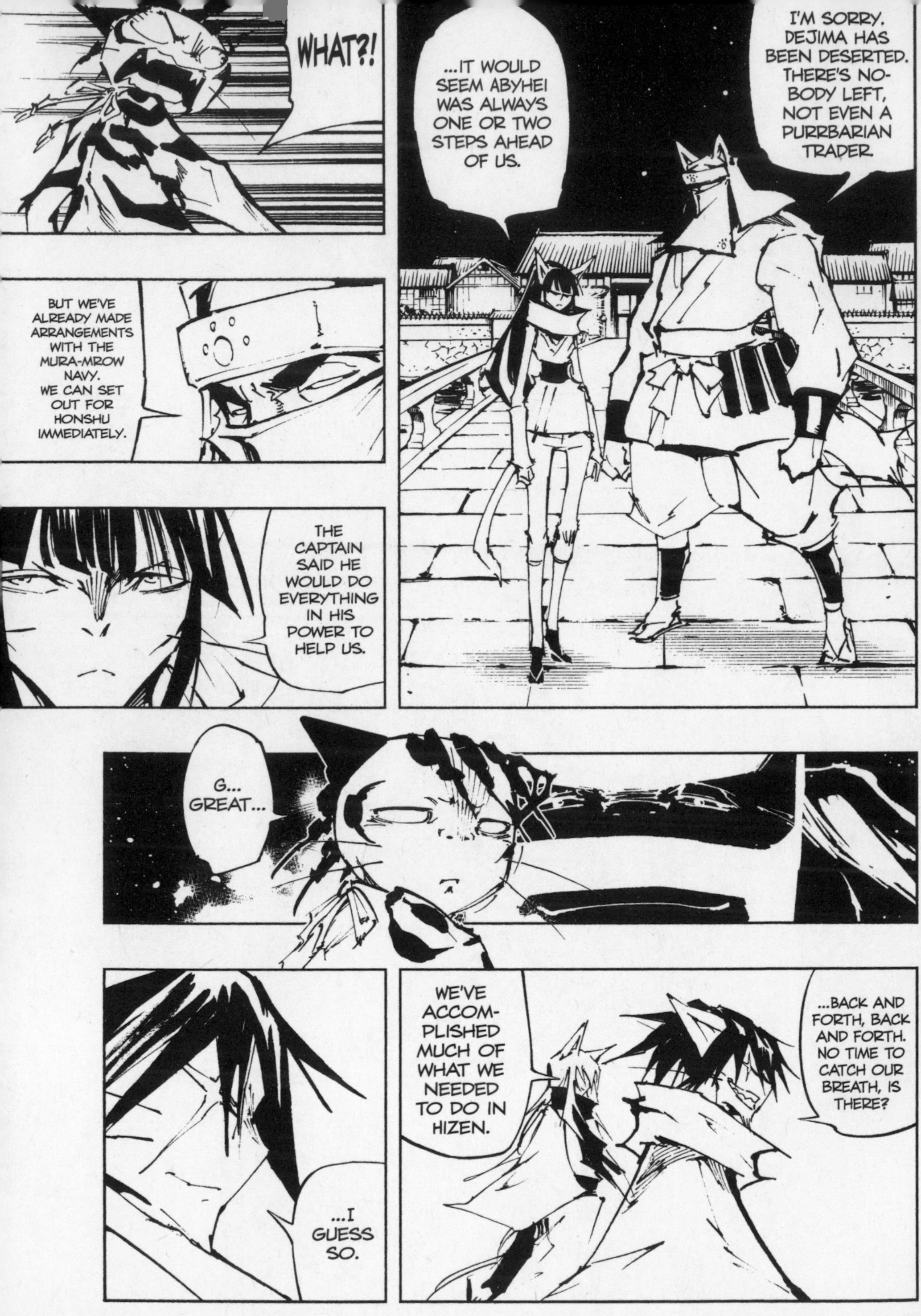
I'M SORRY. DEJIMA HAS BEEN DESERTED. THERE'S NO-BODY LEFT, NOT EVEN A PURRBARIAN TRADER.
...IT WOULD SEEM ABYHEI WAS ALWAYS ONE OR TWO STEPS AHEAD OF US.
WHAT?!
BUT WE'VE ALREADY MADE ARRANGEMENTS WITH THE MURA-MROW NAVY. WE CAN SET OUT FOR HONSHU IMMEDIATELY.
THE CAPTAIN SAID HE WOULD DO EVERYTHING IN HIS POWER TO HELP US.
G... GREAT...
...BACK AND FORTH, BACK AND FORTH. NO TIME TO CATCH OUR BREATH, IS THERE?
WE'VE ACCOM-PLISHED MUCH OF WHAT WE NEEDED TO DO IN HIZEN.
...I GUESS SO.

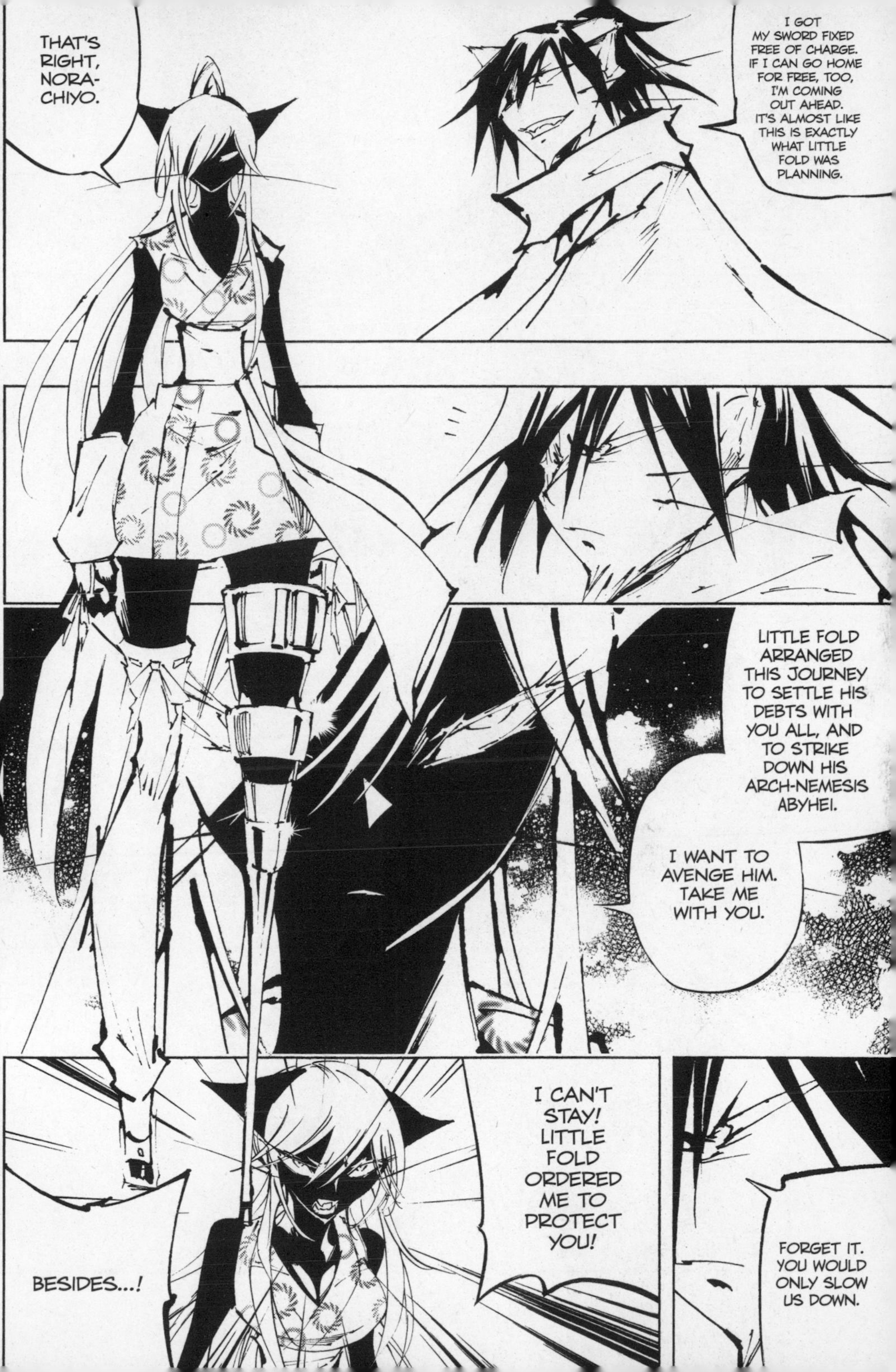
I GOT MY SWORD FIXED FREE OF CHARGE. IF I CAN GO HOME FOR FREE, TOO, I'M COMING OUT AHEAD. IT'S ALMOST LIKE THIS IS EXACTLY WHAT LITTLE FOLD WAS PLANNING.
THAT'S RIGHT, NORA-CHIYO.
LITTLE FOLD ARRANGED THIS JOURNEY TO SETTLE HIS DEBTS WITH YOU ALL, AND TO STRIKE DOWN HIS ARCH-NEMESIS ABYHEI.
I WANT TO AVENGE HIM. TAKE ME WITH YOU.
FORGET IT. YOU WOULD ONLY SLOW US DOWN.
I CAN'T STAY! LITTLE FOLD ORDERED ME TO PROTECT YOU!
BESIDES...!

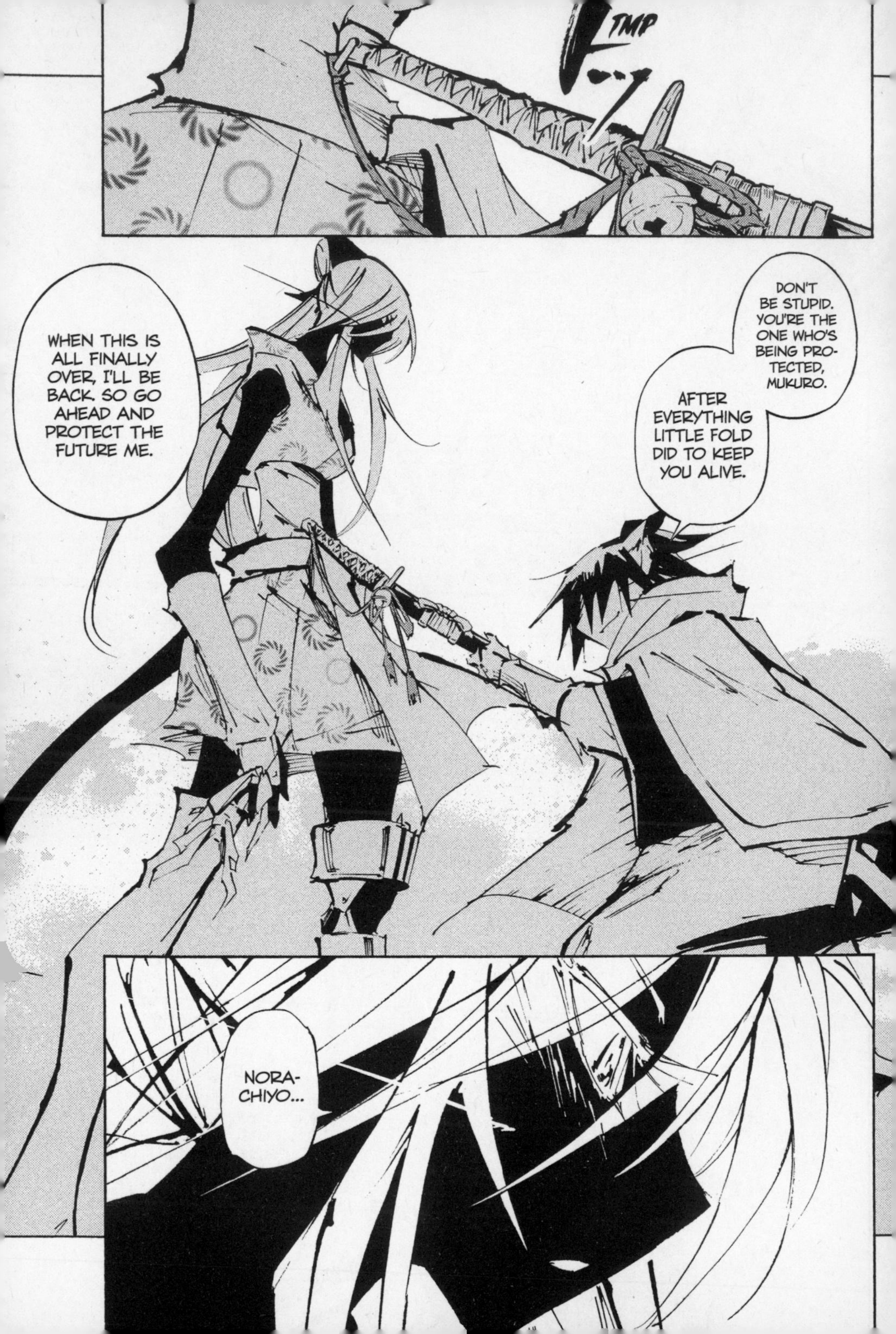
TMP
DON'T BE STUPID. YOU'RE THE ONE WHO'S BEING PRO-TECTED, MUKURO.
AFTER EVERYTHING LITTLE FOLD DID TO KEEP YOU ALIVE.
WHEN THIS IS ALL FINALLY OVER, I'LL BE BACK. SO GO AHEAD AND PROTECT THE FUTURE ME.
NORA-CHIYO...

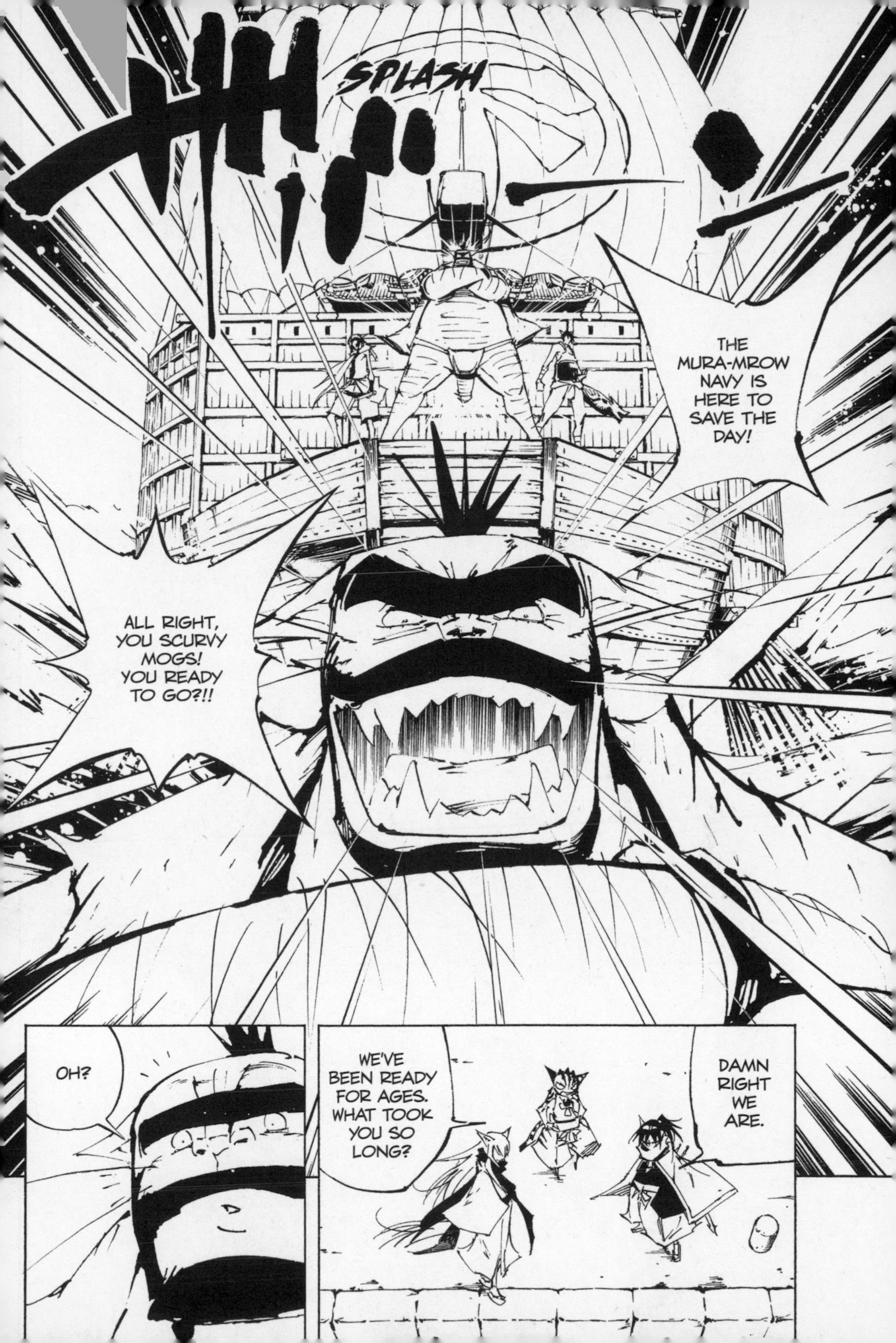
SPLASH
THE MURA-MROW NAVY IS HERE TO SAVE THE DAY!
ALL RIGHT, YOU SCURVY MOGS! YOU READY TO GO?!!
DAMN RIGHT WE ARE.
WE'VE BEEN READY FOR AGES. WHAT TOOK YOU SO LONG?
OH?

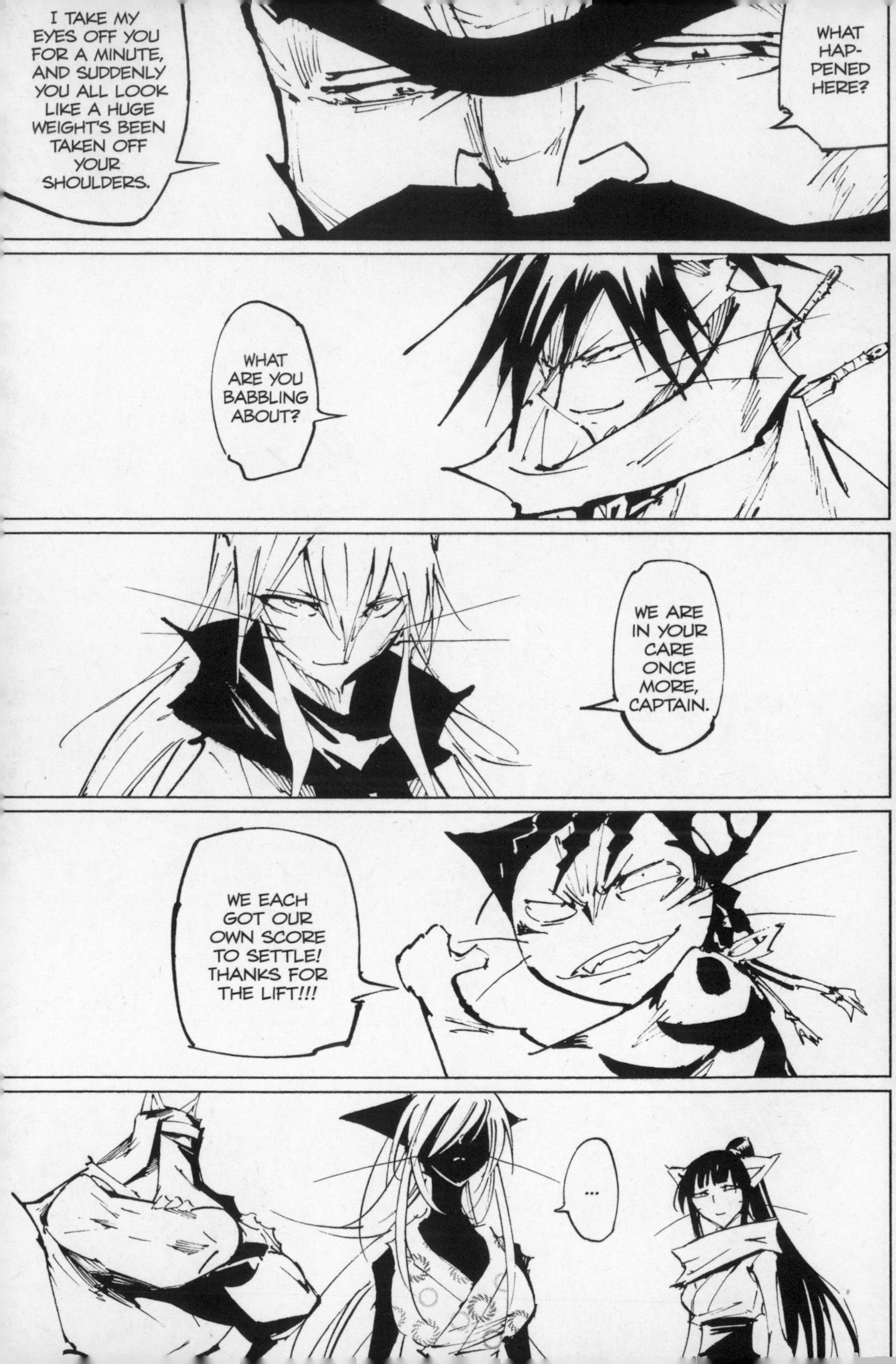
WHAT HAP-PENED HERE?
I TAKE MY EYES OFF YOU FOR A MINUTE, AND SUDDENLY YOU ALL LOOK LIKE A HUGE WEIGHT'S BEEN TAKEN OFF YOUR SHOULDERS.
WHAT ARE YOU BABBLING ABOUT?
WE ARE IN YOUR CARE ONCE MORE, CAPTAIN.
WE EACH GOT OUR OWN SCORE TO SETTLE! THANKS FOR THE LIFT!!!
...

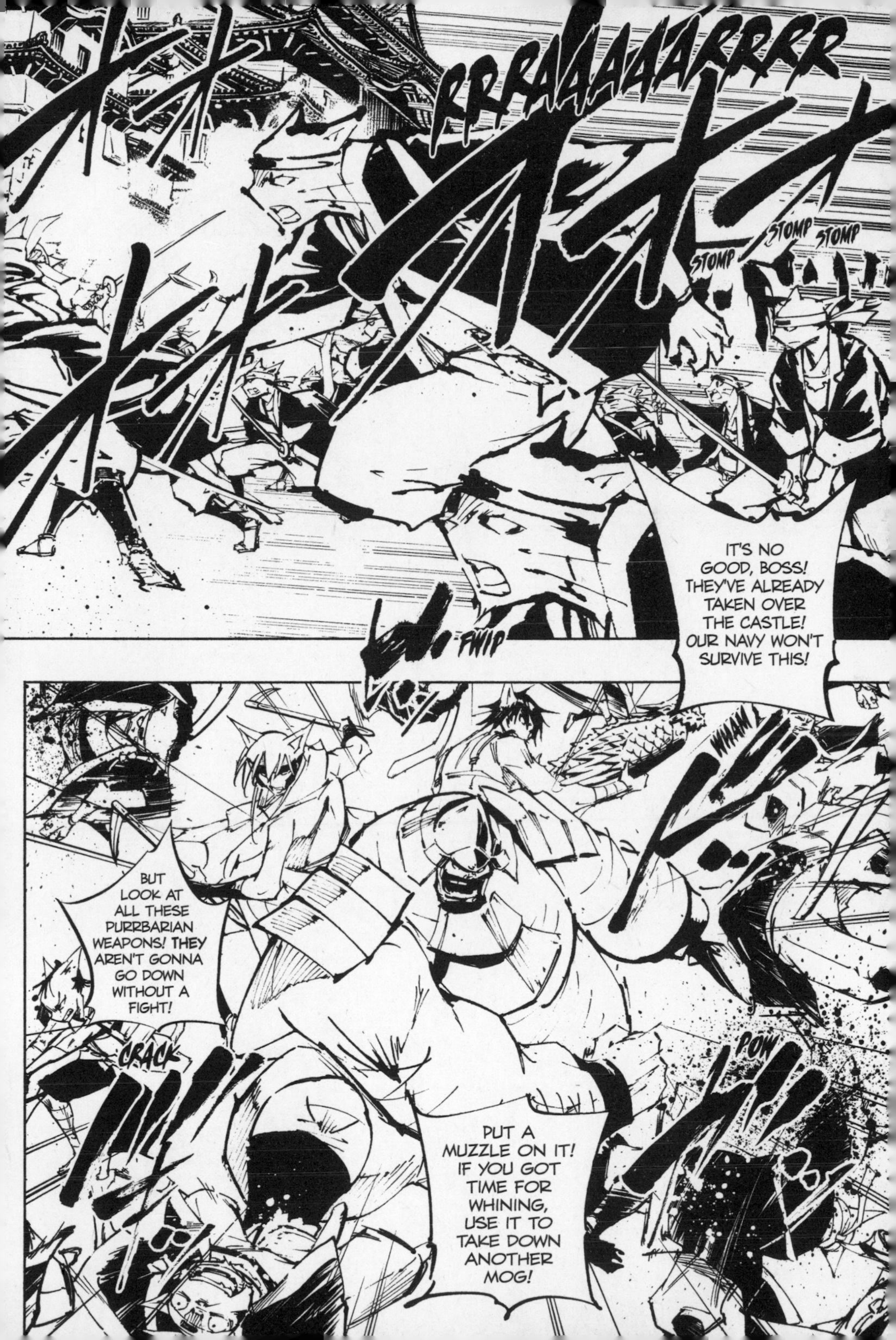
RRRAAAAARRRR
STOMP
STOMP
STOMP
IT'S NO GOOD, BOSS! THEY'VE ALREADY TAKEN OVER THE CASTLE! OUR NAVY WON'T SURVIVE THIS!
FWIP
WHAM
BUT LOOK AT ALL THESE PURRBARIAN WEAPONS! THEY AREN'T GONNA GO DOWN WITHOUT A FIGHT!
POW
PUT A MUZZLE ON IT! IF YOU GOT TIME FOR WHINING, USE IT TO TAKE DOWN ANOTHER MOG!
CRACK

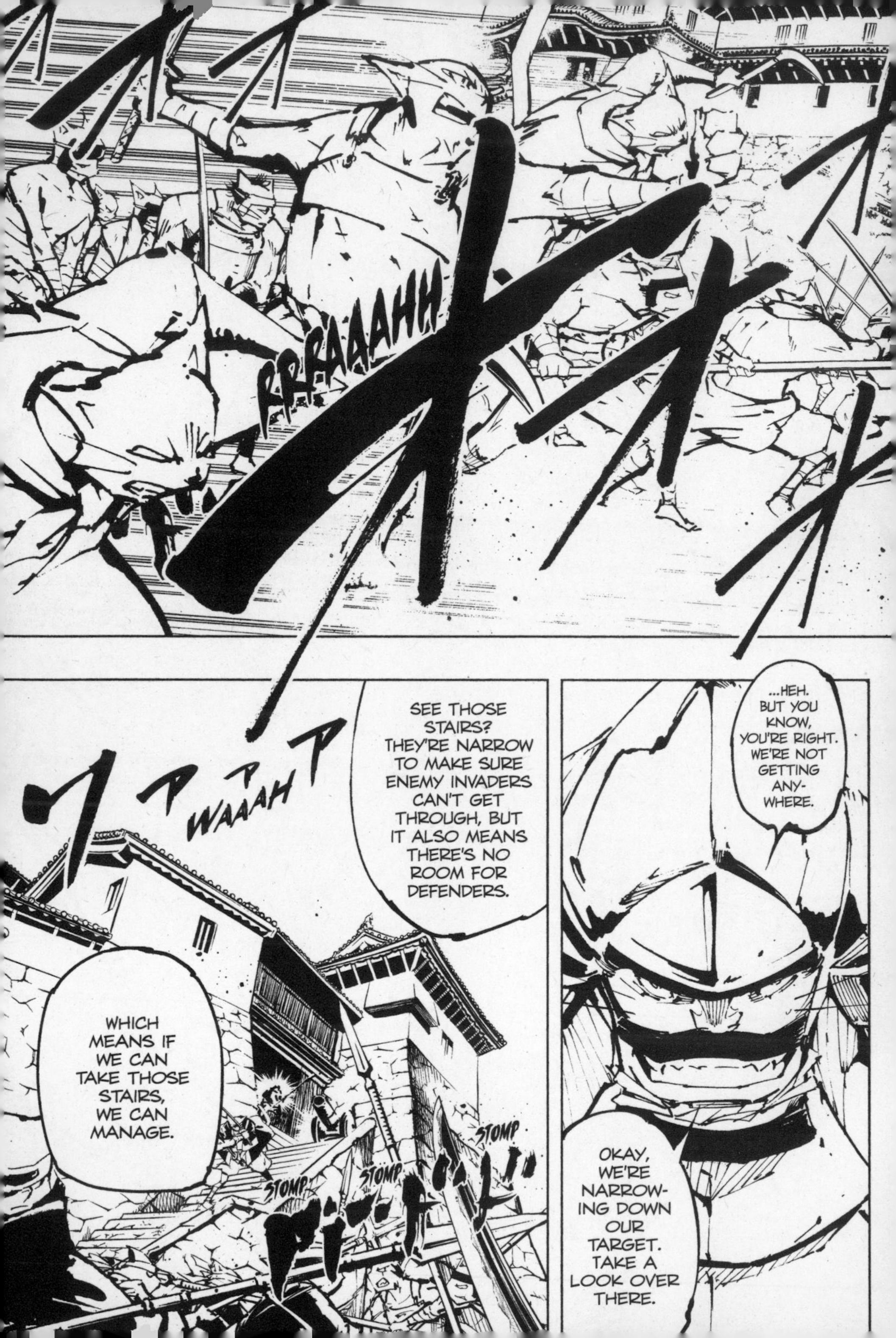
RRRAAAHH
...HEH. BUT YOU KNOW, YOU'RE RIGHT. WE'RE NOT GETTING ANY-WHERE.
OKAY, WE'RE NARROW-ING DOWN OUR TARGET. TAKE A LOOK OVER THERE.
WAAAH
SEE THOSE STAIRS? THEY'RE NARROW TO MAKE SURE ENEMY INVADERS CAN'T GET THROUGH, BUT IT ALSO MEANS THERE'S NO ROOM FOR DEFENDERS.
WHICH MEANS IF WE CAN TAKE THOSE STAIRS, WE CAN MANAGE.
STOMP
STOMP
STOMP

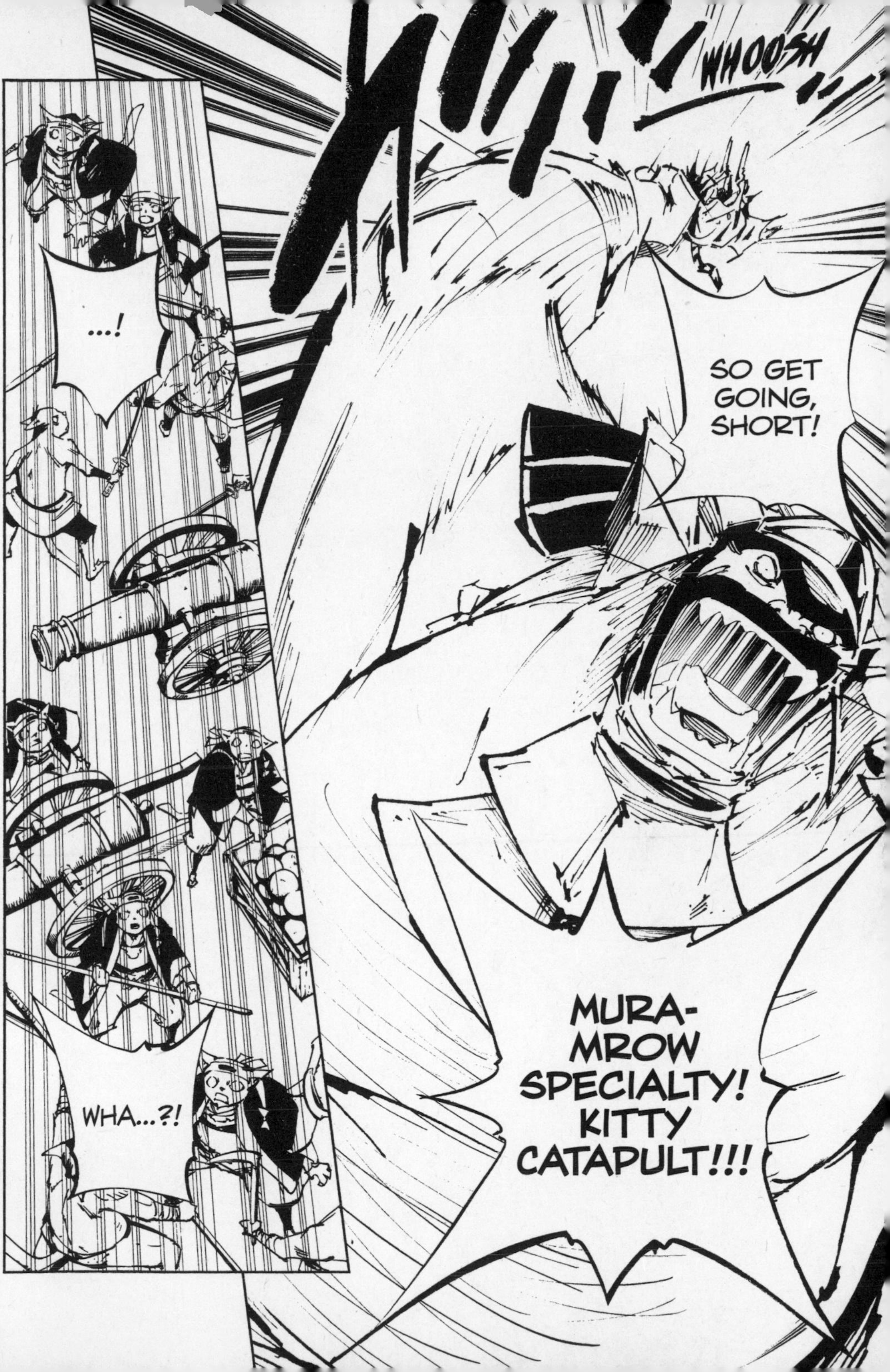
WHOOSH
SO GET GOING, SHORT!
MURA-MROW SPECIALTY! KITTY CATAPULT!!!
...!
WHA...?!

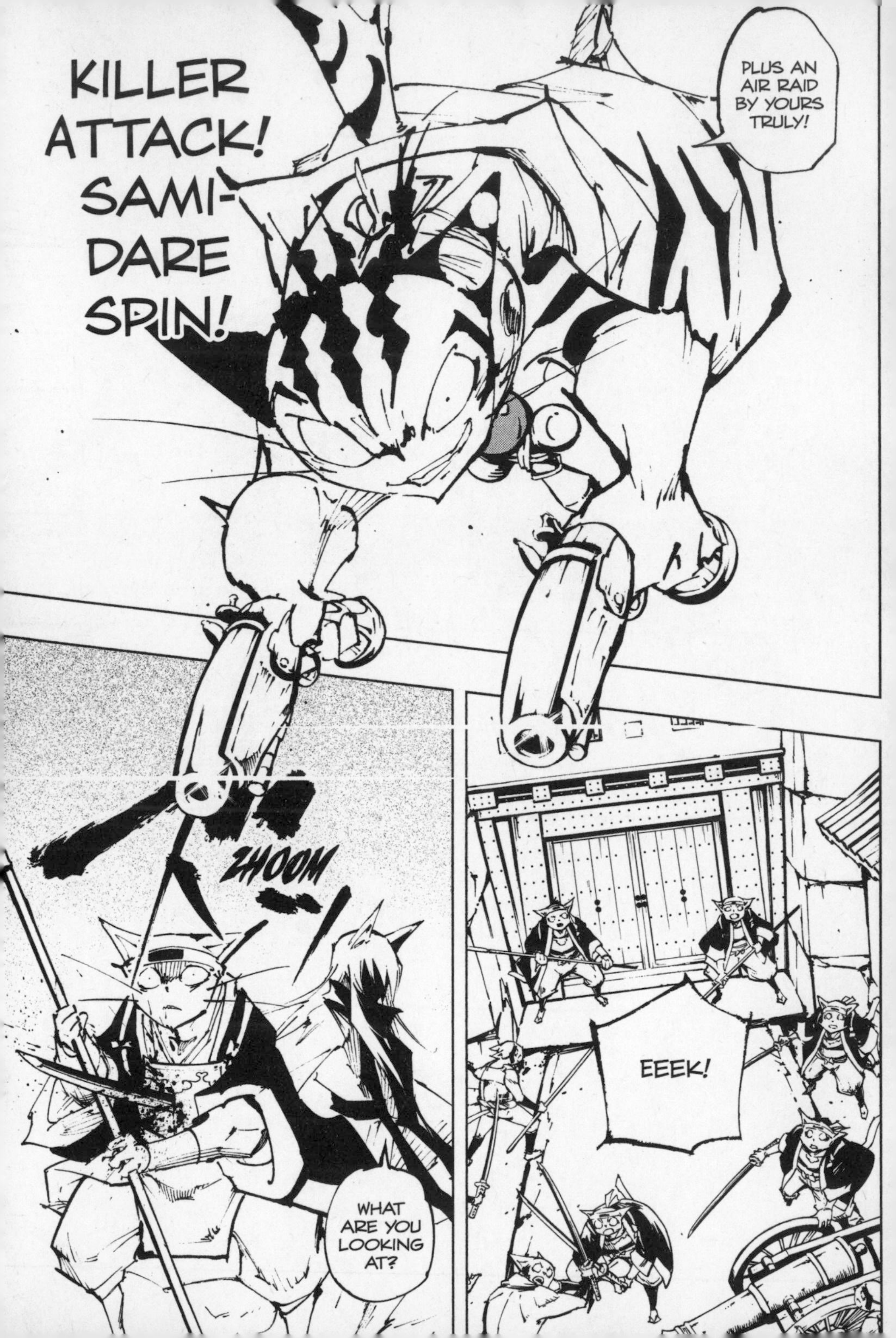
PLUS AN AIR RAID BY YOURS TRULY!
KILLER ATTACK! SAMI-DARE SPIN!
EEEK!
ZHOOM
WHAT ARE YOU LOOKING AT?

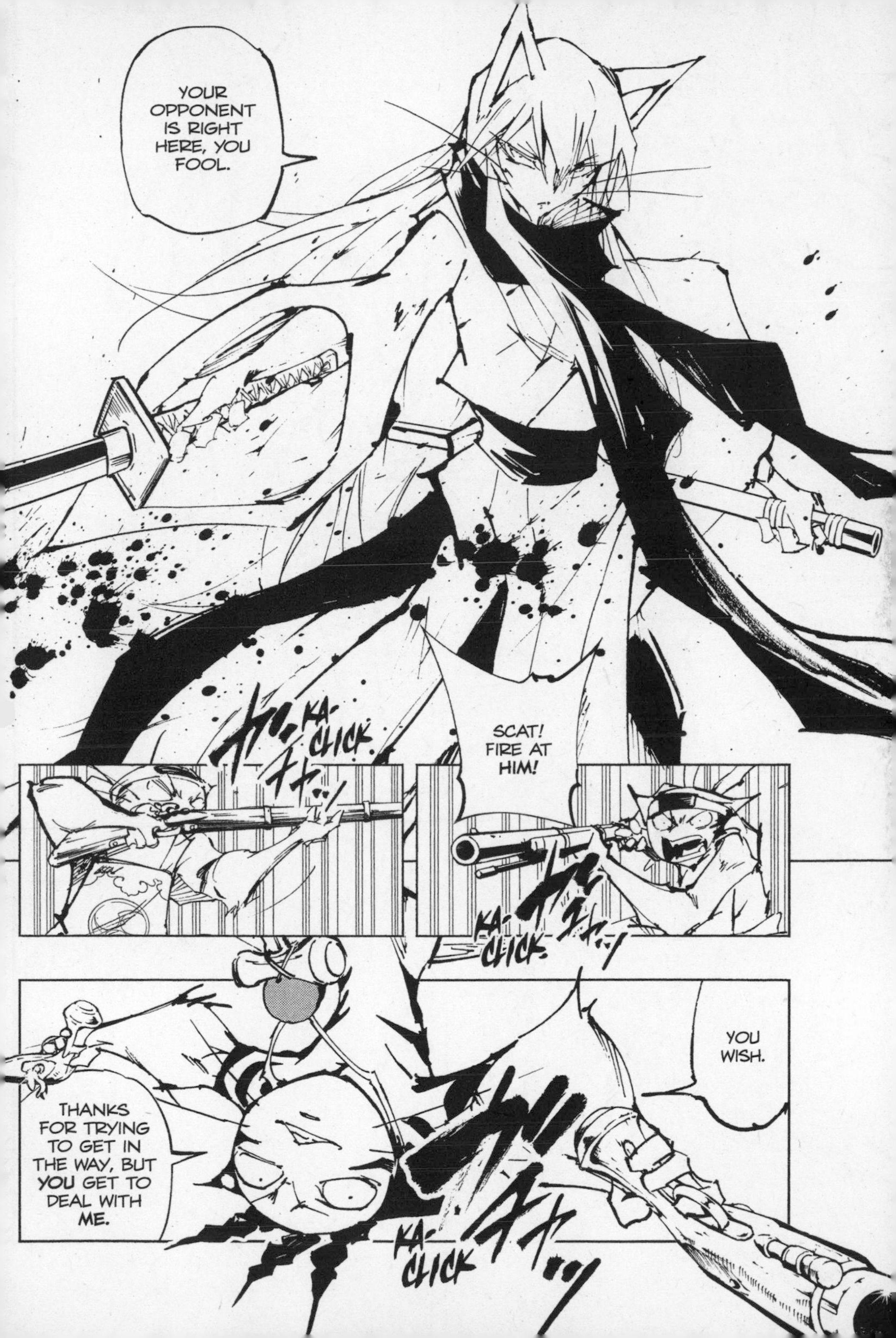
YOUR OPPONENT IS RIGHT HERE, YOU FOOL.
SCAT! FIRE AT HIM!
KA-CLICK
KA-CLICK
YOU WISH.
THANKS FOR TRYING TO GET IN THE WAY, BUT YOU GET TO DEAL WITH ME.
KA-CLICK

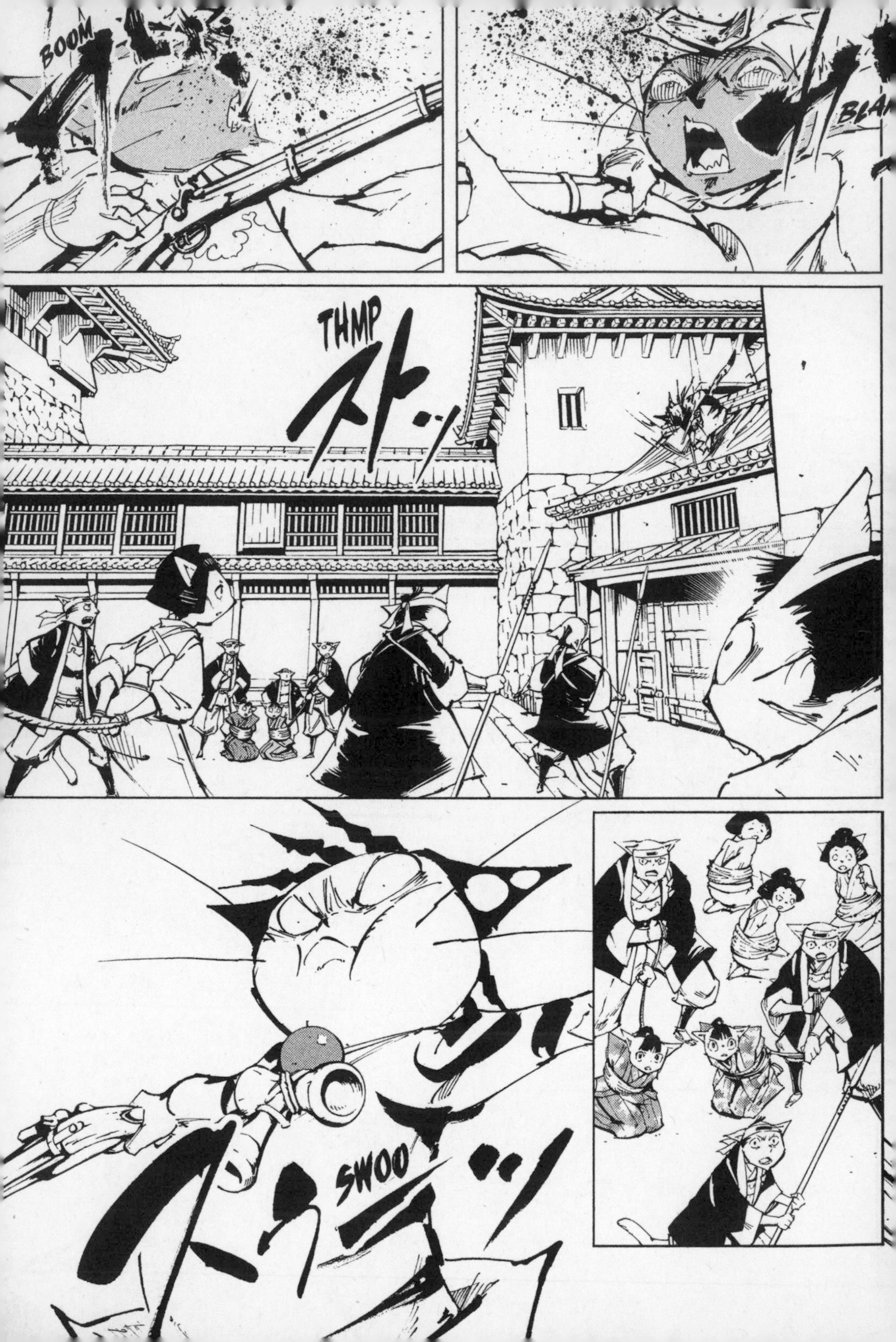
BLA
BOOM
THMP
ストッ
SWOO

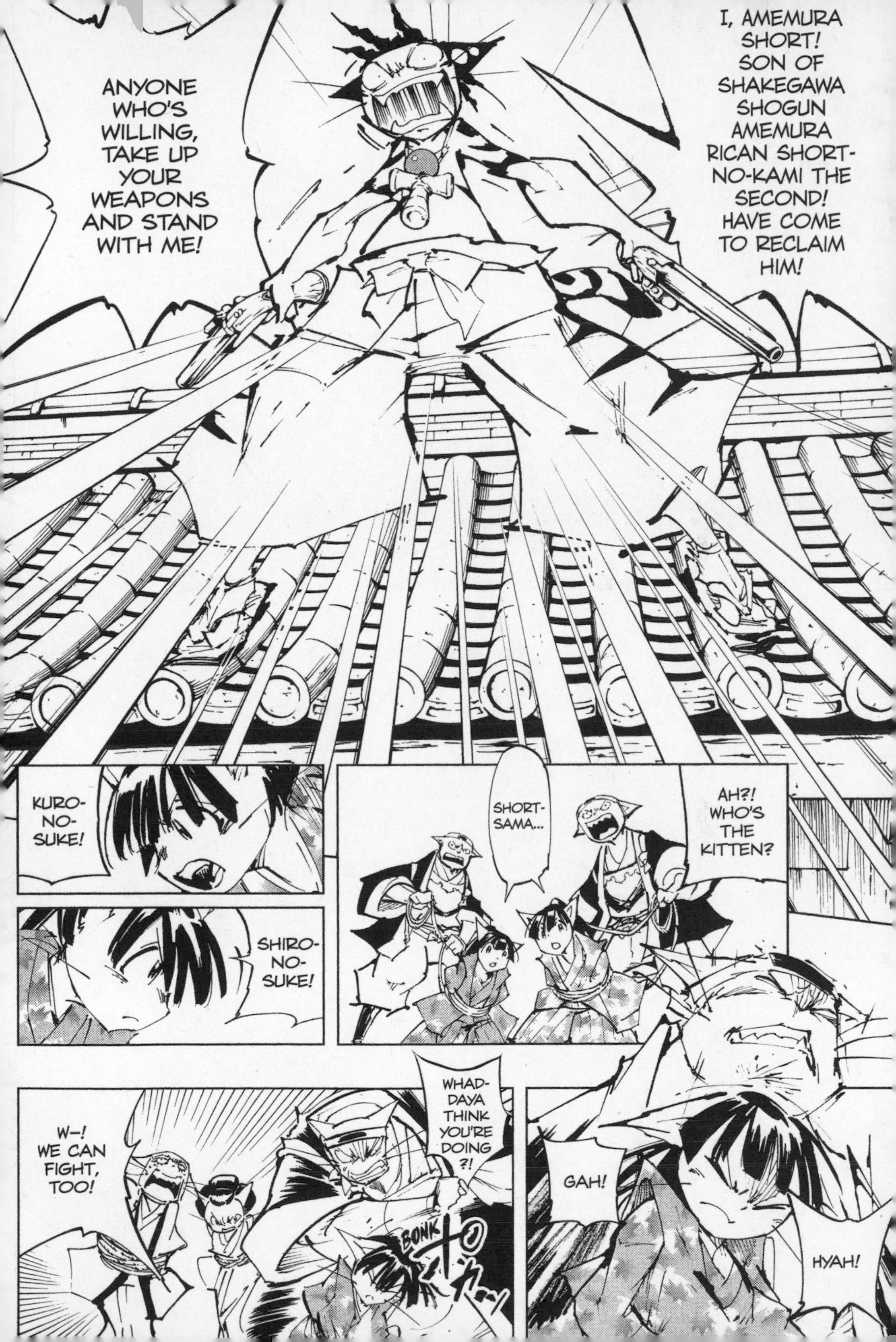
I, AMEMURA SHORT! SON OF SHAKEGAWA SHOGUN AMEMURA RICAN SHORT-NO-KAMI THE SECOND! HAVE COME TO RECLAIM HIM!
ANYONE WHO'S WILLING, TAKE UP YOUR WEAPONS AND STAND WITH ME!
AH?! WHO'S THE KITTEN?
SHORT-SAMA...
KURO-NO-SUKE!
SHIRO-NO-SUKE!
GAH!
HYAH!
WHAD-DAYA THINK YOU'RE DOING?!
BONK
W-! WE CAN FIGHT, TOO!

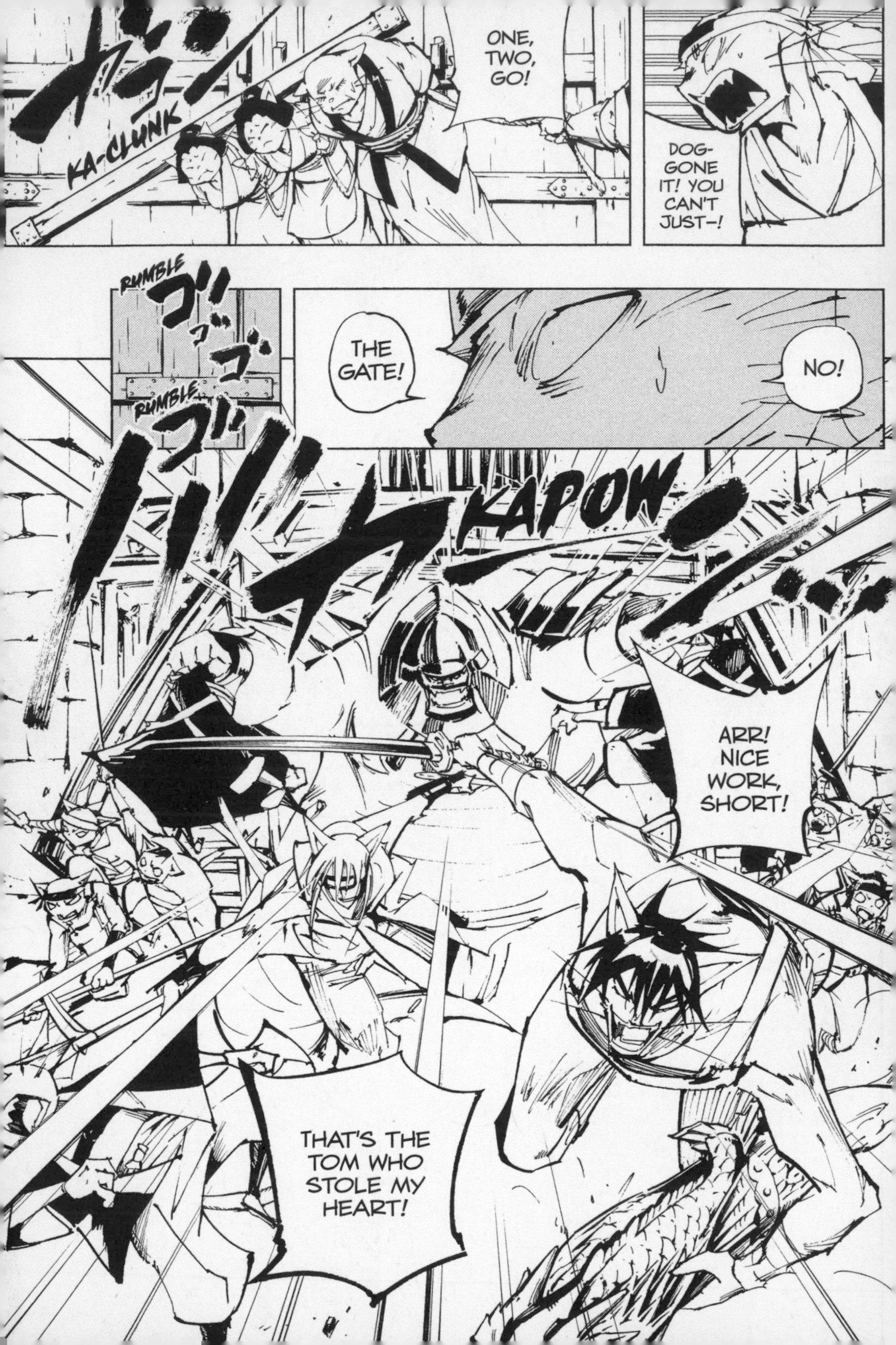
DOG-GONE IT! YOU CAN'T JUST–!
ONE, TWO, GO!
KA-CLUNK
NO!
THE GATE!
RUMBLE
RUMBLE
KAPOW
ARR! NICE WORK, SHORT!
THAT'S THE TOM WHO STOLE MY HEART!

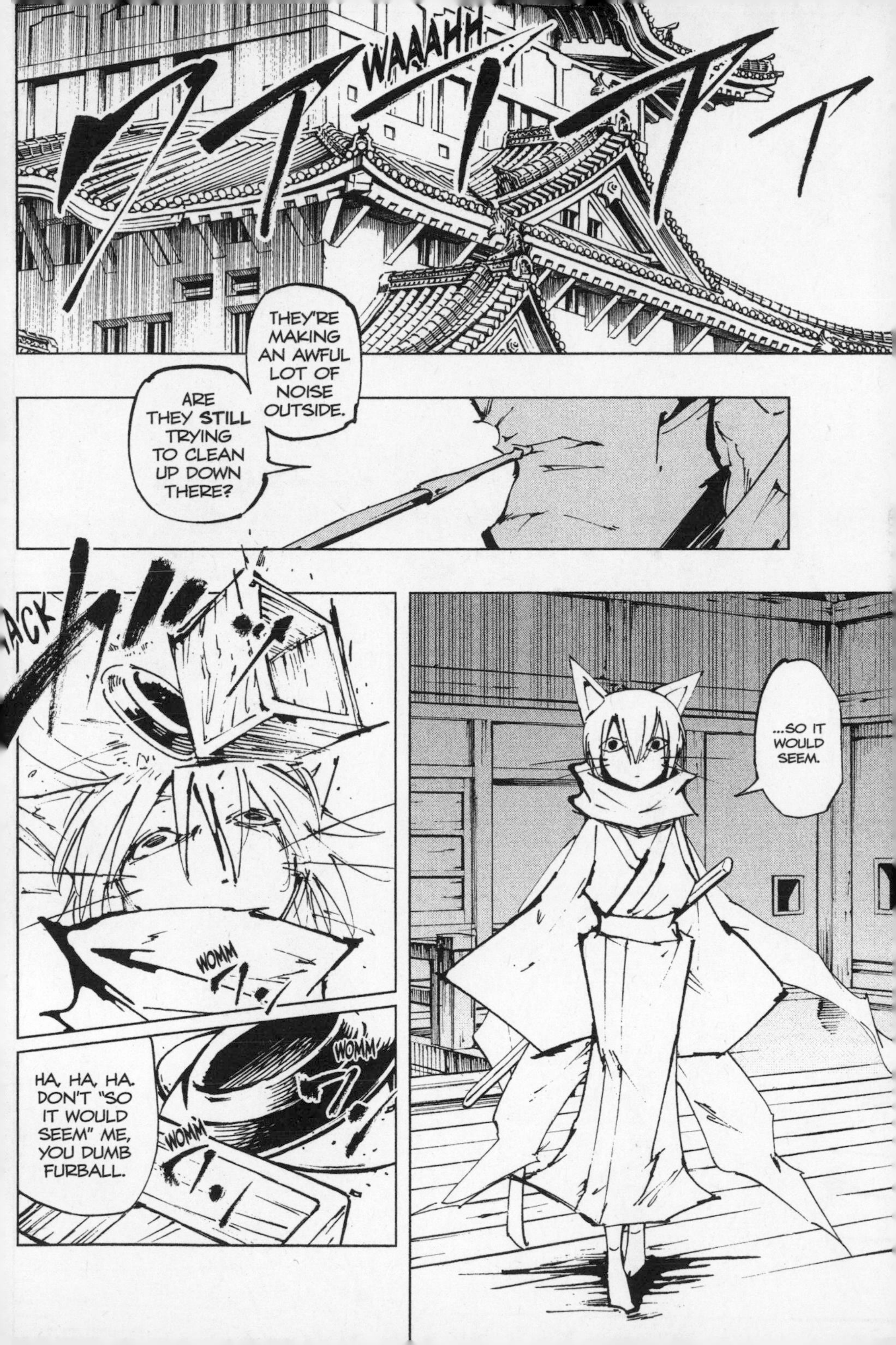
WAAAHH
THEY'RE MAKING AN AWFUL LOT OF NOISE OUTSIDE.
ARE THEY STILL TRYING TO CLEAN UP DOWN THERE?
...SO IT WOULD SEEM.
ACK
WOMM
WOMM
WOMM
HA, HA, HA. DON'T "SO IT WOULD SEEM" ME, YOU DUMB FURBALL.

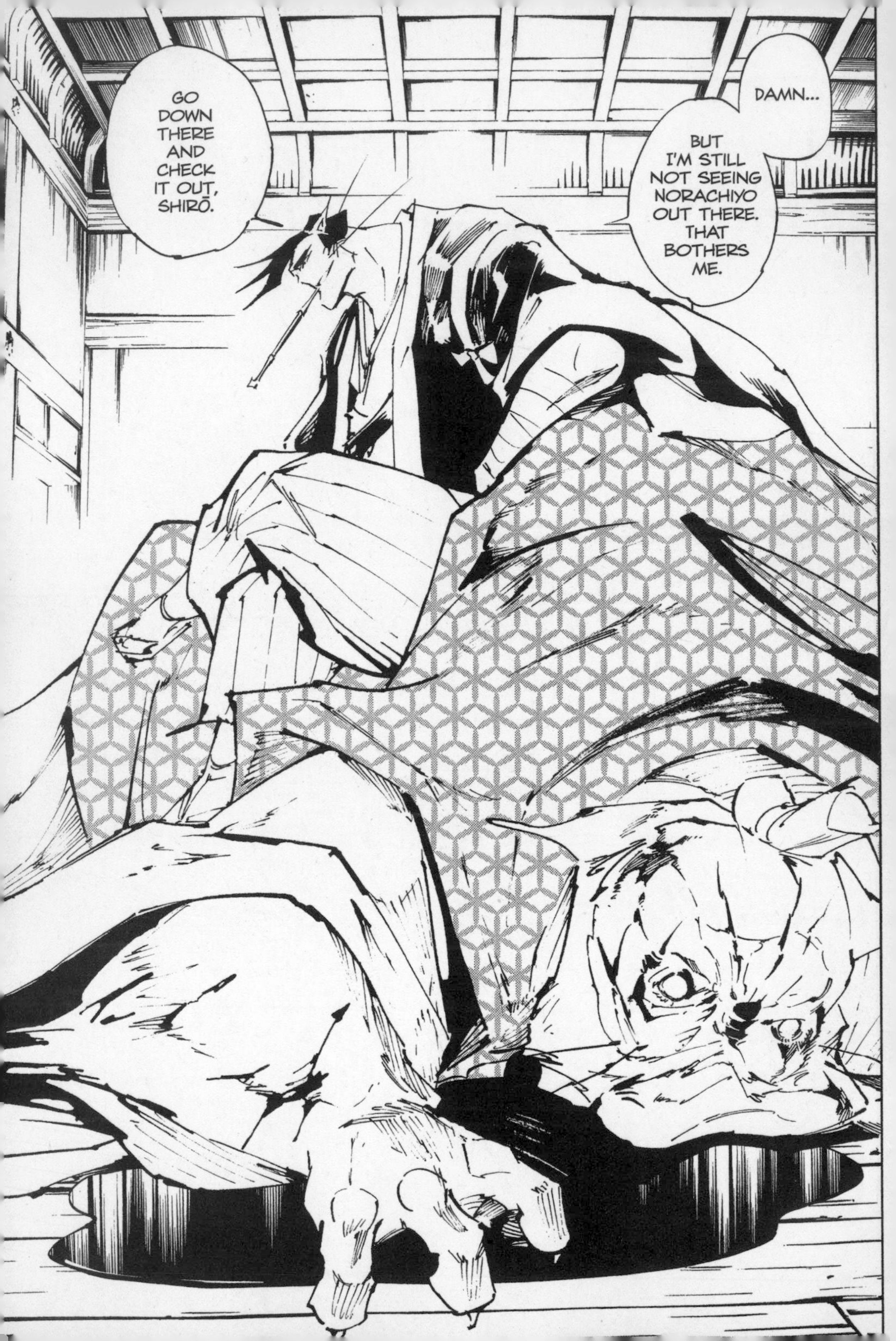
DAMN...
BUT I'M STILL NOT SEEING NORACHIYO OUT THERE. THAT BOTHERS ME.
GO DOWN THERE AND CHECK IT OUT, SHIRŌ.

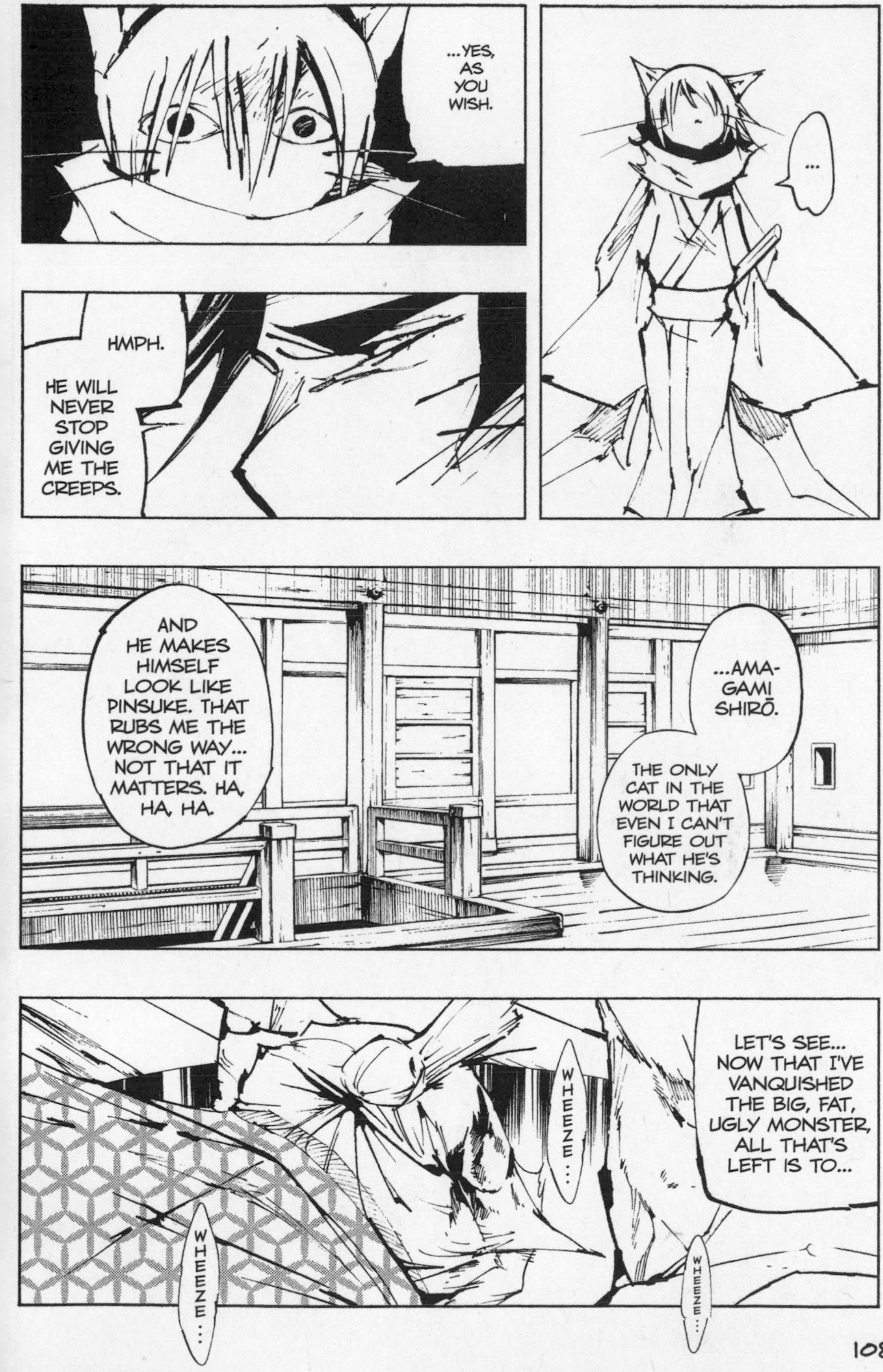
...
...YES, AS YOU WISH.
HMPH.
HE WILL NEVER STOP GIVING ME THE CREEPS.
...AMA-GAMI SHIRŌ.
THE ONLY CAT IN THE WORLD THAT EVEN I CAN'T FIGURE OUT WHAT HE'S THINKING.
AND HE MAKES HIMSELF LOOK LIKE PINSUKE. THAT RUBS ME THE WRONG WAY... NOT THAT IT MATTERS. HA, HA, HA.
LET'S SEE... NOW THAT I'VE VANQUISHED THE BIG, FAT, UGLY MONSTER, ALL THAT'S LEFT IS TO...
WHEEZE...
WHEEZE...
WHEEZE...

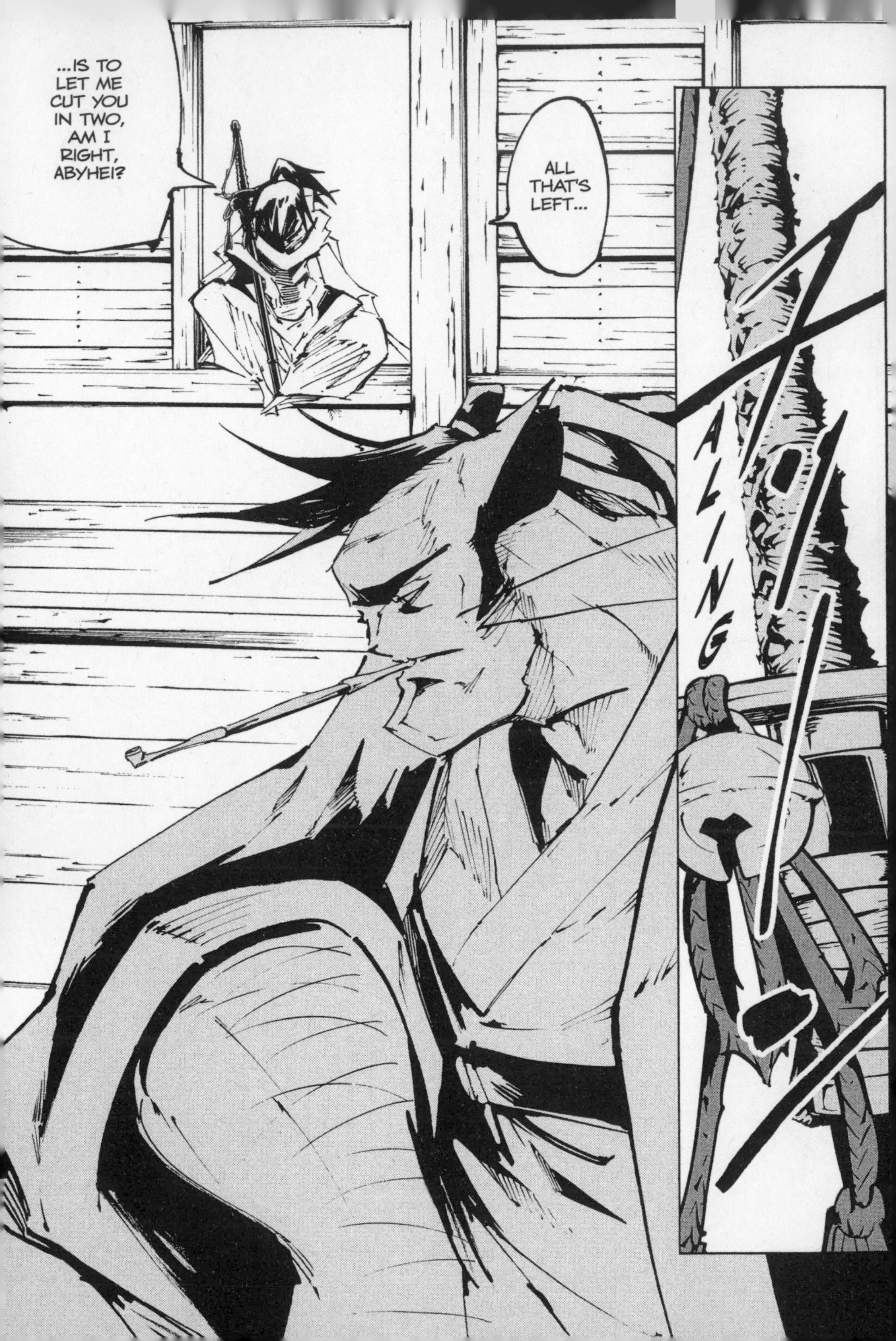
ALL THAT'S LEFT...
...IS TO LET ME CUT YOU IN TWO, AM I RIGHT, ABYHEI?
KALING

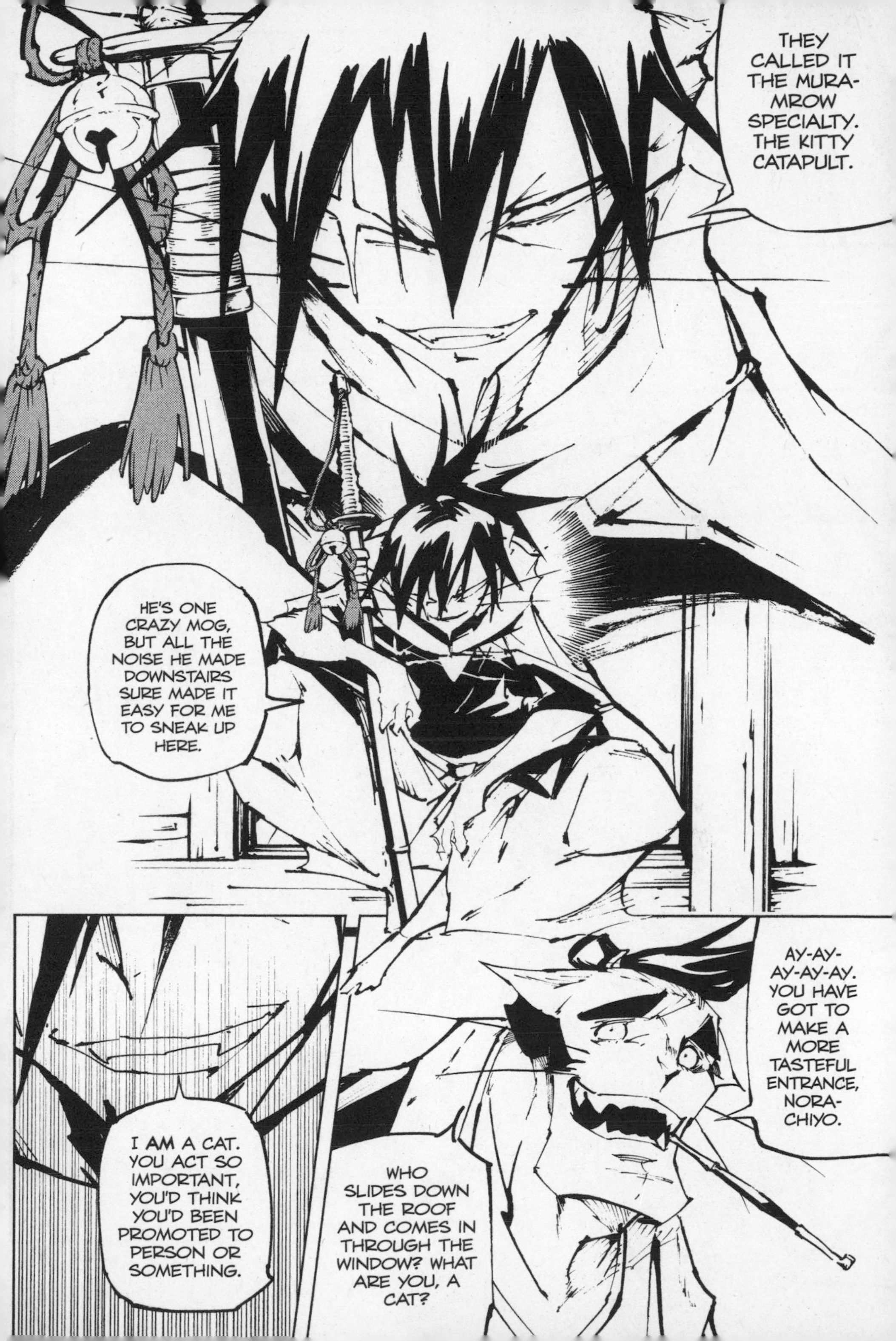
THEY CALLED IT THE MURA-MROW SPECIALTY. THE KITTY CATAPULT.
HE'S ONE CRAZY MOG, BUT ALL THE NOISE HE MADE DOWNSTAIRS SURE MADE IT EASY FOR ME TO SNEAK UP HERE.
AY-AY-AY-AY-AY. YOU HAVE GOT TO MAKE A MORE TASTEFUL ENTRANCE, NORA-CHIYO.
WHO SLIDES DOWN THE ROOF AND COMES IN THROUGH THE WINDOW? WHAT ARE YOU, A CAT?
I AM A CAT. YOU ACT SO IMPORTANT, YOU'D THINK YOU'D BEEN PROMOTED TO PERSON OR SOMETHING.

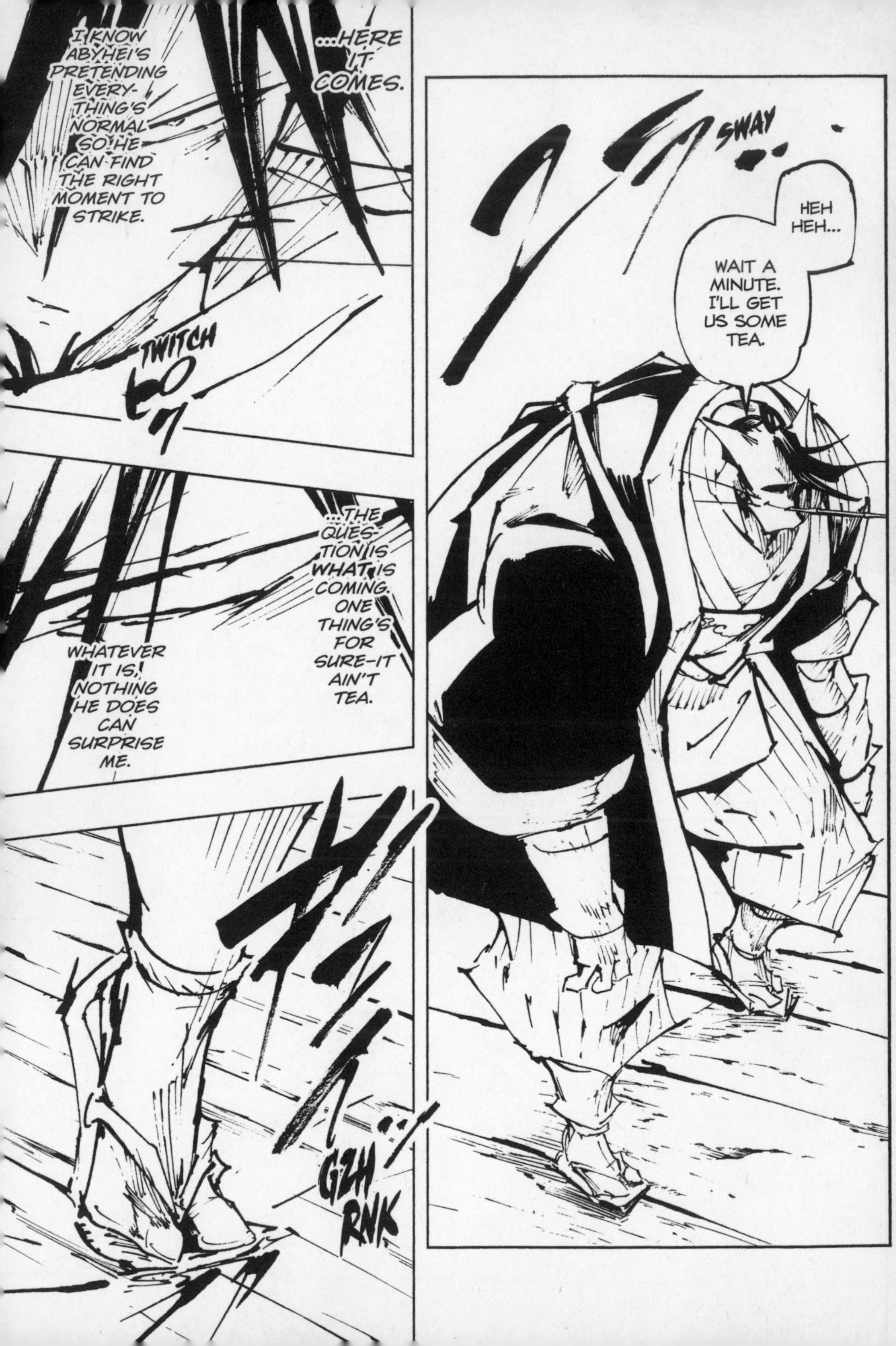
SWAY
HEH HEH...
WAIT A MINUTE. I'LL GET US SOME TEA.
...HERE IT COMES.
I KNOW ABYHEI'S PRETENDING EVERYTHING'S NORMAL SO HE CAN FIND THE RIGHT MOMENT TO STRIKE.
TWITCH
...THE QUESTION IS WHAT IS COMING. ONE THING'S FOR SURE—IT AIN'T TEA.
WHATEVER IT IS, NOTHING HE DOES CAN SURPRISE ME.
GZH RNK

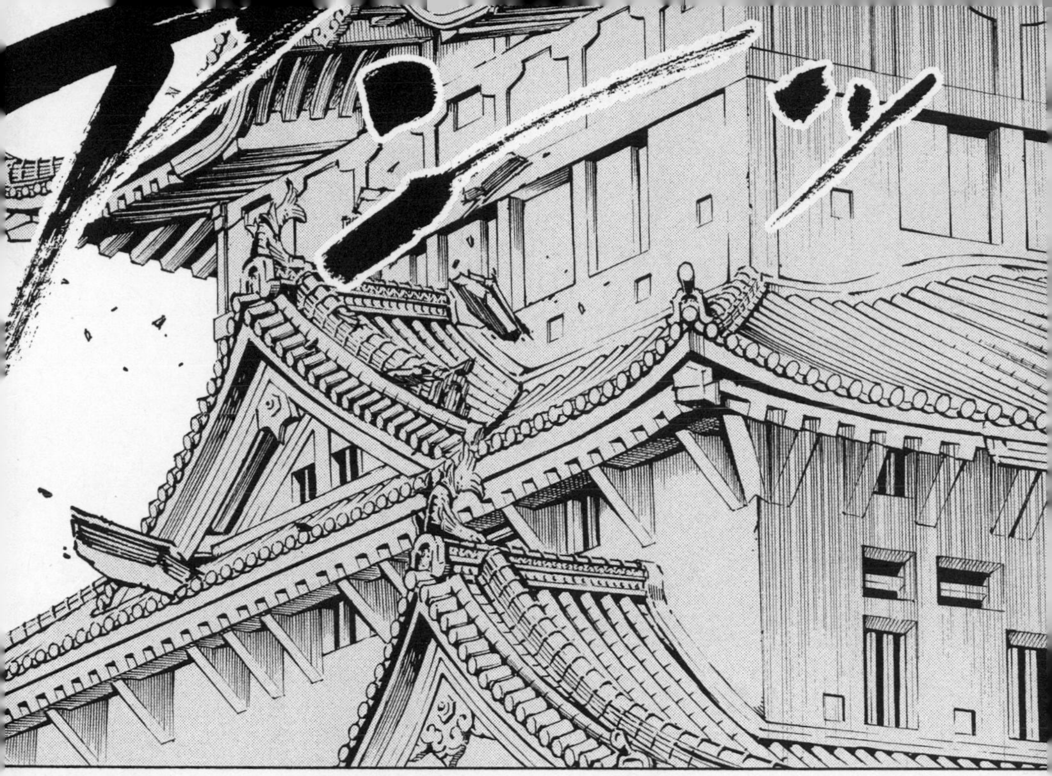

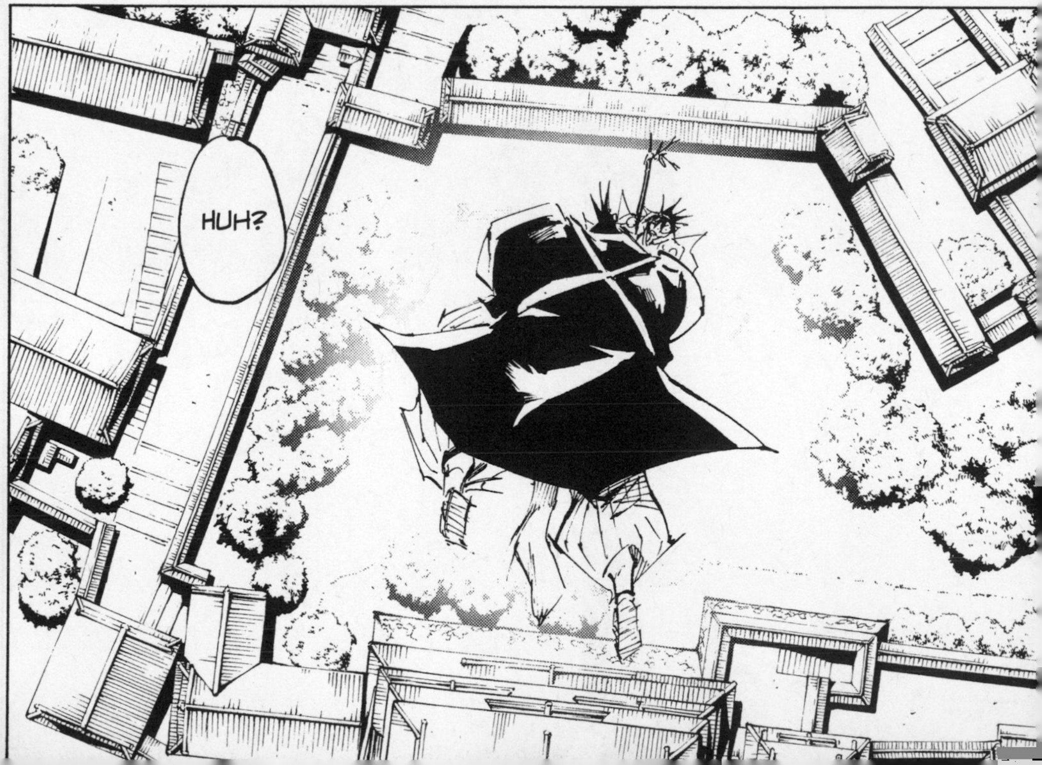
HUH?

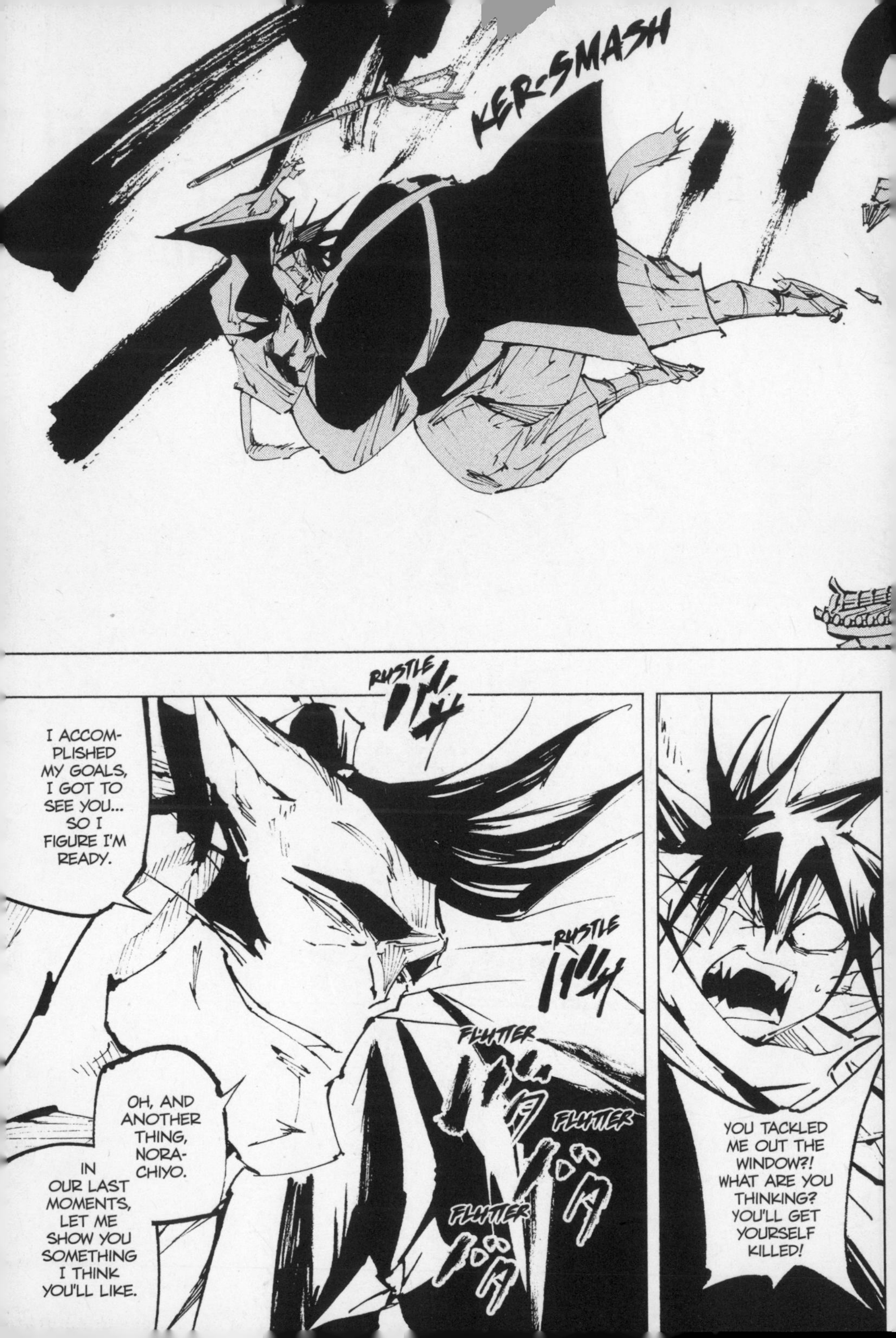
KER-SMASH
YOU TACKLED ME OUT THE WINDOW?! WHAT ARE YOU THINKING? YOU'LL GET YOURSELF KILLED!
RUSTLE
I ACCOMPLISHED MY GOALS, I GOT TO SEE YOU... SO I FIGURE I'M READY.
RUSTLE
FLUTTER
FLUTTER
FLUTTER
OH, AND ANOTHER THING, NORACHIYO.
IN OUR LAST MOMENTS, LET ME SHOW YOU SOMETHING I THINK YOU'LL LIKE.

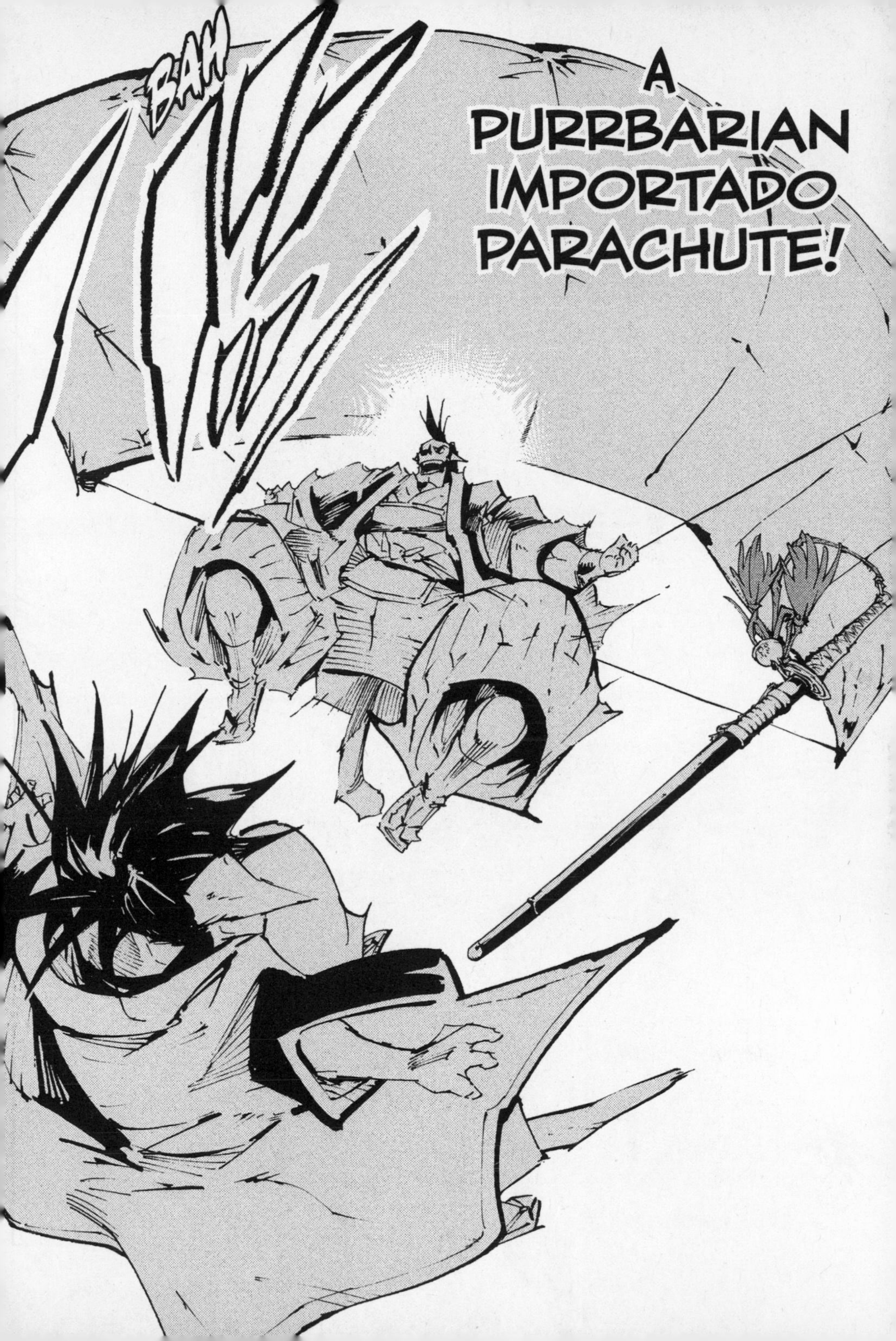
BAH
A PURRBARIAN IMPORTADO PARACHUTE!

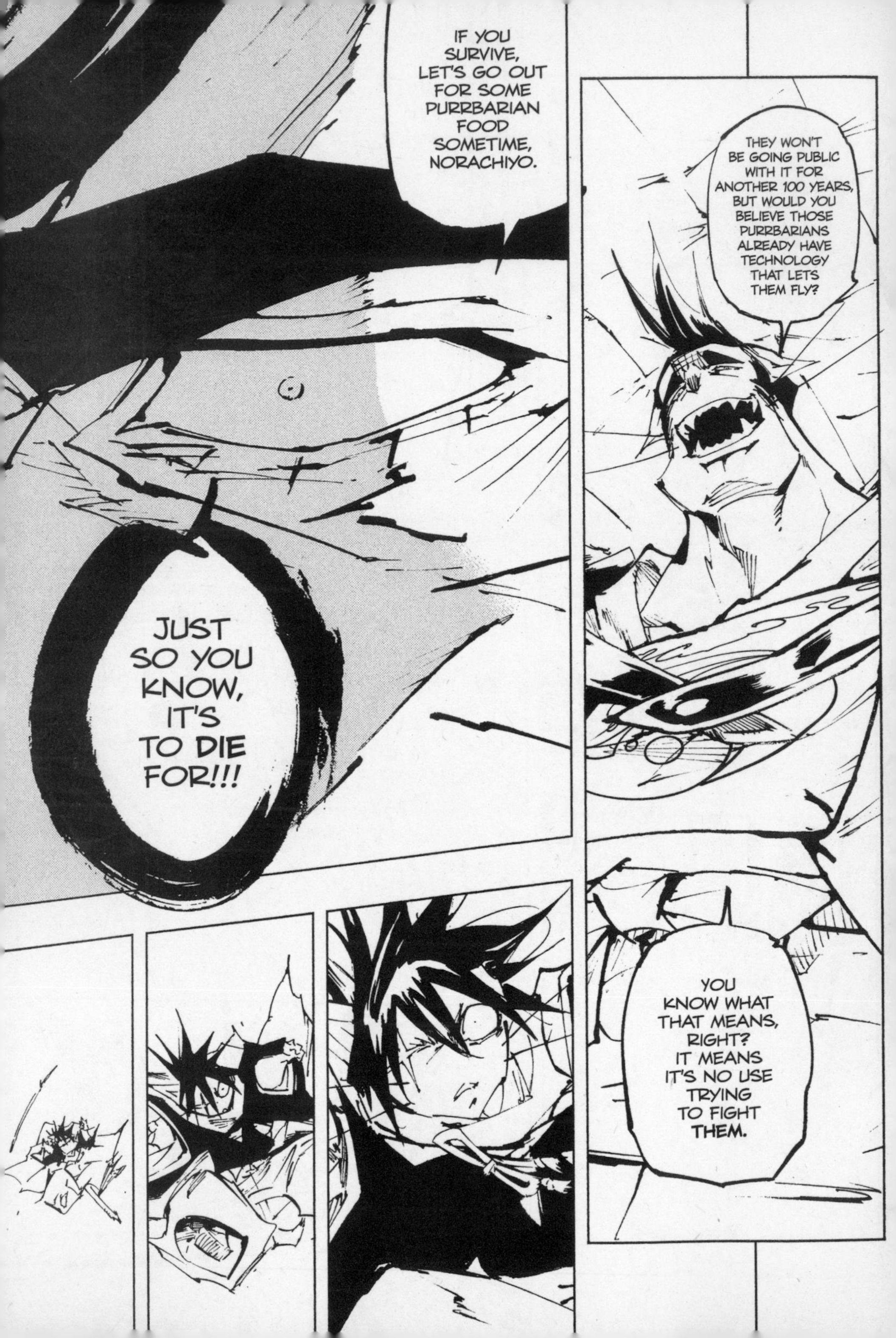
THEY WON'T BE GOING PUBLIC WITH IT FOR ANOTHER 100 YEARS, BUT WOULD YOU BELIEVE THOSE PURRBARIANS ALREADY HAVE TECHNOLOGY THAT LETS THEM FLY?
YOU KNOW WHAT THAT MEANS, RIGHT? IT MEANS IT'S NO USE TRYING TO FIGHT THEM.
IF YOU SURVIVE, LET'S GO OUT FOR SOME PURRBARIAN FOOD SOMETIME, NORACHIYO.
JUST SO YOU KNOW, IT'S TO DIE FOR!!!

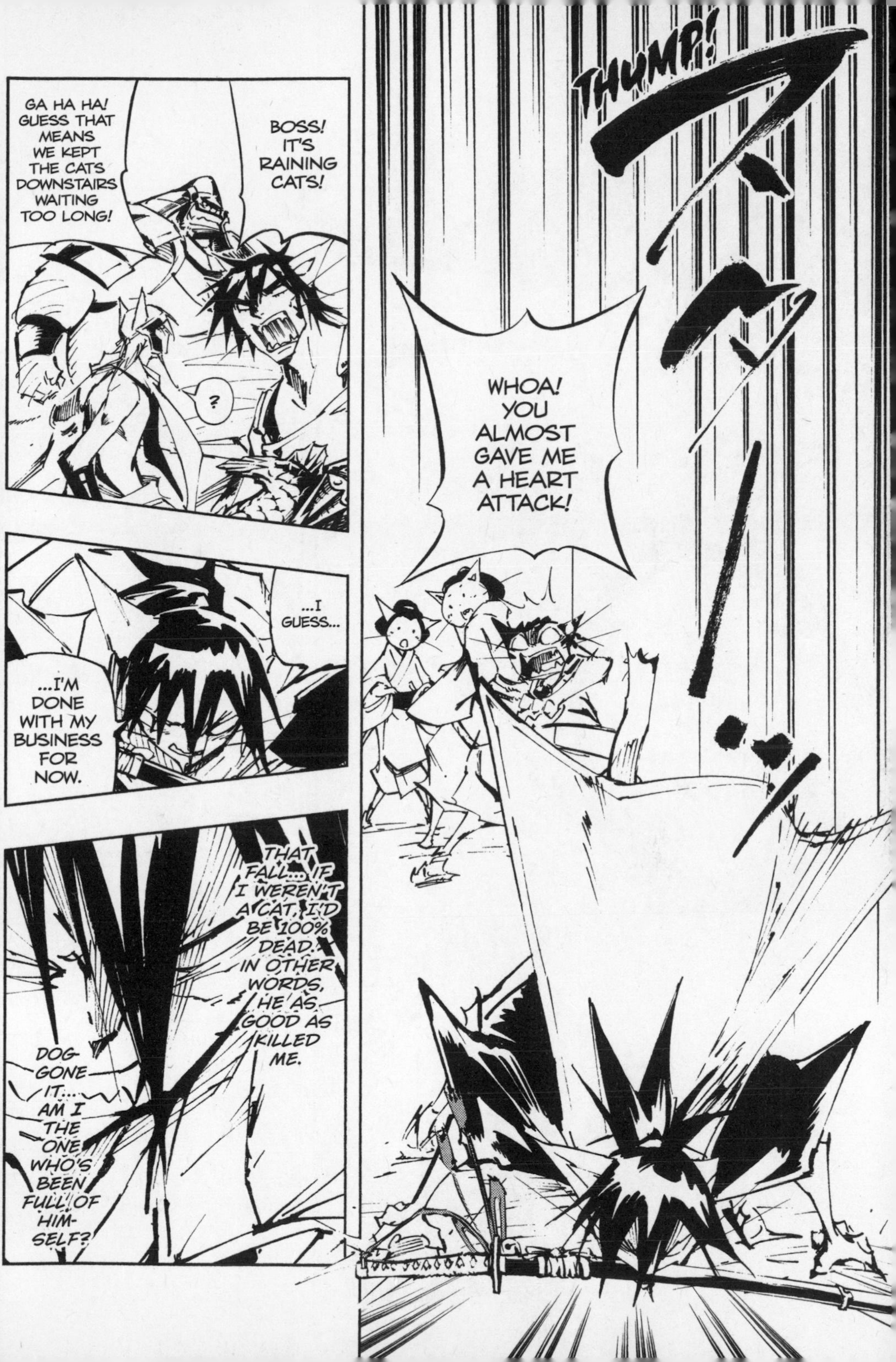
THUMP!
WHOA! YOU ALMOST GAVE ME A HEART ATTACK!
BOSS! IT'S RAINING CATS!
GA HA HA! GUESS THAT MEANS WE KEPT THE CATS DOWNSTAIRS WAITING TOO LONG!
?
...I GUESS...
...I'M DONE WITH MY BUSINESS FOR NOW.
THAT FALL... IF I WEREN'T A CAT, I'D BE 100% DEAD. IN OTHER WORDS, HE AS GOOD AS KILLED ME.
DOG-GONE IT... AM I THE ONE WHO'S BEEN FULL OF HIM-SELF?

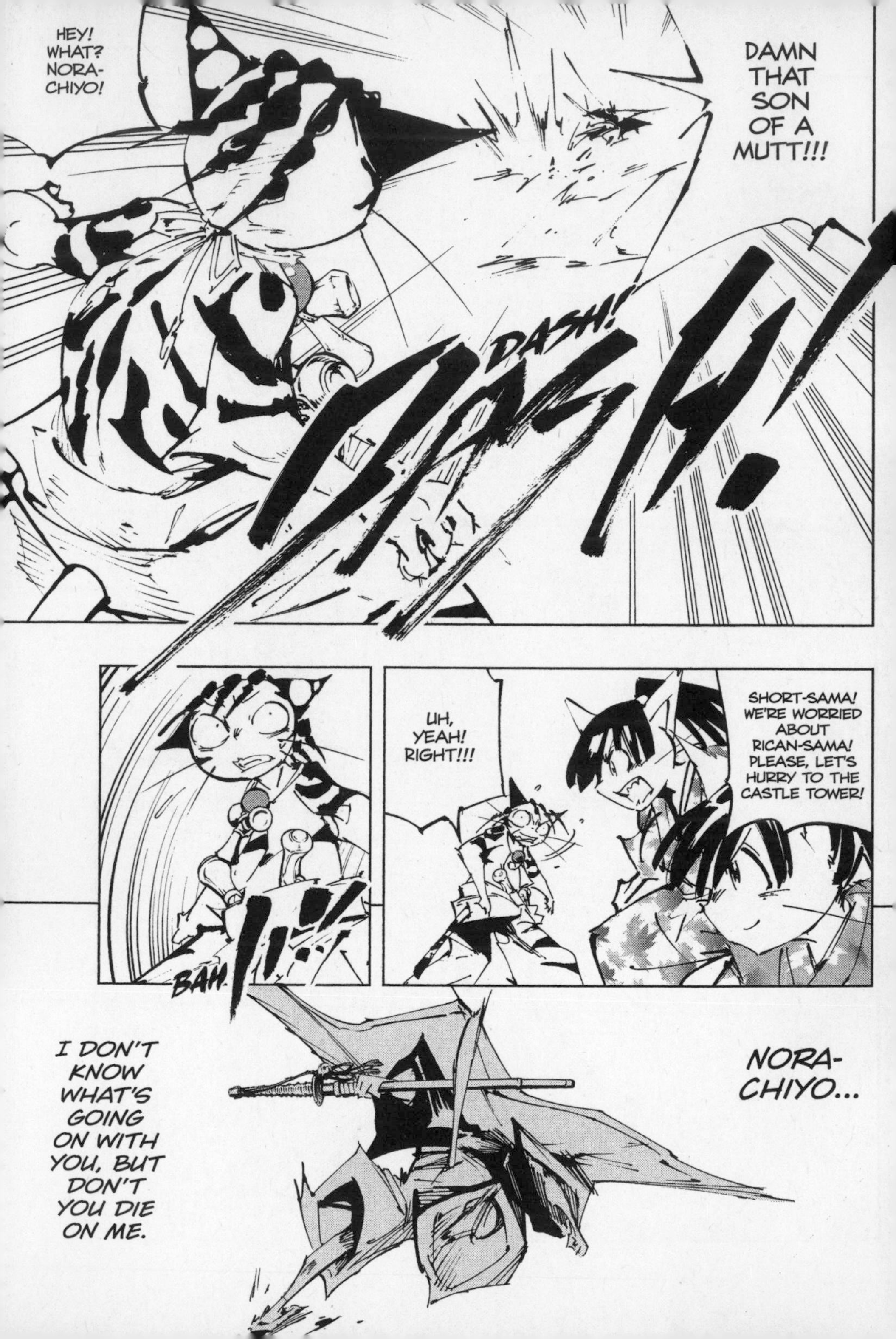
DAMN THAT SON OF A MUTT!!!
HEY! WHAT? NORA-CHIYO!
DASH!
SHORT-SAMA! WE'RE WORRIED ABOUT RICAN-SAMA! PLEASE, LET'S HURRY TO THE CASTLE TOWER!
UH, YEAH! RIGHT!!!
BAH
NORA-CHIYO...
I DON'T KNOW WHAT'S GOING ON WITH YOU, BUT DON'T YOU DIE ON ME.

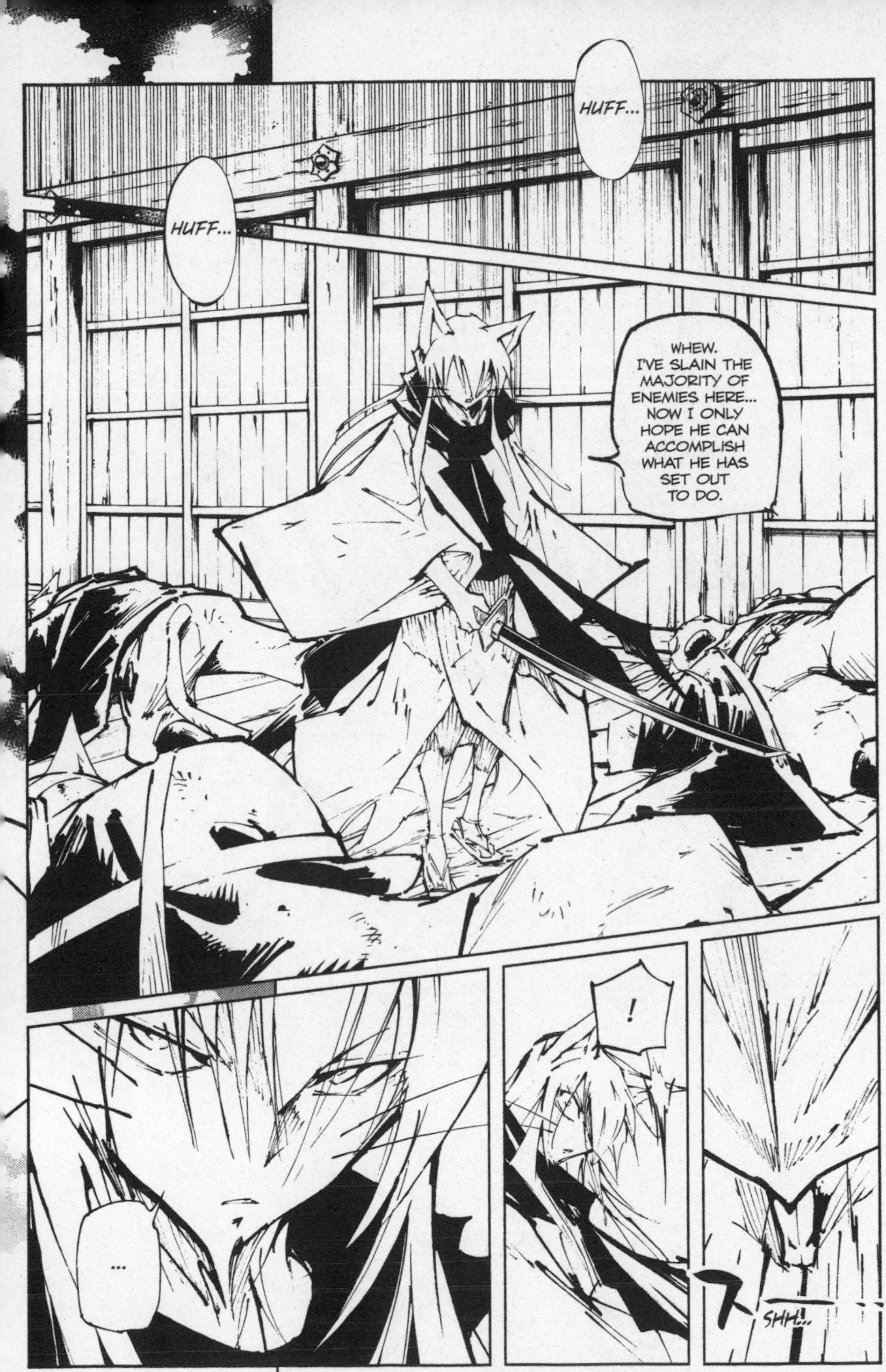
HUFF...
HUFF...
WHEW. I'VE SLAIN THE MAJORITY OF ENEMIES HERE... NOW I ONLY HOPE HE CAN ACCOMPLISH WHAT HE HAS SET OUT TO DO.
SHH!...
!
...

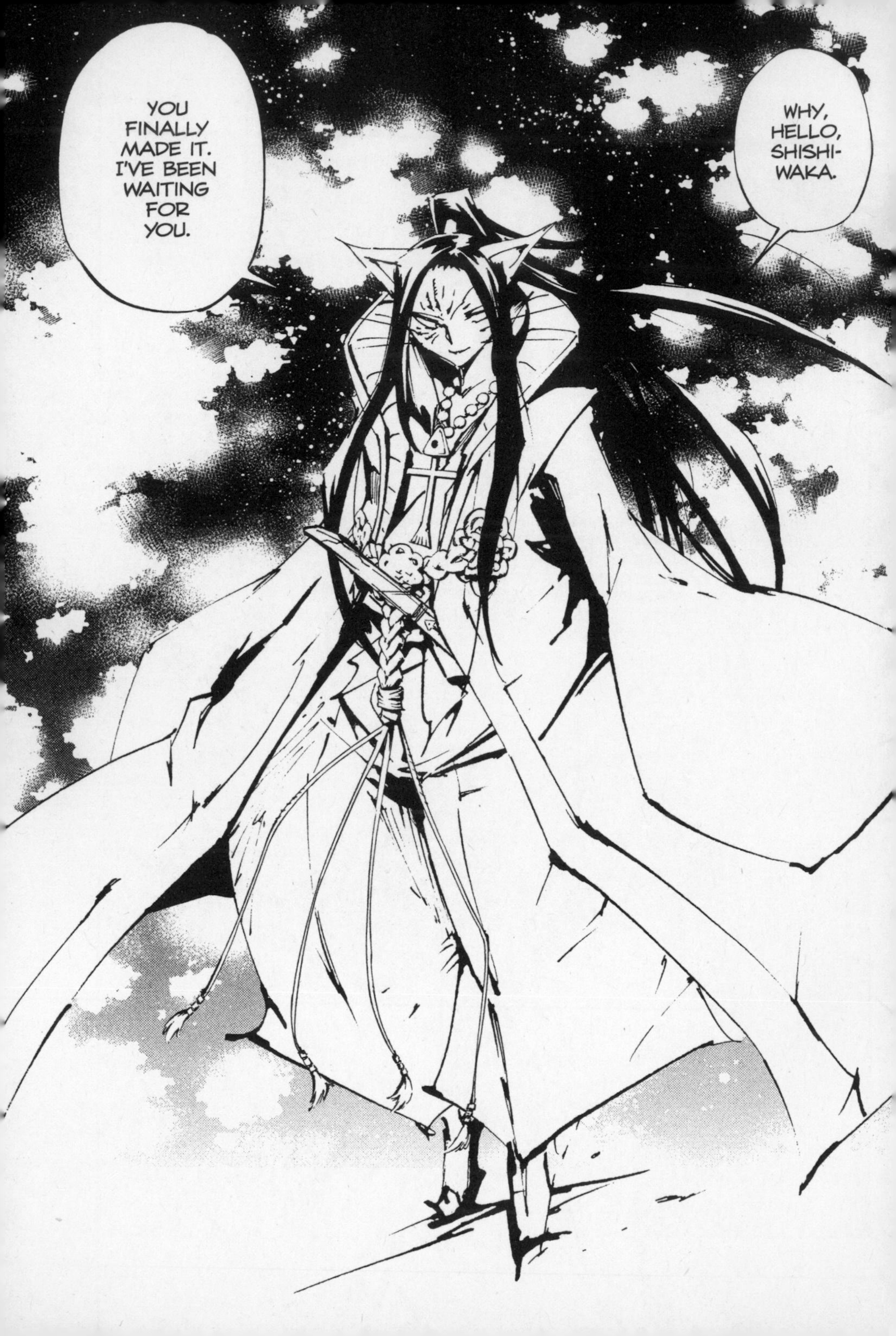
WHY, HELLO, SHISHI-WAKA.
YOU FINALLY MADE IT. I'VE BEEN WAITING FOR YOU.

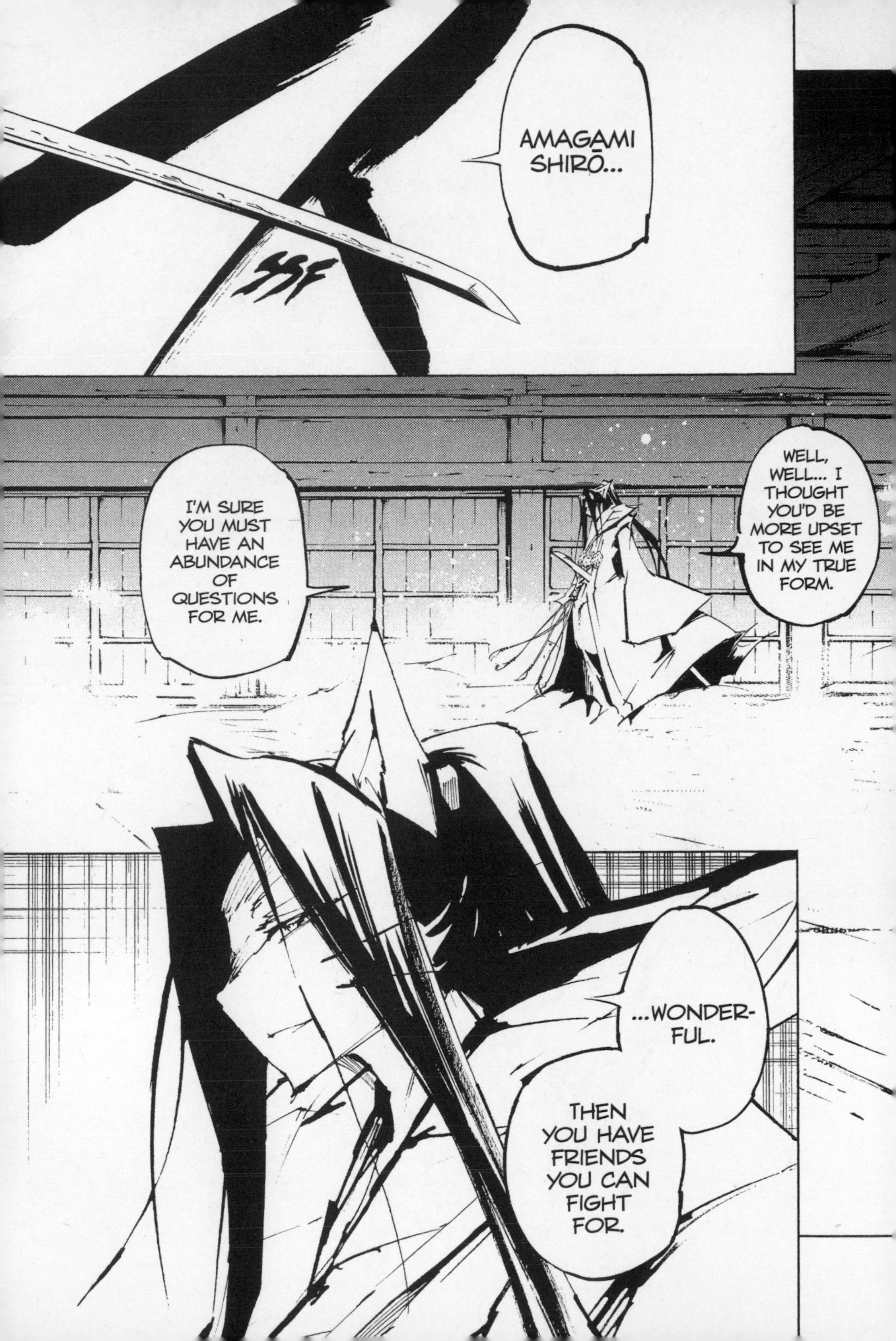
AMAGAMI SHIRŌ...
SSF
WELL, WELL... I THOUGHT YOU'D BE MORE UPSET TO SEE ME IN MY TRUE FORM.
I'M SURE YOU MUST HAVE AN ABUNDANCE OF QUESTIONS FOR ME.
...WONDER-FUL.
THEN YOU HAVE FRIENDS YOU CAN FIGHT FOR.

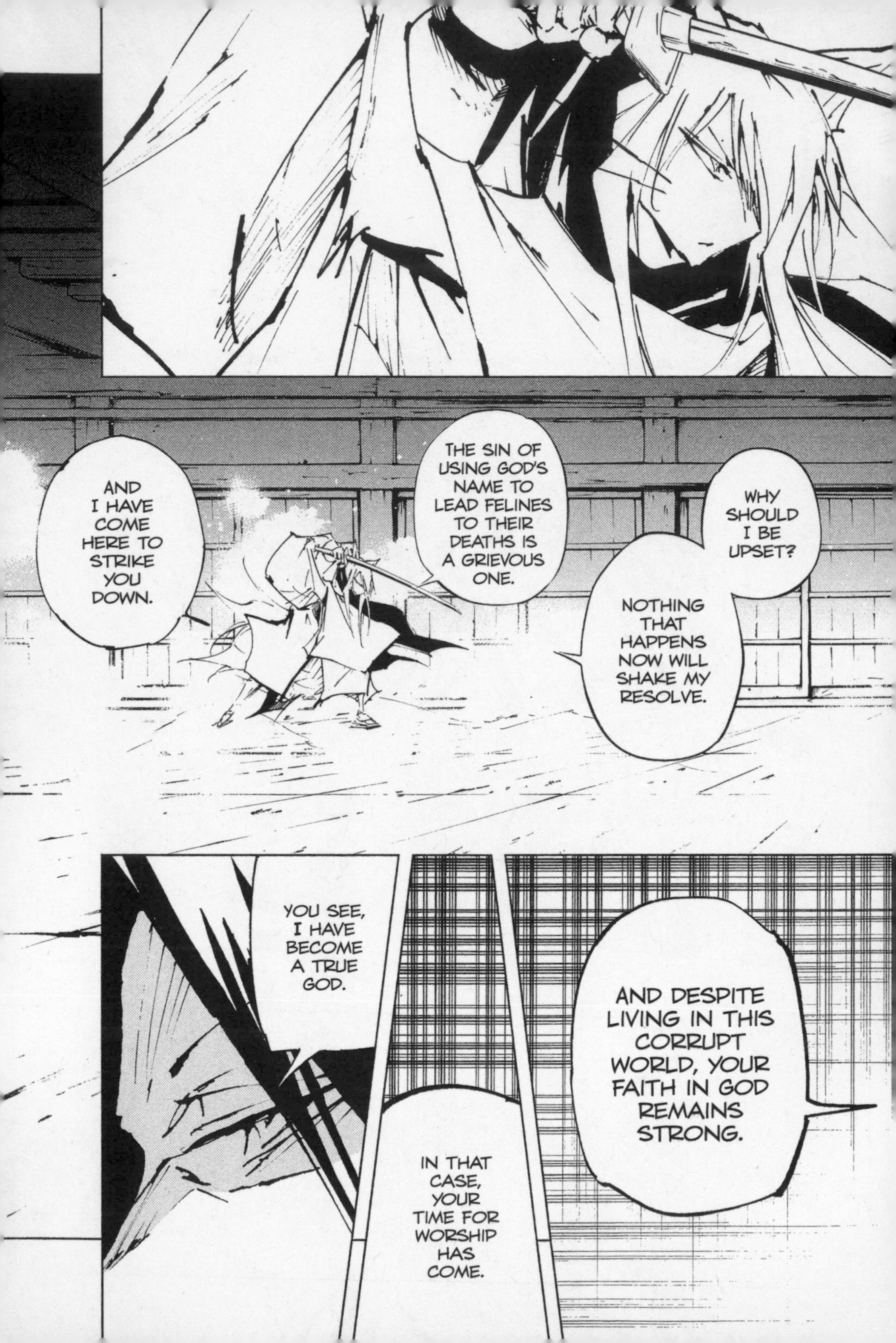
WHY SHOULD I BE UPSET?
NOTHING THAT HAPPENS NOW WILL SHAKE MY RESOLVE.
THE SIN OF USING GOD'S NAME TO LEAD FELINES TO THEIR DEATHS IS A GRIEVOUS ONE.
AND I HAVE COME HERE TO STRIKE YOU DOWN.
AND DESPITE LIVING IN THIS CORRUPT WORLD, YOUR FAITH IN GOD REMAINS STRONG.
IN THAT CASE, YOUR TIME FOR WORSHIP HAS COME.
YOU SEE, I HAVE BECOME A TRUE GOD.

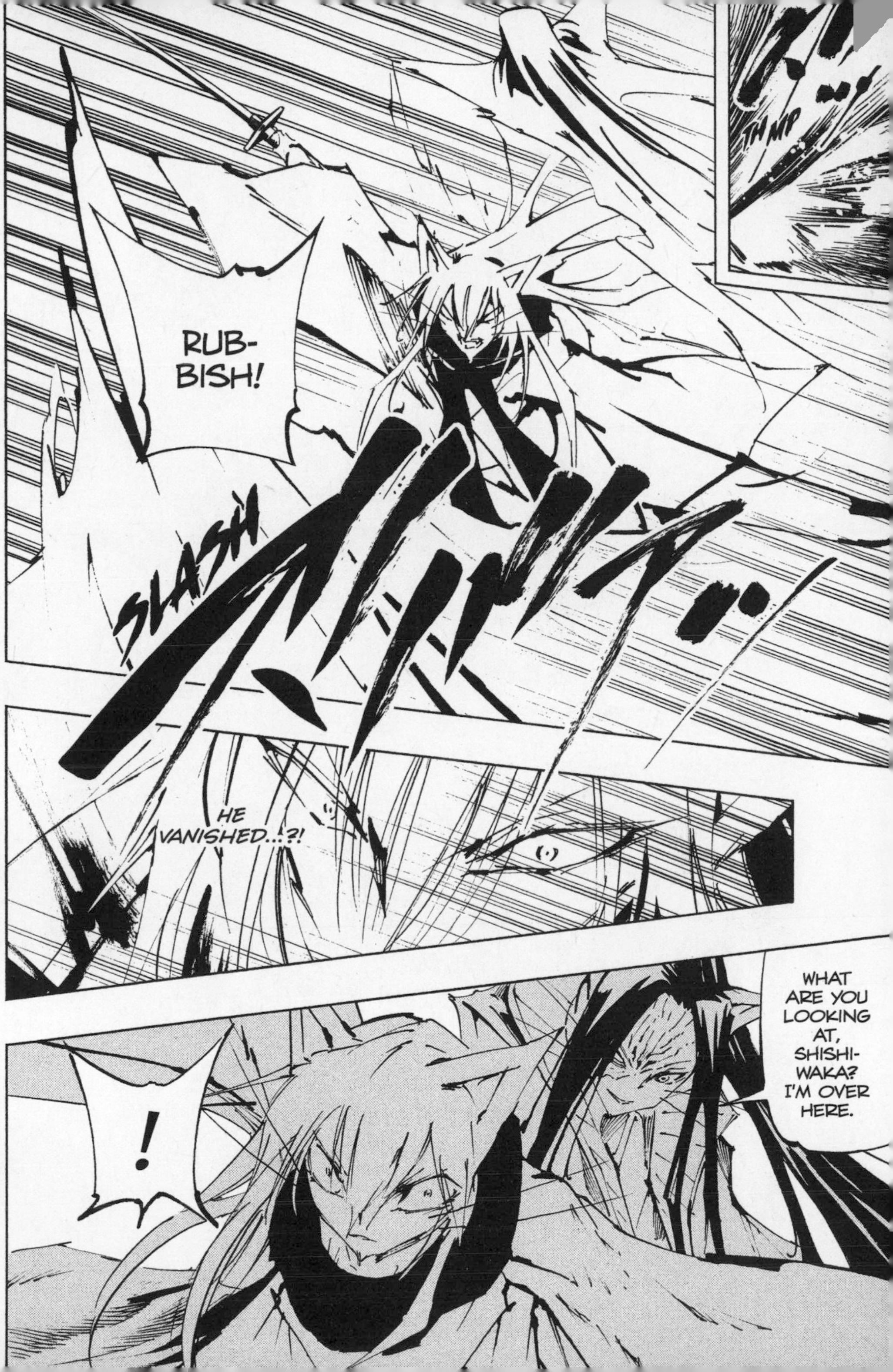
THMP
RUB-BISH!
SLASH
HE VANISHED...?!
WHAT ARE YOU LOOKING AT, SHISHI-WAKA? I'M OVER HERE.
!

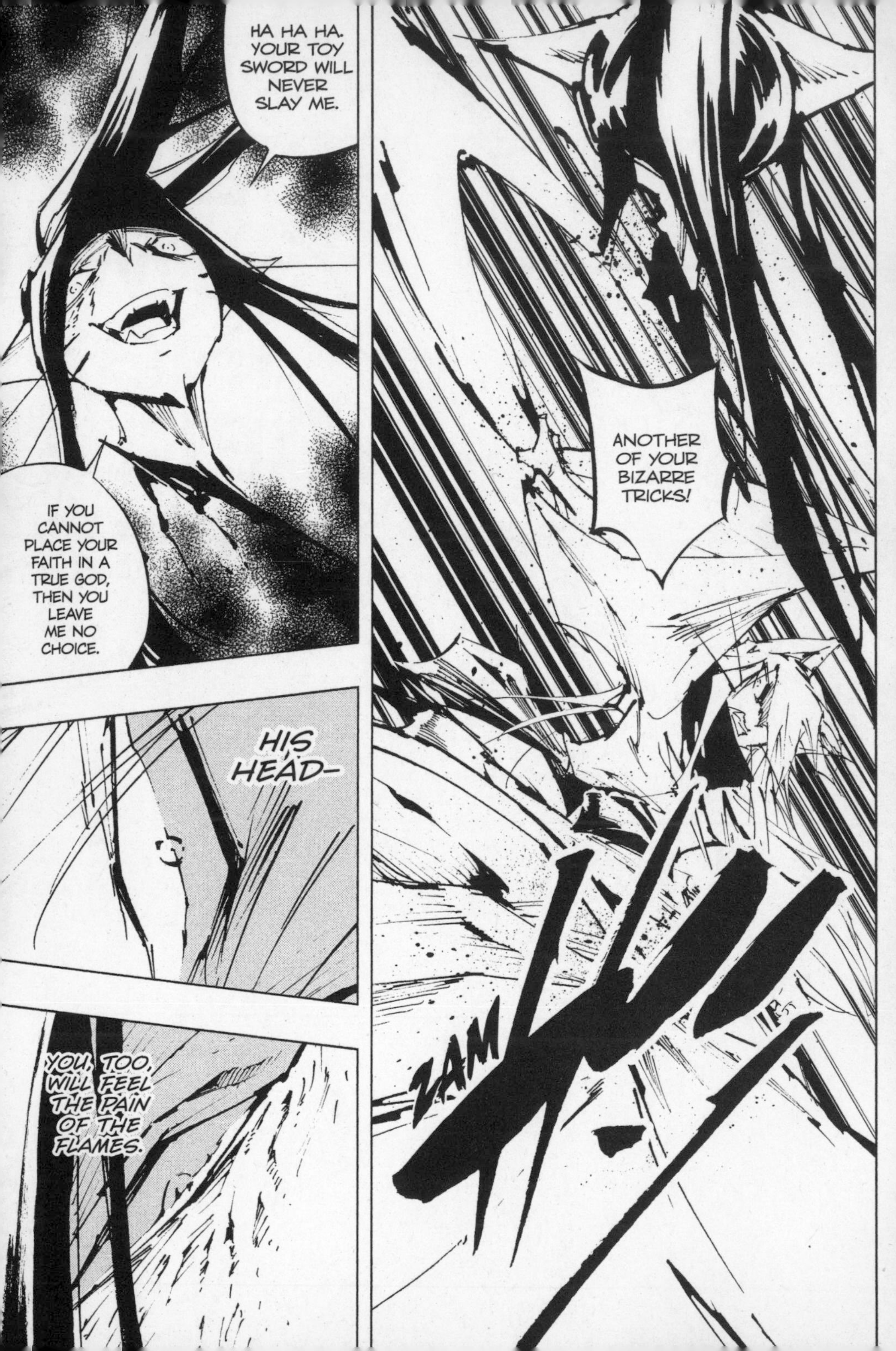
ANOTHER OF YOUR BIZARRE TRICKS!
ZAM
HA HA HA. YOUR TOY SWORD WILL NEVER SLAY ME.
IF YOU CANNOT PLACE YOUR FAITH IN A TRUE GOD, THEN YOU LEAVE ME NO CHOICE.
HIS HEAD-
YOU, TOO, WILL FEEL THE PAIN OF THE FLAMES.

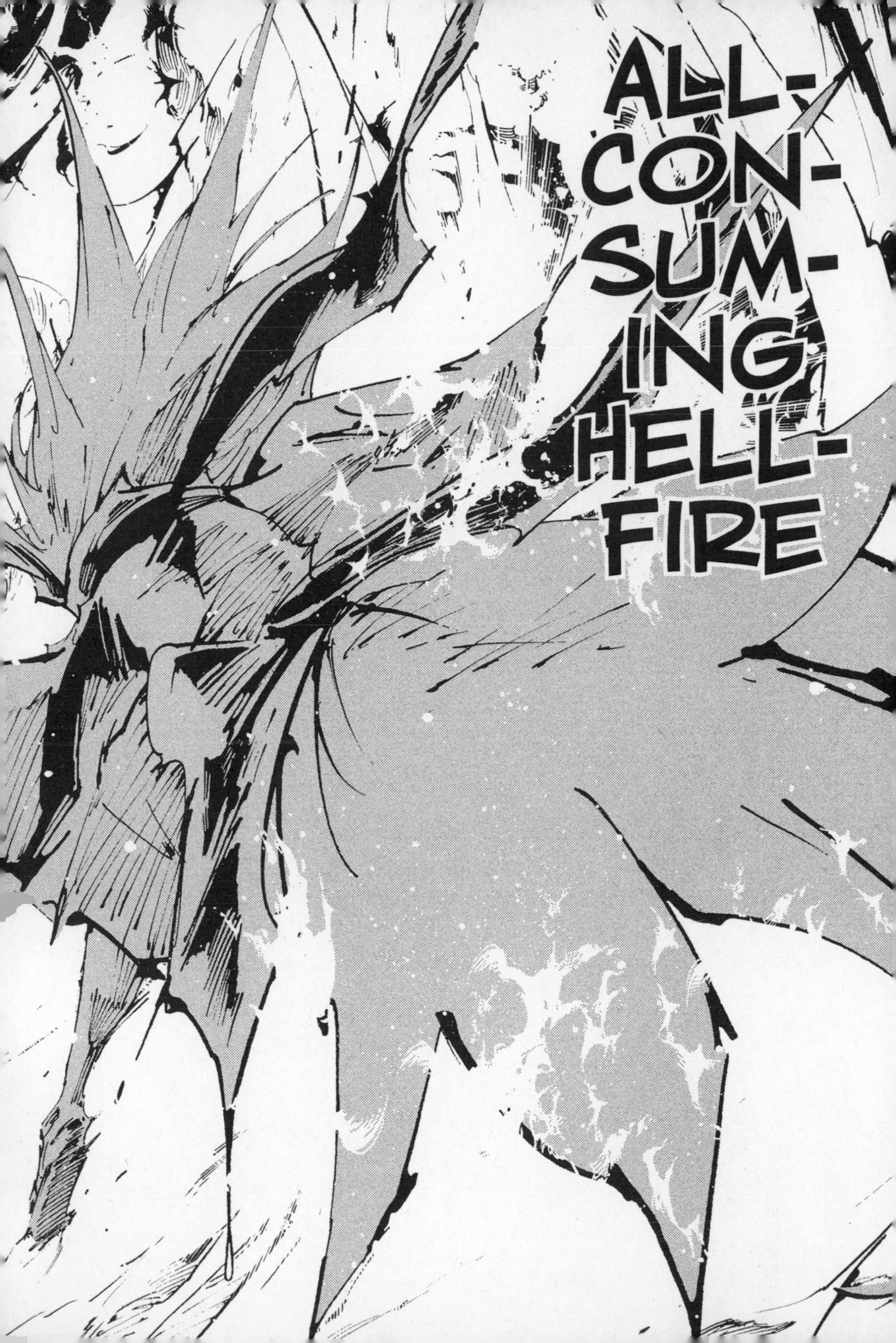
ALL-CON-SUM-ING HELL-FIRE

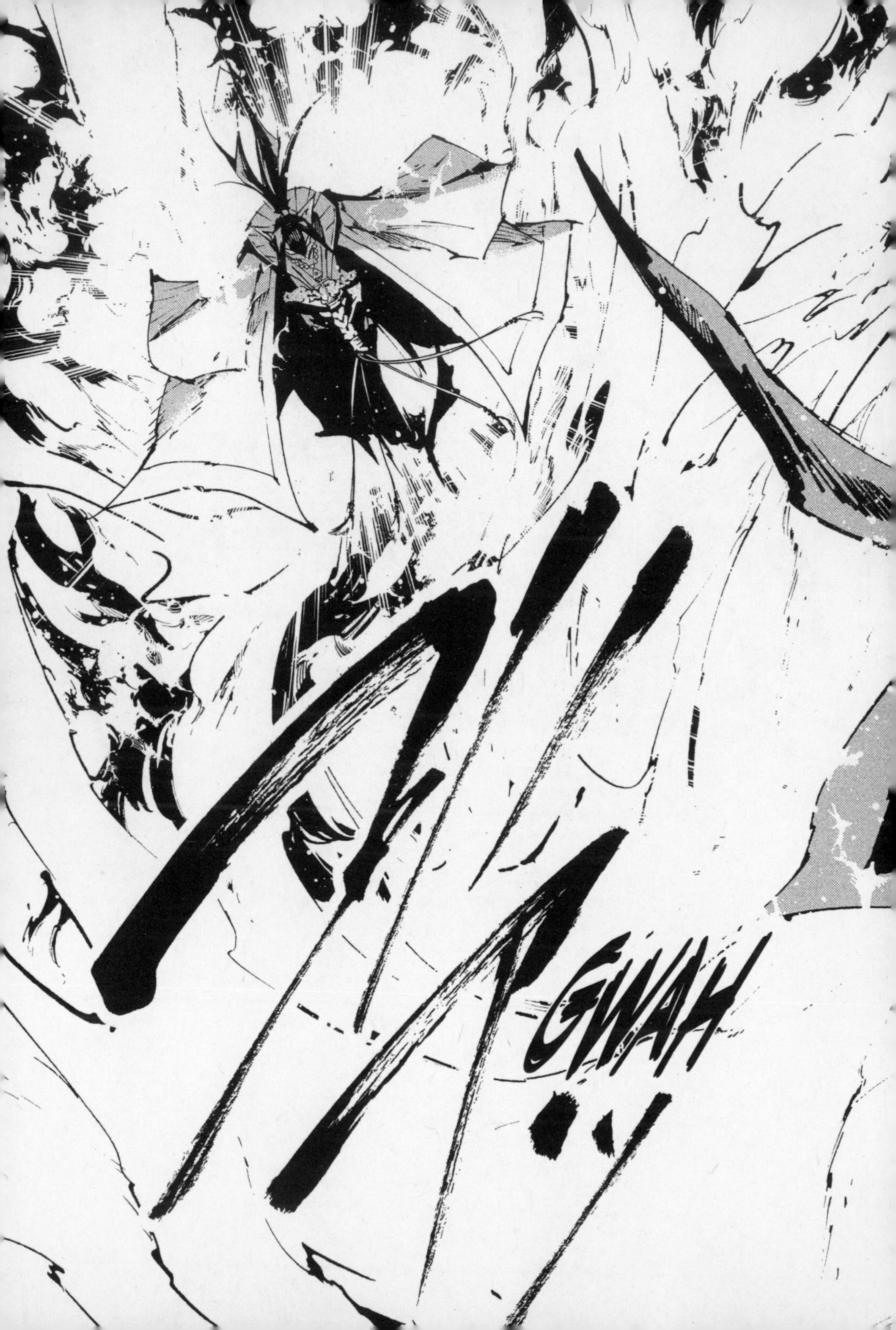
GWAH

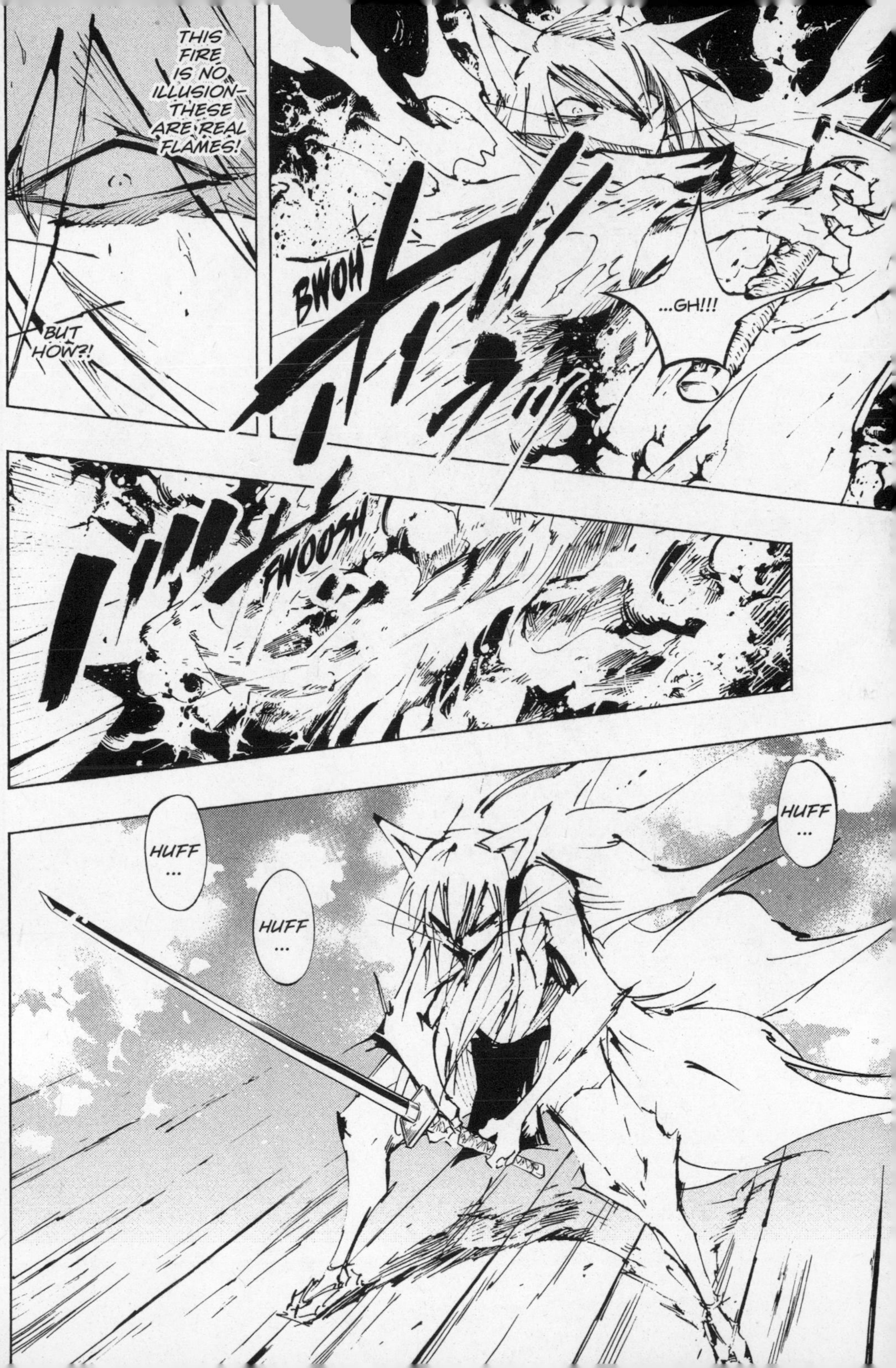
...GH!!!
BWOH
THIS FIRE IS NO ILLUSION-THESE ARE REAL FLAMES!
BUT HOW?!
FWOOSH
HUFF ...
HUFF ...
HUFF ...

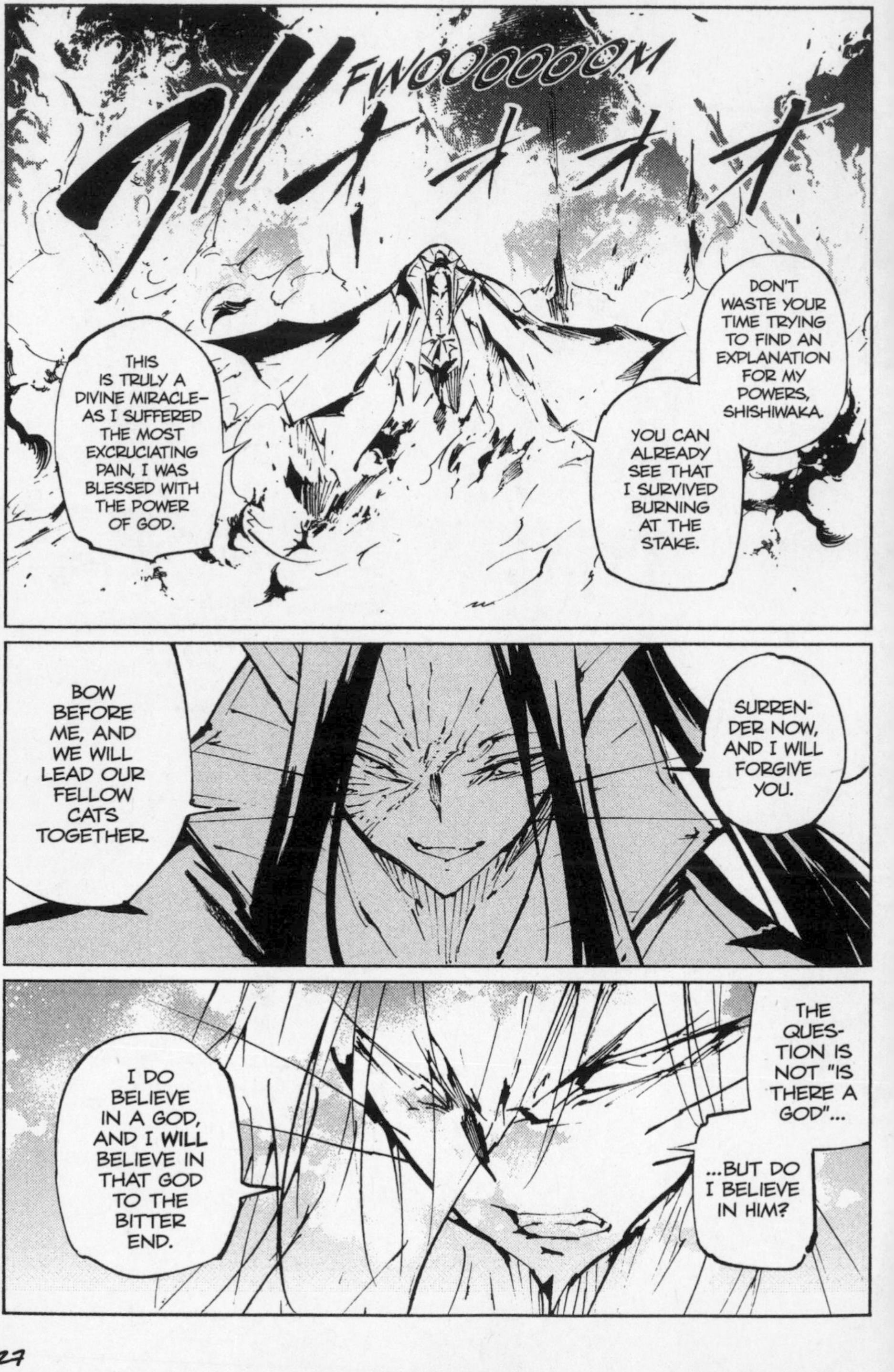
FWOOOOOOOM
DON'T WASTE YOUR TIME TRYING TO FIND AN EXPLANATION FOR MY POWERS, SHISHIWAKA.
YOU CAN ALREADY SEE THAT I SURVIVED BURNING AT THE STAKE.
THIS IS TRULY A DIVINE MIRACLE—AS I SUFFERED THE MOST EXCRUCIATING PAIN, I WAS BLESSED WITH THE POWER OF GOD.
SURRENDER NOW, AND I WILL FORGIVE YOU.
BOW BEFORE ME, AND WE WILL LEAD OUR FELLOW CATS TOGETHER.
THE QUESTION IS NOT "IS THERE A GOD"...
...BUT DO I BELIEVE IN HIM?
I DO BELIEVE IN A GOD, AND I WILL BELIEVE IN THAT GOD TO THE BITTER END.

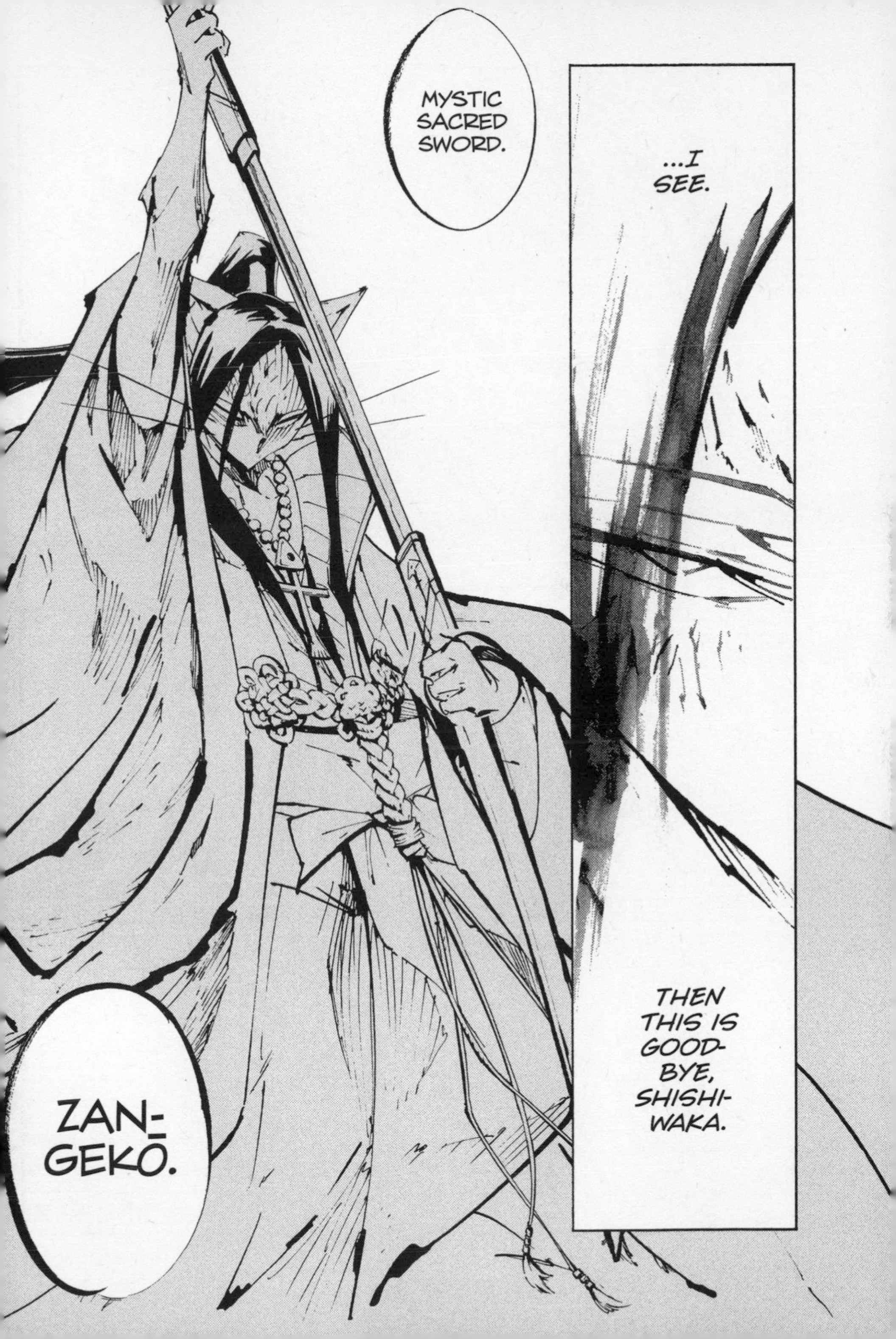
...I SEE.
THEN THIS IS GOOD-BYE, SHISHI-WAKA.
MYSTIC SACRED SWORD.
ZAN-GEKŌ.

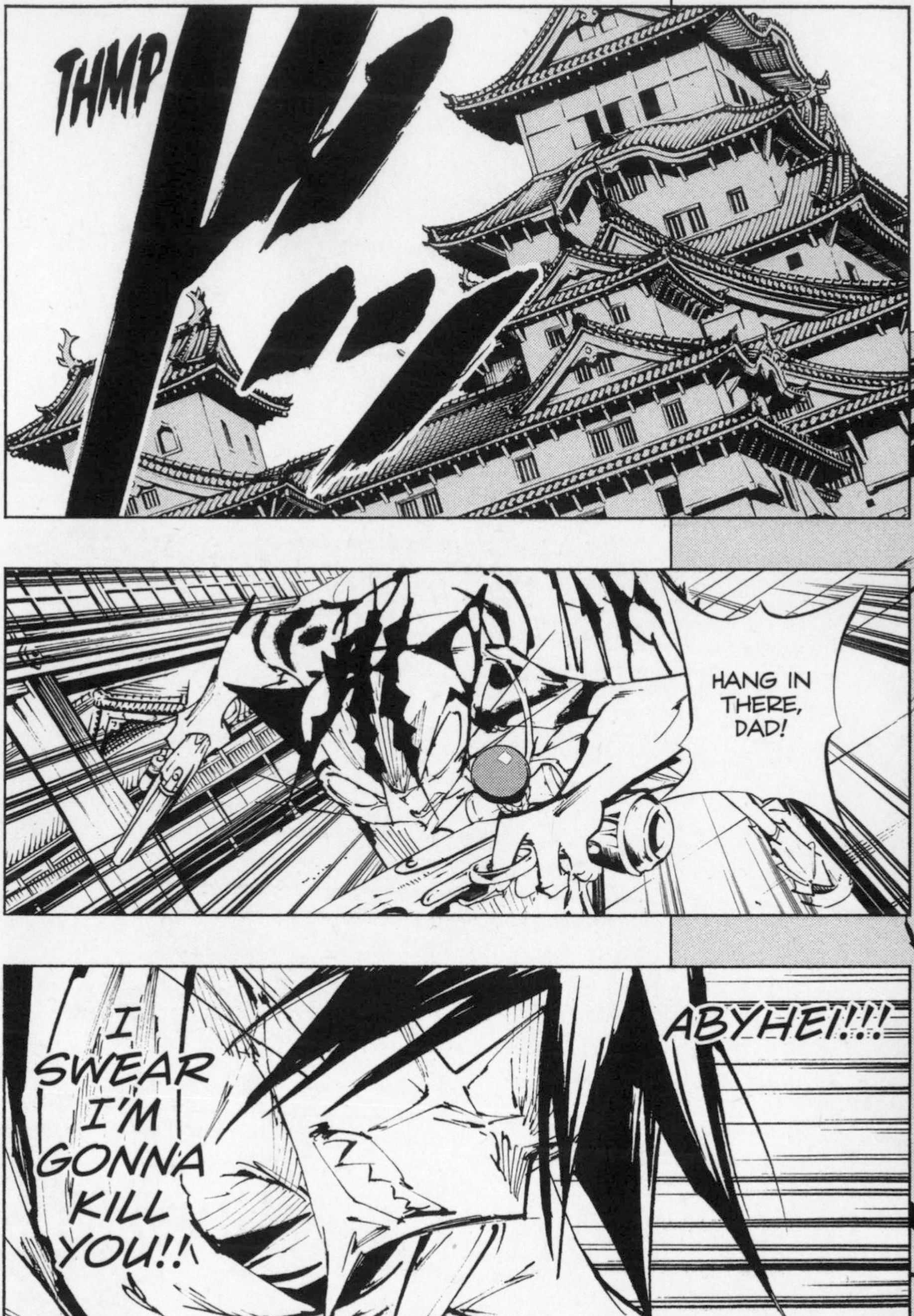
THMP
HANG IN THERE, DAD!
ABYHEI!!!
I SWEAR I'M GONNA KILL YOU!!

猫ヶ原

NEKOGAHARA

ネコガハラ

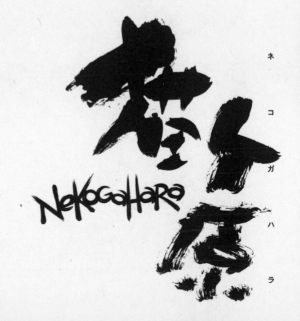

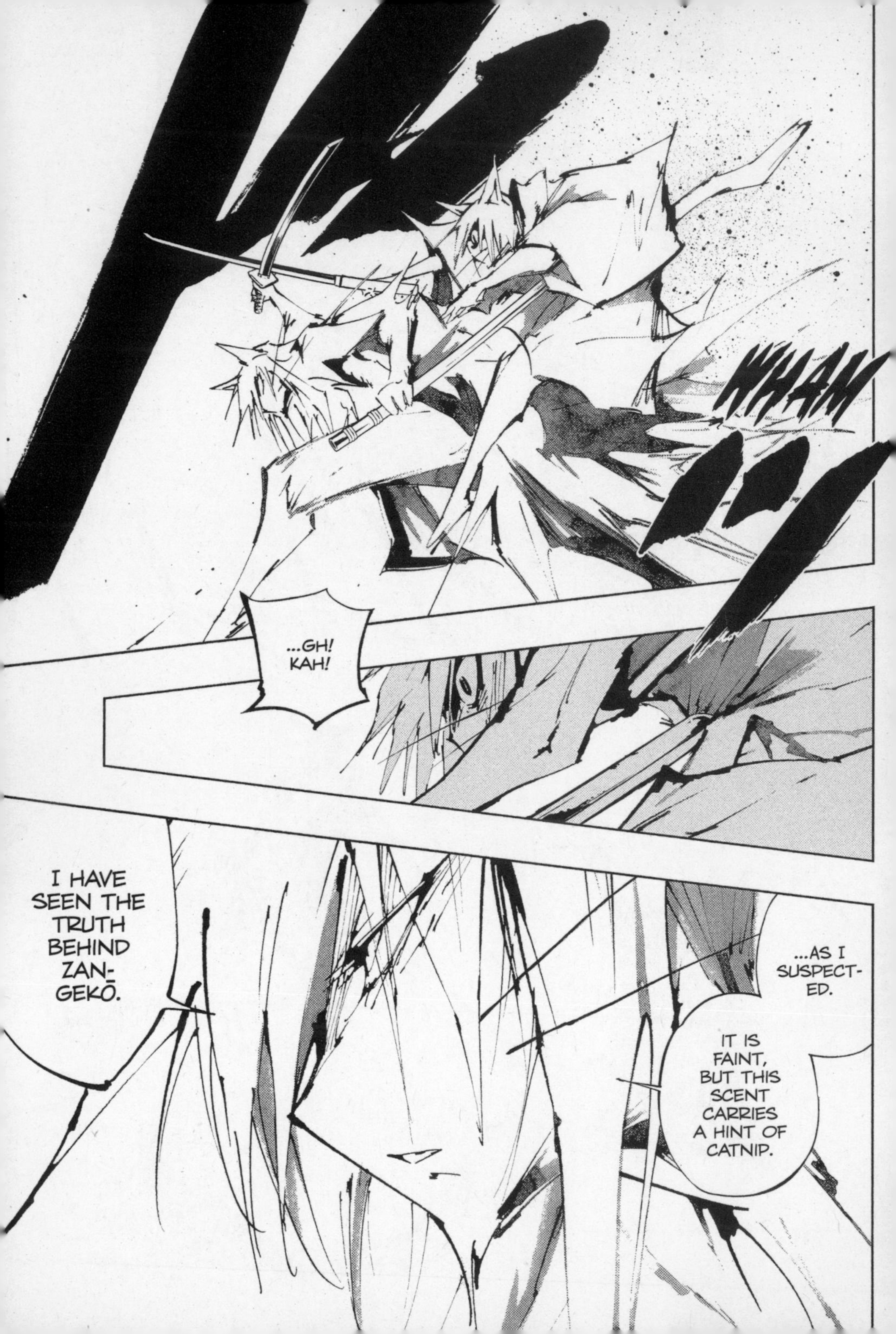
WHAM
...GH! KAH!
...AS I SUSPECTED.
IT IS FAINT, BUT THIS SCENT CARRIES A HINT OF CATNIP.
I HAVE SEEN THE TRUTH BEHIND ZANGEKŌ.

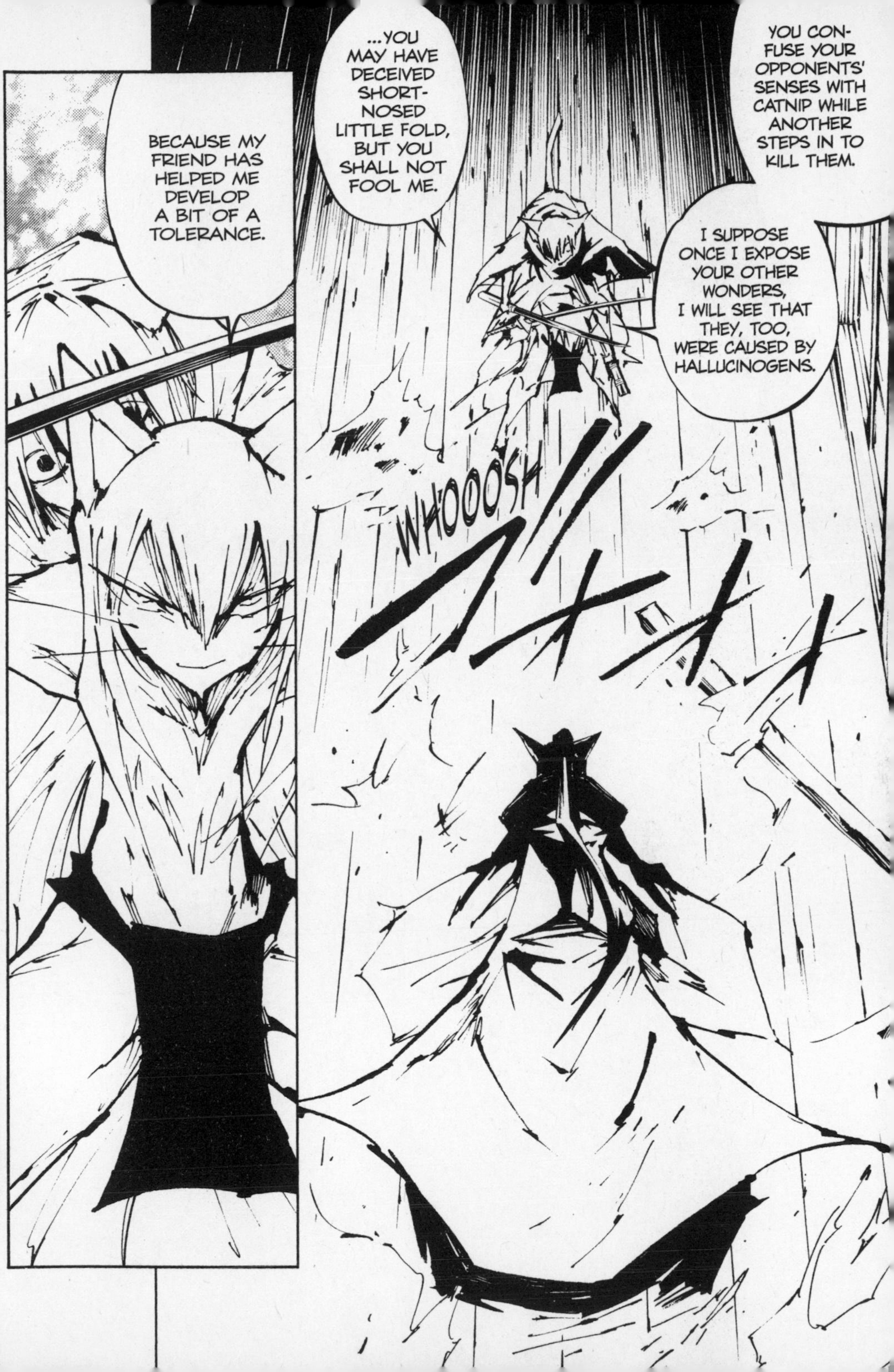
YOU CONFUSE YOUR OPPONENTS' SENSES WITH CATNIP WHILE ANOTHER STEPS IN TO KILL THEM.
...YOU MAY HAVE DECEIVED SHORT-NOSED LITTLE FOLD, BUT YOU SHALL NOT FOOL ME.
I SUPPOSE ONCE I EXPOSE YOUR OTHER WONDERS, I WILL SEE THAT THEY, TOO, WERE CAUSED BY HALLUCINOGENS.
WHOOOSH
BECAUSE MY FRIEND HAS HELPED ME DEVELOP A BIT OF A TOLERANCE.

NEKOGAHARA

CHAPTER 28: "WELCOME TO NEKOGAHARA!"

HIROYUKI TAKEI

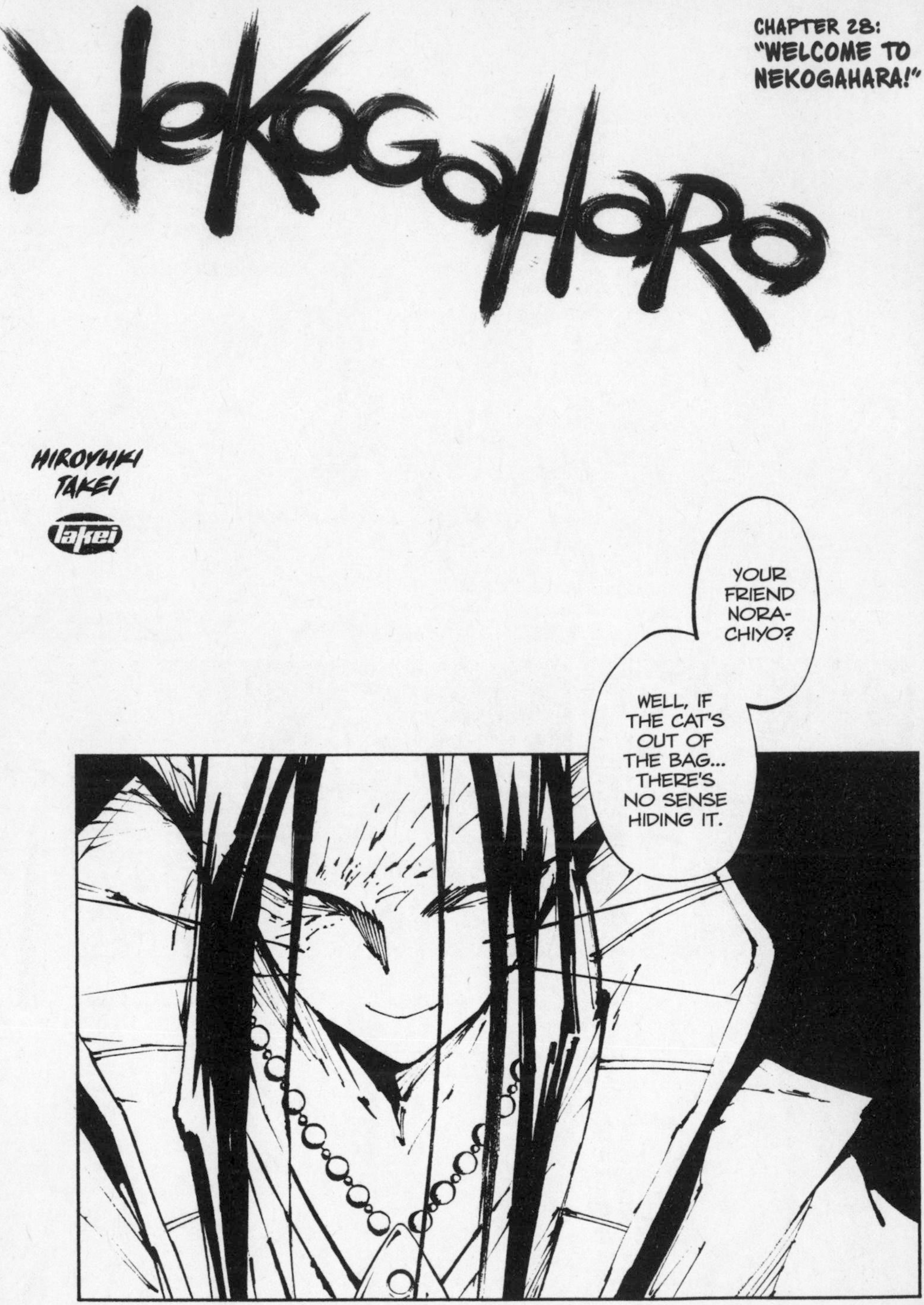
YOUR FRIEND NORA-CHIYO?
WELL, IF THE CAT'S OUT OF THE BAG... THERE'S NO SENSE HIDING IT.

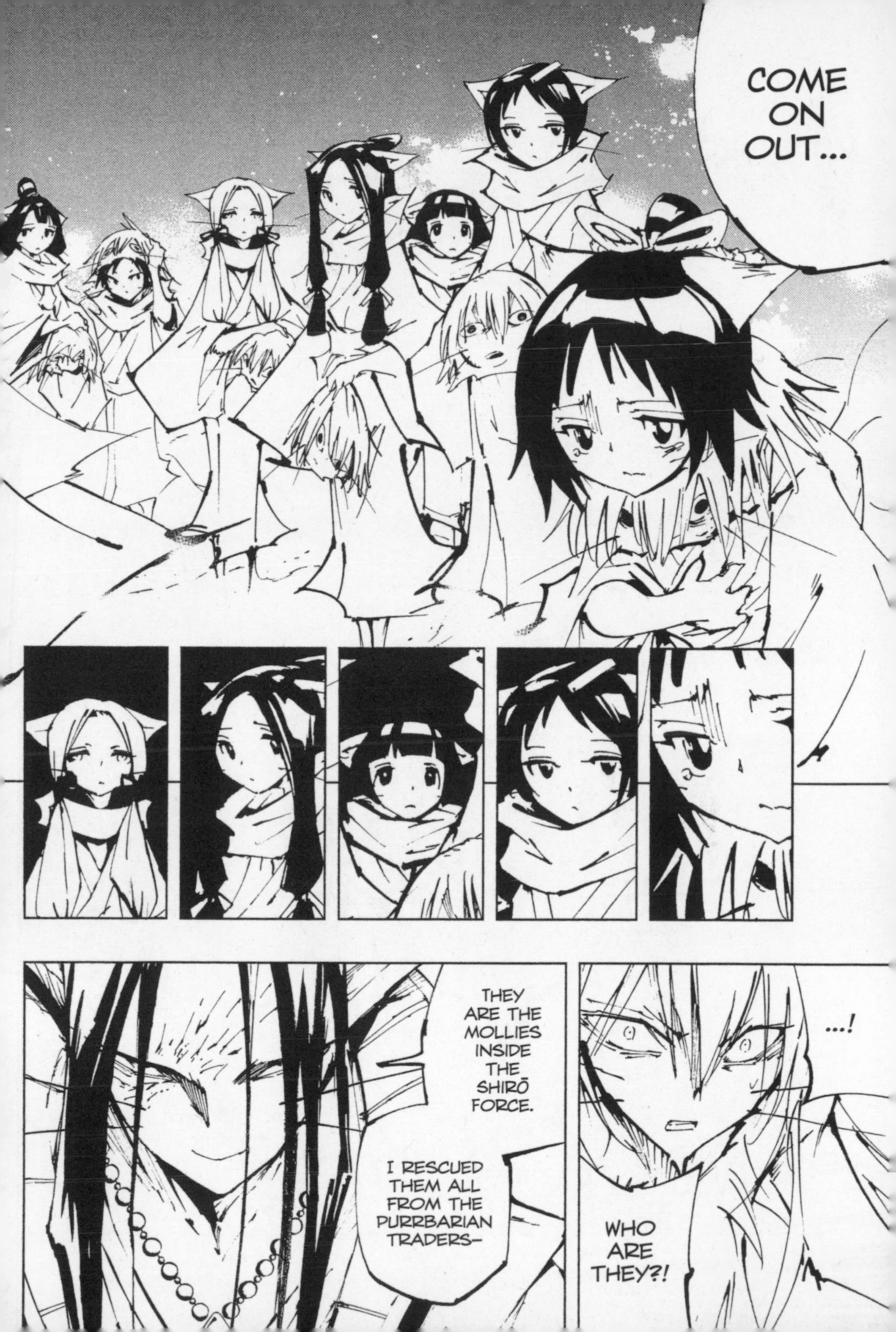
COME ON OUT...
...!
WHO ARE THEY?!
THEY ARE THE MOLLIES INSIDE THE SHIRŌ FORCE.
I RESCUED THEM ALL FROM THE PURRBARIAN TRADERS—

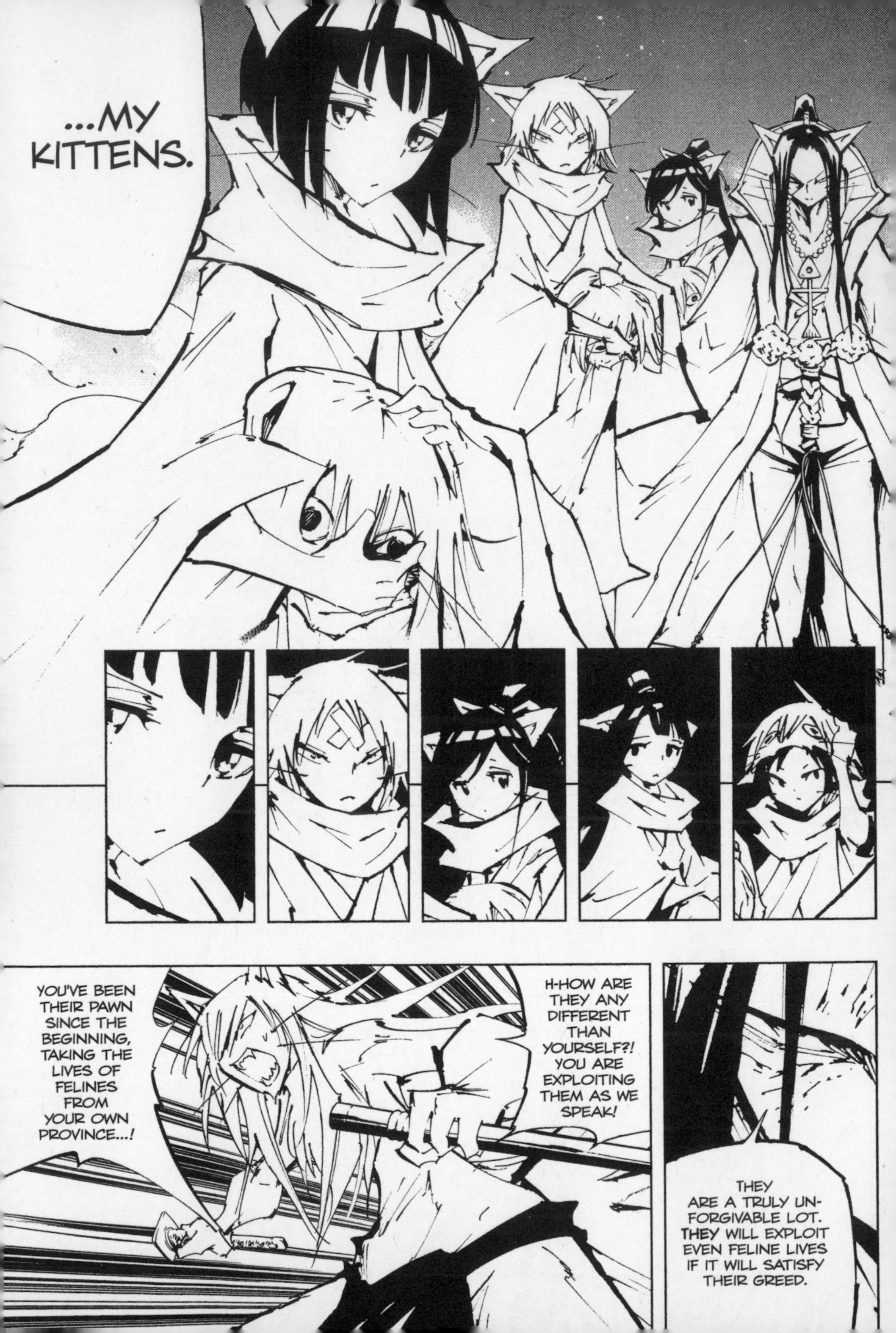
...MY KITTENS.
THEY ARE A TRULY UN-FORGIVABLE LOT. THEY WILL EXPLOIT EVEN FELINE LIVES IF IT WILL SATISFY THEIR GREED.
H-HOW ARE THEY ANY DIFFERENT THAN YOURSELF?! YOU ARE EXPLOITING THEM AS WE SPEAK!
YOU'VE BEEN THEIR PAWN SINCE THE BEGINNING, TAKING THE LIVES OF FELINES FROM YOUR OWN PROVINCE...!

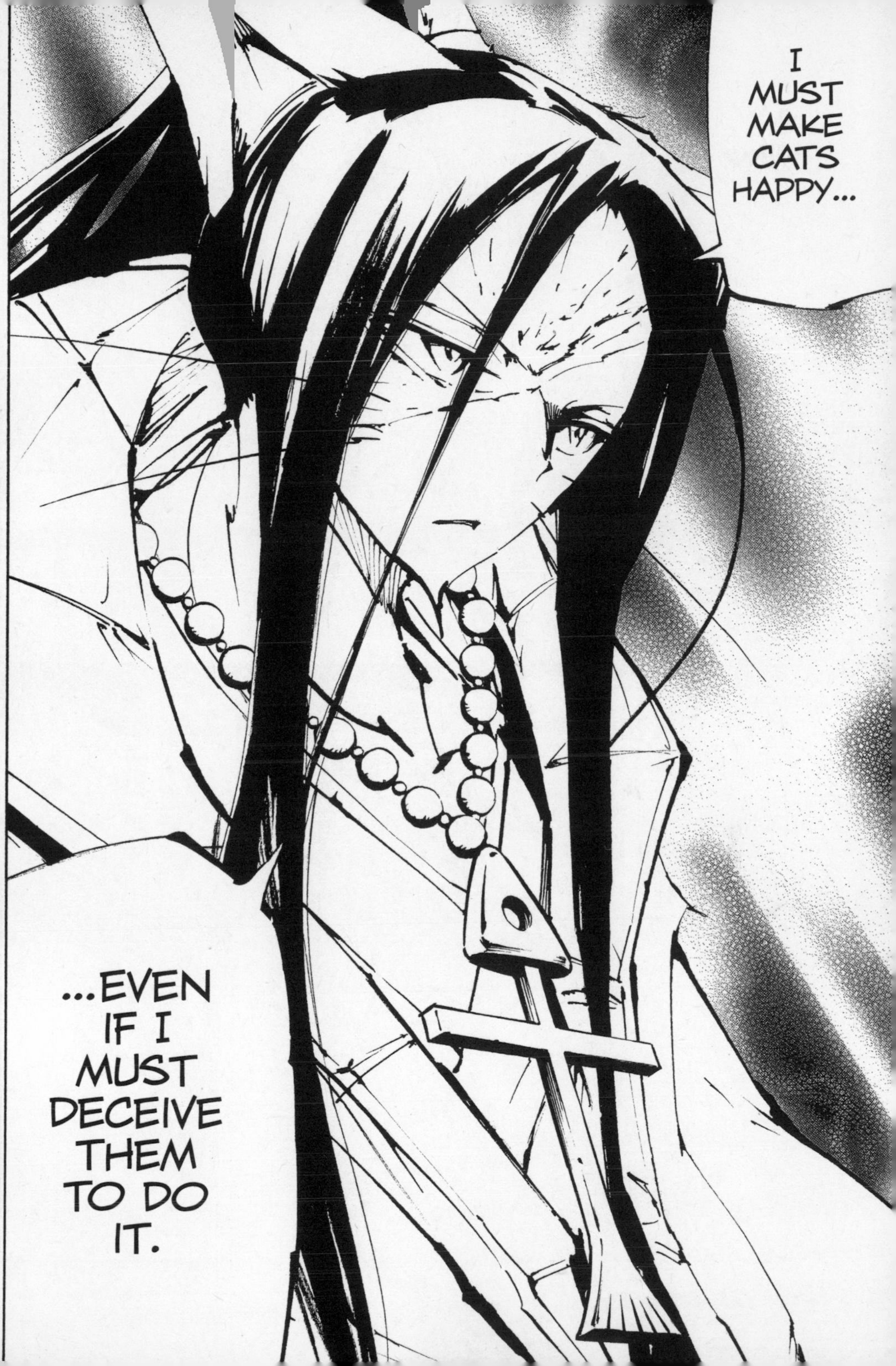
I MUST MAKE CATS HAPPY...
...EVEN IF I MUST DECEIVE THEM TO DO IT.

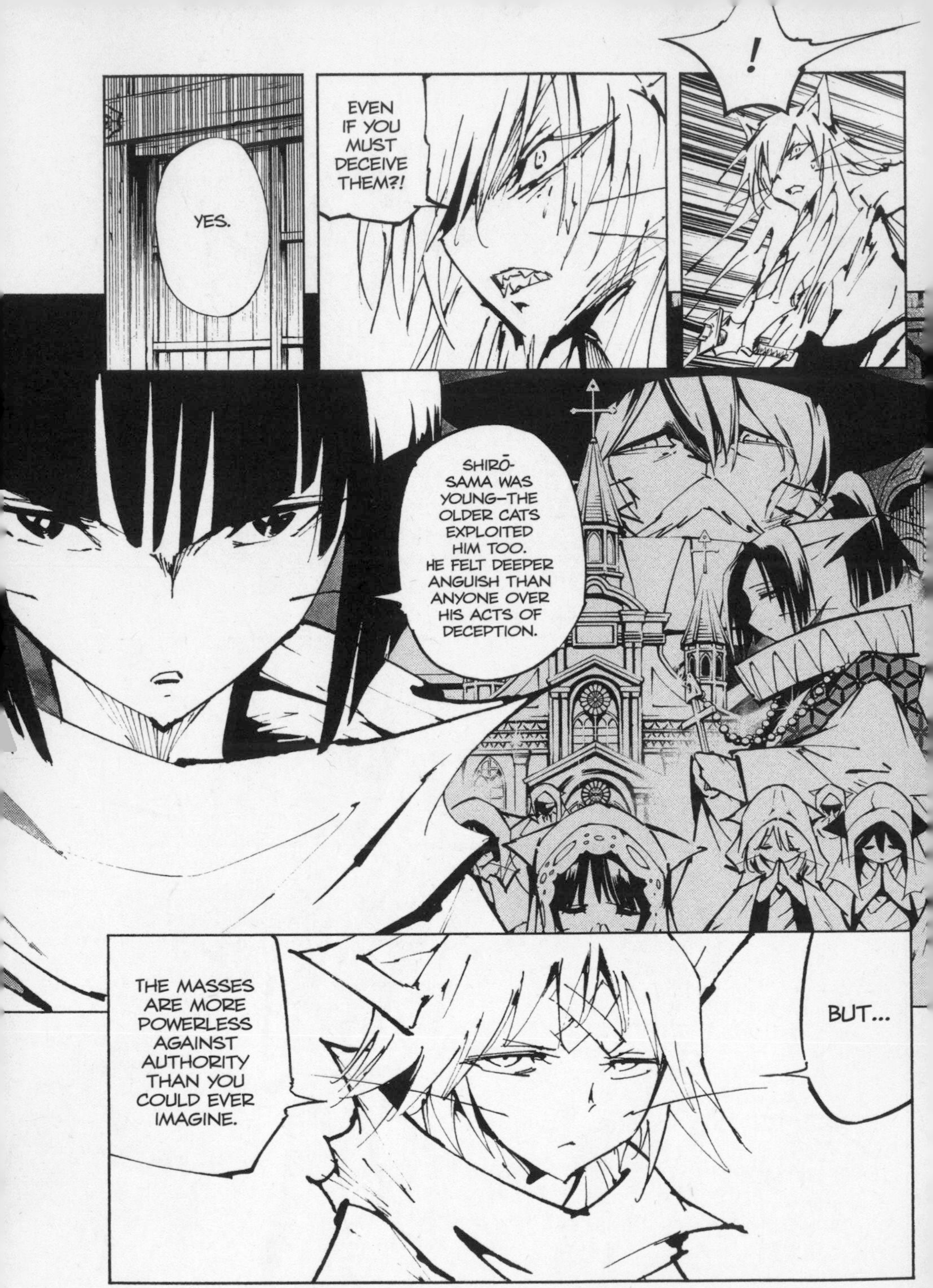
!
EVEN IF YOU MUST DECEIVE THEM?!
YES.
SHIRŌ-SAMA WAS YOUNG—THE OLDER CATS EXPLOITED HIM TOO. HE FELT DEEPER ANGUISH THAN ANYONE OVER HIS ACTS OF DECEPTION.
BUT...
THE MASSES ARE MORE POWERLESS AGAINST AUTHORITY THAN YOU COULD EVER IMAGINE.

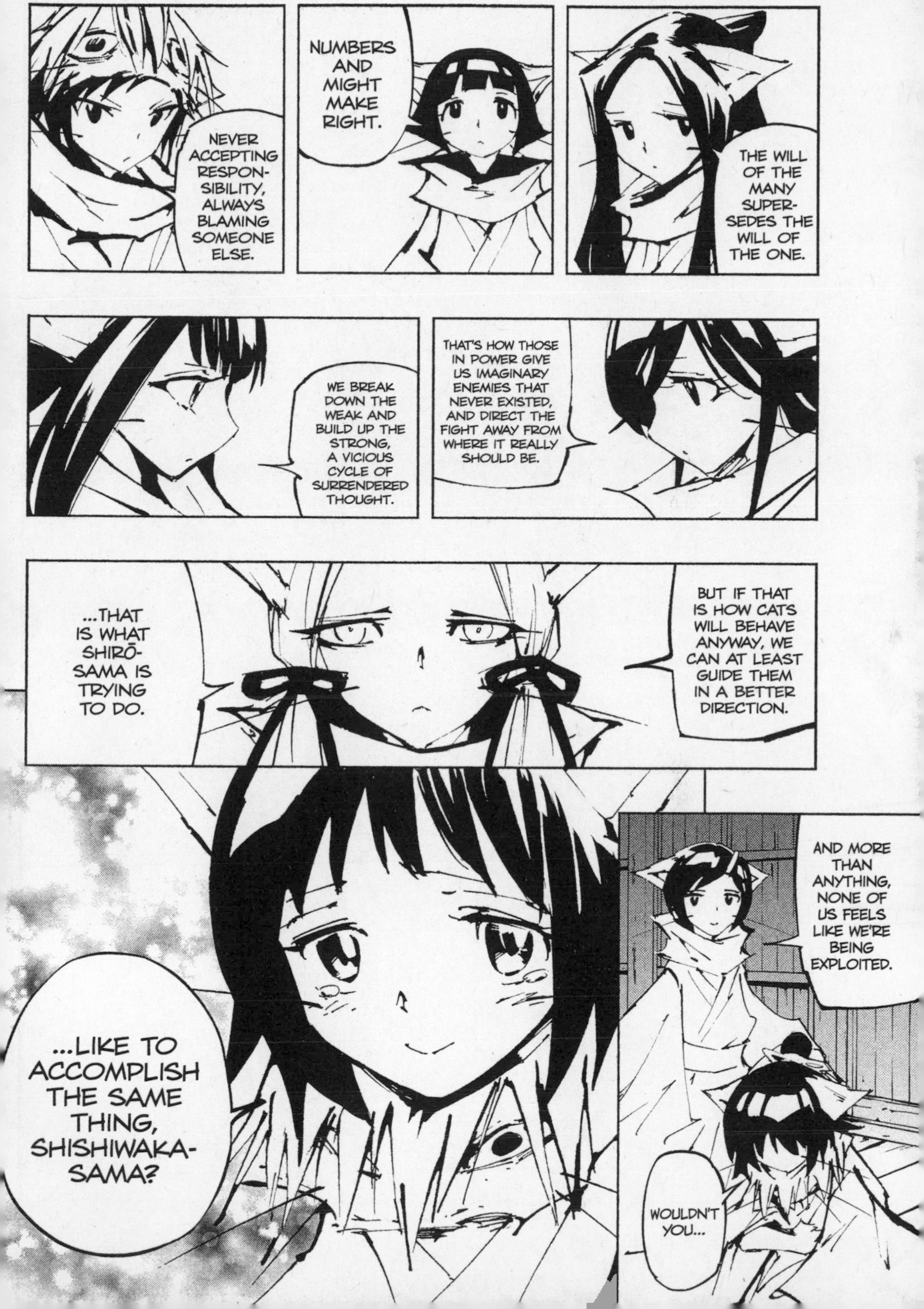
THE WILL OF THE MANY SUPERSEDES THE WILL OF THE ONE.
NUMBERS AND MIGHT MAKE RIGHT.
NEVER ACCEPTING RESPONSIBILITY, ALWAYS BLAMING SOMEONE ELSE.
THAT'S HOW THOSE IN POWER GIVE US IMAGINARY ENEMIES THAT NEVER EXISTED, AND DIRECT THE FIGHT AWAY FROM WHERE IT REALLY SHOULD BE.
WE BREAK DOWN THE WEAK AND BUILD UP THE STRONG, A VICIOUS CYCLE OF SURRENDERED THOUGHT.
BUT IF THAT IS HOW CATS WILL BEHAVE ANYWAY, WE CAN AT LEAST GUIDE THEM IN A BETTER DIRECTION.
...THAT IS WHAT SHIRŌ-SAMA IS TRYING TO DO.
AND MORE THAN ANYTHING, NONE OF US FEELS LIKE WE'RE BEING EXPLOITED.
WOULDN'T YOU...
...LIKE TO ACCOMPLISH THE SAME THING, SHISHIWAKA-SAMA?

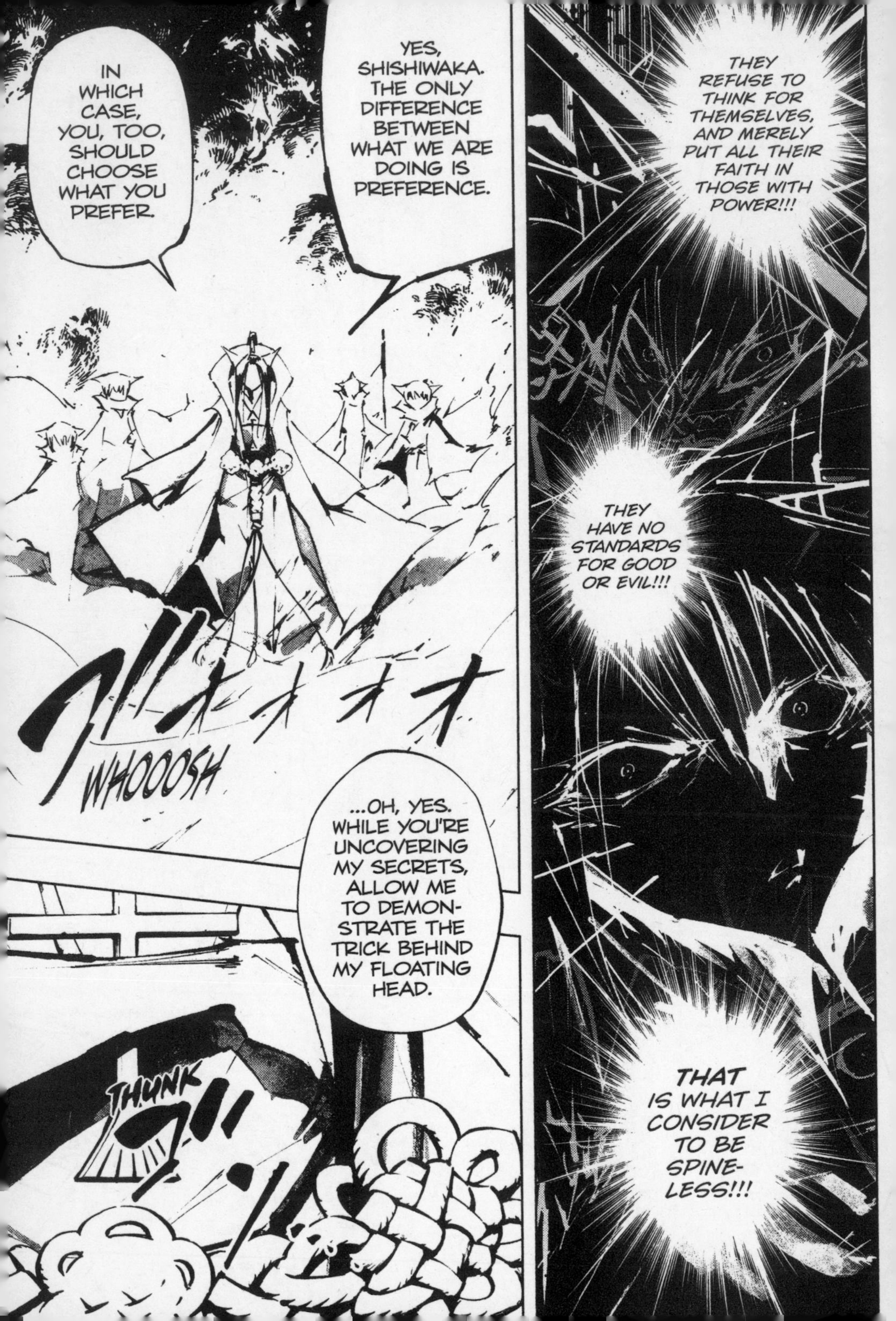
THEY REFUSE TO THINK FOR THEMSELVES, AND MERELY PUT ALL THEIR FAITH IN THOSE WITH POWER!!!
THEY HAVE NO STANDARDS FOR GOOD OR EVIL!!!
THAT IS WHAT I CONSIDER TO BE SPINELESS!!!
YES, SHISHIWAKA. THE ONLY DIFFERENCE BETWEEN WHAT WE ARE DOING IS PREFERENCE.
IN WHICH CASE, YOU, TOO, SHOULD CHOOSE WHAT YOU PREFER.
WHOOOSH
...OH, YES. WHILE YOU'RE UNCOVERING MY SECRETS, ALLOW ME TO DEMONSTRATE THE TRICK BEHIND MY FLOATING HEAD.
THUNK

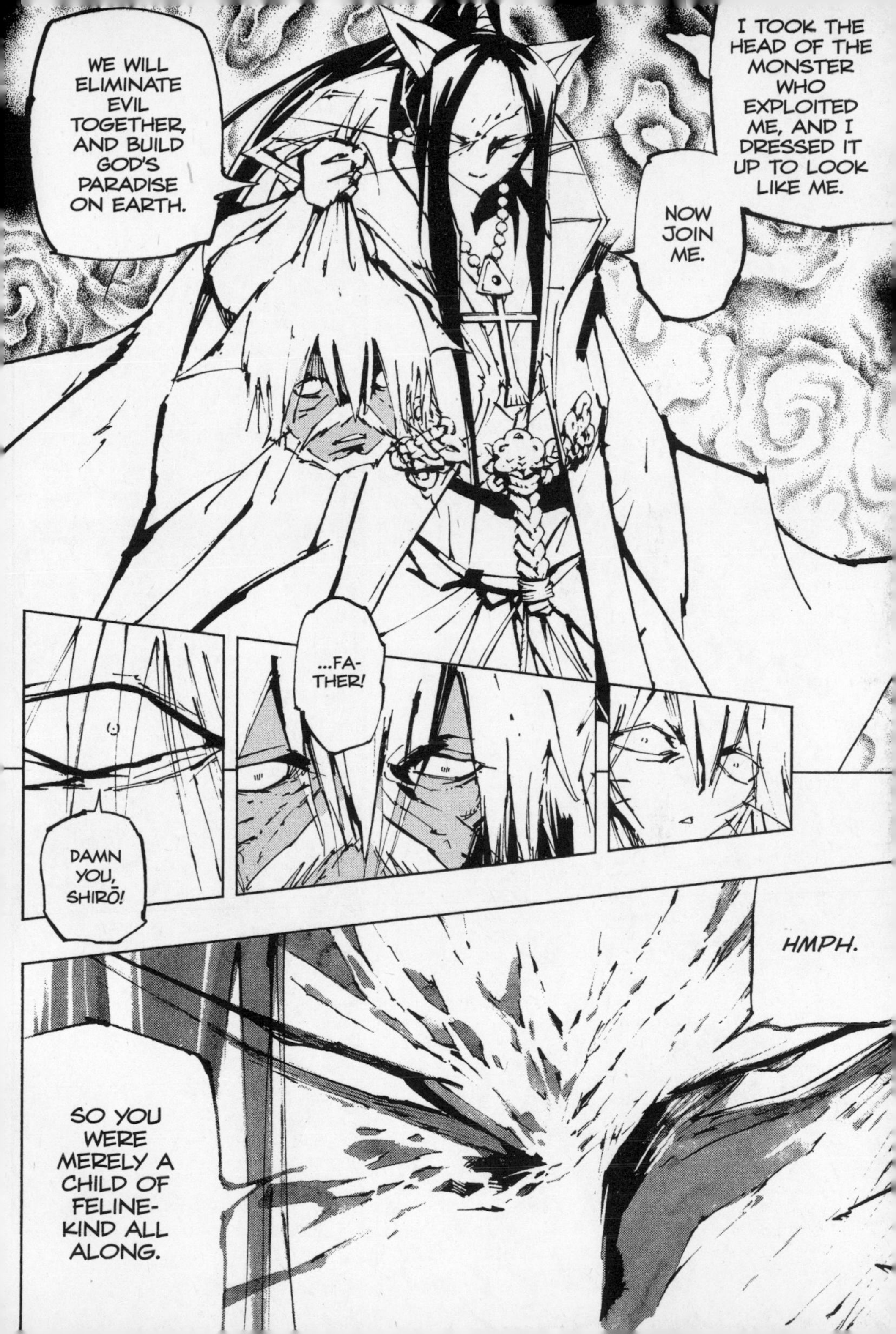
I TOOK THE HEAD OF THE MONSTER WHO EXPLOITED ME, AND I DRESSED IT UP TO LOOK LIKE ME.
NOW JOIN ME.
WE WILL ELIMINATE EVIL TOGETHER, AND BUILD GOD'S PARADISE ON EARTH.
...FA-THER!
DAMN YOU, SHIRŌ!
HMPH.
SO YOU WERE MERELY A CHILD OF FELINE-KIND ALL ALONG.

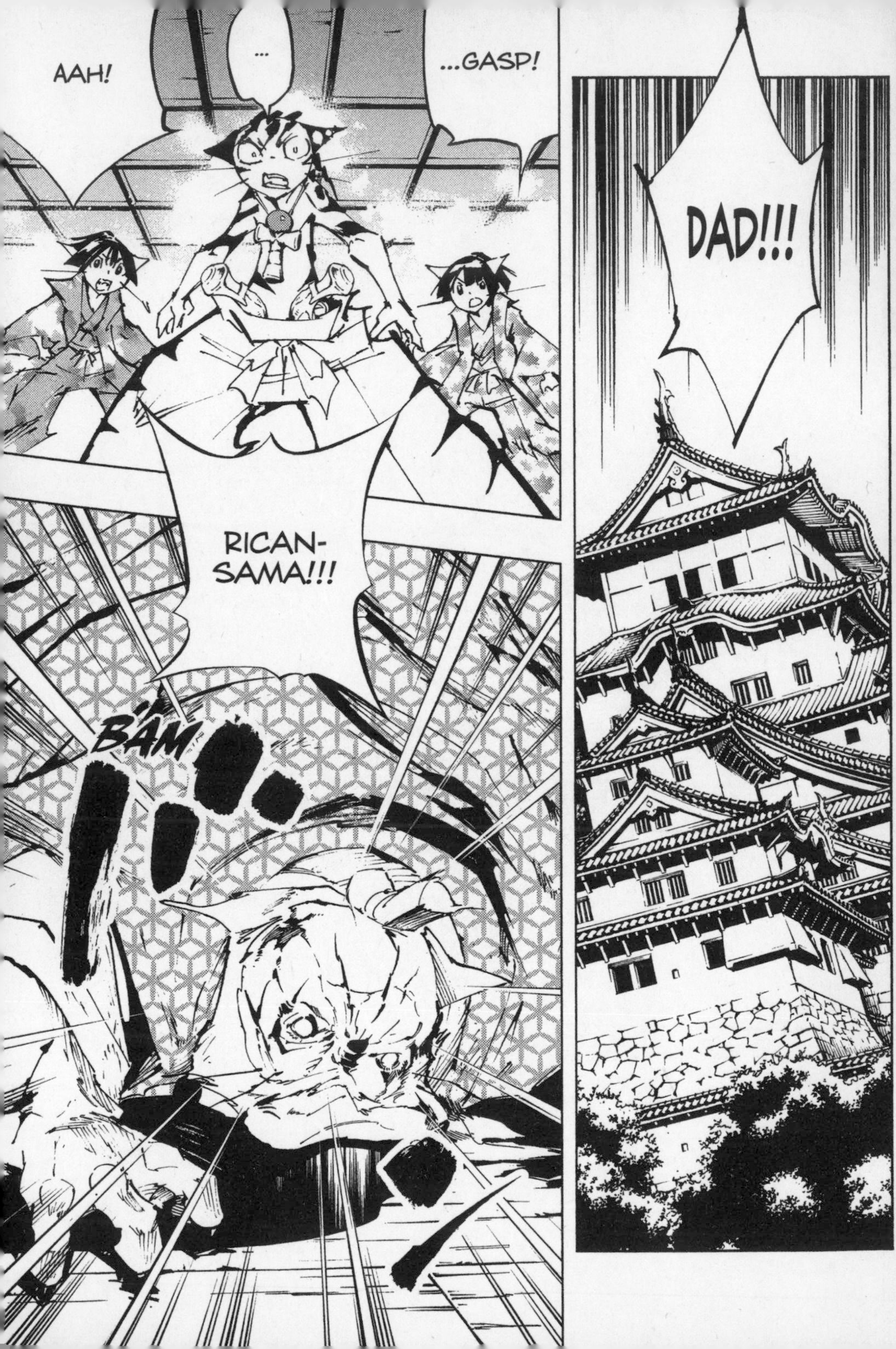
DAD!!!
...GASP!
...
AAH!
RICAN-
SAMA!!!
BAM

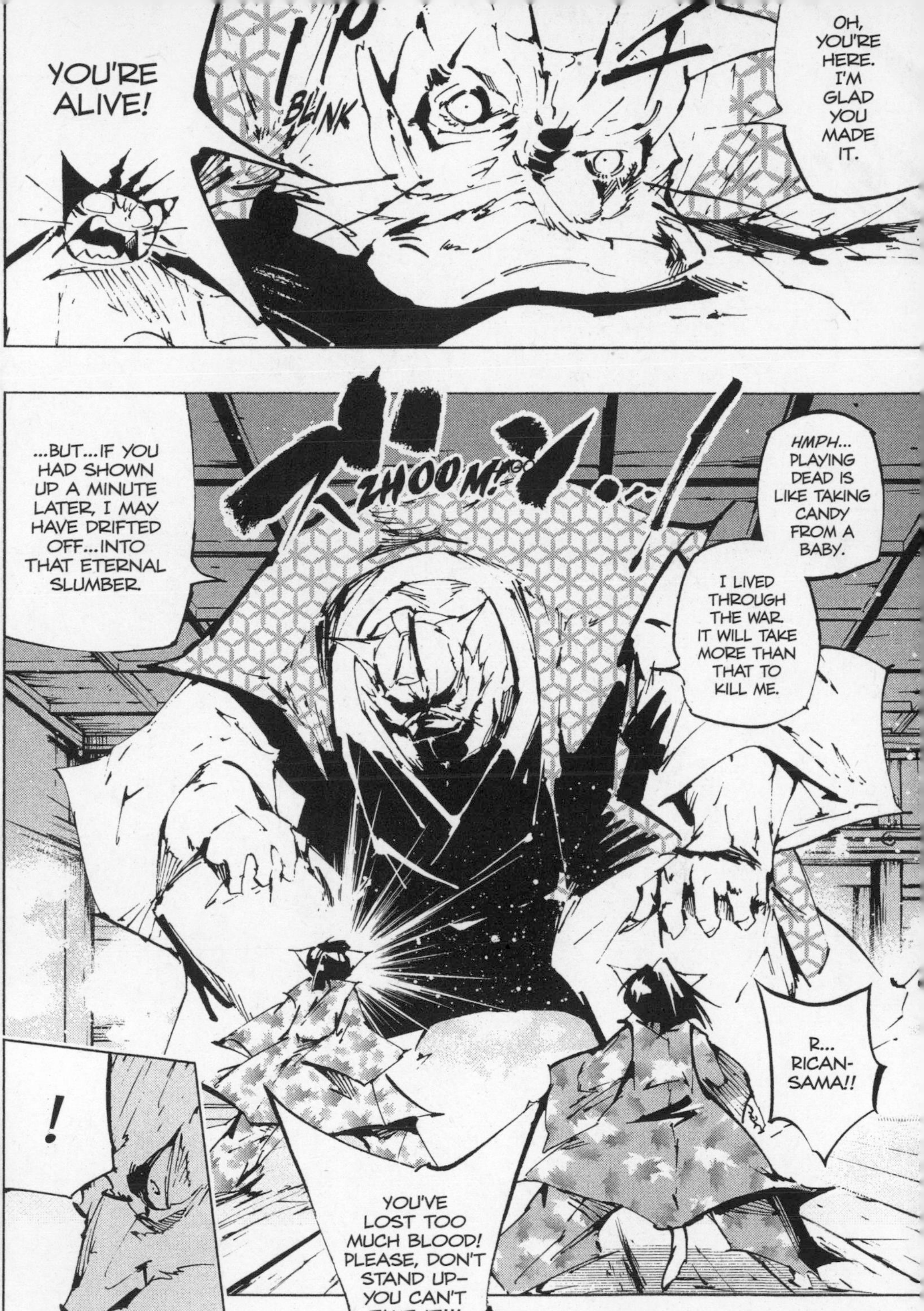
OH, YOU'RE HERE. I'M GLAD YOU MADE IT.
BLINK
YOU'RE ALIVE!
HMPH... PLAYING DEAD IS LIKE TAKING CANDY FROM A BABY.
I LIVED THROUGH THE WAR. IT WILL TAKE MORE THAN THAT TO KILL ME.
ZHOOM!
...BUT...IF YOU HAD SHOWN UP A MINUTE LATER, I MAY HAVE DRIFTED OFF...INTO THAT ETERNAL SLUMBER.
R... RICAN-SAMA!!
YOU'VE LOST TOO MUCH BLOOD! PLEASE, DON'T STAND UP– YOU CAN'T TAKE IT!!!
!

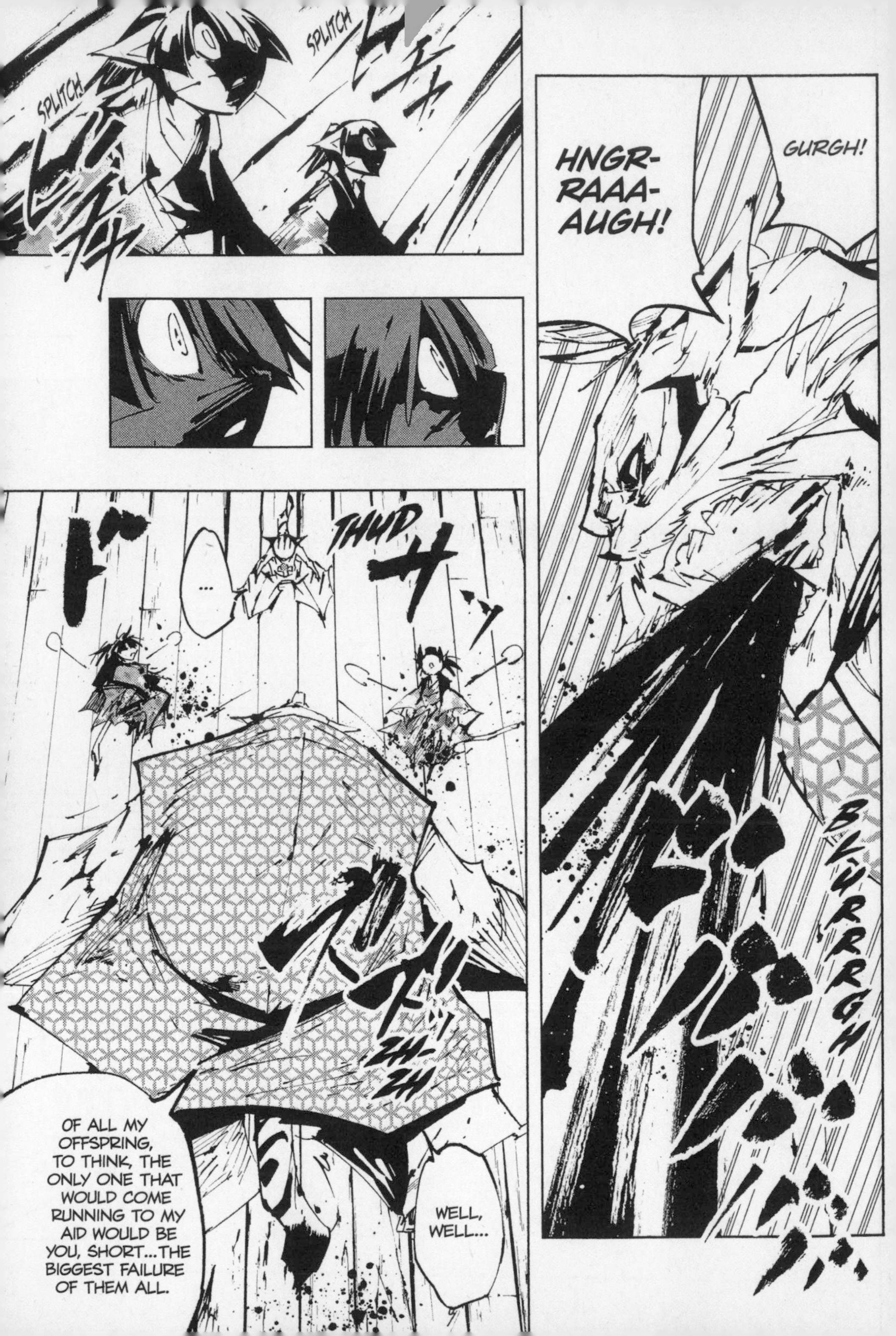
GURGH!
HNGR-RAAA-AUGH!
BLURRRRGH
SPLITCH
SPLITCH
THUD
...
ZAH-ZAH
WELL, WELL...
OF ALL MY OFFSPRING, TO THINK, THE ONLY ONE THAT WOULD COME RUNNING TO MY AID WOULD BE YOU, SHORT...THE BIGGEST FAILURE OF THEM ALL.

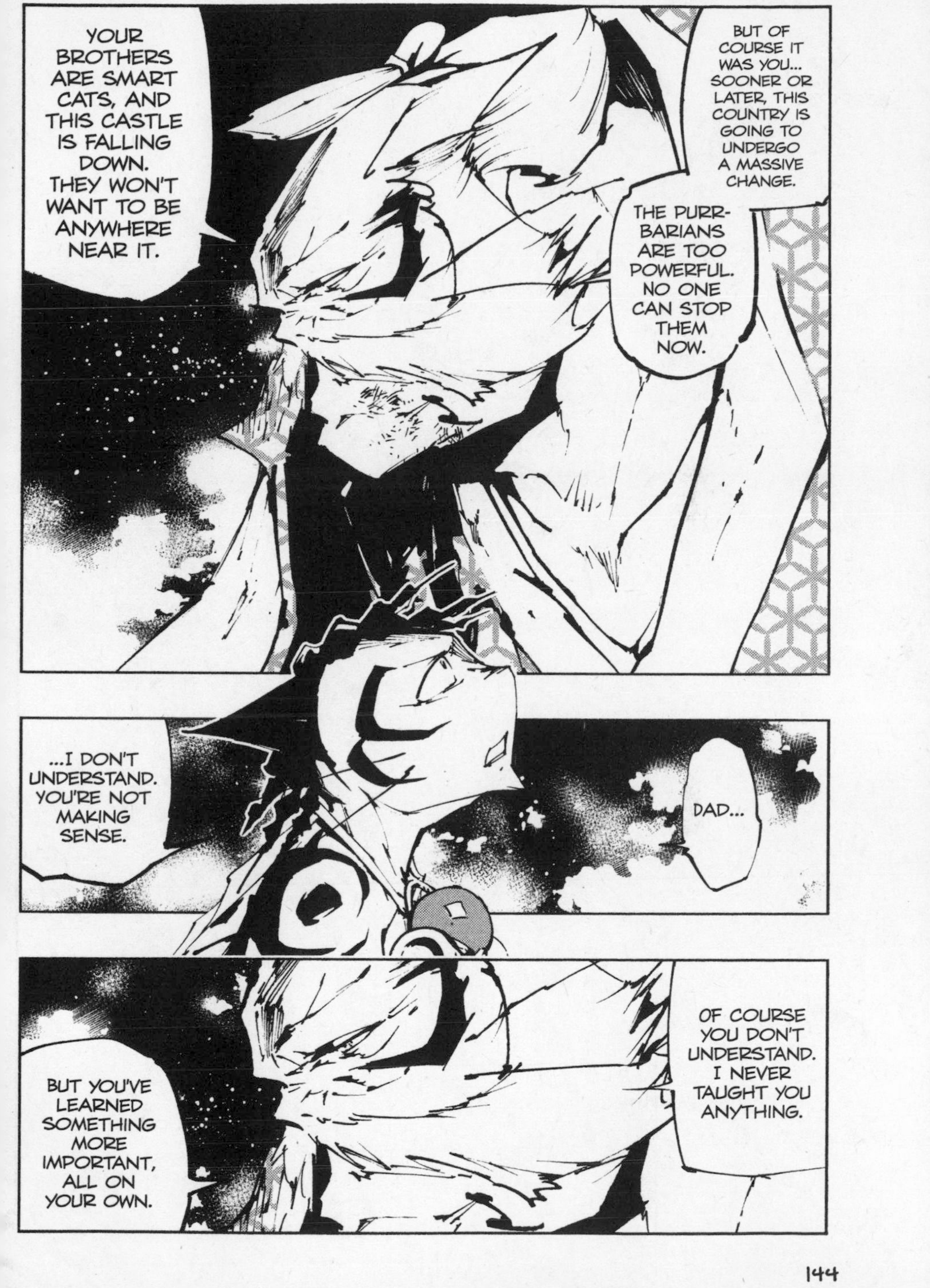
BUT OF COURSE IT WAS YOU... SOONER OR LATER, THIS COUNTRY IS GOING TO UNDERGO A MASSIVE CHANGE.
THE PURR-BARIANS ARE TOO POWERFUL. NO ONE CAN STOP THEM NOW.
YOUR BROTHERS ARE SMART CATS, AND THIS CASTLE IS FALLING DOWN. THEY WON'T WANT TO BE ANYWHERE NEAR IT.
DAD...
...I DON'T UNDERSTAND. YOU'RE NOT MAKING SENSE.
OF COURSE YOU DON'T UNDERSTAND. I NEVER TAUGHT YOU ANYTHING.
BUT YOU'VE LEARNED SOMETHING MORE IMPORTANT, ALL ON YOUR OWN.

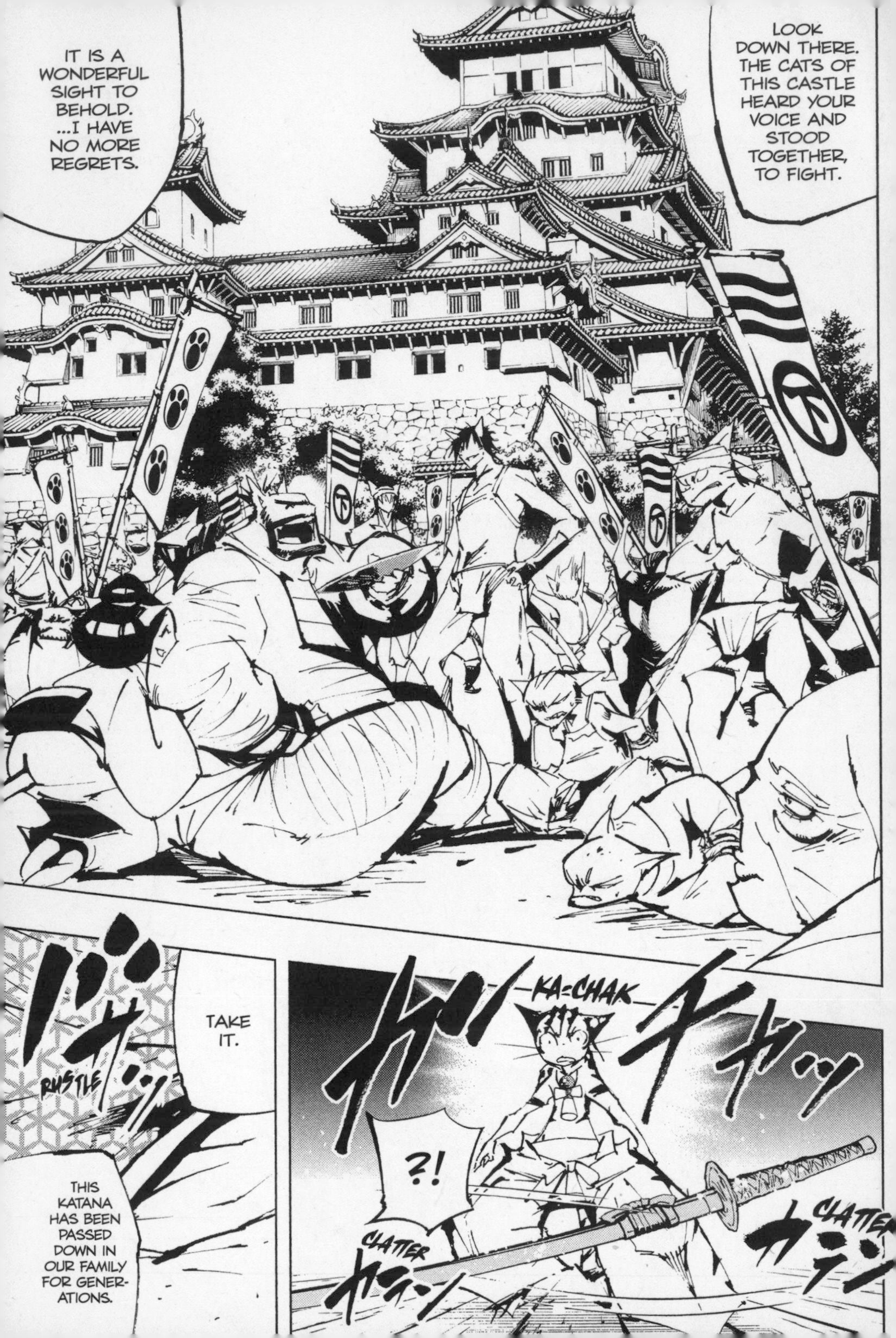
LOOK DOWN THERE. THE CATS OF THIS CASTLE HEARD YOUR VOICE AND STOOD TOGETHER, TO FIGHT.
IT IS A WONDERFUL SIGHT TO BEHOLD. ...I HAVE NO MORE REGRETS.
KA-CHAK
CLATTER
?!
CLATTER
TAKE IT.
RUSTLE
THIS KATANA HAS BEEN PASSED DOWN IN OUR FAMILY FOR GENERATIONS.

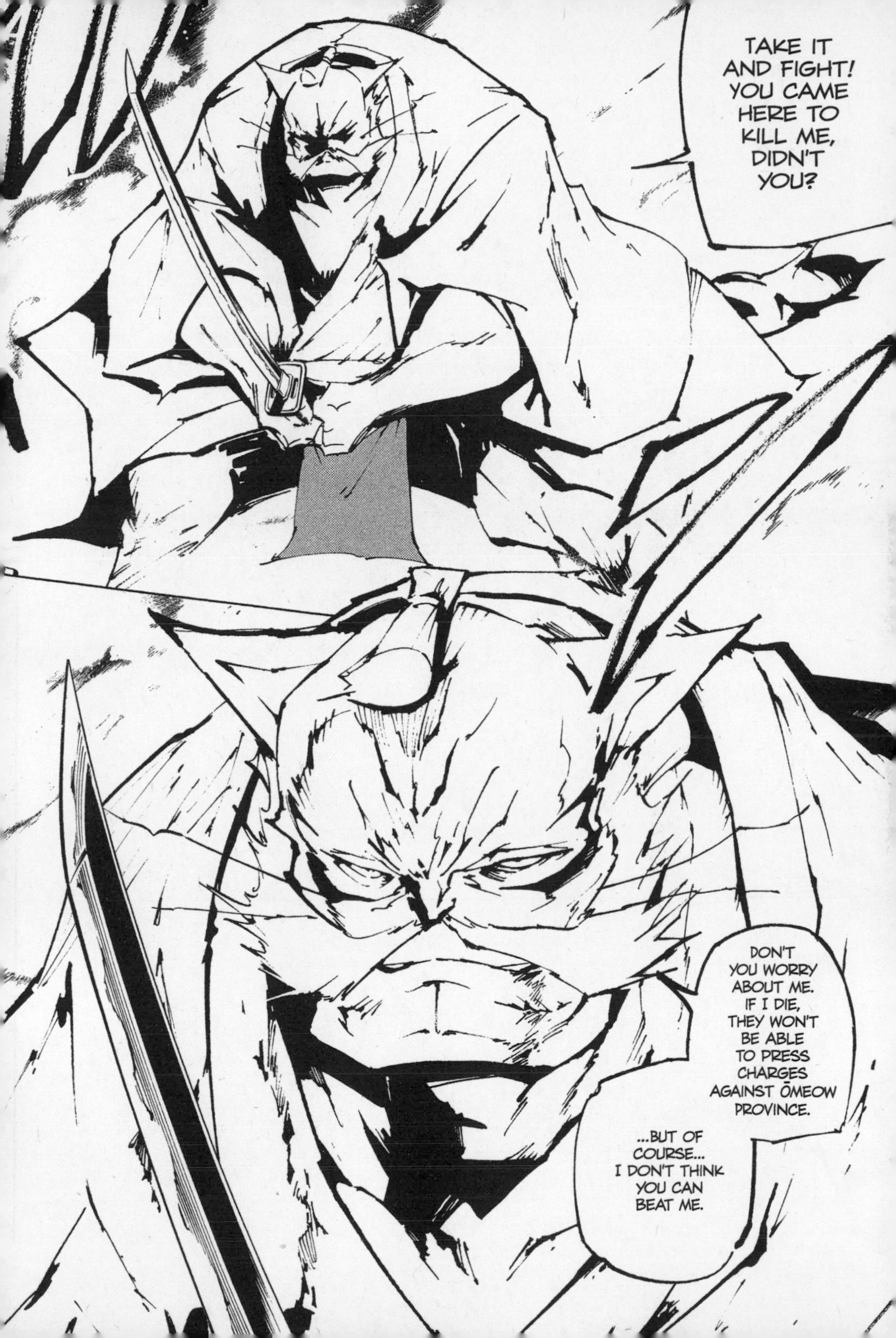
TAKE IT AND FIGHT! YOU CAME HERE TO KILL ME, DIDN'T YOU?
DON'T YOU WORRY ABOUT ME. IF I DIE, THEY WON'T BE ABLE TO PRESS CHARGES AGAINST ŌMEOW PROVINCE.
...BUT OF COURSE... I DON'T THINK YOU CAN BEAT ME.

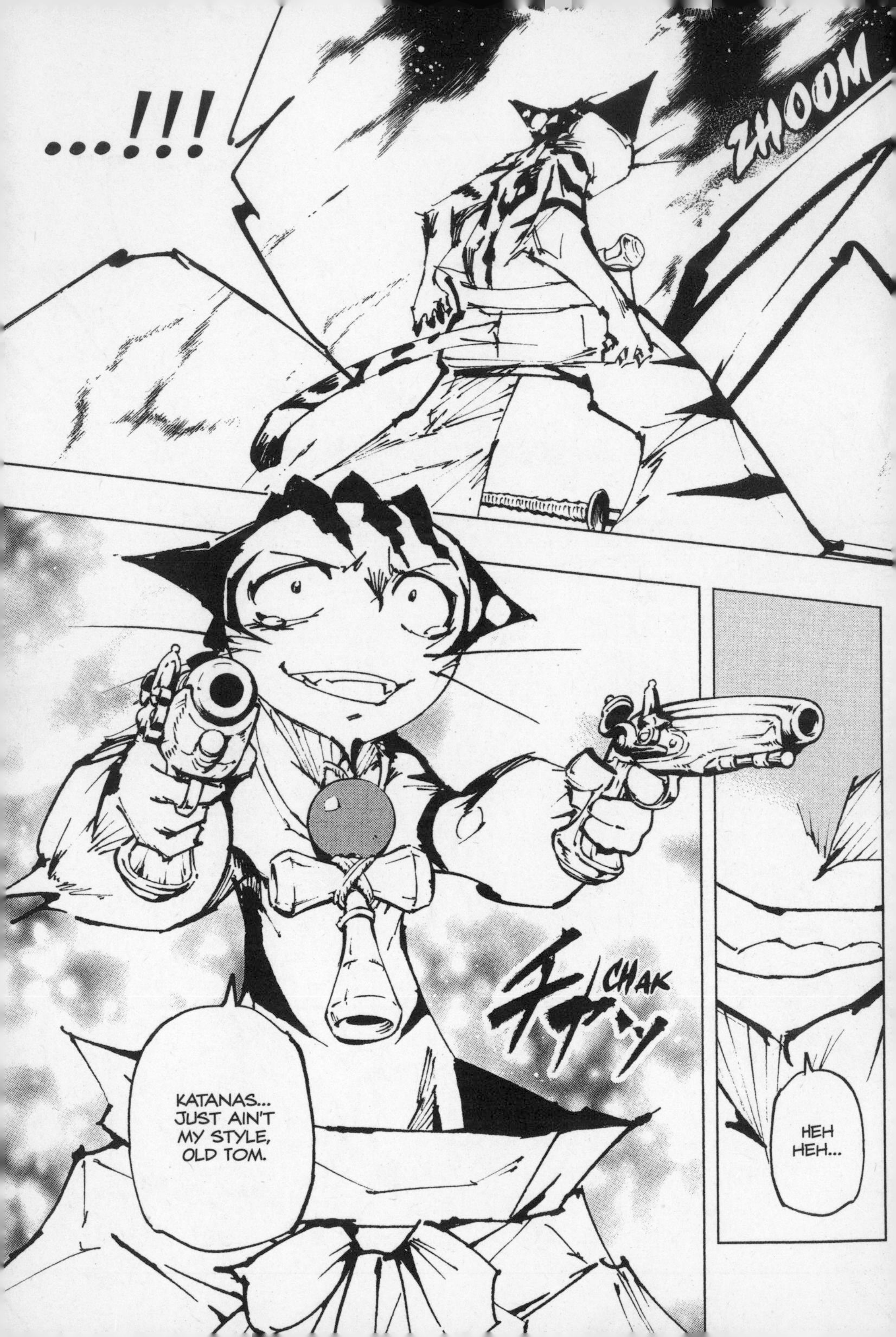
...!!!
ZHOOM
HEH HEH...
CHAK
KATANAS... JUST AIN'T MY STYLE, OLD TOM.

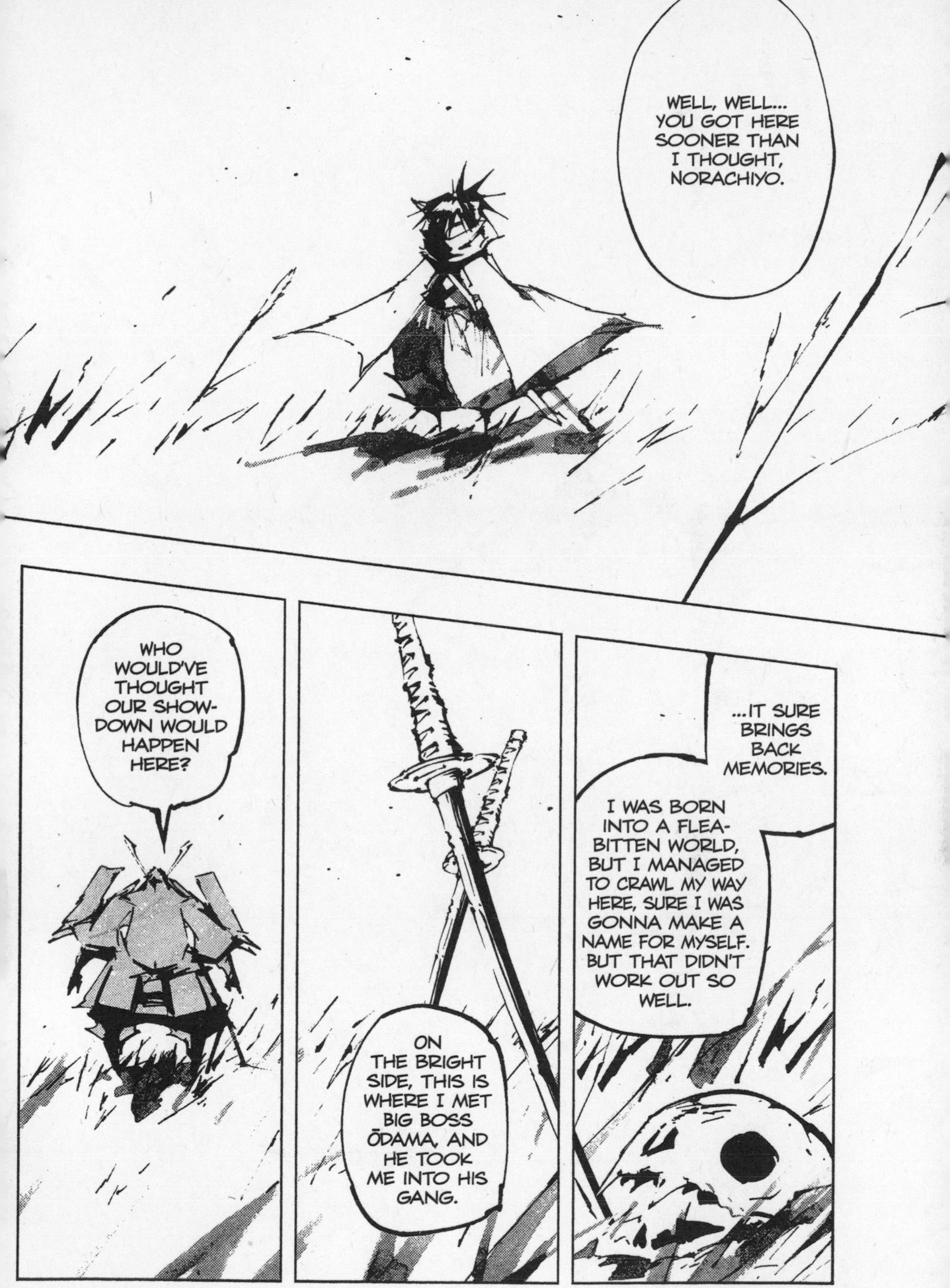
WELL, WELL... YOU GOT HERE SOONER THAN I THOUGHT, NORACHIYO.
...IT SURE BRINGS BACK MEMORIES.
I WAS BORN INTO A FLEA-BITTEN WORLD, BUT I MANAGED TO CRAWL MY WAY HERE, SURE I WAS GONNA MAKE A NAME FOR MYSELF. BUT THAT DIDN'T WORK OUT SO WELL.
ON THE BRIGHT SIDE, THIS IS WHERE I MET BIG BOSS ŌDAMA, AND HE TOOK ME INTO HIS GANG.
WHO WOULD'VE THOUGHT OUR SHOW-DOWN WOULD HAPPEN HERE?

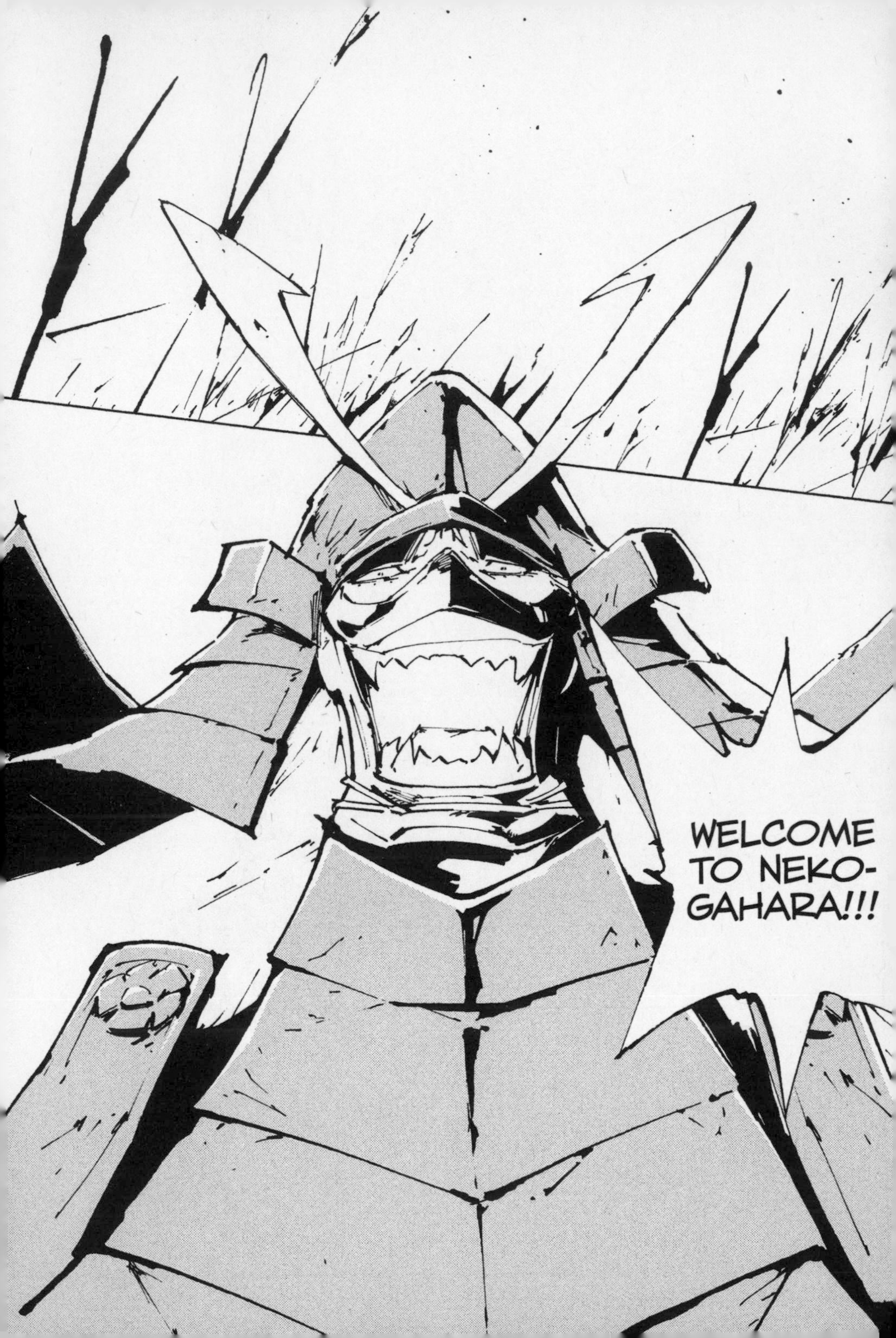
WELCOME TO NEKO-GAHARA!!!

猫ヶ原

NeKoGaHaRa

ネコガハラ

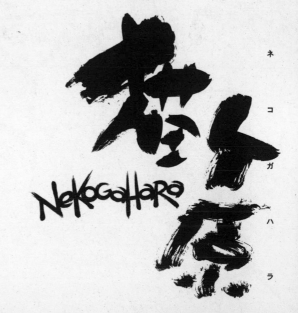

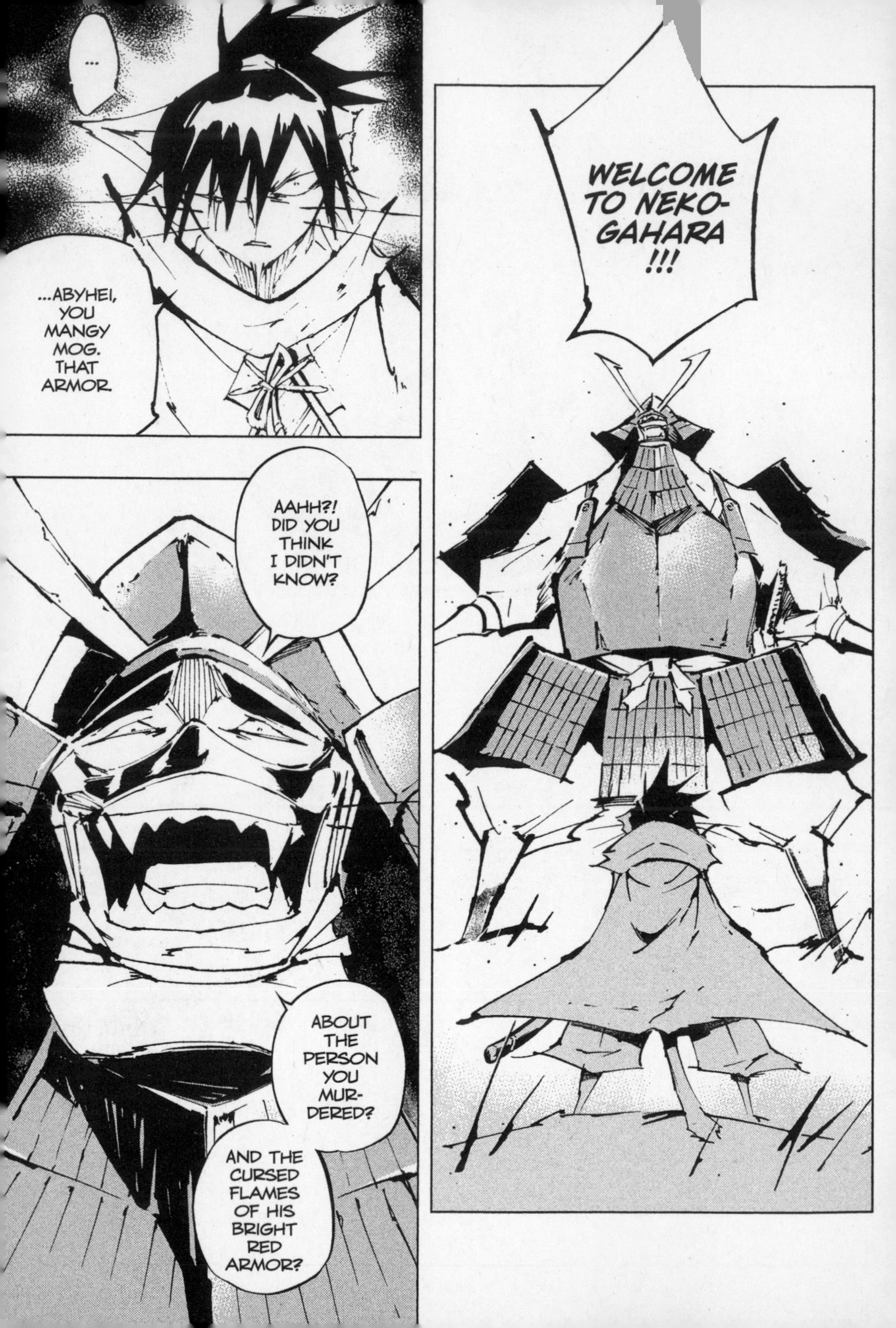
WELCOME TO NEKO-GAHARA !!!
...
...ABYHEI, YOU MANGY MOG. THAT ARMOR.
AAHH?! DID YOU THINK I DIDN'T KNOW?
ABOUT THE PERSON YOU MUR-DERED?
AND THE CURSED FLAMES OF HIS BRIGHT RED ARMOR?

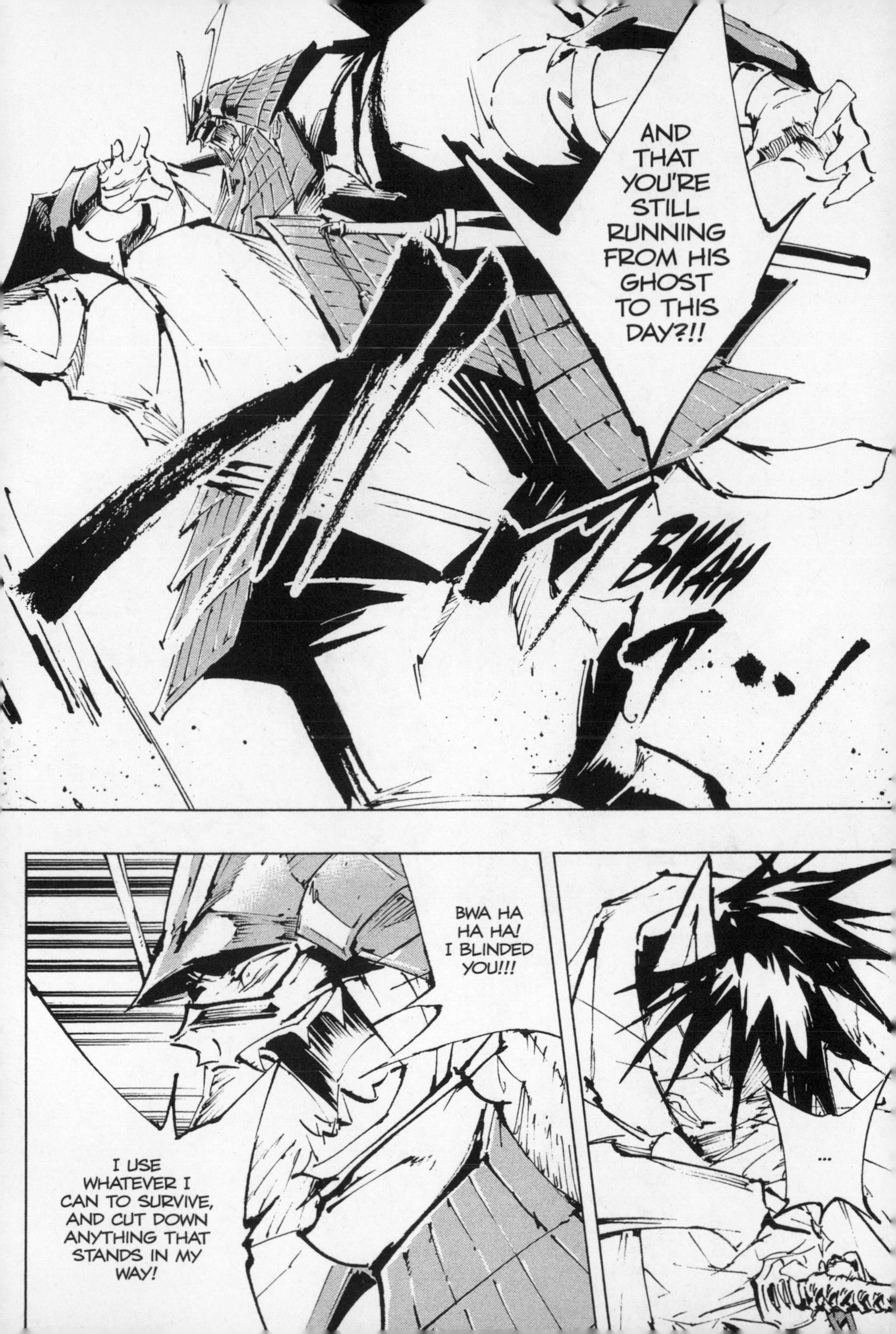
AND THAT YOU'RE STILL RUNNING FROM HIS GHOST TO THIS DAY?!!
BWAH
...
BWA HA HA HA! I BLINDED YOU!!!
I USE WHATEVER I CAN TO SURVIVE, AND CUT DOWN ANYTHING THAT STANDS IN MY WAY!

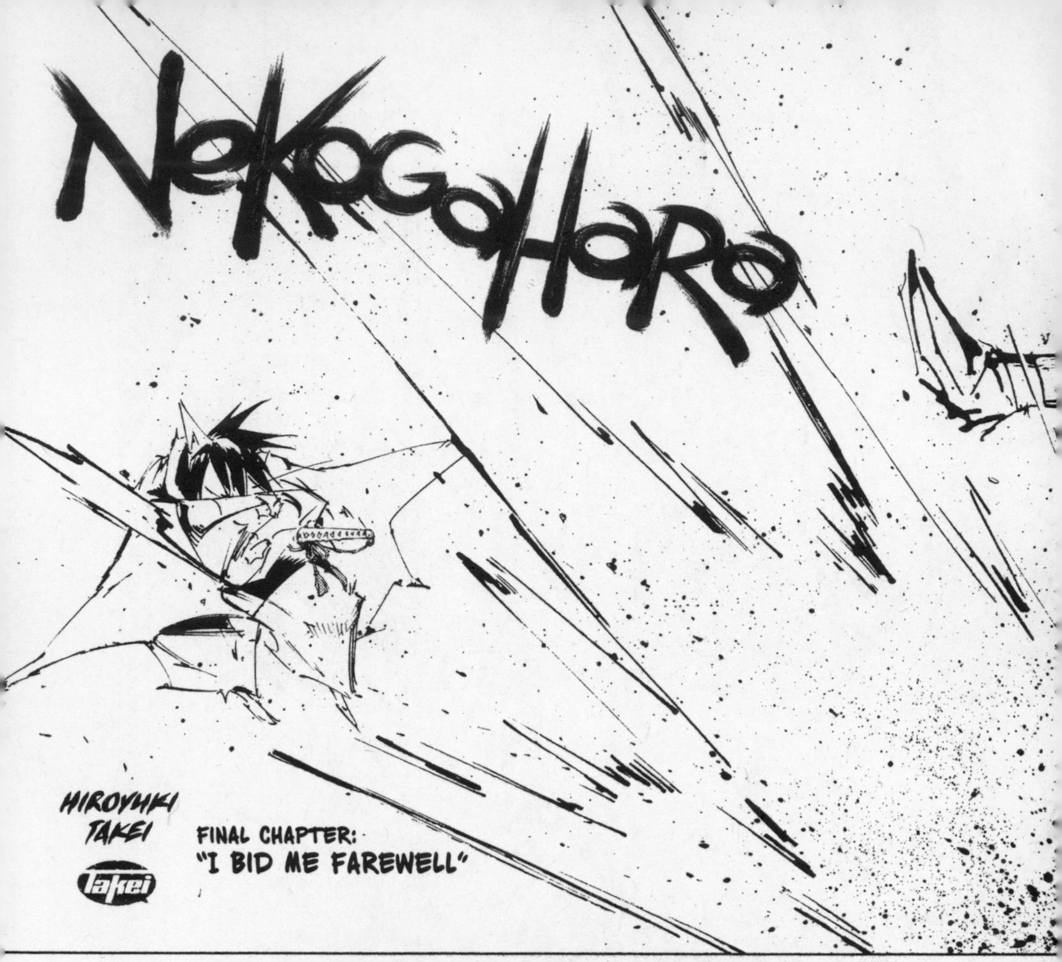
NEKOGAHARA
HIROYUKI TAKEI
FINAL CHAPTER:
"I BID ME FAREWELL"

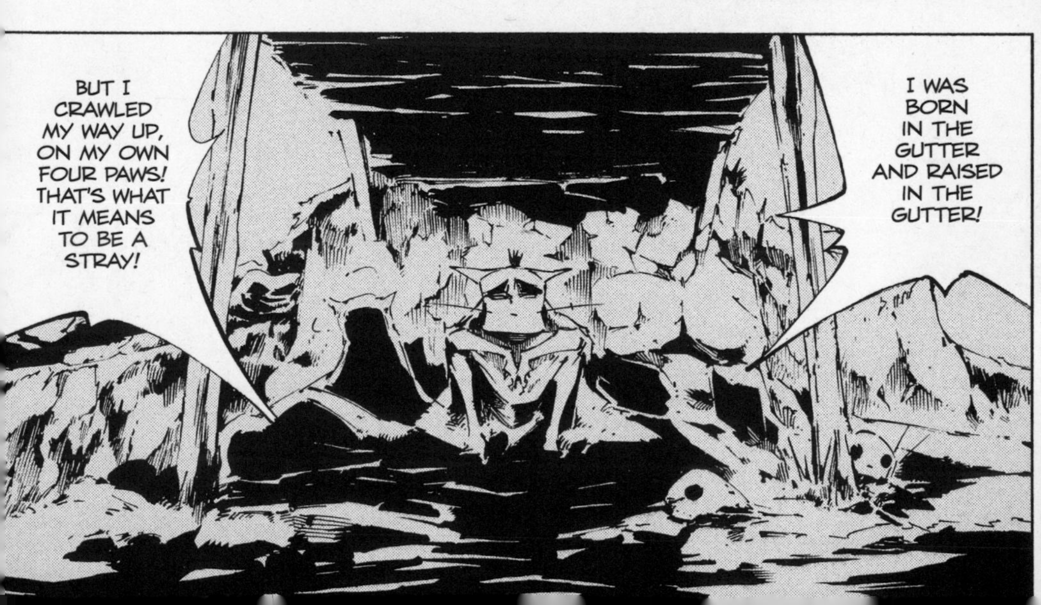
I WAS BORN IN THE GUTTER AND RAISED IN THE GUTTER!
BUT I CRAWLED MY WAY UP, ON MY OWN FOUR PAWS! THAT'S WHAT IT MEANS TO BE A STRAY!

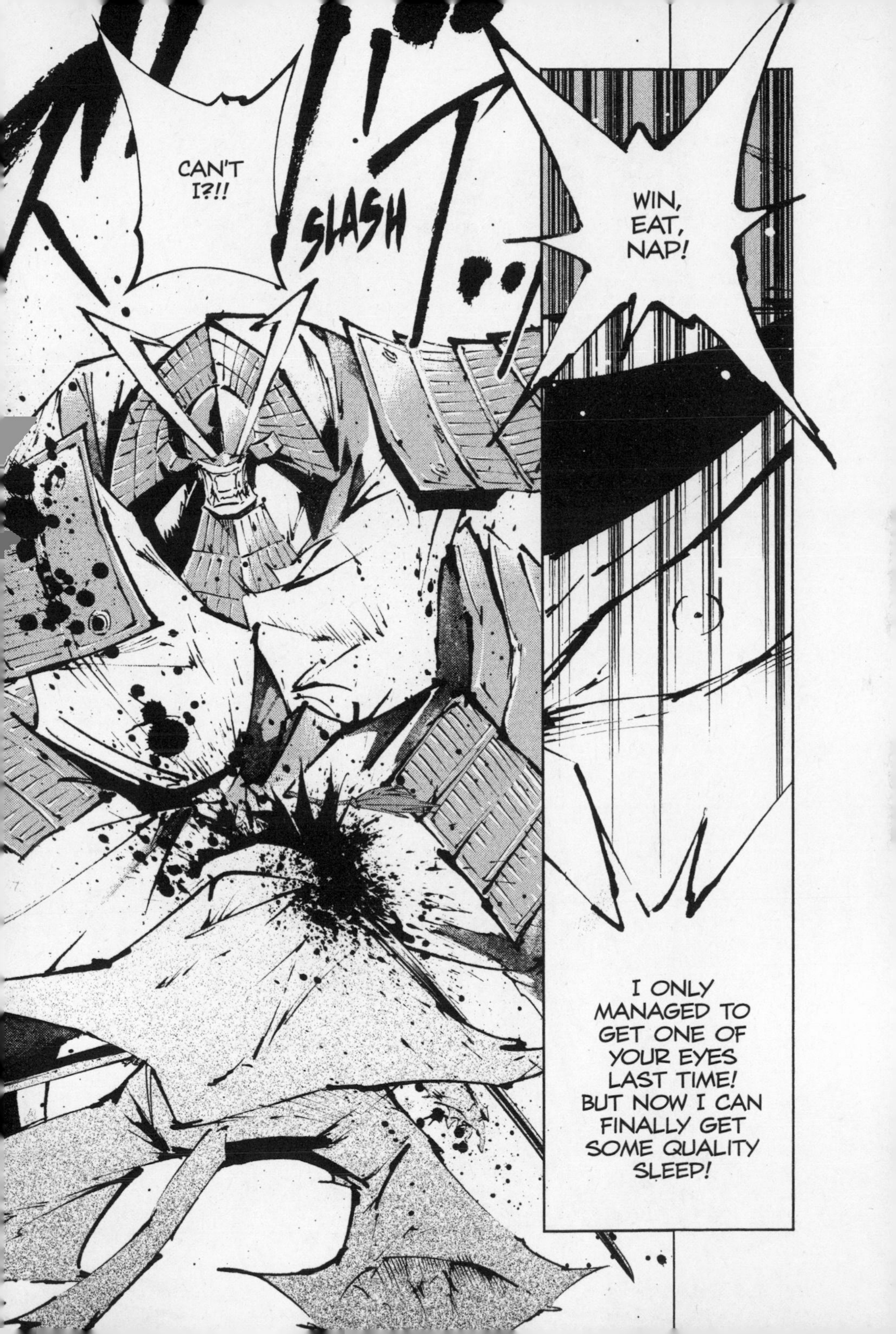
WIN, EAT, NAP!
I ONLY MANAGED TO GET ONE OF YOUR EYES LAST TIME! BUT NOW I CAN FINALLY GET SOME QUALITY SLEEP!
CAN'T I?!!
SLASH

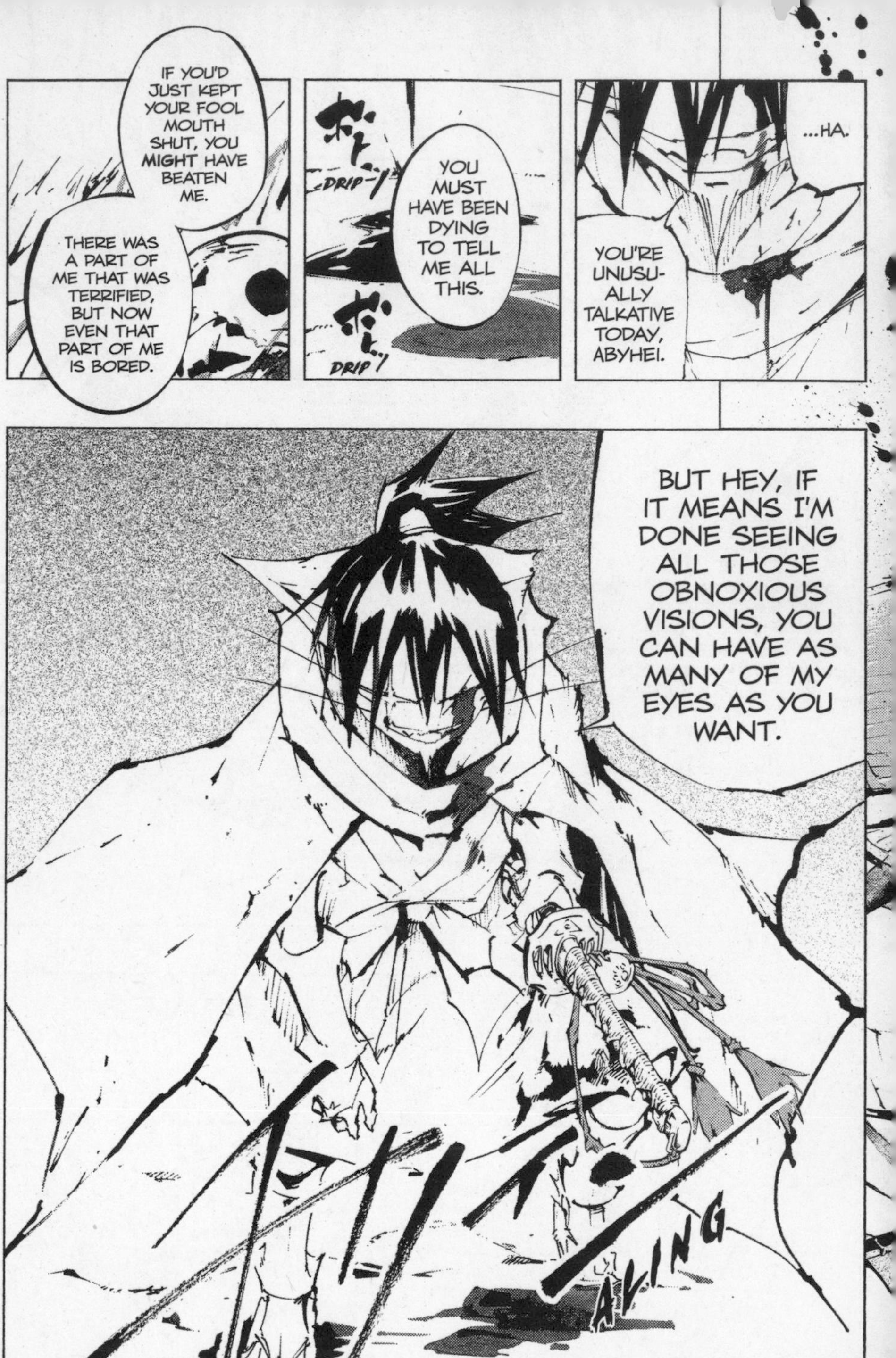
...HA.
YOU'RE UNUSUALLY TALKATIVE TODAY, ABYHEI.
DRIP
YOU MUST HAVE BEEN DYING TO TELL ME ALL THIS.
DRIP
IF YOU'D JUST KEPT YOUR FOOL MOUTH SHUT, YOU MIGHT HAVE BEATEN ME.
THERE WAS A PART OF ME THAT WAS TERRIFIED, BUT NOW EVEN THAT PART OF ME IS BORED.
BUT HEY, IF IT MEANS I'M DONE SEEING ALL THOSE OBNOXIOUS VISIONS, YOU CAN HAVE AS MANY OF MY EYES AS YOU WANT.

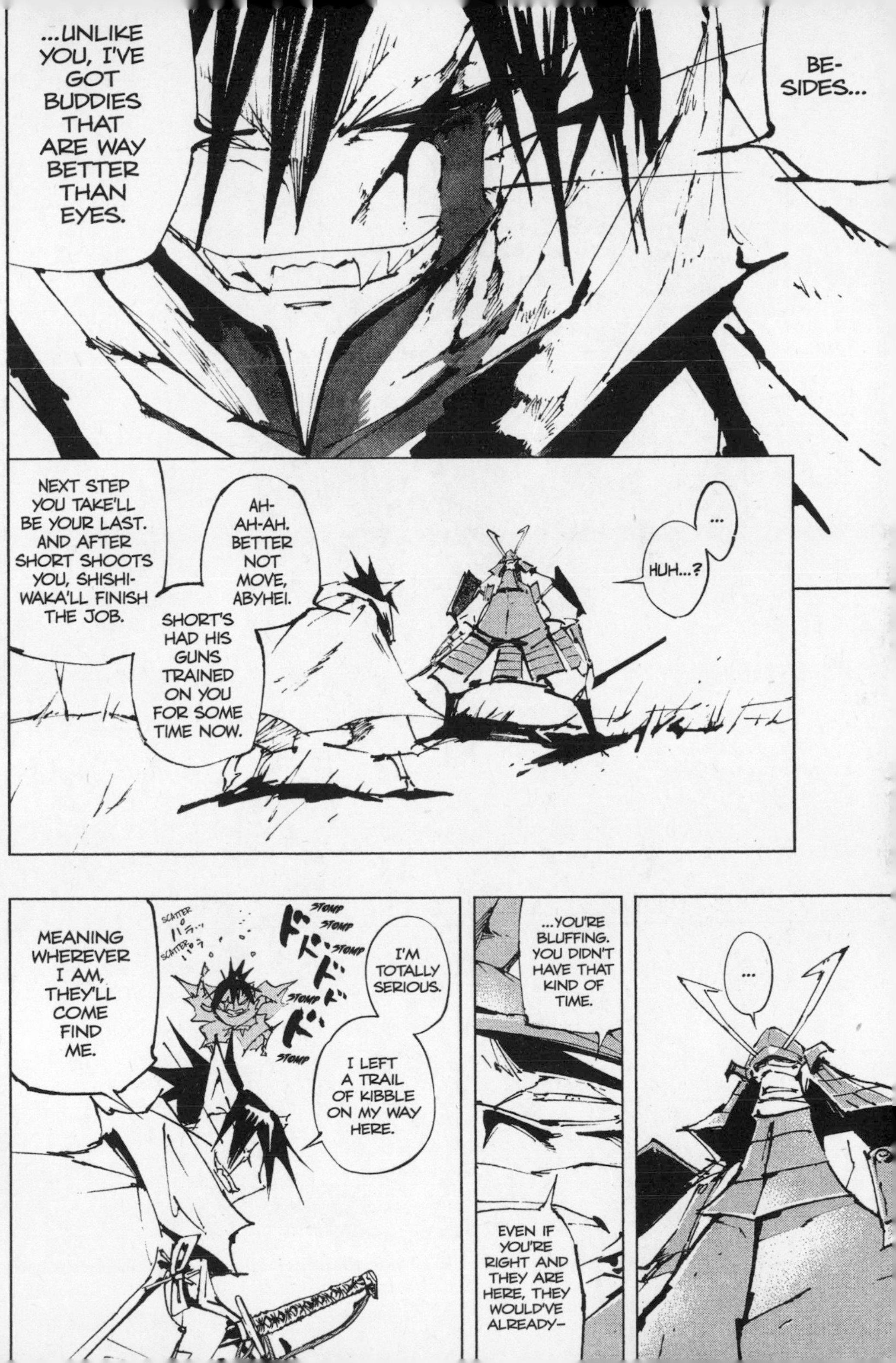
BE-SIDES...
...UNLIKE YOU, I'VE GOT BUDDIES THAT ARE WAY BETTER THAN EYES.
...
HUH...?
AH-AH-AH. BETTER NOT MOVE, ABYHEI.
NEXT STEP YOU TAKE'LL BE YOUR LAST. AND AFTER SHORT SHOOTS YOU, SHISHI-WAKA'LL FINISH THE JOB.
SHORT'S HAD HIS GUNS TRAINED ON YOU FOR SOME TIME NOW.
...
...YOU'RE BLUFFING. YOU DIDN'T HAVE THAT KIND OF TIME.
EVEN IF YOU'RE RIGHT AND THEY ARE HERE, THEY WOULD'VE ALREADY-
I'M TOTALLY SERIOUS.
STOMP STOMP STOMP STOMP STOMP
ドドドド
MEANING WHEREVER I AM, THEY'LL COME FIND ME.
SCATTER SCATTER
I LEFT A TRAIL OF KIBBLE ON MY WAY HERE.

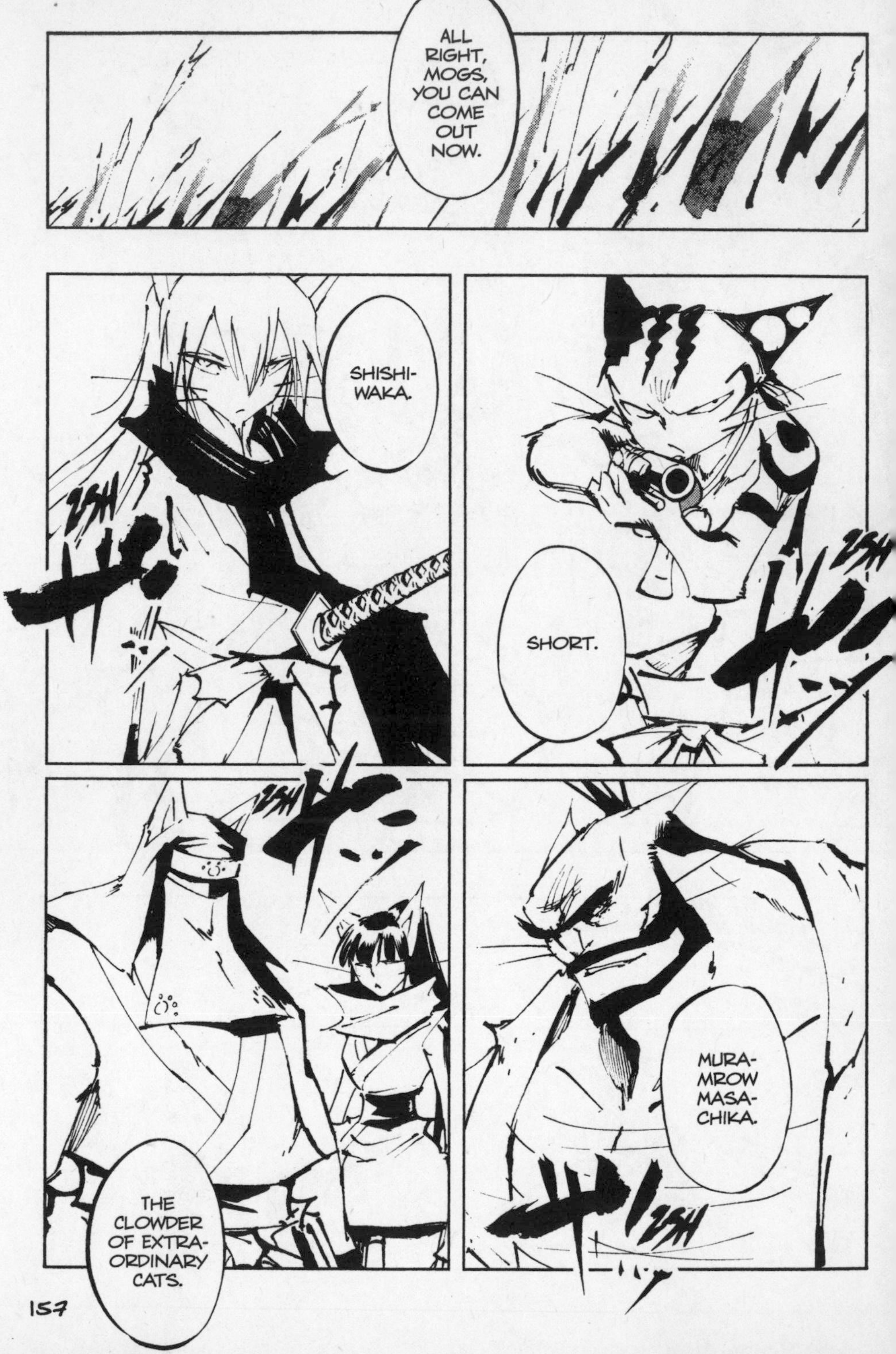
ALL RIGHT, MOGS, YOU CAN COME OUT NOW.
ZSH
SHORT.
SHISHIWAKA.
ZSH
MURAMROW MASACHIKA.
ZSH
ZSH
THE CLOWDER OF EXTRAORDINARY CATS.

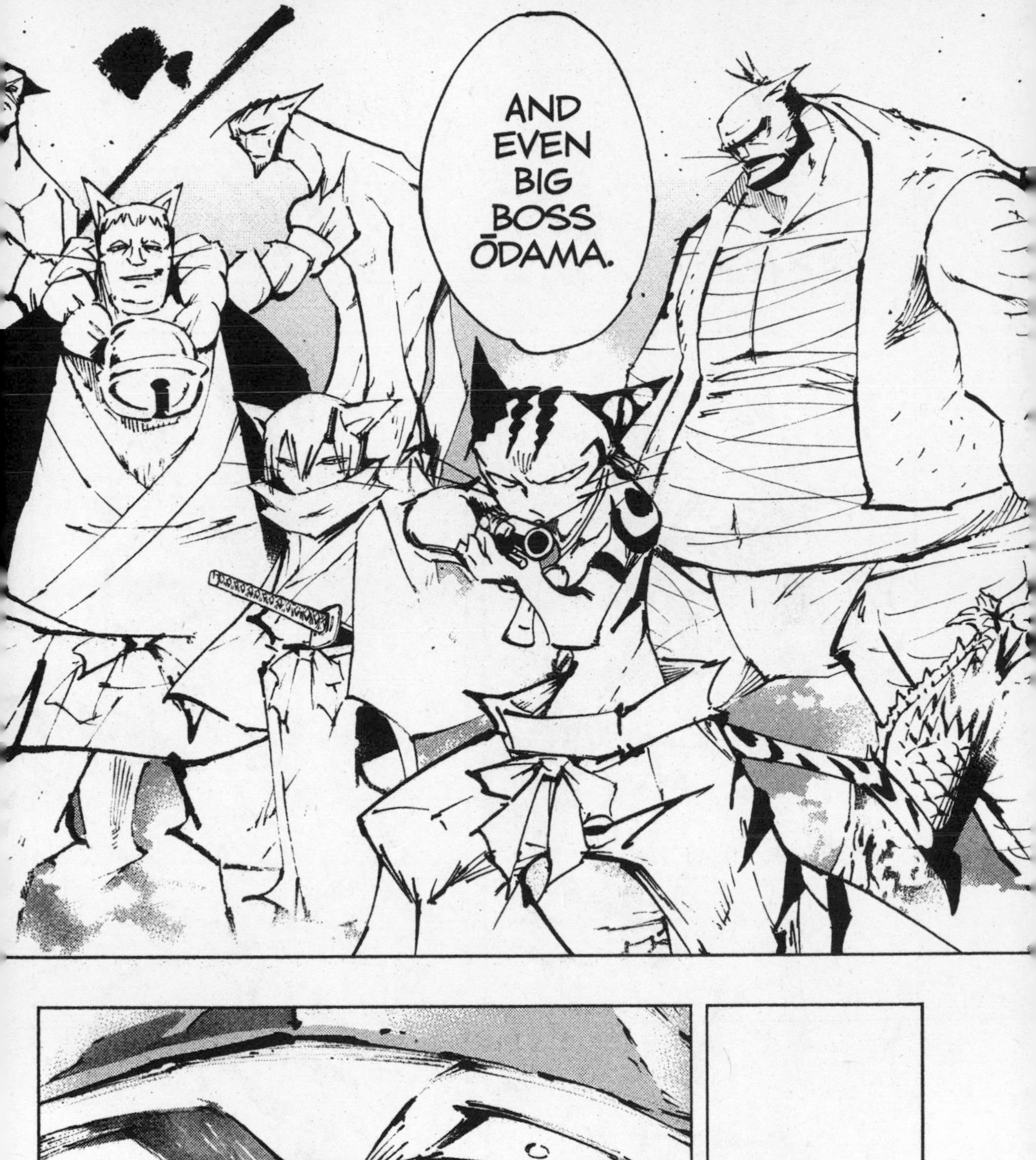
AND EVEN BIG BOSS ŌDAMA.
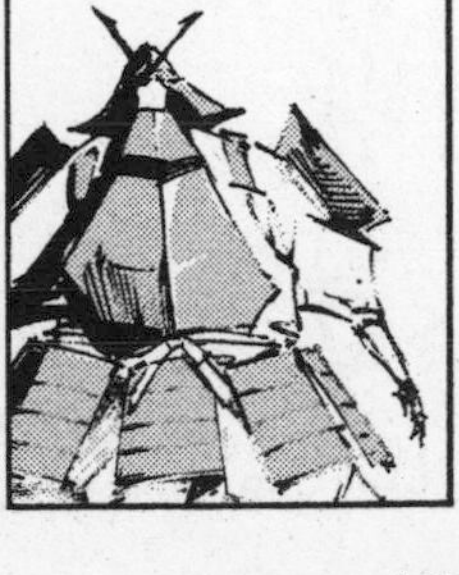
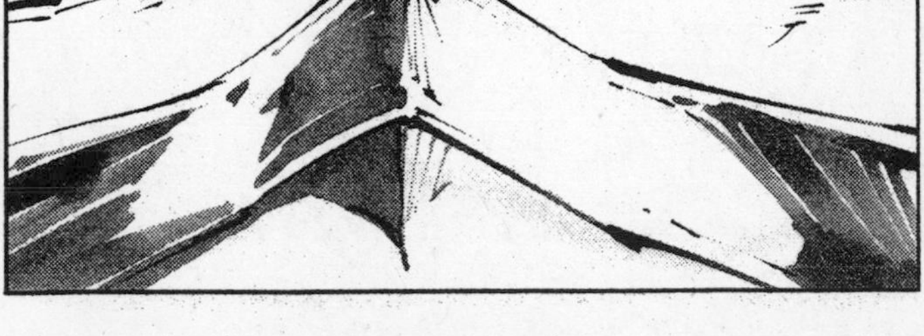

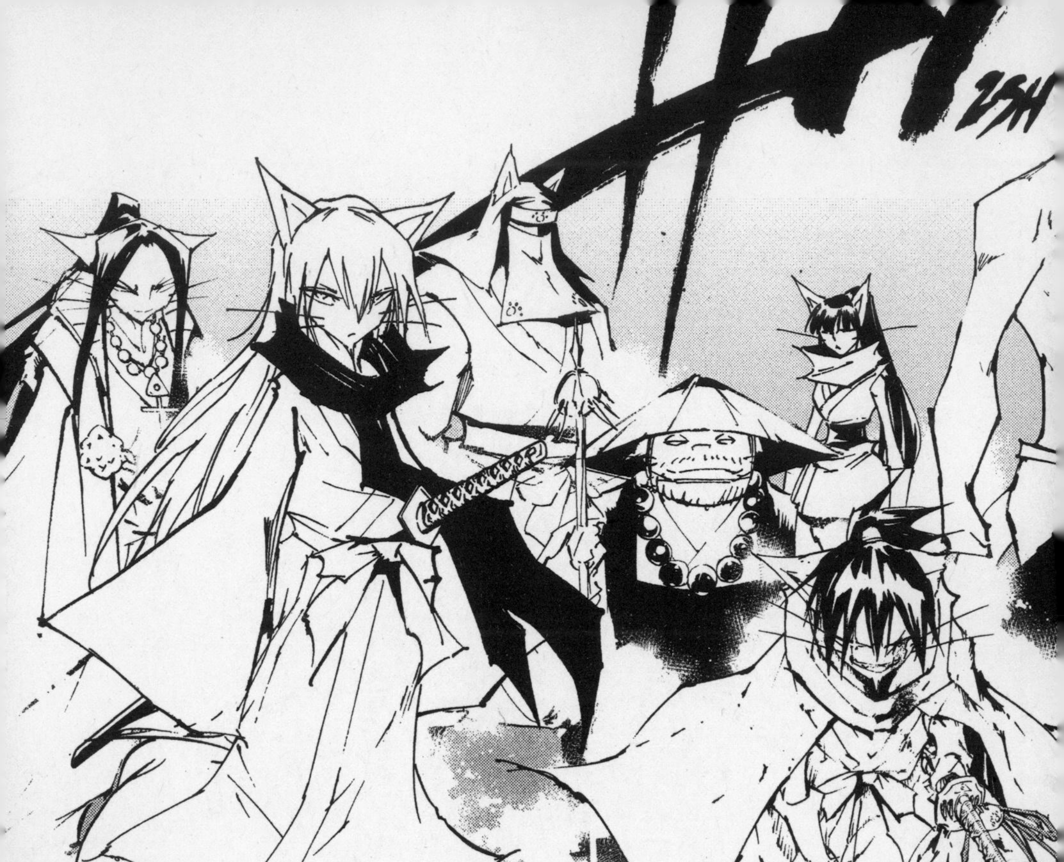
ZSH
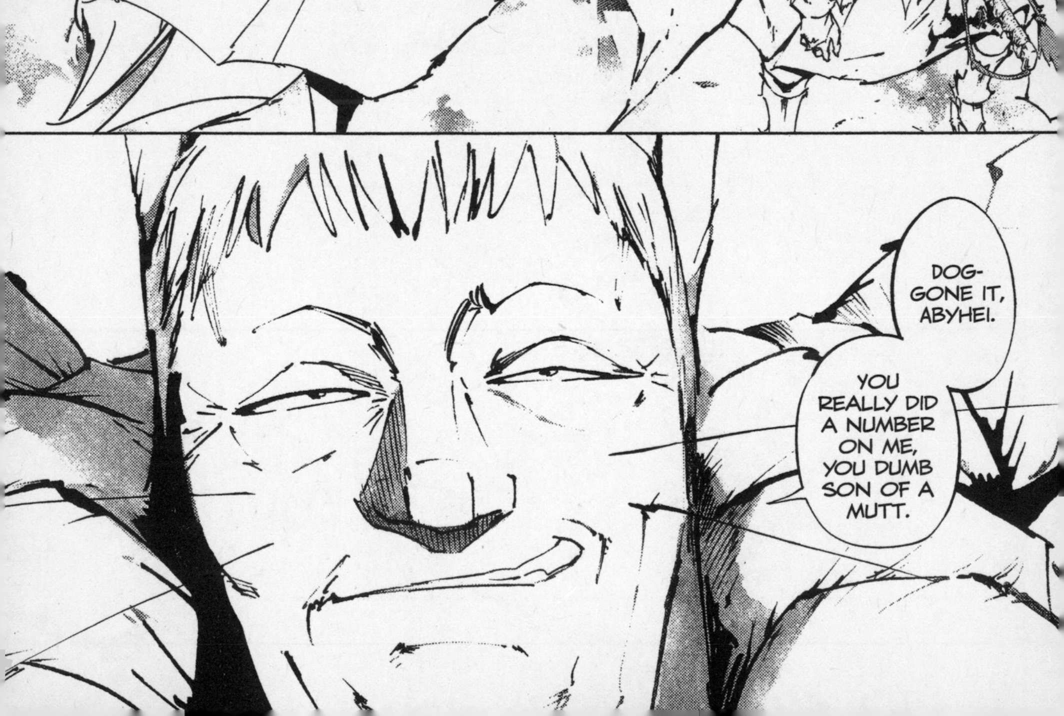
DOG-GONE IT, ABYHEI.
YOU REALLY DID A NUMBER ON ME, YOU DUMB SON OF A MUTT.

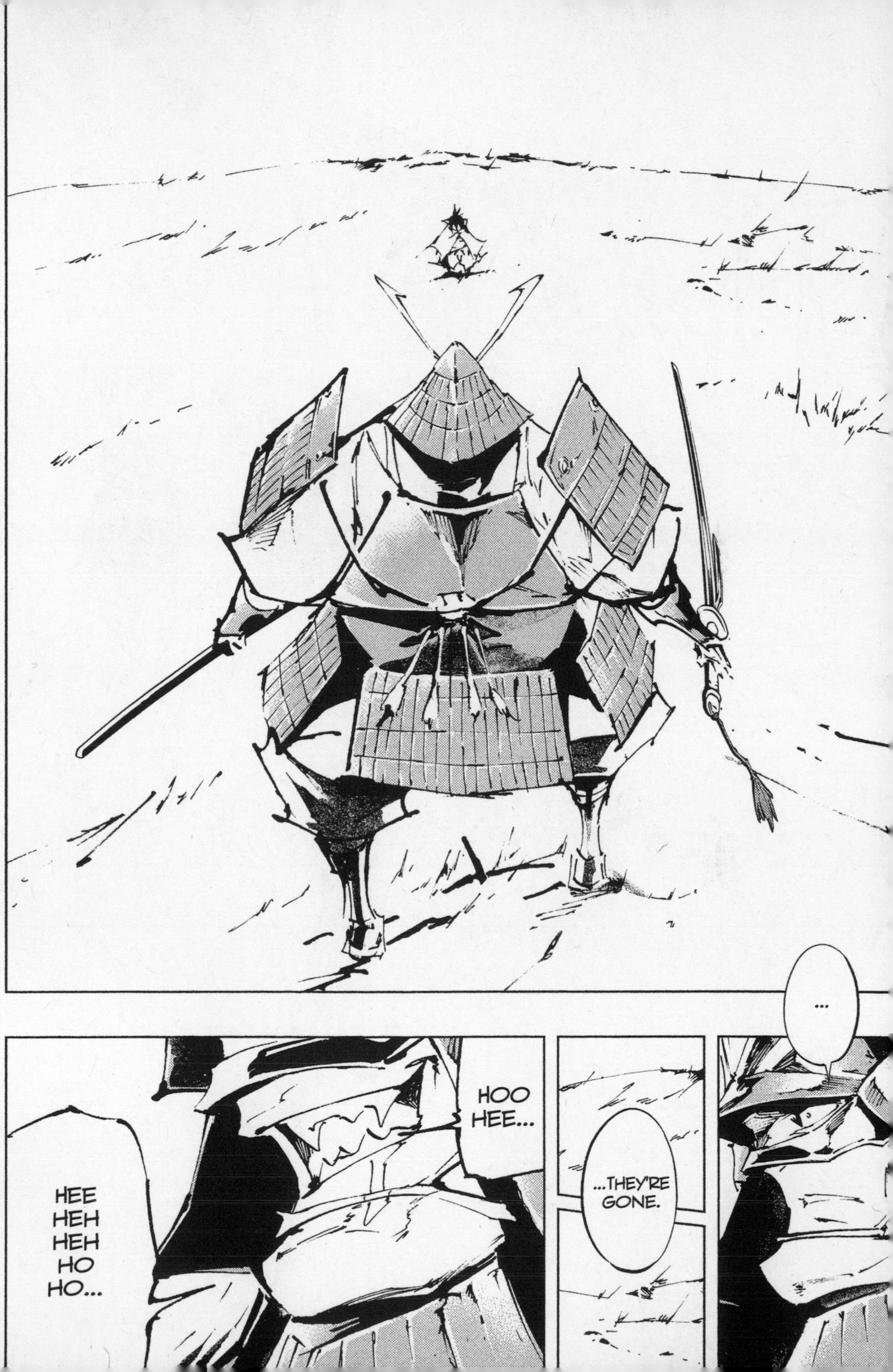
...
...THEY'RE GONE.
HOO HEE...
HEE HEH HEH HO HO...

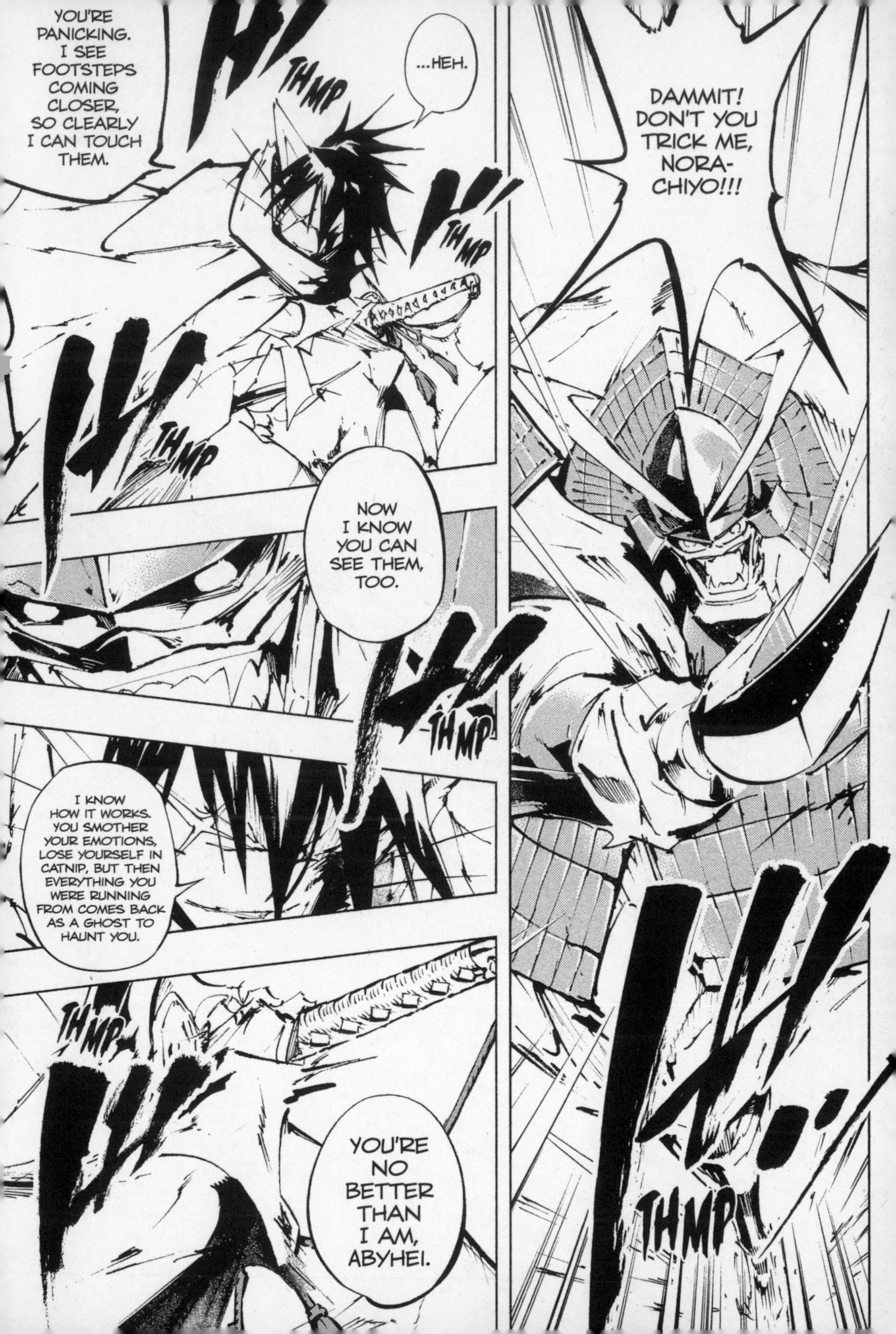
DAMMIT! DON'T YOU TRICK ME, NORA-CHIYO!!!
THMP
...HEH.
YOU'RE PANICKING. I SEE FOOTSTEPS COMING CLOSER, SO CLEARLY I CAN TOUCH THEM.
THMP
THMP
THMP
NOW I KNOW YOU CAN SEE THEM, TOO.
THMP
I KNOW HOW IT WORKS. YOU SMOTHER YOUR EMOTIONS, LOSE YOURSELF IN CATNIP, BUT THEN EVERYTHING YOU WERE RUNNING FROM COMES BACK AS A GHOST TO HAUNT YOU.
THMP
YOU'RE NO BETTER THAN I AM, ABYHEI.

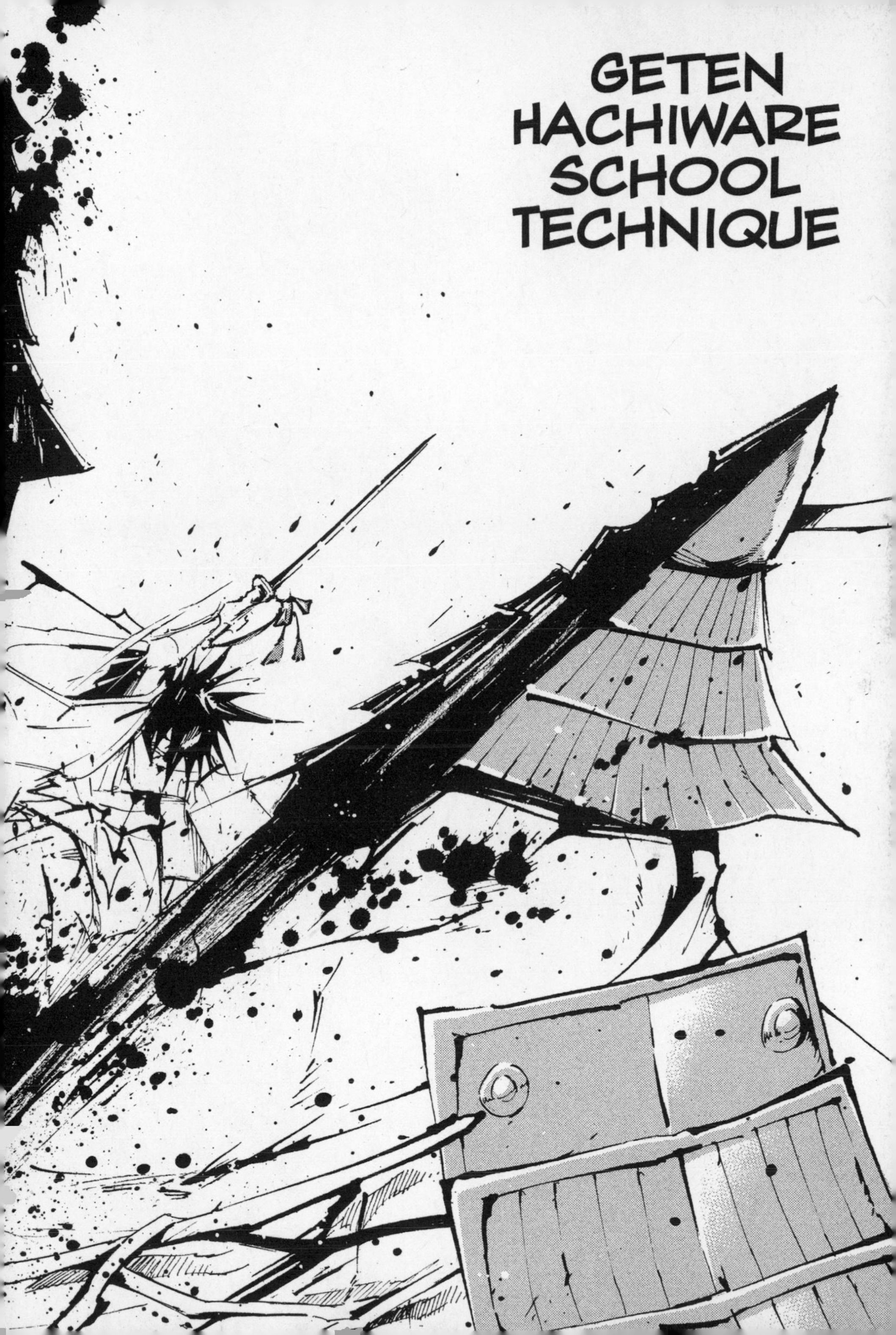
GETEN HACHIWARE SCHOOL TECHNIQUE

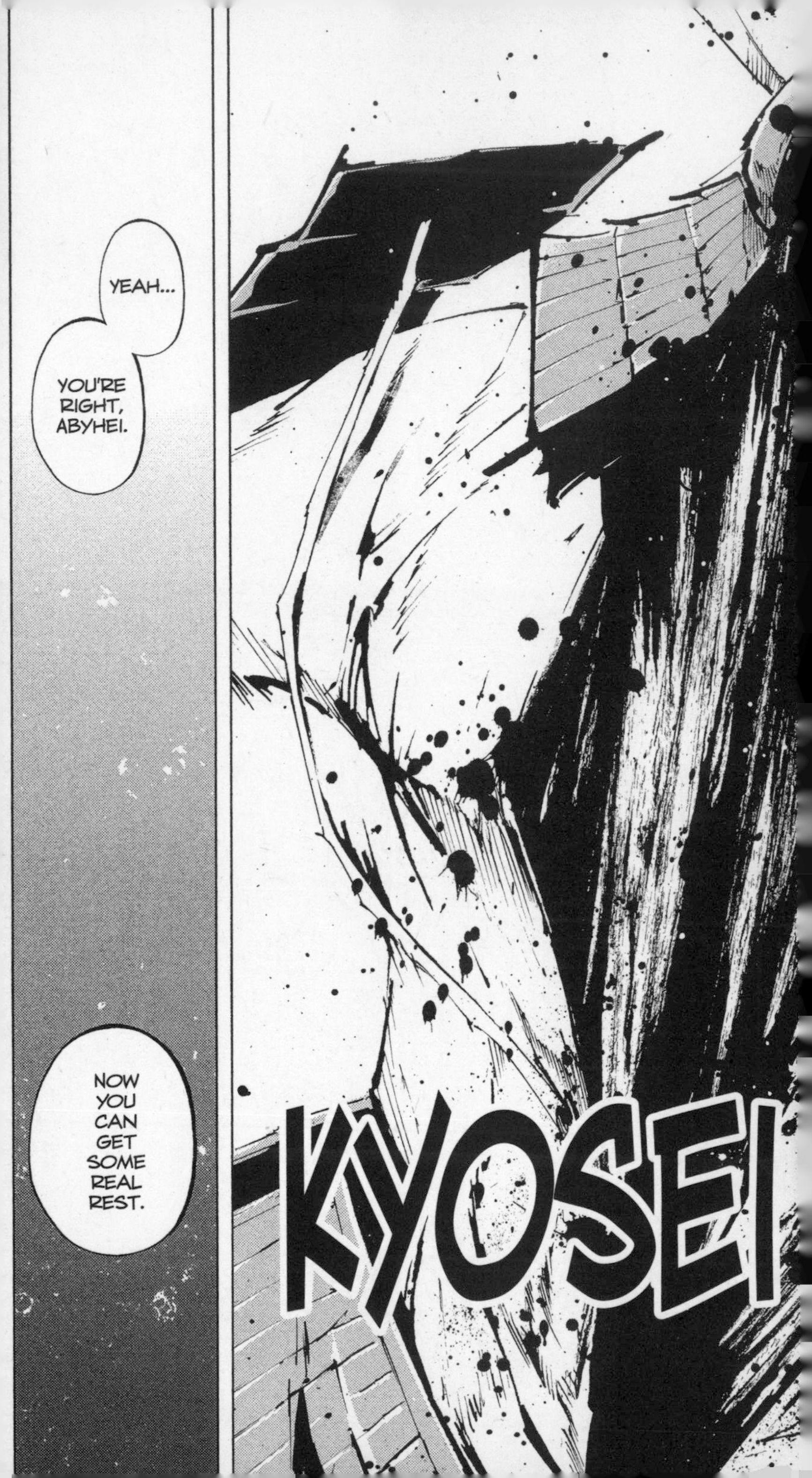
KYOSEI
YEAH...
YOU'RE RIGHT, ABYHEI.
NOW YOU CAN GET SOME REAL REST.

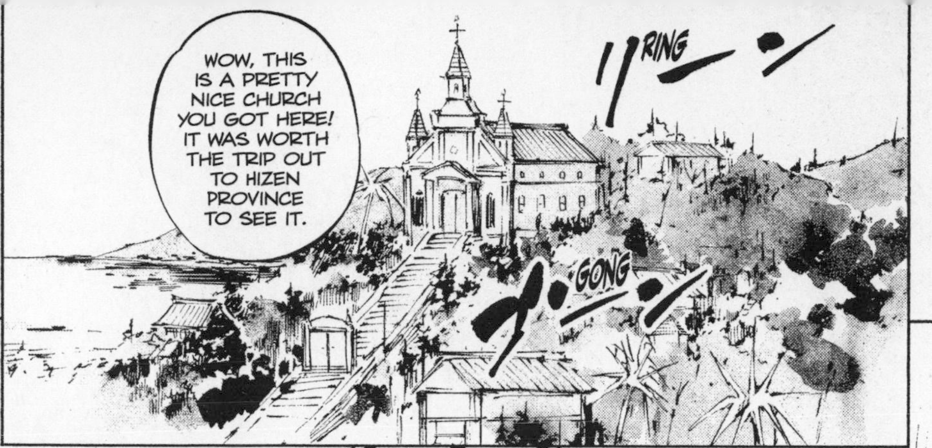
RING
WOW, THIS IS A PRETTY NICE CHURCH YOU GOT HERE! IT WAS WORTH THE TRIP OUT TO HIZEN PROVINCE TO SEE IT.
GONG

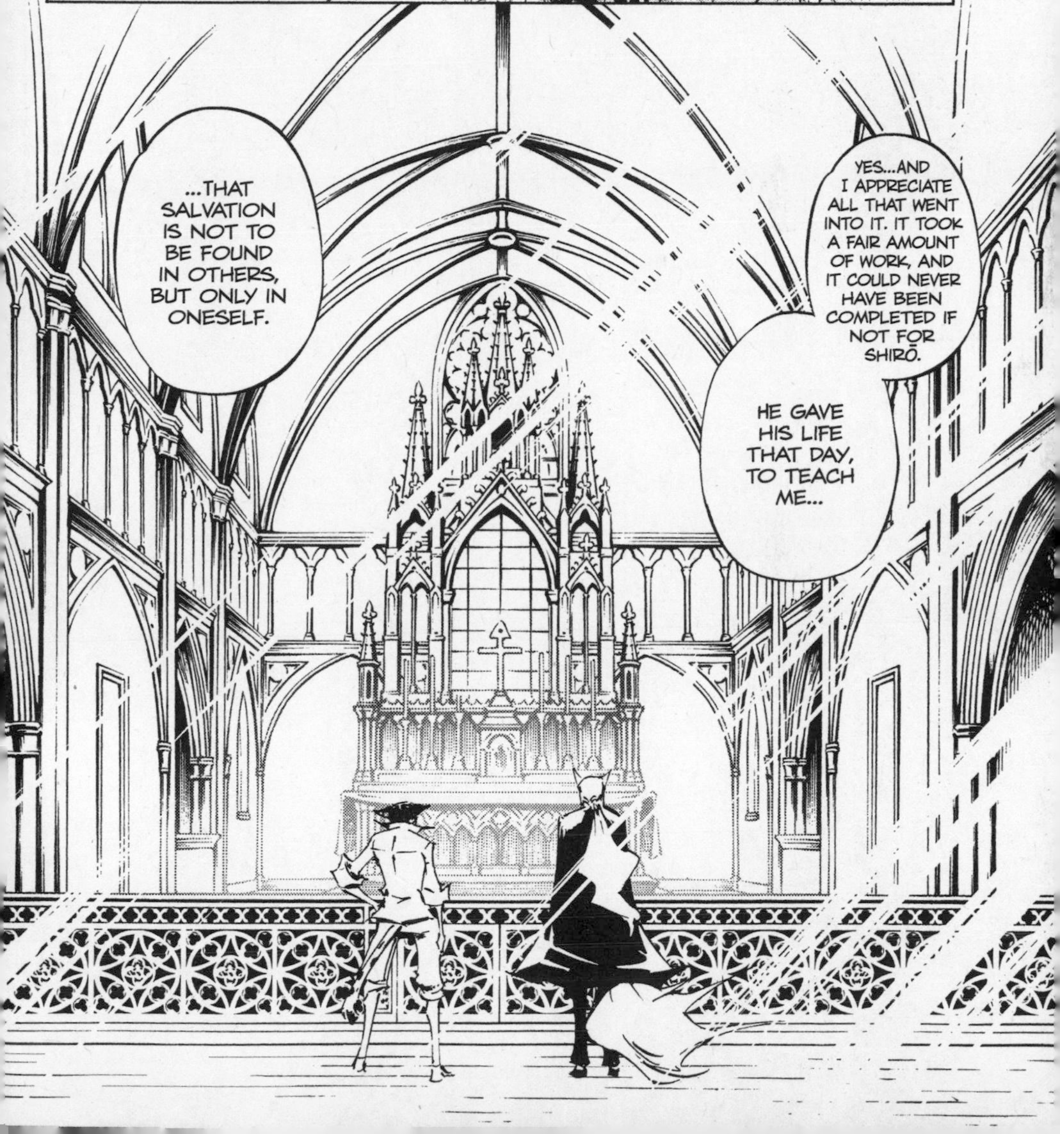
YES...AND I APPRECIATE ALL THAT WENT INTO IT. IT TOOK A FAIR AMOUNT OF WORK, AND IT COULD NEVER HAVE BEEN COMPLETED IF NOT FOR SHIRŌ.
HE GAVE HIS LIFE THAT DAY, TO TEACH ME...
...THAT SALVATION IS NOT TO BE FOUND IN OTHERS, BUT ONLY IN ONESELF.

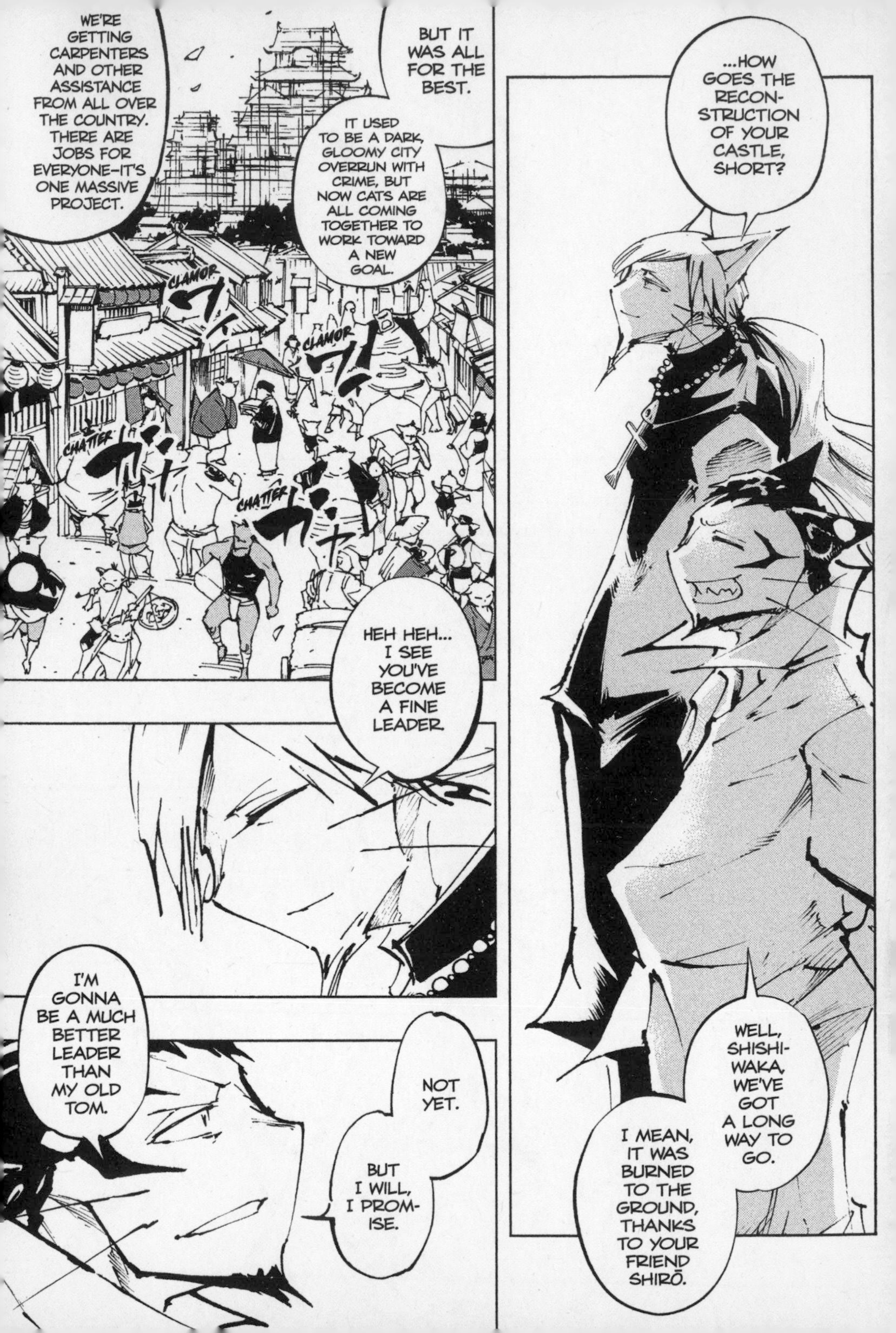
...HOW GOES THE RECONSTRUCTION OF YOUR CASTLE, SHORT?
WELL, SHISHIWAKA, WE'VE GOT A LONG WAY TO GO.
I MEAN, IT WAS BURNED TO THE GROUND, THANKS TO YOUR FRIEND SHIRŌ.
BUT IT WAS ALL FOR THE BEST.
IT USED TO BE A DARK, GLOOMY CITY OVERRUN WITH CRIME, BUT NOW CATS ARE ALL COMING TOGETHER TO WORK TOWARD A NEW GOAL.
WE'RE GETTING CARPENTERS AND OTHER ASSISTANCE FROM ALL OVER THE COUNTRY. THERE ARE JOBS FOR EVERYONE–IT'S ONE MASSIVE PROJECT.
CLAMOR
CLAMOR
CHATTER
CHATTER
HEH HEH... I SEE YOU'VE BECOME A FINE LEADER.
NOT YET.
BUT I WILL, I PROMISE.
I'M GONNA BE A MUCH BETTER LEADER THAN MY OLD TOM.

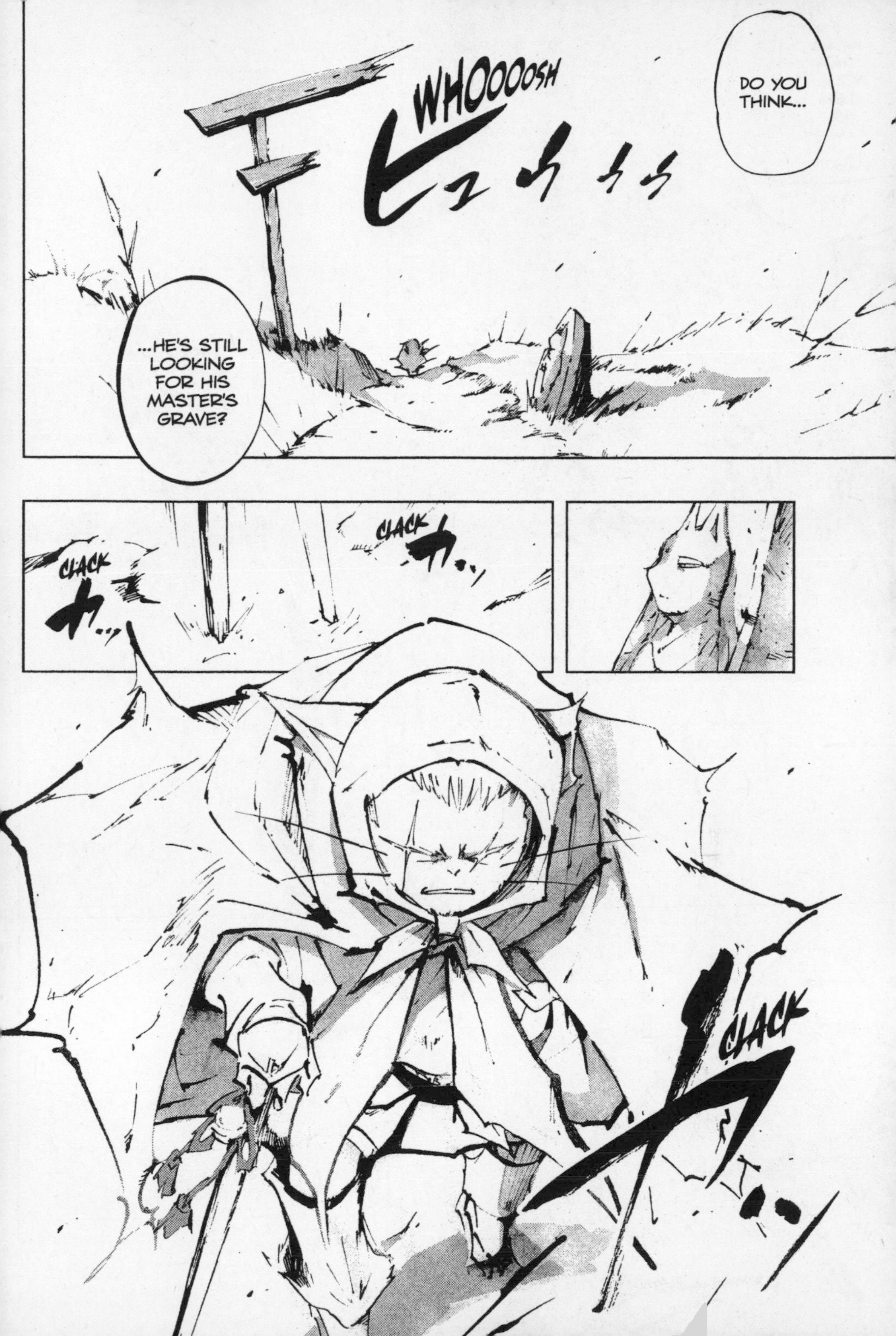
DO YOU THINK...
WHOOOOSH
...HE'S STILL LOOKING FOR HIS MASTER'S GRAVE?
CLACK
CLACK
CLACK

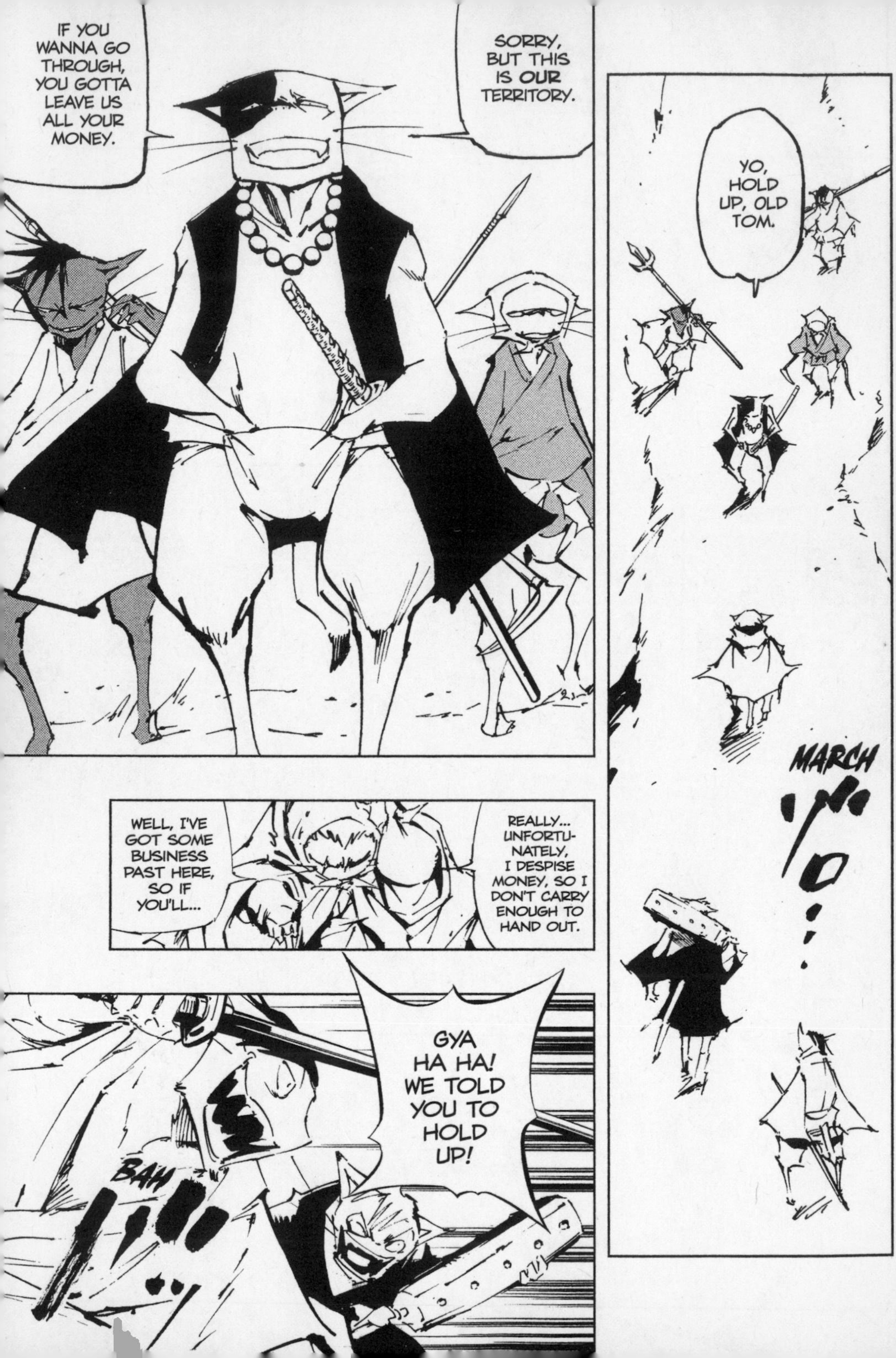
YO, HOLD UP, OLD TOM.
MARCH
SORRY, BUT THIS IS OUR TERRITORY.
IF YOU WANNA GO THROUGH, YOU GOTTA LEAVE US ALL YOUR MONEY.
REALLY... UNFORTU-NATELY, I DESPISE MONEY, SO I DON'T CARRY ENOUGH TO HAND OUT.
WELL, I'VE GOT SOME BUSINESS PAST HERE, SO IF YOU'LL...
GYA HA HA! WE TOLD YOU TO HOLD UP!
BAM

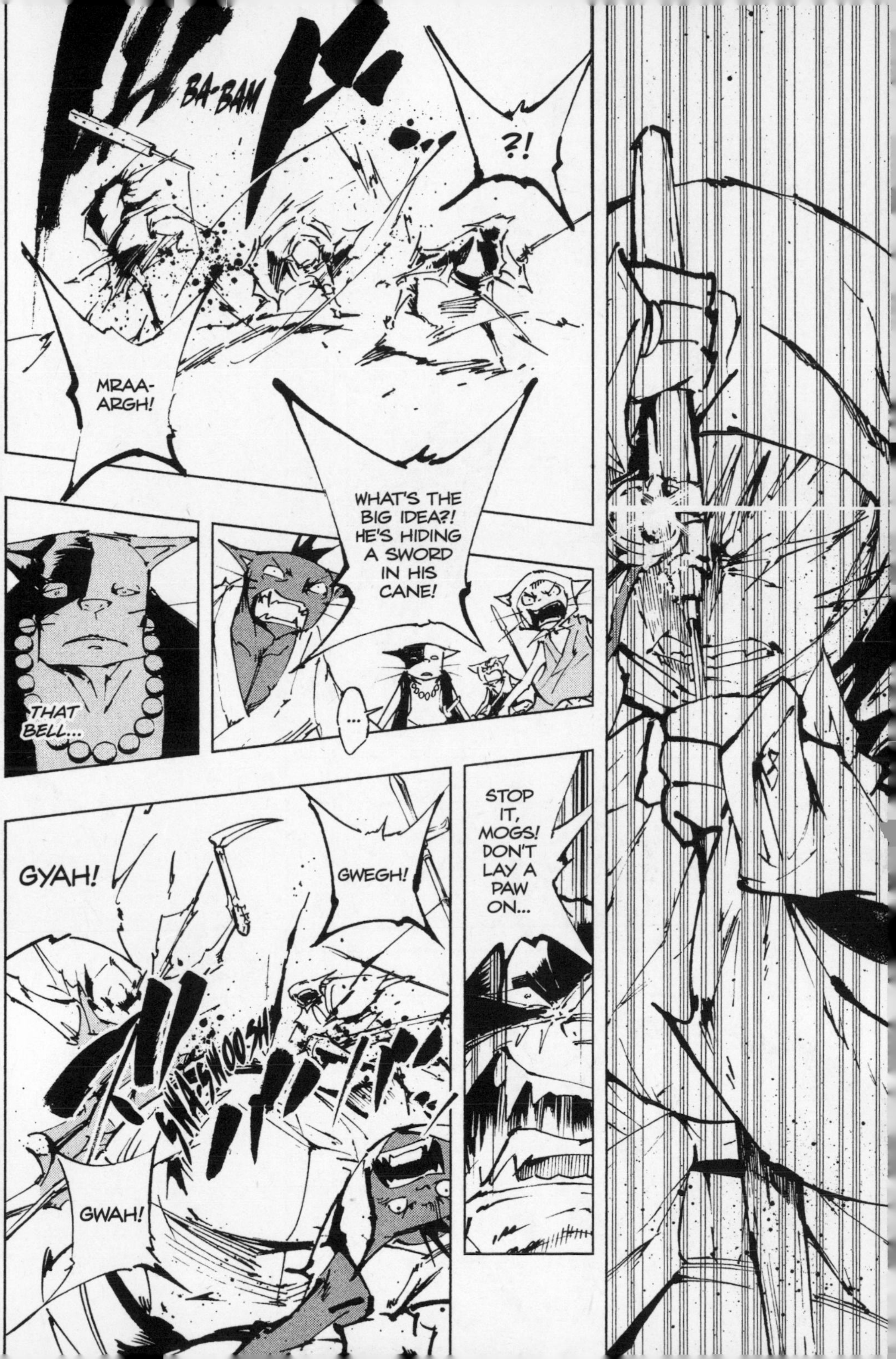
?!
BA-BAM
MRAA-ARGH!
WHAT'S THE BIG IDEA?! HE'S HIDING A SWORD IN HIS CANE!
...
THAT BELL...
STOP IT, MOGS! DON'T LAY A PAW ON...
GWEGH!
GYAH!
SWASH SWOOSH
GWAH!

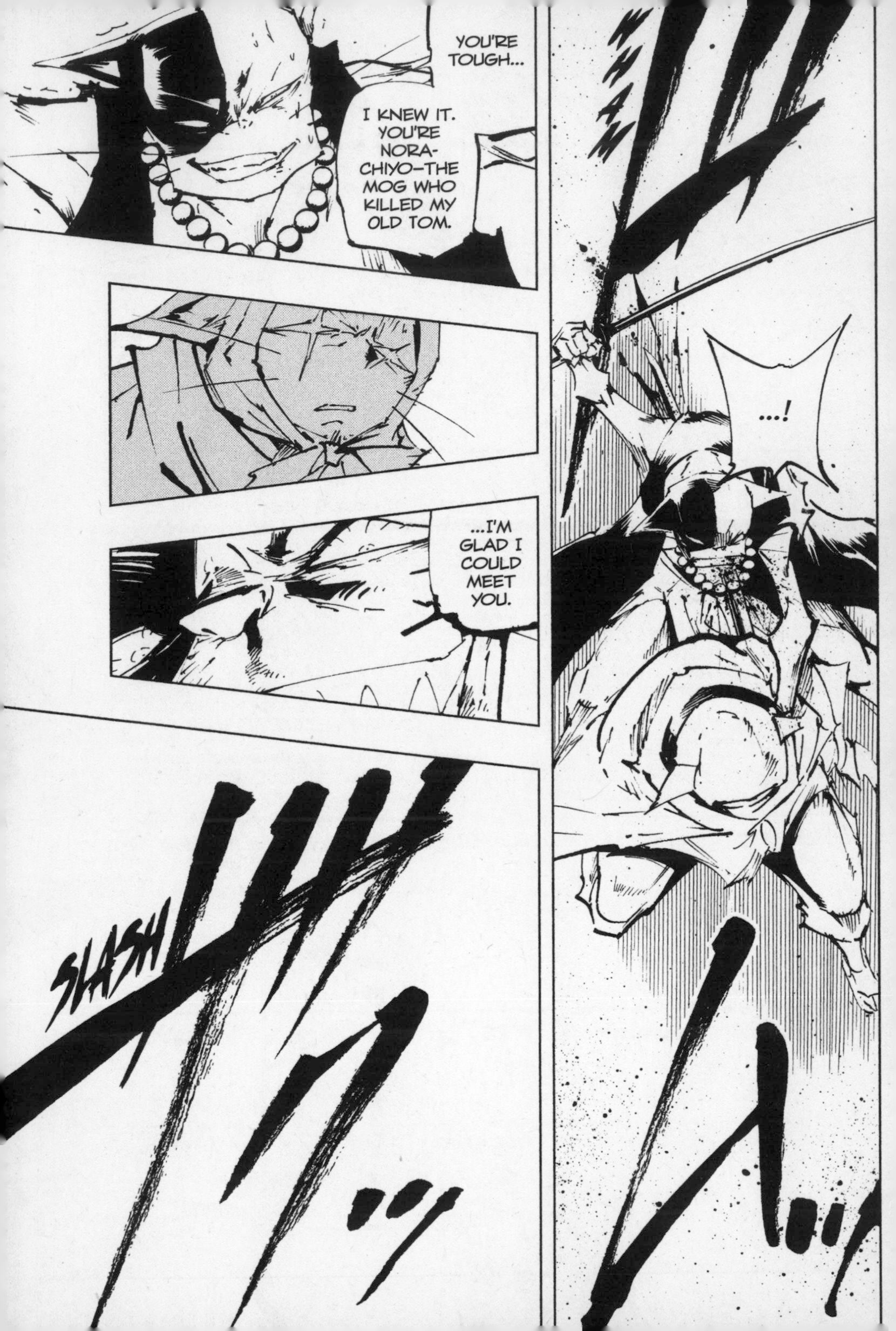
WHAM
...!
YOU'RE TOUGH...
I KNEW IT. YOU'RE NORA-CHIYO—THE MOG WHO KILLED MY OLD TOM.
...I'M GLAD I COULD MEET YOU.
SLASH

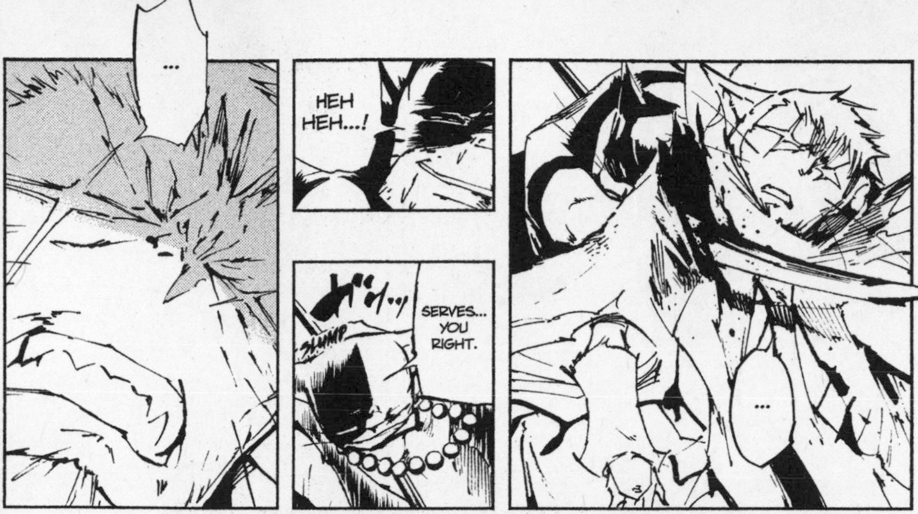
...
HEH HEH...!
SLUMP
SERVES... YOU RIGHT.
...

"NEKOGAHARA"

THE BRAWN IS GONE FROM MY WEAK SHOULDERS, MY TIRED EYES ARE CRUSTED OVER.

A BONY PAW, COARSE AND FLEABITTEN, IS WHAT I HAVE TO LAY MY HEAD ON.

I AM A FERAL CAT. ON A FERAL HIGHROAD, AD-HERRING TO MY DIGNITY, THE ONLY THING THAT BOLSTERS ME.

AT TIMES I BAT AWAY THAT PRIDE, ALL TO KEEP MYSELF ALIVE.

UNTIL THE DAY THAT I ARRIVE, AT NEKOGAHARA.

SINGED FUR WRAPS AROUND MY SKIN, REMAINING UNSWAYED BY THE WIND.

AS I CROSS THE SCORCHING SAND, IT BURNS THE SOFT FLESH OF MY PADS.

I AM A FERAL CAT. ON A FERAL HIGH ROAD.

WETTED BY THE RAIN AND HAIL, I STOP AND WHET MY CLAWS AND NAILS.

I HONE THEM INTO DEADLY KNIVES, ALL TO KEEP MYSELF ALIVE.

UNTIL THE DAY THAT I ARRIVE, AT NEKOGAHARA.

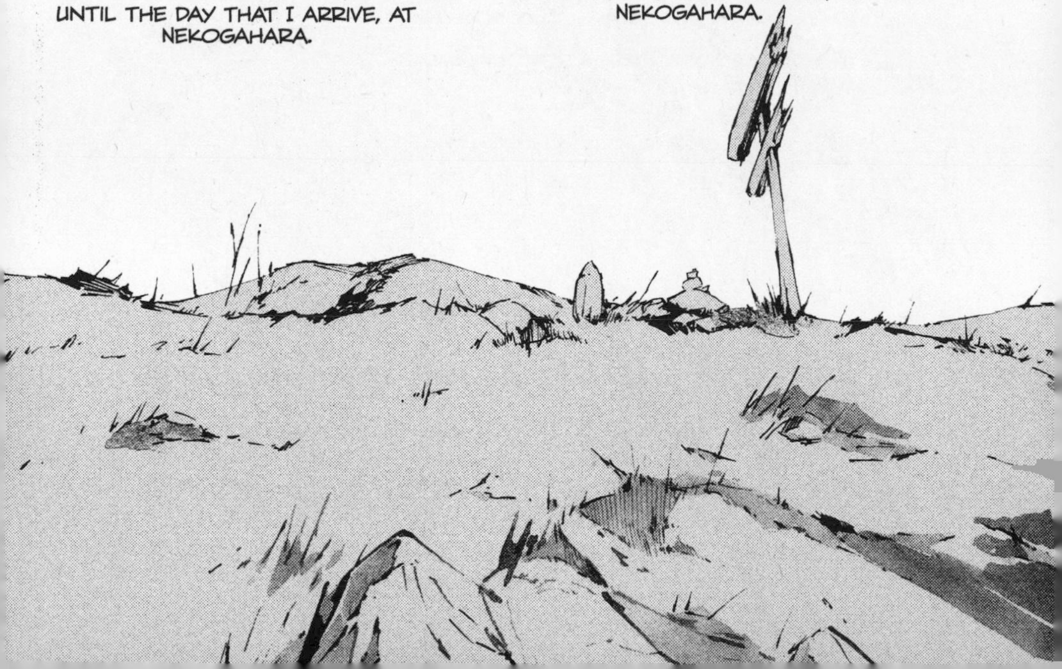

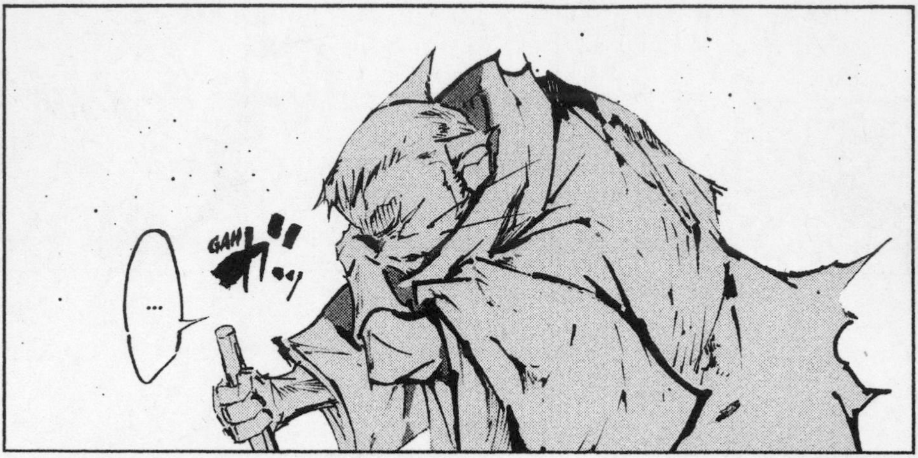
GAH
...

WALKING THROUGH A DARKENED ALLEY, A GANG OF CATS COMES TO SURROUND ME.

I FEEL OUR LOATHING INTERMINGLE. WILL I DIE BENEATH THESE SHINGLES?

I AM A FERAL CAT. ON A FERAL HIGHROAD.

I CARRY ON TOWARD THAT HILL, MY MEMORIES—THEY WARM ME STILL.

MY BROKEN TAIL SWINGS SIDE TO SIDE, AS I KEEP MYSELF ALIVE.

UNTIL THE DAY THAT I ARRIVE, AT NEKOGAHARA.

BEFORE I KNOW IT, HERE I AM, AT NEKOGAHARA.

THE PLACE OF MY SOMEDAY, NEKOGAHARA.

(RECITED) I DON'T WEAR BOOTS.

I'M NO ARISTOCAT.

I NEVER GET WHAT I ORDER.

I DON'T GOTTALOT.

I HAVE MORE WHISKERS NOW THAN EVER.

...AND I DON'T NEED A MILLION LIVES.

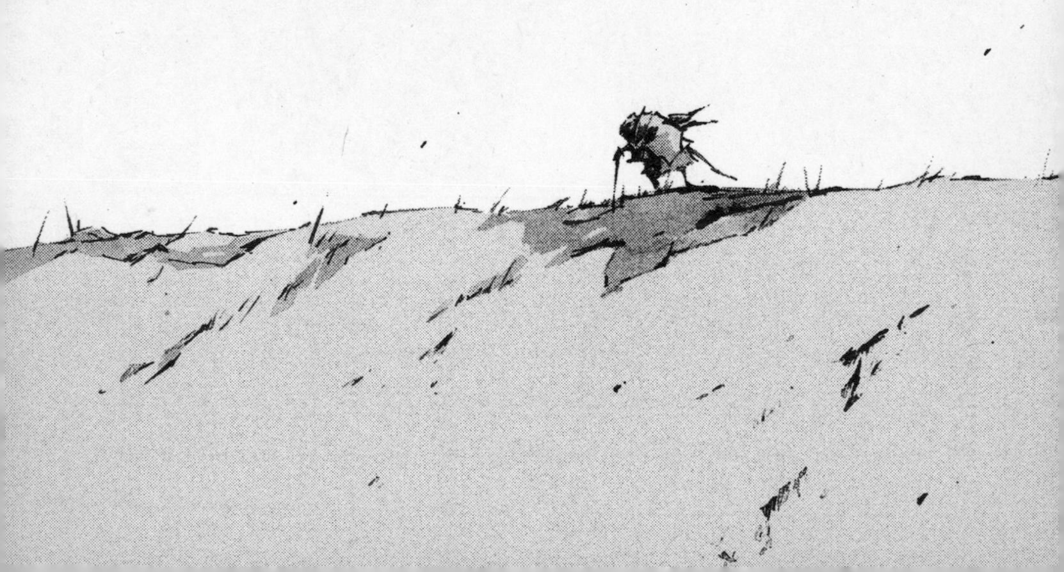

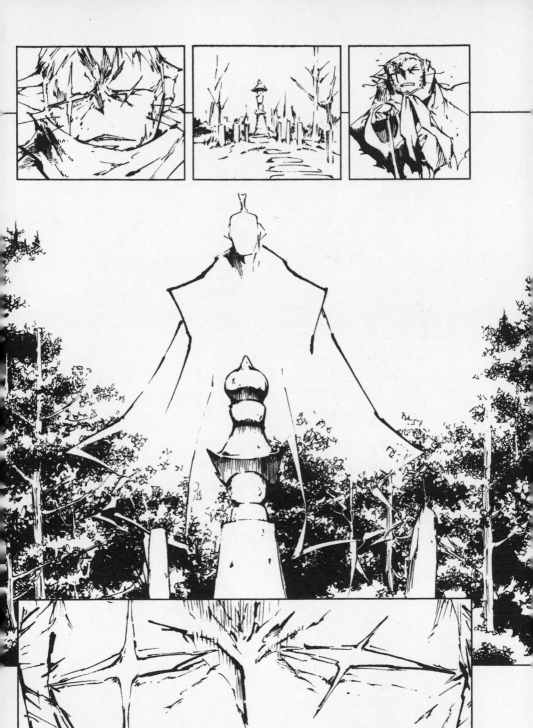

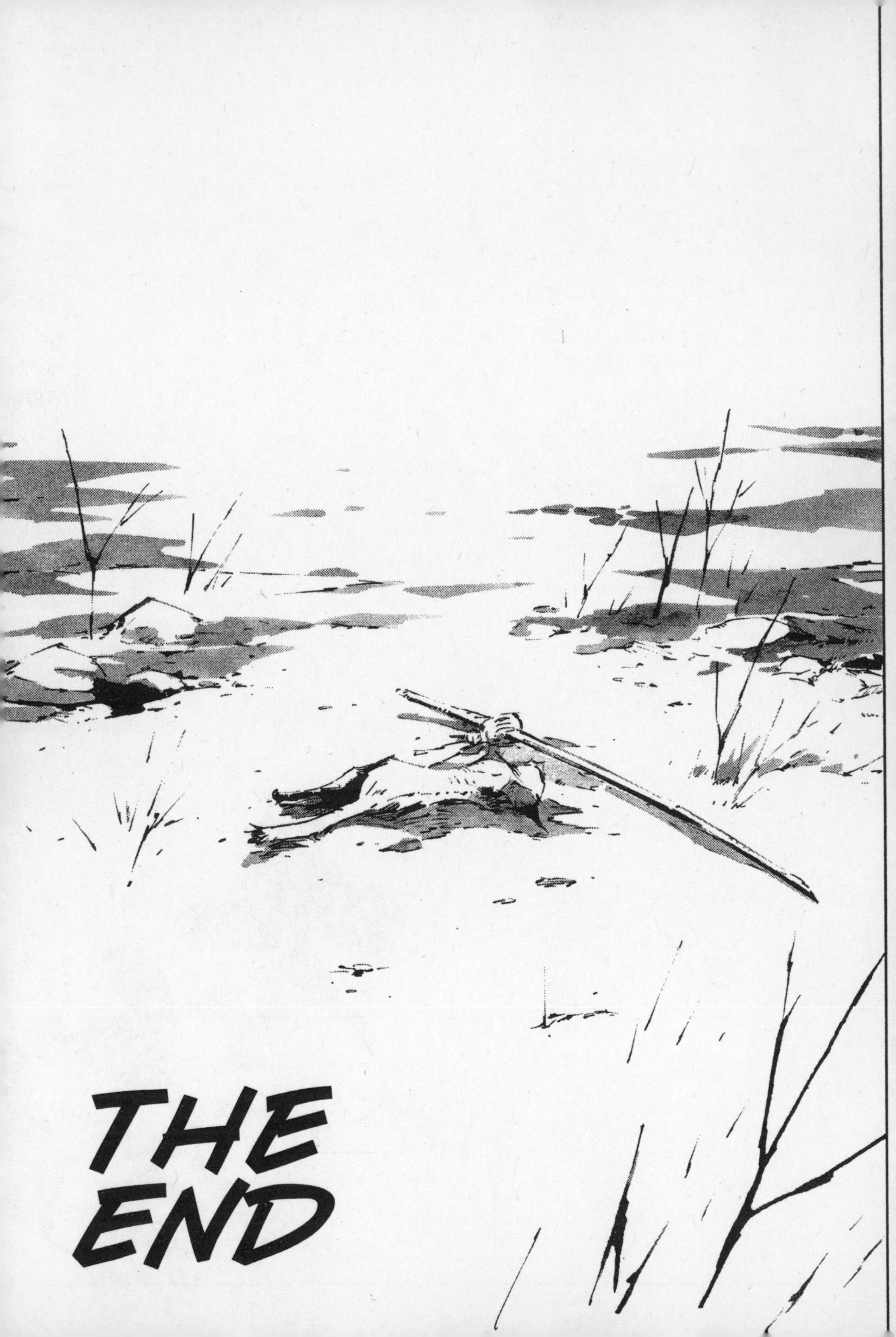
THE END

猫ヶ原

NeKoGaHaRa

ネコガハラ

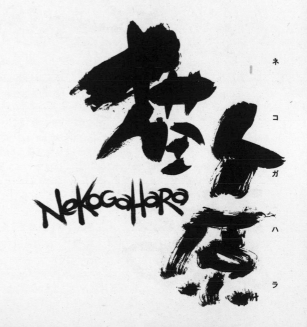

TRANSLATION NOTES

Caragan, page 8

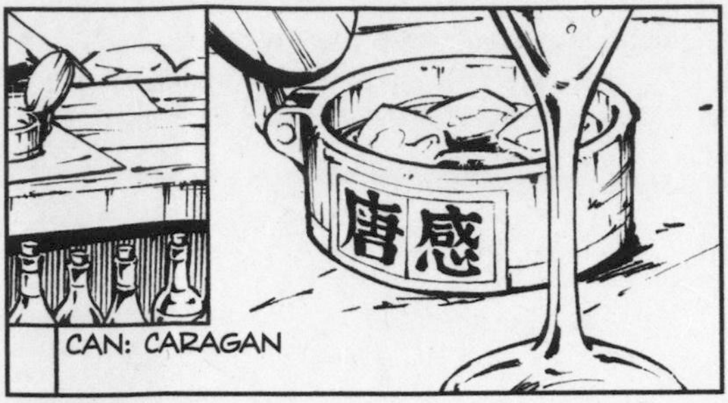
唐感
CAN: CARAGAN

"Cara" is an alternative pronunciation of a character that represents China, so perhaps this is fine imported Chinese food. The name of this food also sounds remarkably like one of the top rated (and expensive) catfood brands in modern-day Japan, Canagan.

Zangekō, page 14

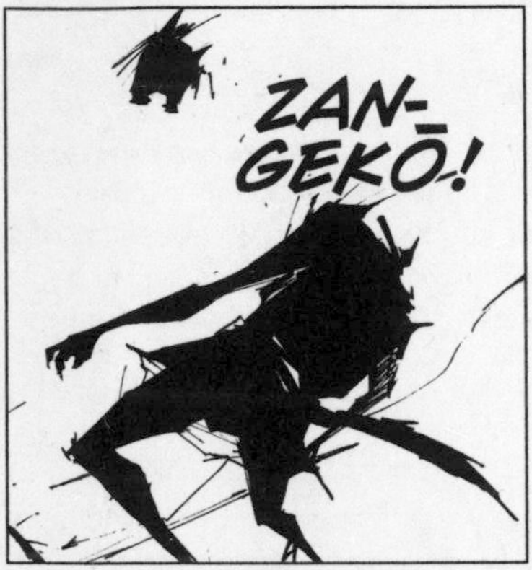
ZAN-GEKŌ!

Based on the *kanji* characters used, the name of Shirō's special attack literally means "lingering summer scent." Phonetically, it is also means "to confess and beg forgiveness."

Southern purrbarian, page 23

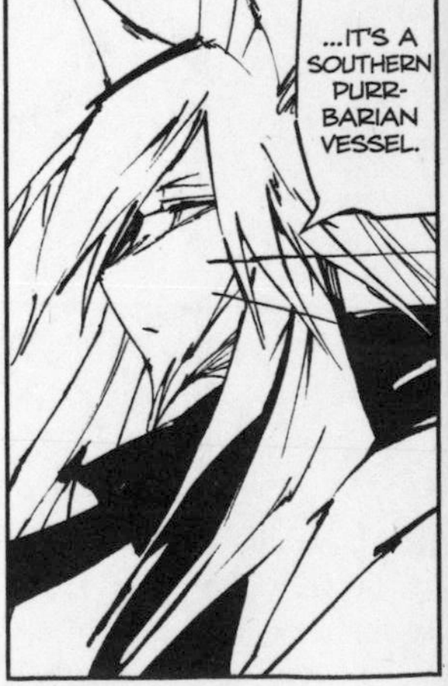
...IT'S A SOUTHERN PURR-BARIAN VESSEL.

When Europeans came to trade with Japan in the 16th century, the Japanese were not impressed with their poor manners (using fingers to eat instead of chopsticks) and inability to read Japanese. The foreign traders came to be known as *Nanban* (or *Nyanban*, as the cats called them), meaning "southern barbarians." Eventually the term lost its negative connotation and became a neutral descriptor for anything exotic and unusual, and today it is still used to refer to a certain kind of cuisine.

The bounty on Abyhei's head, page 33

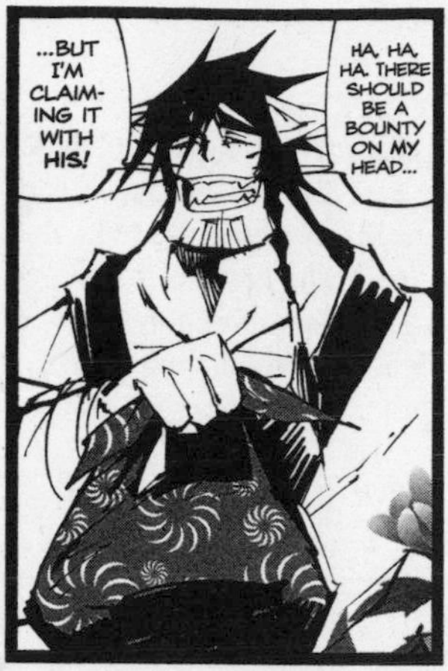
HA, HA, HA. THERE SHOULD BE A BOUNTY ON MY HEAD...
...BUT I'M CLAIMING IT WITH HIS!

The translators admit to speculating about whether or not there should be a bounty on Abyhei's head. The Japanese word for "turning oneself in" is *jishu*, which literally means "one's own head," as in "to offer one's own head to the authorities." The irony that Abyhei is performing *jishu* by turning in another cat's head is not lost on him.

Bye Bye TRAI, page 49

The chapter of this title is a reference to "Bye Bye Dubai," a song by Japanese boy band Sexy Zone. The original title was "Bye Bye DO RAIN," where "DO RAIN" is roughly similar to *torai*, a word meaning "foreign," which is applied to the cats and technology that have come to Japan from other nations. In an attempt to recapture the boy band allusion in a way more familiar to Western readers, the translators have rendered it as "Bye Bye TRAI," which will hopefully sound like N*SYNC's "Bye Bye Bye."

Kyosei, page 50

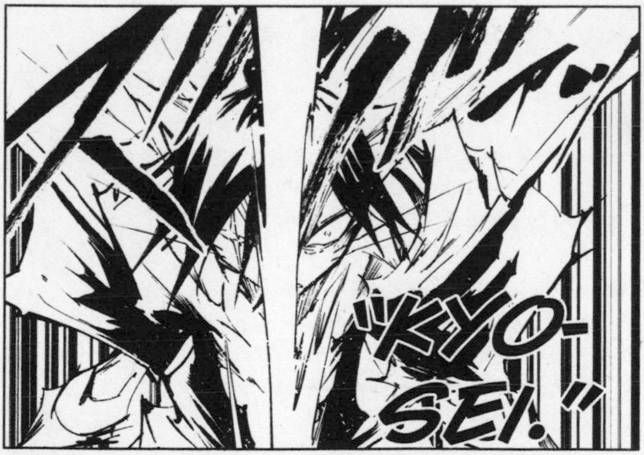
"KYO-SEI!"

The *kanji* characters for this attack provide the meaning of "giant star." As with all the attacks in this series, this, too, has a second meaning. *Kyosei* is also the word for "castration," a technique name fitting of a cat called Tamanashi, or in other words, "no balls."

Shintō new swords, page 52

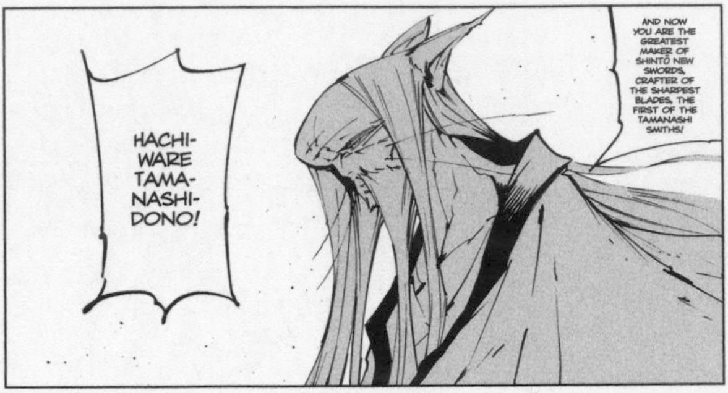
AND NOW YOU ARE THE GREATEST MAKER OF SHINTŌ NEW SWORDS, CRAFTER OF THE SHARPEST BLADES, THE FIRST OF THE TAMANASHI SMITHS!
HACHI-WARE TAMA-NASHI-DONO!

After the long period of war preceding the events of this story, the old style of swordmaking was forgotten, so new blades were made in the *shintō* style. The style was pioneered by Umetada Myōju, whose apprentice was Tadayoshi of Hizen Province. *Shintō* swords were heavier than *kotō* old swords, and all of them were made of the same iron, as opposed to the *kotō* blades, whose origin could be determined by the type of iron used to make them.

Fire-nsmith, page 75

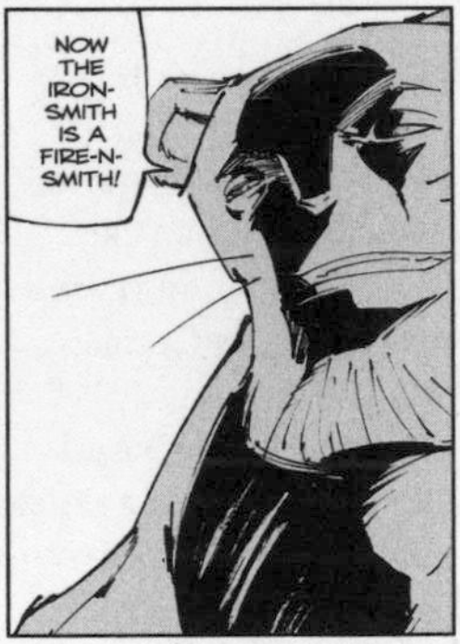
NOW THE IRON-SMITH IS A FIRE-N-SMITH!

The Japanese word for smith is *kajiya*, roughly meaning "one whose job is at the forge." The word for fire, as it applies to buildings that are on fire, is *kaji*. So the original joke was more along the lines of, "A *kajiya* (smith) needs a *kaji* (fire)."

Kendama vs. kendama, page 84

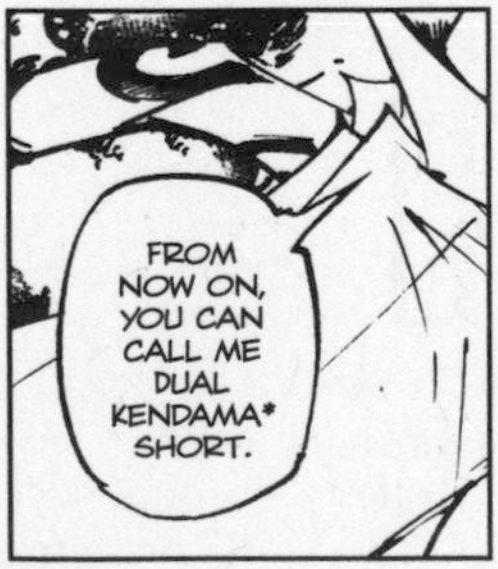
FROM NOW ON, YOU CAN CALL ME DUAL KENDAMA* SHORT.

Short has applied a new meaning to his trademark kendama. The name of the toy he carries around his neck literally means "sword and ball," where the "sword" is the handle of the kendama. He has traded it out for a *kenjū*, meaning handgun, and *tama*, bullets. By combining these two new words, Short has made a new kendama—a handgun that fires bullets.

Samidare Spin, page 101

Samidare is an old-fashioned word for the rain that tends to fall in Japan around May, and can also refer to a barrage of something, like bullets. In this attack, Short is acting kind of like a sprinkler, raining bullets on his enemies.

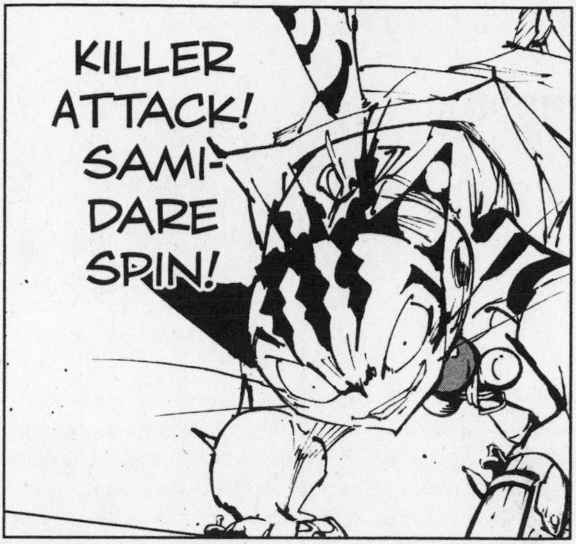
KILLER ATTACK! SAMI-DARE SPIN!

Norachiyo's recitation, page 171

Here Norachiyo is comparing himself with other well-known feline figures. The first, of course, is *Puss in Boots* from the fairy tale of the same name. Second, he compares himself to the narrator of Natsume Soseki's *I Am a Cat*, who uses *wagahai*, a very noble, aristocratic way of saying "I." Next, Norachiyo appears to be referring to a pair of famous internet cats, who have been trained to ring a bell to "order" cat treats. There is a children's book translated into English as *Rudolf the Black Cat*, about a little cat and his friend Ippaiattena, or Gottalot, as he is known in the English version. After that, he suggests that he has no reason to say "*A Farewell to Whiskers*," alluding to either the book or the stop-motion animated series based on the book, *Hige yo, Saraba*, about a group of stray cats who band together to survive against the dogs and rats of the area. Finally, Norachiyo says he doesn't need a million lives, referring to *The Cat that Lived a Million Times*, about a feline who was reincarnated one million times in an ongoing quest to find a better owner.

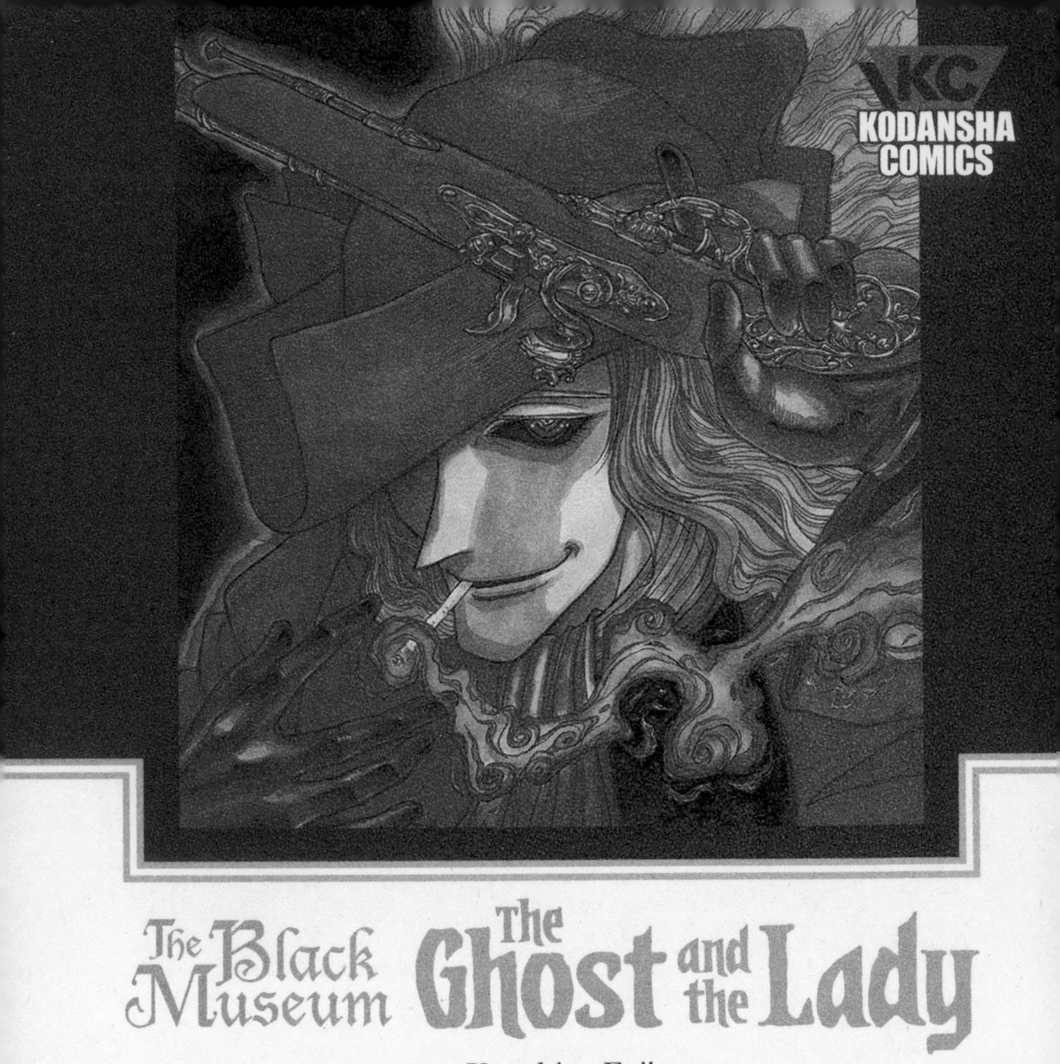
KC
KODANSHA COMICS

The Black Museum: The Ghost and the Lady

By Kazuhiro Fujita

Deep in Scotland Yard in London sits an evidence room dedicated to the greatest mysteries of British history. In this "Black Museum" sits a misshapen hunk of lead–two bullets fused together–the key to a wartime encounter between Florence Nightingale, the mother of modern nursing, and a supernatural Man in Grey. This story is unknown to most scholars of history, but a special guest of the museum will tell the tale of The Ghost and the Lady...

Praise for Kazuhiro Fujita's *Ushio and Tora*

"A charming revival that combines a classic look with modern depth and pacing... **Essential viewing both for curmudgeons and new fans alike.**" — Anime News Network

"**GREAT!** The first episode of Ushio and Tora captures the essence of '90s anime." — IGN

A Kodansha Comics Trade Paperback Original.

Published in the United States by Kodansha Comics,
an imprint of Kodansha USA Publishing, LLC, New York.

Publication rights for this English edition arranged through Kodansha Ltd.,
Tokyo.

First published in Japan in 2018 by Kodansha Ltd., Tokyo, as *Nekogahara*
volume 5.

ISBN 978-1-63236-503-3

Printed in the United States of America.

www.kodanshacomics.com

9 8 7 6 5 4 3 2 1

Translation: Alethea Nibley & Athena Nibley
Lettering: Scott O. Brown
Editing: Ajani Oloye
Kodansha Comics edition cover design: Phil Balsman

D0556465